Authors & Artists for Young Adults

ISSN 1040-5682

Authors & Artists for Young Adults

VOLUME 36

 *GALE GROUP*

Detroit
New York
San Francisco
London
Boston
Woodbridge, CT

Scot Peacock, *Managing Editor, Literature Product*
Mark Scott, *Publisher, Literature Product*

Alan Hedblad, *Managing Editor*
Susan Trosky, *Literature Content Coordinator*

Thomas McMahon, *Editor*
Kristen Dorsch, Shayla Hawkins, Simone Sobel, *Associate Editors*

Mark Springer, *Technical Training Specialist*

Victoria B. Cariappa, *Research Manager*
Tracie A. Richarson, *Project Coordinator*
Andrew Guy Malonis, Gary J. Oudersluys, Cheryl L. Warnock, *Research Specialists*
Tamara C. Nott, *Research Associate*, Tim Lehnerer, *Research Assistant*

Maria Franklin, *Permissions Manager*
Edna Hedblad, *Permissions Specialist*
Shalice Shah, *Permissions Associate*

Mary Beth Trimper, *Production Director*
Stacy L. Melson, *Buyer*

Randy Bassett, *Image Database Supervisor*
Michael Logusz, *Graphic Artist*
Robert Duncan, *Imaging Specialist*
Pamela A. Reed, *Imaging Coordinator*
Dean Dauphinais, Robyn V. Young, *Senior Image Editors*
Kelly A. Quin, *Image Editor*

The paper used in this publication meets the minimum requirements of
American National Standard for Information Sciences—Permanence Paper
for Printed Library Materials, ANSI Z39.48-1984.

Library of Congress Catalog Card Number 89-641100
ISBN 0-7876-3236-8
ISSN 1040-5682

10 9 8 7 6 5 4 3 2 1

Printed in the United States of America

Authors and Artists for Young Adults

TEEN BOARD ADVISORS

Contents

Introduction

Authors and Artists for Young Adults is a reference series designed to serve the needs of middle school, junior high, and high school students interested in creative artists. Originally inspired by the need to bridge the gap between Gale's *Something about the Author,* created for children, and *Contemporary Authors,* intended for older students and adults, *Authors and Artists for Young Adults* has been expanded to cover not only an international scope of authors, but also a wide variety of other artists.

Although the emphasis of the series remains on the writer for young adults, we recognize that these readers have diverse interests covering a wide range of reading levels. The series therefore contains not only those creative artists who are of high interest to young adults, including cartoonists, photographers, music composers, bestselling authors of adult novels, media directors, producers, and performers, but also literary and artistic figures studied in academic curricula, such as influential novelists, playwrights, poets, and painters. The goal of *Authors and Artists for Young Adults* is to present this great diversity of creative artists in a format that is entertaining, informative, and understandable to the young adult reader.

Entry Format

Each volume of *Authors and Artists for Young Adults* will furnish in-depth coverage of twenty to twenty-five authors and artists. The typical entry consists of:

—A detailed biographical section that includes date of birth, marriage, children, education, and addresses.

—A comprehensive bibliography or filmography including publishers, producers, and years.

—Adaptations into other media forms.

—Works in progress.

—A distinctive essay featuring comments on an artist's life, career, artistic intentions, world views, and controversies.

—References for further reading.

—Extensive illustrations, photographs, movie stills, cartoons, book covers, and other relevant visual material.

A cumulative index to featured authors and artists appears in each volume.

Compilation Methods

The editors of *Authors and Artists for Young Adults* make every effort to secure information directly from the authors and artists through personal correspondence and interviews. Sketches on living authors and artists are sent to the biographee for review prior to publication. Any sketches not personally reviewed by biographees or their representatives are marked with an asterisk (*).

Highlights of Forthcoming Volumes

Among the authors and artists planned for future volumes are:

Berenice Abbott
Mitch Albom
Amelia Atwater-Rhodes
Avi
Gary L. Blackwood
Lewis Carroll
Chris Crutcher
Christopher Paul Curtis
Fedor Dostoevsky
Daphne du Maurier
Shelby Foote
Jack Gantos

Edward Gorey
Adele Griffin
Libby Hathorn
Will Hobbs
Kimberly Willis Holt
Nalo Hopkinson
Ji-Li Jiang
William Joyce
Gail Carson Levine
Janet Lunn
Peter Matthiessen
Lurlene McDaniel

Hayao Miyazaki
Gloria Naylor
I. M. Pei
Rick Reilly
Diego Rivera
Charles Schulz
William Sleator
Gary Soto
Andrew Lloyd Webber
Orson Welles
Lois-Ann Yamanaka
Paul Zindel

Contact the Editor

We encourage our readers to examine the entire *AAYA* series. Please write and tell us if we can make AAYA even more helpful to you. Give your comments and suggestions to the editor:

BY MAIL: The Editor, *Authors and Artists for Young Adults*, 27500 Drake Rd., Farmington Hills, MI 48331-3535.

BY TELEPHONE: (800) 347-GALE

Acknowledgments

Grateful acknowledgment is made to the following publishers, authors, and artists for their kind permission to reproduce copyrighted material.

JOAN ABELOVE. From a jacket of *Go and Come Back*, by Joan Abelove. DK Ink Books, 1998. Jacket painting copyright © 1998 Elly Simmons. Reproduced by permission of DK Publishing, Inc./ Manley, Matt, illustrator. From a jacket of *Saying It Out Loud*, by Joan Abelove. DK Ink Books, 1999. Jacket art © 1999 by Matt Manley. Reproduced by permission./ Simmons, Elly, illustrator.

BRUCE BROOKS. Brooks, Bruce (seated in leather chair wearing polka dot tie, round glasses), photograph. Reproduced by permission of Mr. Brooks.

STEVEN K. BRUST. Rakeland, Sam, illustrator. From a cover of *The Phoenix Guards*, by Steven Brust. TOR Books, 1992. Reproduced by permission./ Rakeland, Sam, illustrator. From a cover of *The Gypsy*, by Steven Brust and Megan Lindholm. TOR Books, 1993. Reproduced by permission./ Burns, Jim, illustrator. From a cover of *Agyar*, by Steven Brust. TOR Books, 1994. Reproduced by permission./ Rakeland, Sam, illustrator. From a cover of *Five Hundred Years After*, by Steven Brust. TOR Books, 1995. Reproduced by permission./ Brust, Steven, photograph. Reproduced by permission./ Hickman, Stephen, illustrator. From a jacket of *Dragon*, by Steven Brust. TOR Books, 1998. Reproduced by permission./ Brust, Steven K., photograph by David Dyer-Bennet. Reproduced by permission.

ALBERT CAMUS. Burne-Jones, Sir Edward, illustrator. From a cover of *The Myth of Sisyphus and Other Essays*, by Albert Camus. Vintage International, 1991. Reproduced by permission./ Hall, Barnaby, photographer. From a cover of *The Fall*, by Albert Camus. Vintage International, 1991. Reproduced by permission./ Reinberg, Tracey, photographer. From a cover of *The Plague*, by Albert Camus. Vintage International, 1991. Reproduced by permission./ Bullaty, Sonja, and Angelo Lomeo, photographers. From a cover of *The First Man*, by Albert Camus. Vintage International, 1996. Cover photograph © Sonja Bullaty and Angelo Lomeo. Reproduced by permission./ Camus, Albert, photograph. AP/Wide World Photos. Reprinted by permission.

PAULA DANZIGER. Csatari, Joe, illustrator. From a cover of *Not for a Billion Gazillion Dollars* by Paula Danziger. Yearling, 1992. Copyright © 1992 by Paula Danziger. Jacket illustration © 1992 by Joe Csatari. Reproduced by permission of Random House Children's Books, a division of Random House, Inc./ Colin, Paul, illustrator. From a jacket cover of *P. S. Longer Letter Later* by Paula Danziger and Ann M. Martin. Scholastic Press, 1998. Jacket illustrated copyright © 1998 by Paul Colin. Reprinted by permission of Scholastic Inc./ Cover of *Amber Brown Goes Fourth*, by Paula Danziger. Little Apple Paperbacks, 1995. Reproduced by permission./ Danziger, Paula (wearing beaded scarf around head), photograph by Paul Abdoo. Reproduced by permission.

CYNTHIA DEFELICE. Lill, Debra, illustrator. From a jacket of *The Strange Night Writing of Jessamine Colter*, by Cynthia DeFelice. Macmillan Publishing Company, 1988. © 1988 by Macmillan Publishing Company. © 1988 by Debra Lill. Reproduced by permission./ Cover of *Lostman's River*, by Cynthia DeFelice. Avon Camelot Books, 1995. Reproduced by permission./ Dooling, Michael, illustrator. From a jacket of *The Apprenticeship of Lucas Whitaker*, by Cynthia DeFelice. Farrar, Straus, & Giroux, 1996. Jacket illustration © 1996 by Michael Dooling. Reproduced by permission./ DeFelice, Cynthia (wearing white crew neck sweater underneathblack blazer), photograph by Neil Sjoblom. Reproduced by permission of Cynthia DeFelice.

STEPHEN R. DONALDSON. Herring, Michael, illustrator. From a cover of *The Illearth War*, by Stephen R. Donaldson. Del Rey Books, 1978. Reproduced by permission./ Herring, Michael, illustrator. From a cover of *The Wounded Land*, Stephen R. Donaldson. Del Rey Books, 1981. Reproduced by permission./ Whelan, Michael, illustrator. From a cover of *The Mirror of Her Dreams*, by Stephen R. Donaldson. Del Rey Books, 1987. Reproduced by permission./ Cover of *A Man Rides Through*, by Stephen R. Donaldson. Del Rey Books, 1988. Reproduced by permission./ Yuoll, Stephen, illustrator. From a cover of *A Dark and Hungry God Arises*, by Stephen R Donaldson. Bantam Books, 1993. Cover art © 1993 by Stephen Youll. Reproduced by permission.

SYLVIA LOUISE ENGDAHL. Engdahl, Sylvia Louise, photograph. Reproduced by permission.

DAVID FINCHER. Norton, Edward and Brad Pitt in the movie *Fight Club*, photograph by David Fincher. The Kobal Collection. Reproduced by permission./ Scene from the film, *The Fight Club*. The Kobal Collection. Reproduced by permission./ Weaver, Sigourney in the film *Alien III*, 1992, photograph by David Fincher. The Kobal Collection. Reproduced by permission./ Freeman, Morgan, and Brad Pitt in the movie *Seven*, 1995, photograph. The Kobal Collection. Reproduced by permission./ Douglas, Michael in the film *The Game*, 1997, photograph by Tony Friedkin. The Kobal Collection. Reproduced by permission.

ERIK CHRISTIAN HAUGAARD . Cover of *Cromwell's Boy*, by Erik Christian Haugaard. Houghton Mifflin Company, 1978. Reproduced by permission./ Cover of *A Boy's Will*, by Erik Christian Haugaard. Houghton Mifflin Company, 1983. Reproduced by permission./ Cover of *The Samurai's Tale*, by Erik Christian Haugaard. Houghton Mifflin Company, 1984. Reproduced by permission./ Evans, Leslie, illustrator. From a jacket of *The Boy and the Samurai*, by Erik Christian Haugaard. Houghton Mifflin Company, 1991. Jacket art © 1991 by Leslie Evans. Reproduced by permission./ Evans, Leslie, illustrator. From a jacket of *The Revenge of the Forty-Seven Samurai*, by Erik Christian Haugaard. Houghton Mifflin Company, 1995. Jacket art © 1995 by Leslie Evans. Reproduced by permission./ Haugaard, Erik, photograph. Reproduced by permission of Erik Haugaard.

GUY GAVRIEL KAY. Cover of *Tigana*, by Guy Gavriel Kay. Roc Books, 1991. Reproduced by permission./ Cover of *The Darkest Road*, by Guy Gavriel Kay. Roc Books, 1992. Reproduced by permission./ Cover of *The Summer Tree*, by Guy Gavriel Kay. Roc Books, 1992. Reproduced by permission./ Odom, Mel, illustrator. From a cover of *A Song for Arbonne*, by Guy Gavriel Kay. Roc Books, 1994. Reproduced by permission.

HARRY MAZER. Cover of *Snow Bound*, by Harry Mazer. Laurel-Leaf Books, 1975. Reproduced by permission./ Freeman, Tom, illustrator. From a cover of *The Last Mission*, by Harry Mazer. Laurel-Leaf Books, 1981. Reproduced by permission./ Cover of *Who Is Eddie Leonard?* by Harry Mazer. Laurel-Leaf Books, 1995. Reproduced by permission of Random House Children's Books, a division of Random House, Inc./ Buzelli, Christopher, illustrator.From a cover of *The Dog in the Freezer*, by Harry Mazer. Simon & Schuster Books for Young Readers, 1997. Cover illustration © 1997 by Christopher Buzelli. Reproduced by permission of the illustrator./ Lanino, Deborah, illustrator. From a jacket of *The Wild Kid*, by Harry Mazer. Simon & Schuster Books for Young Readers, 1998. Jacket illustration © 1998 by Deborah Lanino. Reproduced by permission of the illustrator./ Mazer, Harry (looking up to the left), photograph by Ruth Putter. Reproduced by permission.

NORMA FOX MAZER. Gallagher, S. Saelig, illustrator. From a jacket of *When She Was Good*, by Norma Fox Mazer. Arthur A. Levine Books, 1997. Jacket art © 1997 by S. Saelig Gallagher. Reproduced by permission of Scholastic Inc./ Mazer, Norma Fox (body facing left), photograph by Darkroom on Wheels. Reproduced by permission of Norma Fox Mazer.

COLLEEN MCCULLOUGH. Laurie, Piper, and Mel Gibson, in the film *Tim*. The Kobal Collection. Reproduced by permission./ McCullough, Colleen, 1981, photograph. AP/Wide World Photos. Reproduced by permission./ Villarreal, William L. From a jacket of *The Thornbirds*, by Colleen McCullough. Gramercy Books, 1998. Reproduced by permission./ Ward, Rachel, and Richard Chamberlain, in the film *The Thornbirds*. The Kobal Collection. Reproduced by permission.

GORDON PARKS. Parks, Gordon, photograph. Corbis-Bettmann. Reproduced by permission./ Parks, Gordon, photographer. "Homeless Couple." From a photograph in *Half Past Autumn: A Retrospective*, by Gordon Parks and Philip Brookman. Bullfinch Press Books, 1997. © 1997 by Gordon Parks. Reproduced by permission./ Parks, Gordon, photographer. "Black Muslim Rally, New York, 1963." From a photograph in *Half Past Autumn: A Retrospective*, by Gordon Parks and Philip Brookman. Bullfinch Press Books, 1997. © 1997 by Gordon Parks. Reproduced by permission./ Parks, Gordon, photographer. "Child and Doll, North Carolina." From a photograph in *Half Past Autumn: A Retrospective*, by Gordon Parks and Philip Brookman. Bullfinch Press Books, 1997. © 1997 by Gordon Parks. Reproduced by permission./ Roundtree, Richard, in the film *Shaft*, photograph. AP/Wide World Photo. Reproduced by permission.

J. D. SALINGER. Jacket of *Nine Stories*, by J. D. Salinger. Little, Brown and Company, 1953. Reproduced by permission./ Jacket of *Franny and Zooey*, by J. D. Salinger. Little, Brown and Company, 1961. Reproduced by permission./ Jacket of *Raise High the Roof Beams*, Carpenters, and Seymour: An Introduction, by J. D. Salinger. Little, Brown and Company. Reproduced by permission./ Salinger, J.D., photograph. The Library of Congress.

TOM SHADYAC. Carrey, Jim, Sean Young, and Jon Capodice, in the film *Ace Ventura: Pet Detective*, photograph by Tom Shadyac. The Kobal Collection. Reproduced by permission./ Murphy, Eddie, in the film *The Nutty Professor*, 1996, photograph by Bruce McBroom. The Kobal Collection. Reproduced by permission./ Tilly, Jennifer, and Jim Carrey in the film *Liar Liar,* photograph by Melinda Sue Gordon. The Kobal Collection. Reproduced by permission./ Shadyac, Tom, photograph. AP/Wide World Photo. Reproduced by permission.

JOHN UPDIKE. Updike, John (turned to his right, looking forward), 1990, photograph by Wyatt Counts. AP/Wide World Photos. Reproduced by permission./ Adam and Eve Sleeping, byengraving by William Blake. From a cover of *Couples*, by John Updike. Fawcett Columbine, 1996. Reproduced by permission./Cover of *Rabbit Is Rich*, by John Updike. Fawcett Columbine, 1996. Reproduced by permission./ Hashimoto, K., photographer. From a cover of *The Centaur*, by John Updike. Fawcett Columbine, 1996. Cover photograph © K. Hashimoto/Photonica. Reproduced by permission./Scholz, William, photographer. From a cover of *Pigeon Feathers and Other Stories,* by John Updike. Fawcett Columbine, 1996. Cover photograph © William Scholz/Photonica. Reproduced by permission./ Roth, Arnold, illustrator. From a cover of *Bech: A Book*, by John Updike. Fawcett Columbine, 1998. Reproduced by permission.

WENDELIN VAN DRAANEN. Yaccarino, Dan, illustrator. From a cover of *Sammy Keyes and the Hotel Thief*, by Wendelin Van Draanen. Knopf, 1998. Cover art © 1998 by Dan Yaccarino. Reproduced by permission./ Yaccarino, Dan, illustrator. From a cover of *Sammy Keyes and the Skeleton Man*, by Wendelin Van Draanen. Knopf, 1999. Cover art © 1998 by Dan Yaccarino. Reproduced by permission./ Yaccarino, Dan, illustrator. From a cover of *Sammy Keyes and the Sisters of Mercy*, by Wendelin Van Draanen. Knopf, 1999. Cover art © 1999 by Dan Yaccarino. Reproduced by permission./ Van Draanen, Wendelin, photograph. Reproduced by permission.

PHYLLIS A. WHITNEY. Cover of *The Golden Unicorn*, by Phyllis A. Whitney. Fawcett Crest, 1983. Reproduced by permission./ Cover of *Amethyst Dreams*, by Phyllis A. Whitney. Fawcett Crest, 1998. Reproduced by permission./ Cover of *Listen for the Whisperer*, by Phyllis A. Whitney. Fawcett Crest, 1989. Reproduced by permission./ Cover of *Feather on the Moon*, by Phyllis A. Whitney. Fawcett Crest, 1989. Reproduced by permission./ Cover of *Daughter of the Stars*, by Phyllis A. Whitney. Fawcett Crest, 1995. Reproduced by permission./ Whitney, Phyllis, photograph by Jerry Bauer . © Jerry Bauer. Reproduced by permission./ Whitney, Phyllis A., photograph by Malice Domestic. Reproduced by permission of the author.

DIANE WIELER. McGaw, Laurie, illustrator. From a cover of *Bad Boy* by Diana Wieler. A Groundwood Book, Douglas & McIntyre, 1989. Copyright © 1989 by Diana Wieler. Reproduced by permission./ Temertey, Ludmilla, illustrator and Emilio De Cesaris, photographer. From a cover of *Ranvan: A Worthy Opponent*, by Diana Wieler. Copyright © 1998 by Julia Bell. Groundwood Books, 1995. Reproduced by permission./ Temertey, Ludmilla, illustrator. From a cover of *Ran Van: Magic Nation* by Diana Wieler. A Groundwood Book, Douglas & McIntyre, 1997. Copyright © 1997 by Julia Bell. Reproduced by permission./ Bell, Julia, illustrator. From a jacket of *Drive*, by Diana Wieler. Groundwood Books, 1998. Illustration copyright © 1998 by Julia Bell. Reproduced by permission./ Wieler, Diana, photograph. Towne Studios Ltd. Reproduced by permission.

SIMON WIESENTHAL. Corbett, Jay, photographer. From a cover of *The Sunflower* by Simon Wiesenthal. Revised edition. Schocken Books, 1998. © 1997 by Simon Wiesenthal. Reproduced by permission./ Wiesenthal, Simon (head and shoulders), photograph. UPI/Corbis-Bettmann. Reproduced by permission.

ELLEN WITTLINGER. Wittlinger, Ellen, photograph, outdoors. Reproduced by permission.

Authors & Artists for Young Adults

Joan Abelove

■ Personal

Raised in New York; daughter of a businessman; married Steve Hoffman, 1987; children: Andrew. *Education:* Barnard College, B.A., 1966; City University of New York, Ph.D. (anthropology), 1978.

■ Addresses

E-mail—JoanAndy@aol.com.

■ Career

Taught emotionally disturbed boys in a state hospital, New York; part-time teacher of anthropology at colleges in New York City, c. 1978-84; technical writer, 1984—.

■ Member

Society of Children's Book Writers and Illustrators, Authors Guild.

■ Awards, Honors

Notable Children's Books and Best Books for Young Adults selections, both American Library Association, and Best Books commendations, *Publishers Weekly* and *School Library Journal*, Editor's Choice designation, *Booklist*, named Blue Ribbon Book, *Bulletin of the Center for Children's Books*, Fanfare selection, *Horn Book*, Book of Distinction, *Riverbank Review*, Pick of the Lists, American Booksellers Association, Editors' Choice, *Kliatt*, Booklinks' Lasting Connections, Pick of the Lists selection, American Booksellers Association, and *Los Angeles Times* Book Prize finalist, all 1999, all for *Go and Come Back*; Best Books for Young Adults selection, American Library Association, 2000, Best Book of the Year commendation, *Publishers Weekly*, and Books for the Teenage designation, New York Public Library, all for *Saying ItOut Loud*.

■ Writings

Go and Come Back, DK Ink, 1998.
Saying It Out Loud, DK Ink, 1999.

Contributor of story, "Sproing!," to *Lost and Found*, Forge, 2000.

■ Work in Progress

A novel.

■ Sidelights

An encounter experienced over two decades before in the jungles of Peru would serve as the foundation for Joan Abelove's first work of fiction. The author of *Go and Come Back,* an award-winning novel about a young Isabo woman whose village becomes the home for two American anthropology students, Abelove herself spent two years in the Amazon jungle in the 1970s while doing her doctoral research in cultural anthropology. Hailing the debut work of fiction as being "Full of life and packed with characters that by turns irritate and enlighten," *Booklist* reviewer Ilene Cooper deemed *Go and Come Back* "a startling, vibrant read." Abelove would follow the success of *Go and Come Back* with 1999's *Saying It Out Loud,* a book that also draws heavily upon the author's own experiences.

Raised in upstate New York, Abelove enjoyed reading as a child, and her first efforts at writing came early on. "I wrote short stories in elementary school," she told an interviewer for *AAYA,* "but never showed them to anyone. I wrote a lot of school papers but never fiction." It wasn't until 1991, after working for several years as a technical writer, that Abelove began to experiment with the novel genre. "A friend had decided to take a writing class at [New York City's] New School, and I took it with him. I still take the class. So my writing really came late in life, but I have always loved to read."

Visit to Peru Makes Lasting Impression

After high school graduation, Abelove enrolled at Barnard College, and graduated in 1966. Six years later, in 1972, as a Ph.D. candidate in clinical psychology at the City University of New York, Abelove and a friend went to live in the Peruvian jungle. After spending two years in the Amazon basin studying local tribes, Abelove returned to the United States and changed her academic focus to cultural anthropology. Receiving her doctorate in 1978, she taught undergraduate anthropology for several years before leaving the field to begin a new career as a technical writer.

Although she would never return to the Peruvian jungle, Abelove realized she had been through something that would change her life. As she told *AAYA,* "The experience has transformed my life in many ways—mainly in noticing the incredible way my own culture has shaped my views, and how these views seem so natural, so correct and true, but are, in reality, learned." She wanted to share this new understanding by writing about the

people she had lived among for two years, "and especially," she added, "about one young woman who had become my friend."

Abelove made several efforts to write her story, but "it came out pedantic and preachy. I put it away, began it again, put it away." In 1991 she started another book, the story of a teen coping with the death of her mother that would eventually become her second novel, 1999's *Saying It Out Loud.* "All the while, I had this other book, this jungle book, in the back of my head," the novelist recalled. "Then one day, while I was on the treadmill at my gym, a voice whispered `Two old white ladies came to live in my village today.'" Abelove recognized the voice: it was that of her Peruvian friend Alicia. "And I knew that I could write the book I wanted, that . . . it was through Alicia that I could tell my story."

Fictionalizes Experiences in *Go and Come Back*

Alicia, the teen narrator of *Go and Come Back,* is a member of the fictional Isabo tribe in the jungle village of Poincushmana. Promised in marriage to her sister's husband, Alicia does not welcome becoming a second wife to an old man. When a sickly *nawa* infant—a child not of Isabo blood—is abandoned in her village, she adopts the child, creating a sense of maturity and independence for herself while also saving the child's life.

Soon Joanna and Margarita, two American graduate students in their twenties, come to the village, and ask permission to live there for one year while they take notes on agriculture and babies. "Joanna is basically me, Margarita is basically the anthropologist friend I did my field work with, who happens to still be one of my closest friends," Abelove explained. "The `basically' is important. Since the book is a novel, I made one character more likeable than the other." In the book, the white women are seen to be somewhat out of their element by the villagers with whom they have come to study, and their own lessons quickly extend beyond agriculture and babies.

The villagers agree to build Joanna and Margarita a house and kitchen; until the buildings are finished the two students live at the home of Chawa, the daughter of Papaisi, the village sage. While their strange habits cause the Isabo much amusement, the two white women are also found to be stingy, refusing to share their vast stores of sugar, string, spirits, and otherthings with the tribe. Sharing, not trade, is the Isabo way; Isabo culture dictates that food and supplies be divided among kinsmen, and the villagers consider stealing from those who will not share to be a lesser sin than not sharing. It is not until the village decides that, because of their stinginess, the white women should be asked to leave that Joanna and Margarita realize how their own ignorance has allowed them to be perceived.

Other aspects of Western culture come under the microscope of the Isabo perspective. The white women are looked at askance for not participating in the same bathing rituals as the tribe. Finally, Alicia tells them why they are laughed at: "[Y]ou are dirty in the morning. Dirty at the most important bath time. Dirty to begin the day. That is why people have been laughing at you in the morning." However, explanations of such things as indoor plumbing, American dating and mating habits, and views of death in Western culture are unfathomable to the Peruvian natives. Just before they depart for the United States, the two women take Alicia for a plane ride and she sees her village from high above. Through this trip, as well as through her year-long relationship, she also gains new perspectives on the world.

Visit Provides Readers with Fresh Perspective

By describing her own view of the white women—considered "old white ladies" by the Isabo—Alicia reveals to readers a fresh take on their own culture. As a bridge between her own tribe and the white women, Alicia learns to appreciate the differences she and her Isabo friend had at first ridiculed; meanwhile Joanna and Margarita are also transformed by the tribal culture as they begin to understand and accept its practices. A large part of Abelove's purpose in writing the novel was, as she once explained, "to describe theexperience of living with people who at first seemed so different from me and anyone I had known, and of discovering that we were more the same than not."

While *Go and Come Back* is a work of fiction, much of it is based on actual people and occurrences. "The character Alicia is based on a woman who was really a bit older than Alicia in the book," Abelove explained to *AAYA*; "and every event described in the book actually happened: Margarita did have terrible stomach pains that were cured [by the village healer after our medicines would not work]; we really did get hookworm; Alicia did adopt a Peruvian baby that died (although the baby she adopted was a boy, even more remarkable, since boy babies are not nearly as valued as girl babies)."

The character of Papaisi is also based on an actual person, an old man in the village who was a curer. In the book, Papaisi's role extends beyond mere medicine man; he is the glue holding the village together, exhibiting great common sense, dispensing justice fairly in disagreements that surface among the villagers, and serving as spokes-

Two U.S. anthropologists learn more about the world and themselves while studying a Peruvian tribe in Abelove's first novel, published in 1998.

person when necessary. When Margarita becomes ill with a terrible stomachache, the medicines brought by the two white women do no good— only the ministrations of Papaisi cure her. Infestations of lice, hookworm, and other insects caught from the sands or river water are dealt with as a matter of course among the Isabo, as is death, which happens with frequency. "These people have survived for centuries on what they know and continue to learn about the healing powers of the medicinal herbs they live around," Abelove told *AAYA*. "They are also enormously interested in any Western medicine that works for them. They are extremely practical and pragmatic about healing illnesses."

Visits by Westerners to Peruvian villages have brought with them new influences and the gradual introduction of technology, as Abelove illustrates in her story. Modern gadgetry given by the young anthropologists, as well as well-meaning advice from a group of missionaries, is cheerfully accepted, then discarded because of its uselessness or because the Isabo realize that it will harm some other facet of their existence. While they are ignorant of most modern technology, the Isabo are never portrayed as foolish in Abelove's narrative. "I was very impressed with the natives' ability to pick and choose from what was offered by fairly well-intentioned visitors," the novelist explained in her interview. "Alicia stopped 'believing' in the missionaries' god when the tape recorder some Swiss missionaries gave her broke, [while] the man who cured Margarita asked me for some aspirin for his stomachache. The people I lived with in that village were extremely practical. If aspirin worked, they took it. If believing got you a tape recorder, they believed."

Sixteen-year-old Mindy finds solace in her friends as she struggles with her terminally ill mother and grief-stricken father in this 1999 novel.

Human Connection Transcends Language Barrier

One of the strongest themes in *Go and Come Back* is the indefinable quality that draws human beings to one another as friends, which is "based on some ineffable human emotional connection that cut[s] through the differences created by language, culture and history," according to Abelove. "I can't say that we became fluent in the language," the author added in her interview. "We had daily lessons with a woman who I called Elena in the book. But what I learned from the experience is that it takes a lot more than words

to communicate. And there are certainly times when words can become a hindrance to really sensing what is going on in someone else's mind and heart. After all, you can't lie unless you are using language to do it."

Another of the interesting aspects of Abelove's book is the way it illustrates the development of language. The Isabos have no word that equals "goodbye." Their word used in parting is *catanhue,* which translated means "go and come back."

In addition to earning its author several awards, including the American Library Association's Best Book for Young Adults citation, *Go and Come Back* was lauded by reviewers. Abelove's novel "provides countless opportunities for misunderstandings by the observer and the observed, most of them a source of humor for the reader and tension for the participants," asserted *Horn Book* reviewer Nancy Vasilakis. "By juxtaposing these two radically different cultures, Abelove provides humorous yet respectful insight into both." Pam Gosner added in *School Library Journal* that the anecdotal information "never overwhelms the narrative," and called *Go and Come Back* a "compelling novel."

While *New York Times Book Review* contributor Jen Nessel criticized the novel for its lack of a strong plot line, the critic added that "by its end the reader has nonetheless become attached to the characters and their relationships. We are left with a lot to think about in our own culture—why we think the things we think and do the things we do." Since writing *Go and Come Back*, Abelove has been asked to visit schools and libraries, where she gives a presentation that includes slides of her trip to the Amazon, showing pictures of the actual people whom she has woven into her story.

Saying It Out Loud

The inspiration for *Saying It Out Loud* was the tragic death of Abelove's mother, who died of a brain tumor when Abelove was sixteen. By turns poignant and humorous, the novel finds sixteen-year-old Mindy attempting the adolescent task of navigating a changing and sometimes conflicting relationship with her mother while also dealing with her mother's imminent death. Her father, a rigid, bigoted, chauvinistic, and unemotional man, provides her with neither guidance nor comfort during the final months of her mother's life. Isolated from her father's efforts to part with his wife, Mindy goes to the hospital on her own to make her peace with a mother who, after her final surgery, is unable to communicate with the outside world. "This woman, whose hand I was holding was still staring at the wall, oblivious... She hadn't even noticed my touch. I closed my eyes again. Maybe if I just sit here... just be near her, she will wake up, she will shake her head and say `Hi, sweetie.'"

The character of Mindy's father, a man who would disown his own daughter should she marry a Gentile boy, looms over her narrative like an impenetrable wall. But as her father withdraws into his own grief, Mindy fills the void he creates by finding solace in friendships; her best friend Gail, Gail's happy-go-lucky little brother Andrew, a caring neighbor, a schoolmate named Bobby who shows a growing interest in her, and Mindy's own recollections of episodes with her mother all allow her to express her sadness, guilt, and sometimes even anger. While many of the book's episodes, such as those that relate to Mindy's mom's increased suffering due to her developing brain tumor, are sad, others reflect the experiences of many teens growing up in the 1960s, and even today.

Saying It Out Loud received praise from critics for its realistic depiction of adolescent emotion. Deborah Stevenson, a contributor to *Bulletin of the Center for Children's Books,* commended the novel's "particularly authentic . . . depiction of strain laying bare a family's secrets." Praising Abelove's second novel as "a quiet book," *Voice of Youth Advocates* reviewer Judy Sasges added that "Mindy copes with death and spiritual questions, and challenges authority with strength and maturity." "[Mindy's] isolation is palpable," declared *Horn Book* critic Nancy Vasilakis. *School Library Journal* contributor Barbara Auerbach described *Saying It Out Loud* as "a beautifully written and tender portrayal of one young woman coming to grips with loss."

The character of Mindy reflects Abelove a great deal, and the author drew on many specific memories of her own adolescence in writing the book. "The books Mindy talks about are some of my favorite books as a kid," she told *AAYA;* she also "had first hand experience being raised by a father who adamantly did not want his daughter to marry anyone who wasn't Jewish." The character of Andrew, an exuberant young boy, is based on the author's own son, as well as "a number of other children I have known over the years, many of whom are now adults."

Career as Writer Takes Several Forms

While much of her energy has lately been put into writing novels for young adults, Abelove has worked as a technical writer since the 1980s. "I work every day, 9 to 5, writing technically," she explained to *AAYA.* "Writing fiction is entirely dissimilar," she added. "The skills barely overlap." While technical writing requires reviewing and distilling factual information, fiction is a creative

If you enjoy the works of Joan Abelove, you may also want to check out the following books:

Louise Moeri, *The Forty-Third War*, 1989.
Suzanne Fisher Staples, *Shabanu: Daughter of the Wind*, 1989.
Frances Temple, *A Taste of Salt*, 1992.

act, the first step of which is finding the right voice. "Once I find the voice of the storyteller, the story tells itself," Abelove once explained. "But it is my experience that you have to do a lot of writing before you find the voice. A good writing class and a good critique group help with finding the voice. I have been taking a writing workshop since 1991, and have been in a critique group since 1993. They are both indispensable to my work, as is my incomparable editor, Dick Jackson. My work is indelibly enriched by the experience of working with him."

Abelove plans to continue writing for young audiences. "My next book is very much in process," she told *AAYA*. "I am not sure at all where it is going. All I can say is that I will continue to write novels. It's what I love to do."

■ **Works Cited**

Abelove, Joan, *Go and Come Back*, DK Publishing, 1998.

Abelove, Joan, *Saying It Out Loud*, DK Publishing, 1999.
Abelove, Joan, interview with *Authors and Artists for Young Adults*, May, 2000.
Auerbach, Barbara, review of *Saying It Out Loud*, *School Library Journal*, September, 1999, p. 218.
Cooper, Ilene, review of *Go and Come Back*, *Booklist*, March 1, 1998, p. 1129.
Gosner, Pam, review of *Go and Come Back*, *School Library Journal*, March, 1998, p. 208.
Nessel, Jen, review of *Go and Come Back*, *New York Times Book Review*, June 21, 1998.
Sasges, Judy, review of *Saying It Out Loud*, *Voice of Youth Advocates*, October, 1999, p. 254.
Stevenson, Deborah, review of *Saying It Out Loud*, *Bulletin of the Center for Children's Books*, October, 1999, pp. 44-45.
Vasilakis, Nancy, review of *Go and Come Back*, *Horn Book*, May-June, 1998, p. 337.
Vasilakis, Nancy, review of *Saying It Out Loud*, *Horn Book*, September-October, 1999, p. 605.

■ **For More Information See**

PERIODICALS

Kirkus Reviews, January 15, 1998, p. 108.
Kliatt, September, 1999. p. 4.
Magpies, July, 1999, p. 36.
Publishers Weekly, February 2, 1998, p. 91.

—*Sketch by J. Sydney Jones*

Bruce Brooks

■ Personal

Born September 23, 1950, in Washington, DC; son of Donald D. Brooks and Lelia Colleen Collins; married Penelope Winslow, June 17, 1978; children: Alexander. *Education:* University of North Carolina at Chapel Hill, B.A., 1972; University of Iowa, M.F.A., 1982. *Politics:* "Certainly." *Religion:* "Lapsed Baptist." *Hobbies and other interests:* Music, nature study, sports, reading.

■ Addresses

Home and office—11208 Legato Way, Silver Spring, MD 20901.

■ Career

Writer. Has worked variously as a letterpress printer, newspaper and magazine reporter, and teacher.

■ Awards, Honors

Best Books, *School Library Journal,* and Notable Books, *New York Times,* both 1984, Newbery Honor, American Library Association (ALA), and *Boston Globe-Horn Book* Award, both 1985, and Notable Books, ALA, all for *The Moves Make the Man;* Best Books, *School Library Journal,* and Best Books for Young Adults, ALA, both 1986, Fanfare Honor List, *Horn Book,* and teacher's choice, National Council of Teachers of English, both 1987, young adult choice, International Reading Association, 1988, and Best Books for Young Adults of the 1980s, ALA/*Booklist,* all for *Midnight Hour Encores;* Best Books for Young Adults, ALA, young adult editor's choice, ALA/*Booklist,* Best Books, *School Library Journal,* and Notable Children's Trade Book in the Field of Social Studies, National Council for the Social Studies-Children's Book Council, all for *No Kidding;* Notable Books, ALA, and Best Books, *School Library Journal,* both for *Everywhere;* Best Books for Young Adults, ALA, 1990, for *On the Wing: The Life of Birds from Feathers to Flight;* Best Books for Young Adults, ALA, 1992, for *Predator!;* John Burroughs Award, 1992, for *Nature By Design;* Newbery Honor Book, Notable Books, and Best Books for Young Adults, all ALA, and Fanfare book, *Horn Book,* all 1993, all for *What Hearts.*

■ Writings

YOUNG ADULT FICTION

The Moves Make the Man, Harper, 1984.
Midnight Hour Encores, Harper, 1986.
No Kidding, Harper, 1989.
What Hearts, HarperCollins, 1992.

Asylum for Nightface, HarperCollins, 1996.
Vanishing, HarperCollins, 1999.

"THE WOLFBAY WINGS" SERIES

Woodsie, HarperCollins, 1997.
Zip, HarperCollins, 1997.
Cody, HarperCollins, 1997.
Boot, HarperCollins, 1998.
Prince, HarperCollins, 1998.
Shark, HarperCollins, 1998.
Billy, HarperCollins, 1998.
Dooby, HarperCollins, 1998.
Reed, HarperCollins, 1998.
Subtle, HarperCollins, 1999.
Barry, HarperCollins, 1999.
Woodsie, Again, HarperCollins, 1999.

JUVENILE FICTION

Everywhere, Harper, 1990.
Each a Piece, illustrated by Elena Pavlov, Harper Collins, 1996.
Throwing Smoke, HarperCollins, 2000.

NONFICTION

On the Wing: The Life of Birds from Feathers to Flight, Scribner, 1989.
Predator!, Farrar, Straus, 1991.
Nature by Design, Farrar, Straus, 1991.
Making Sense: Animal Perception and Communication, Farrar, Straus, 1993.
Boys Will Be, Holt, 1993.
(With Glenn Rivers) *Those Who Love the Game*, Holt, 1994.
NBA by Numbers, Scholastic, 1997.
(Editor) *The Red Wasteland: A Personal Selection of Writings about Nature for Young Readers*, Holt, 1998.

OTHER

Author of introductions to reprinted sports fiction of John R. Tunis, including *The Kid from Tomkinsville*, *Rookie of the Year*, *World Series*, and *Keystone Kids*. Brooks's work has been translated into German.

■ Sidelights

Two-time Newbery Honor book winner Bruce Brooks is an author of nonfiction, novels, and stories for both YA and younger readers. Called "an outstandingly perceptive writer," by a critic for *Kirkus Reviews*, Brooks has blended interests in sports and in nature to create a diverse body of work for readers of a wide range of ages. A graduate of the prestigious University of Iowa writing program, Brooks put his prodigious talents to work in his first novel, *The Moves Make the Man*, an interracial tale of hoops and hopes, to create an impressive debut; the book won a Newbery Honor and a *Boston Globe-Horn Book* Award. Since that 1984 novel, Brooks has gone on to pen some thirty books in genres from serious fiction to series fiction, from picture books to detailed accounts of the lives of birds.

In his fiction, Brooks often deals with outsider themes, placing his young protagonists in the crosshairs of adult incompetence—victims of a broken home or of alcoholic abuse. In this respect, Brooks writes out of his own personal experience. Even in his "Wolfbay Wings" series about a high-school hockey team, Brooks manages to invest his prose with depth, both in characterization and in ideas. As Michael Cart put it in *St. James Guide to Young Adult Writers*, "Bruce Brooks is that rarity in the world of books for young readers—a novelist of ideas. But he is also a rare stylist whose writer's razzle always dazzles thanks to his uncanny ear for voice and his powerful imagery and unforgettable simile and metaphor."

Brooks was born on September 23, 1950, in Richmond, Virginia, but spent much of his childhood in North Carolina, where he moved after the divorce of his parents when he was six years old. The child of a divided family, Brooks shuttled back and forth between parents, learning to adapt to different surroundings in the process. At his father's in Washington, D.C., he was part of a "smaller, urban-oriented family" as he once told *Authors and Artists for Young Adults* (*AAYA*). In North Carolina with his mother, he belonged to a "larger Southern clan." Moving back and forth, he felt he never had the chance to develop close friendships with his peers; he was always the new kid, learning to grab friendship fast when he could. He developed fast-talking, story-telling skills to this end.

Lessons Learned

"Belonging to both worlds but not belonging completely to either was really an experience that made me an observer and a student of social situations," Brooks told *AAYA*. "[I]t made me learn how to apply myself to people and activities and to figure out how to belong, after figuring out which natural parts of me belonged and which did not." But such chameleon-like skills also had their cost. "I could never really relax and just say, 'Ah, this is me, I'm among my peers.' I was never among my peers. I was always somewhat different from everyone else. I was always the Yankee kid in the South, and when I went back to the North I was always the Southern kid. It led me to simply be very watchful." It also led to an early love of books and reading, constants in an otherwise ever-changing world.

"Bruce Brooks is that rarity in the world of books for young readers—a novelist of ideas. But he is also a rare stylist whose writer's razzle always dazzles thanks to his uncanny ear for voice and his powerful imagery and unforgettable simile and metaphor."

—Michael Cart

Brooks attended college at the University of North Carolina at Chapel Hill, graduating in 1972. He had long harbored the notion of becoming a writer, but upon graduation, he quickly understood the realities of simply making a living. Working variously as a letterpress printer and journalist, Brooks used the hours before and after work to hone his writing skills. Then in the late 1970s he attended the Iowa Writer's Workshop, an experience that not only trained him in the technique of writing, but that also afforded him two years to simply write. "I went there very aggressive intellectually," Brooks once told Christine McDonnell of *Horn Book*, "and came out very ambitious and increasingly confident. I used the workshop to boost my feeling that anything is possible. The only things I want to do are books that are unique and different."

Like so many authors for young adults, Brooks never intended to write for a niche audience. The fact that his first novel had teenage protagonists

was enough to prompt editors to advise Brooks to send it to the children's divisions of their houses. "I've never written *for* kids," Brooks told Leonard S. Marcus in a *Publishers Weekly* interview. Instead, as he put it, he writes for "intelligent people. I write *about* kids because my own childhood is still something that I am very much wondering about." Overcoming initial surprise over his YA audience, Brooks quickly came to prize this readership. "They don't just read a book," Brooks told Marcus, " they *use* it. And reading matters so much to the kids themselves that it's enthralling to have them respond to my books."

Debut Work Draws Praise

Brooks's first novel was *The Moves Make the Man*, set against the historical background of the 1950s school desegregation in the South. Brooks's own childhood spent moving between the South and the North gave him an eyewitness perspective from which to view the budding interracial friendship between two boys, Jerome and Bix. The boys discover that their racial differences prove less important than their common personality traits. Both loners, they frequent a secluded basketball court where Jerome teaches Bix how to play the game. Through this activity, Jerome learns about his new friend's unfortunate domestic situation. Bix's confidence and happiness has eroded since his mother suffered a nervous breakdown and entered the hospital. In addition, his stepfather refuses to take Bix tosee her. Determined to visit his mother, Bix proposes a deal to his stepfather. If Bix beats him at a game of one-on-one, they will go to the hospital. Although Bix wins and invites Jerome along for the ensuing trip, the reunion is not what Bix had expected and he runs away from home, leaving Jerome alone to sort out the jarring events.

The Moves Make the Man earned enthusiastic critical response; it was named a Newbery honor book and won a *Boston Globe-Horn Book* Award. Writing in the *New York Times*, Mel Watkins declared that "we get one of the most charming, witty protagonists you're likely to encounter" in this "excellent novel about values and the way people relate to each other." Robert E. Unsworth noted in *School Library Journal* that this first novel was more than just a sports story. "The sport is merely the vehicle for delivering a serious story of friendship and madness," Unsworth wrote. "The description of the basketball action is simply excellent, but all the writing is top rank. Brooks is, indeed, a major new talent in the YA field." *Booklist's* Denise M. Wilms pointed to "savvy monologue," while Allan A. Cuseo in *Voice of Youth Advocates* commented on the "fast hilarious prose" and *Horn Book*'s Nancy Hammond enjoyed the "breezy, irreverent first-person narration." It seemed there was something for everyone in Brooks's first novel.

Yet Brooks confessed that such praise was not as heady as might be expected for a first-time novelist. At the times the awards were bestowed, the author explained to *AAYA*, "I hadn't written a word of fiction in three years. I'd been working out the story on my second book, *Midnight Hour Encores*, for three years mentally, but I had not written anything because I was too busy earning a living and I had a new child. So when the awards came, I felt like a hypocrite. Here everybody was saying `Oh, brilliant new writer' and I didn't *feel* like a *writer*." Nonetheless, Brooks's success afforded him new career opportunities; he decided to quit his job and write full-time.

Brooks's next, and equally successful, venture was *Midnight Hour Encores*, a story narrated by Sibilance (Sib for short), a sixteen-year-old musical prodigy. Sib, whose parents separated after her birth, lives with her father, Taxi, in Washington DC, and has never met her mother. The self-absorbed Sib, one of the top-ranked cello players in the world, is wrapped up in her practices, competitions, and concerts, and is preparing to attend the prestigious Juilliard School of Music in New York City. While searching for a mentor after her cello teacher dies, Sib discovers that a brilliant but reclusive player may accept a teaching post at a new music school in California. Under the guise of visiting her mother, who also lives in the state, Sib travels to California to audition for the institution. Taxi drives her there, afraid all the while that his daughter will leave him. Sib initially considers Taxi's fears unfounded, but after an enjoyable and educational stay with her mother, she gradually becomes aware of what her father means to her. *Midnight Hour Encores* ends as Sib decides what school to attend and, consequently, which parent to live with.

Midnight Hour Encores was favorably received by critics. Deeming the work "another terrific book" from Brooks, *Washington Post Book World* contribu-

tor Katherine Paterson acknowledged the welcome complexity of the novel. "This is a book the reader will have to fool around with, poke into, and tell in his own accents," Paterson insisted. Although several reviews of the book focused on the novel's coming-of-age slant, Brooks remarked in *AAYA* that "to me *Midnight Hour Encores* is about being a father. I wrote that book in the year after my son was born. The most important thing in my life was being a father. . . . My curiosity about the future—of what you get when you invest certain things in the very early days of your child's life—inspired my imagination to come up with those characters and that story."

Dystopian Novel

Brooks's 1989 literary enterprise, *No Kidding,* again tackles a sophisticated topic. Set in twenty-first-century Washington, D.C., *No Kidding* presents a bleak environment in which alcoholics compose the majority of the population. Society is overwhelmed by this problem and schools have curriculum geared specifically toward alcoholics' offspring, more commonly referred to as AOs. The fourteen-year-old protagonist, an AO named Sam, has been forced to assume adult-level responsibility in his fatherless home. He previously committed his mother to a rehabilitation program and placed his younger brother, Ollie, with foster parents. Now that his mother's stint is completed, Sam must decide whether to reunite the family. Complicating Sam's decision is the knowledge that his mothermay revert to her old behavior and that Ollie, who is unaware of her alcoholism, may experience emotional problems. At book's end, however, Sam's mother manipulates events to generate the outcome, giving Sam the chance to assume the role of a child once again. Elizabeth S. Watson, favorably reviewed the novel in *Horn Book,* and noted that "Brooks is a fine writer."

In 1990 Brooks published a short novel titled *Everywhere.* In this book, a nameless young protagonist frets about his beloved grandfather, who has suffered a heart attack and is near death. As the boy keeps a vigil, a local nurse arrives with her nephew, Dooley, who suggests killing an animal in a soul-switching ceremony to save the grandfather. During the course of the story, the boy ponders his grandfather's fate, his own mortality, and the ethics of taking one life to save another. Recognizing *Everywhere* for both its accessibility and complex issue, *Horn Book* contributor Nancy Vasilakis dubbed the work a "masterly novella" and added that "Brooks's precise use of language is a tour de force." Carolyn Phelan noted in a *Booklist* review of this novel for younger readers that the "magnetic force of Brooks's graceful prose seems to increase right to the end, drawing readers further into the hearts of his characters and into the mystery of the human heart."

Brooks won a second Newbery Honor for his 1992 *What Hearts,* a volume of four short stories all dealing with crucial events in the life of young Asa. Asa experiences the breakup of his home at age seven, when his mother takes him to live with a stepfather named Dave; he falls in love at age twelve; and he experiences a rivalry with his stepfather until finally he and his mother leave Dave behind to find a new life. "The book defies category and asks much of the reader," observed Vasilakis in *Horn Book.* "As with an important truth, its meaning comes slowly and stays forever." Eric Kraft noted in the *New York Times Book Review* that Brooks "writes with great respect for his audience, a respect that shows in the richness and subtlety of expression throughout *What Hearts* and in the complexity of the characters' emotions and their attempts to make sense of themselves and their lives." *Kirkus Reviews* declared that the book was a "brilliant demonstration that childhood's battles are less important than what one brings to them."

Produces Challenging Books

Brooks continued his unique and thoughtful approach to literature for young adults with 1996's *Asylum for Nightface* and the 1999 *Vanishing.* In the former novel, Brooks delves into "philosophical and theological questions rarely raised in children's literature," according to Deborah Stevenson in *Bulletin of the Center for Children's Books.* Zim, short for Zimmerman (named after Bob Dylan) is fourteen and religious—a cipher to his fun-loving parents. But when they suddenly acquire a religion on a vacation and hope to use Zim as a poster child for their cult, he takes it into his own hands to escape becoming "his parents' holy relic," as Stevenson put it. Incorporating a sub-plot about a local card shop and the display of artwork there, Brooks, "a brilliant and original writer," fashioned an "intriguing" book for young readers "hungry for philosophical chal-

lenges," according to Stevenson. Michael Cart, writing in *Booklist,* felt that despite some structural problems there were still "many moments of Brooks's signature brilliance here, and since he has tackled a difficult subject with passion, the novel is sure to provoke heated—and welcome—discussion."

Vanishing is the story of two eleven-year-olds sharing a hospital room. Rex is dying of cancer while Alice is floating in a hallucinatory world as a result of a self-imposed hunger strike to avoid being sent home to her alcoholic mother and bitter stepfather. Both youngsters are "vanishing" in a sense, but it is Rex—"a fiery outspoken boy who rages against his terminal illness with all his energy," according to Grace Anne A. DeCandido in *Booklist*—who is truly alive. Ultimately it is Rex who brings Alice back to the world of the living. A critic for *Horn Book* called the novel a "trenchant and powerful fable," while a *Kirkus Reviews* contributor commented that Brooks "deftly fills in a complex background, peopled by adults who have failed his protagonist in various ways, and, without forcing an agenda onto events, presents Alice with reasons to take up her life again. . . ."

Brooks has also turned his fictional hand to series writing, with his "Wolfbay Wings" hockey books. Each book in the series, which is geared for readers between nine and twelve, focuses on a different member of the squad, from new member Dixon Woods, AKA Woodsie, to the rude goalie, Zip, to team captain and coach's son, Cody. Readers also meet Boot, the right wing; Prince, the sole black player on the team; Shark, the weak link on the team; and Billy with the sports dad from hell, among other players. Reviewing the first in the series, *Woodsie,* a *Kirkus Reviews* commentator noted that Brooks's "knowledge and love of the sport, in all its thrilling complexity, and his respect for his audience and athletes, comes through on every page," while "[w]it and intelligence run as undercurrents to the game." Reviewing the second book, *Zip,* a reviewer for *Horn Book Guide* commented that "the well-individuated protagonists relate their experience in loosely structured plots that contain hockey tips, comic riffs, schoolboy vulgarity, and lots of action on the ice." In a review of *Shark,* the sixth in the series, a critic for *Kirkus Reviews* called the "Wolfbay Wings" series "thoughtful though action-oriented," noting the "intelligence that informs the book is every bit as sharp as the action. . . ."

If you enjoy the works of Bruce Brooks, you may also want to check out the following books:

Aidan Chambers, *Nik: Now I Know*, 1988.
Norma Fox Mazer, *Someone to Love*, 1985.
Michael Murpurgo, *The War of Jenkins' Ear*, 1995.

Brooks is also the author of several nonfiction works, including the nature and wildlife books *On the Wing: The Life of Birds from Feathers to Flight, Predator!, Nature by Design,* and *Making Sense: Animal Perception and Communication;* and a book of essays on boyhood and fatherly concerns, *Boys Will Be.* In a *Publishers Weekly* interview with Leonard Marcus, the author commented that he wrote *On the Wing* because "by explaining why [birds] have the equipment they do . . . we can begin to understand their behavior while still enjoying that wonderful sense of difference." Brooks added two more works about facets of animal life to his corpus with his 1991 publications *Predator!* and *Nature by Design.* Reviewers admired the colorful photographs in both books and praised the author for his grasp of his subjects and for injecting humor into the narratives. A third book in the "Knowing Nature" series was *Making Sense*, a book "[p]acked with surprising examples," according to Roger Sutton in *Bulletin of the Center for Children's Books,* with "a vibrantly synthesizing approach."

Reviewing *Boys Will Be*, Hazel Rochman noted in *Booklist* that this "thoughtful celebration of growing up male now" was "[p]art parenting book for fathers, part self-help book for boys. . . ." Brooks tackles subjects from sports to the wearing of baseball caps to dangerous friends in these essays which a *Kirkus Reviews* contributor characterized as a "funny, thoughtful miscellany." Additionally, Brooks has penned a rhyming picture book, illustrated by Elena Pavlov, *Each a Piece,* described as a "valentine of a picture book" by a critic for *Kirkus Reviews.*

With each of his literary endeavors, Brooks has shown his versatility. The opportunity for variety pleases the author, who concluded in *AAYA*: "One of the nice things about being a writer is also the biggest challenge about being a writer: You're al-ways going to be a beginner as soon as you finish something. You wrap up one book and immediately you are a rookie againbecause you've never written your next book." Respect for the reader is a hallmark of Brooks's literary production. "I leave my books open-ended on purpose," Brooks explained to *AAYA*, "because I want my readers to continue to think about the characters. I want the characters to come to life in the imagination of the readers."

■ Works Cited

Review of *Boys Will Be, Kirkus Reviews*, October 1, 1993, p. 1270.

Cart, Michael, review of *Asylum for Nightface, Booklist*, June 1, 1996, p. 1696.

Cart, Michael, in *St. James Guide to Young Adult Writers*, edited by Tom Pendergast and Sara Pendergast, St. James Press, 1999, pp. 102-4.

Cuseo, Allan A., review of *The Moves Make the Man, Voice of Youth Advocates,* February, 1983, p. 322.

DeCandido, Grace Anne A., review of *Vanishing, Booklist,* May 15, 1999.

Review of *Each a Piece, Kirkus Reviews,* September 15, 1998, p. 1381.

Hammond, Nancy C. review of *The Moves Make the Man, Horn Book,* March-April, 1985, p. 185.

Kraft, Eric, "Thrown Out at Home," *New York Times Book Review,* November 9, 1992, p. 40.

Marcus, Leonard, interview with Brooks for *Publishers Weekly,* July 29, 1990, pp. 214-15.

McDonnell, Christine, "New Voices, New Visions: Bruce Brooks," *Horn Book,* March-April, 1987, pp. 188-90.

Paterson, Katherine, "Heart Strings and Other Attachments," *Washington Post Book World,* November 9, 1986, p. 17.

Phelan, Carolyn, review of *Everywhere, Booklist,* October 15, 1990, p. 441.

Rochman, Hazel, review of *Boys Will Be, Booklist,* December 1, 1993, p. 687.

Review of *Shark, Kirkus Reviews,* April 1, 1998.

Stevenson, Deborah, review of *Asylum for Nightface, Bulletin of the Center for Children's Books,* June, 1996, p. 328.

Sutton, Roger, review of *Making Sense, Bulletin of the Center for Children's Books,* June, 1994, pp. 148-49.

Unsworth, Robert E., review of *The Moves Make the Man, School Library Journal,* December, 1984, p. 103.

Review of *Vanity, Horn Book,* May-June, 1999.

Review of *Vanity, Kirkus Reviews,* June 1, 1999.

Vasilakis, Nancy, review of *Everywhere, Horn Book,* January, 1991, pp. 72-73.

Vasilakis, review of *What Hearts, Horn Book,* January-February, 1993, p. 89.

Watkins, Mel, "A Trickster and His Upright Friend," *New York Times Book Review,* November 11, 1984, p. 54.

Watson, Elizabeth S., review of *No Kidding, Horn Book,* July, 1989, p. 486.

Review of *What Hearts, Kirkus Reviews,* October 15, 1992, p. 1307.

Wilms, Denise M., review of *The Moves Make the Man, Booklist,* February 1, 1985, pp. 782-83.

Review of *Woodsie, Kirkus Reviews,* October 1, 1997.

Review of *Zip, Horn Book Guide,* Spring, 1998, p. 68.

■ For More Information See

BOOKS

Children's Books and Their Creators, edited by Anita Silvey, Houghton, 1995.

Children's Literature Review, Volume 25, Gale, 1991.

PERIODICALS

Publishers Weekly, September 27, 1993, p. 65; May 1, 1995, p. 60; June 3, 1996, p. 84; October 26, 1998.

School Library Journal, June, 1996, p. 150; June, 1998, p. 143; July, 1998, p. 92; September, 1998, p. 120; October, 1998, p. 87; June, 2000, p. 142.

Voice of Youth Advocates, October, 1999, pp. 255-56.*

—Sketch by J. Sydney Jones

Steven K. Brust

Middle-Eastern and Oriental dancers; folk guitarist, banjoist, singer, and songwriter.

■ **Member**

Science Fiction Writers of America, Interstate Writers Workshop, Minnesota Science Fiction Society (executive vice-president), Pre-Joycean Fellowship.

■ **Personal**

Born November 23, 1955, in St. Paul, MN; son of William Z. (a professor) and Jean (Tilsen) Brust; separated; children: Corwin Edward, Aliera Jean and Carolyn Rocza (twins), Antonia Eileen. *Education:* Attended University of Minnesota—Twin Cities. *Politics:* "Trotskyist." *Religion:* "Materialist." *Hobbies and other interests:* Cooking, poker, Middle-Eastern drumming.

■ **Writings**

SCIENCE FICTION AND FANTASY NOVELS

To Reign in Hell, Steel Dragon, 1984.
Brokedown Palace, Ace Books, 1985.
The Sun, the Moon, and the Stars, Armadillo Press, 1987.
Cowboy Feng's Space Bar and Grille, Ace Books, 1990.
The Phoenix Guards, Tor Books, 1991.
(With Megan Lindholm) *The Gypsy,* Tor Books, 1992.
Agyar, Tor Books, 1992.
Athyra, Ace Books, 1993.
Five Hundred Years After (sequel to *The Phoenix Guards*), Tor Books, 1994.
ORCA, Ace Books, 1996.
(With Emma Bull) *Freedom and Necessity,* Tor Books, 1997.

■ **Addresses**

Home—3248 Portland Avenue S., Minneapolis, MN 55407. *E-mail*—kzb@dreamcafe.com. *Agent*—Valerie Smith, Route 44-55, RD Box 160, Modena, NY 12548.

"VLAD TALTOS" SERIES

Jhereg, Ace Books, 1983.
Yendi, Ace Books, 1984.

■ **Career**

Employed as systems programmer, 1976-86, including Network Systems, New Brighton, MN, 1983-86; full-time writer, 1986—. Former actor for local community theater; rock 'n' roll drummer; drummer for

Teckla, Ace Books, 1986.
Taltos, Ace Books, 1988.
Phoenix, Ace Books, 1990.
Dragon, Tor Books, 1998.
The Book of Jhereg (contains *Jhereg, Yendi,* and *Teckla*),
     Ace Books, 1999.

Work represented in anthologies, including *Liavek Anthology*, 1985.

■ Sidelights

In the realms of science fiction and fantasy, Steven K. Brust's fans have become accustomed to discovering exciting, and strange, yet believable new worlds. "It is very easy to cheat when writing fantasy—to say, 'This is magic, it just works,' " Brust once commented. "But if one is able to avoid this trap, one has the power to work real magic with the story. For me, magic must be either an alternate set of physical laws, used to express something about how we view our tools, or else a metaphor for Mystery, or the Unknown, or whatever."

Brust's own Hungarian ancestry is evident in many of his books, especially his popular five-book series that chronicles the adventures of Vlad Taltos, a warlock and hired assassin educated by a swordsman and a sorceress, who carries out assignments on behalf of the Dragonlords of the Dragaeran Empire.

In *Jhereg* (1983), the first book in the series, young Vlad is left to fend for himself when his father dies. The young man quickly discovers that his early education comes in handy when he has to rely on his own cunning and wit to survive among the powerful Dragaerans. In his *Booklist* review, Roland Green notes that "the book features intelligent world building" and "good handling of the assassin character."

Brust uses flashbacks to establish the chronology and setting of *Yendi* (1984), the second book in the series, which is actually a prequel. Here, readers discover how Vlad has risen through the ranks from his start as a small-time mobster to his current status as a major criminal. *Yendi* also chronicles the romance and courtship of Vlad and Cawti, the Dagger of the Jhereq, who would become his wife. Roland Green, again writing in *Booklist*, says that *Yendi* "is as intelligent, witty, and generally well written as its predecessor."

In this 1991 adventure, Khaavren, a young master swordsman and son of landless nobles, finds danger and excitement within Dragaera.

The third book in the series, *Teckla* (1986), picks up where the first, *Jhereg*, left off. This time, Vlad becomes involved in a revolution against the Dragaeran Empire along with the Teckla, the Empire's lowest class of citizens. During the rebellion, Vlad finds himself in the role of Cawti's protector, which only exacerbates their rocky relationship. The chronology of the series shifts again as the fourth novel, *Taltos* (1988), goes back to Vlad's early life. Writing about *Taltos* in *Voice of Youth Advocates*, Carolyn Caywood states, "This is one of the four novels of Taltos which will be of interest to the fantasy fan who discovers any one of them."

Phoenix, the fifth book in the series, finds Vlad embroiled once again in revolution and upheaval. This novel, which *Voice of Youth Advocates* reviewer Caywood describes as "more somber and more straightforward" than Brust's previous efforts, finds Vlad questioning his life-long beliefs and occupation. Caywood adds that some fans may be disappointed by the introspective nature of this book, but that "readers who are willing to follow the author's lead will discover that his conclusion has added depth to the entire series."

The Dragaeran Empire is not the only fantasy world that Brust envisions in rebellion and turmoil. *To Reign in Hell,* published just after *Jhereg* in 1984, takes place in Heaven where some of the angels are in the midst of their own revolution. "There are many fantasy novels that are thinly disguised Christian metaphors," Brust once stated. "So I wrote *To Reign in Hell,* which is a Christian metaphor that is really a thinly disguised fantasy novel." *Voice of Youth Advocates* reviewer Janet R. Mura applauds *To Reign in Hell* and declares that Brust "has created an engaging story with consummate skill and ability."

Retells Hungarian Folk Tales

Another of Brust's tales derived from Hungarian folklore is *Brokedown Palace* (1985), a story of magic and determination set in a crumbling palace on the banks of the river of Faerie. The plot follows four brothers who share power in the land of Fenario. Writing in *Voice of Youth Advocates,* Jean Kaufman remarks, "The author creates a land where magic is expected if not really loved." Kaufman goes on to call the book "a sophisticated and rewarding fantasy."

The Sun, the Moon, and the Stars (1987) is another retelling of a Hungarian folktale in the idiom of modern fantasy. Three brothers are on a quest to return the sun, moon, and stars to the sky, thereby bringing light to the world. Interestingly, Brust uses the folktale in this case as the framework for a novel depicting the struggle of five young artists to achieve the impossible. A reviewer for *Library Journal* explains how the author utilized his "Fantasist" conventions and generated a book that is "recommended for general fiction and fantasy collections."

With *Cowboy Feng's Space Bar and Grille* (1990), in which a fiendish paranoiac named the Physician

decides to destroy his native planet in order to stop the spread of a deadly illness called Hags Disease, Brust proves that he can write science fiction as well as fantasy. The setting is Feng's, a bar and grille that features Jewish cooking, a dance floor, and the ability to travel through time and space. A contributor in *Publishers Weekly* notes that "Brust's fantasy landscape seems truer than the backdrops of many realistic novels" and, in *Voice of Youth Advocates,* Mary R. Voors calls the work "a compelling and humorous science fiction novel."

The Phoenix Guards (1991) is set in Dragaera, the same world that was home to Vlad Taltos in Brust's earlier books. Though a *Publishers Weekly* reviewer

"Steven Brust might just be America's best fantasy writer!"
—Tad Williams

STEVEN BRUST

AGYAR

"A marvelous fantasy...Brust is a master stylist!"
—Publishers Weekly

Brust entangles readers with this 1992 contemporary vampire tale.

notes that the book "shares the wit and exuber-
ance of the Taltos books," don't expect to find Vlad
here; *The Phoenix Guards* is set a thousand years
earlier. Even its sequel, *Five Hundred Years After*
(1992), is set too early for Vlad to make an appearance. "Full of flamboyant action and arch dialogue,
this latest adventure in Brust's popular 'Dragaeran'
novels pits sword against sorcery in classic swashbuckling style," according to a critic for *Library Journal*.

In *The Gypsy* (1992), a collaborative effort between
Brust and Megan Lindholm, a sinister being called

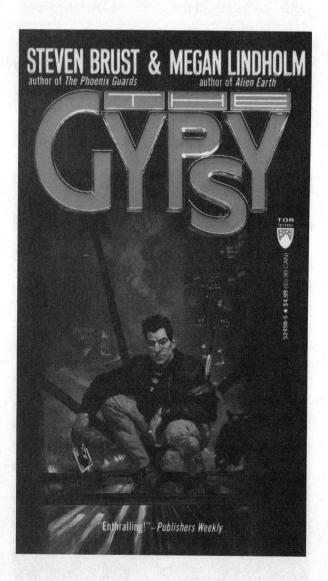

The Queen of the Underworld, Fair Lady, pulls a
gypsy and a veteran cop into her dark world in this
1992 fantasy by Brust and Megan Lindholm.

Khaavren, along with his loyal friends Pel, Aerich,
and Tazendra, help save the Dragaeran Empire in
Steven Brust's 1994 sequel to *The Phoenix Guards*.

Fair Lady reaches out from a parallel universe seeking to extend her shadowy dominion through
magic, corruption, and murder. Opposing her is a
cast of magical archetypes fronted by the Gypsy. A
reviewer in *Publishers Weekly* calls the book "a powerful and memorable fantasy" and Scott Winnett
writing in *Locus* notes that it is "an exciting fan-
tasy/mystery crossover," referring to Brust's and
Lindholm's work as "one of the best jobs yet com-
bining these contrasting genres. The marriage of the
two genres is near-perfect."

If you enjoy the works of Steven K. Brust, you may also want to check out the following books:

Suzy McKee Charnas, *The Vampire Tapestry*, 1980.
Spider Robinson, *Callahan's Crosstime Saloon*, 1977.
Joan D. Vinge, *The Summer Queen*, 1981.

"Different" Vampire Novel

Brust created something of a puzzle in *Agyar* (1992), an impressively wrought modern vampire/redemption yarn. The novel is presented as a collection of narrative fragments, like a diary, written by John Agyar, an amateur with time on his hands and an old Royal typewriter, in the abandoned house where he is staying. The pieces of the puzzle are shaped by the Agyar's first-person point of view; the clues lie more in what he doesn't say than what he does. Agyar's secret is obvious, but Brust tantalizes, holding off on a firm confirmation for much of the novel. Eventually the puzzle pieces fall together, as events come to a head. *Locus* reviewer Carolyn Cushman considers *Agyar* "a different vampire novel, a striking contemporary dark fantasy." *Kirkus Reviews* notes that the work is "compact, understated, and highly persuasive. Brust accomplishes with a wry turn of phrase or a small flourish what others never achieve despite hundreds of gory spatters." *Washington Post Book World* reviewer Robert K. J. Killheffer refers to *Agyar* as "good, fast-moving, intelligent fun."

Brust collaborated with Emma Bull for his next book, *Freedom and Necessity* (1997). The story, which a *Publishers Weekly* critic describes as a "romantic mystery-adventure," unfolds in nineteenth-century England after a young man gets a letter from his cousin two months after his supposed death. Writing in *Booklist*, reviewer Roland Green calls *Freedom and Necessity* "an exceptionalpage-turner" that "deserves a place in every self-respecting fantasy collection."

In his next book, *Dragon* (1998), Brust brings back Vlad Taltos, his most popular protagonist. A prequel to *Yendi* and a sequel to *Jhereg*, *Dragon* recounts Vlad's early career as an assassin. When Vlad accepts an assignment to search for a stolen sword, his actions start a war between two dragonlords, and Vlad becomes a soldier in one of the dragonlord's armies. *Booklist*'s Green complains that in *Dragon*, "Brust's writing style has changed noticeably," but he concedes that "Vlad's devotees will not be put off by anything so petty as stylistic dissonance." Writing for *Library Journal*, reviewer Jackie Cassada states that *Dragon* "belongs in libraries" where the Vlad Taltos series is popular. A *Publishers Weekly* reviewer praises *Dragon* and the skill with which Brust incorporates his literary influences into the story: "As always, Brust invests Vlad with the panache of a Dumas musketeer and the colloquial voice of one of Roger Zelazny's Amber heroes. This is a rousing adventure with

Popular assassin Vlad Taltos's job of guarding a magical weapon turns into something more serious in this 1998 sequel to *Jhereg*.

enough humor, action, and sneaky plot twists to please newcomers as well as longtime fans."

"There appears to be a split in literature between work with strong story values and nothing else, and work that has depth and power but no story values," Brust has said. "The stuff I enjoy reading most can be read as simple entertainment, but rewards more intense reading as well. Since I try to write the sort of stories I like to read, that is what I attempt to do in my own work. Science fiction is a category that allows and even encourages this, which is one of the reasons I write it."

■ Works Cited

Review of *Agyar, Kirkus Reviews,* December 15, 1992, p. 1517.

Cassada, Jackie, review of *Dragon, Library Journal,* November 15, 1998, p. 95.

Caywood, Carolyn, review of *Taltos, Voice of Youth Advocates,* August, 1988, p. 137.

Caywood, Carolyn, review of *Phoenix, Voice of Youth Advocates,* February, 1991, p. 361.

Review of *Cowboy Feng's Space Bar and Grille, Publishers Weekly,* December 8, 1989, p. 50.

Cushman, Carolyn, review of *Agyar, Locus,* February, 1994, p. 75.

Review of *Dragon, Publishers Weekly,* October 19, 1998, p. 60.

Review of *Five Hundred Years After, Library Journal,* March 15, 1994, p. 104.

Review of *Freedom and Necessity, Publishers Weekly,* January 27, 1997, p. 77.

Green, Roland, review of *Jhereg, Booklist,* July, 1983, p. 1387.

Green, Roland, review of *Yendi, Booklist,* September 15, 1984, p. 108.

Green, Roland, review of *Freedom and Necessity, Booklist,* March 15, 1997, p. 1231.

Green, Roland, review of *Dragon, Booklist,* September 15, 1998, p. 205.

Review of *The Gypsy, Publishers Weekly,* May 25, 1992, p. 43.

Kaufman, Jean, review of *Brokedown Palace, Voice of Youth Advocates,* June, 1986, p. 86.

Killheffer, Robert K. J., review of *Agyar, Washington Post Book World,* May 2, 1993, p. 8.

Mura, Janet R., *To Reign in Hell, Voice of Youth Advocates,* February, 1986, p. 393.

Review of *The Phoenix Guards, Publishers Weekly,* August 2, 1991, p. 66.

Review of *The Sun, the Moon, and the Stars, Library Journal,* March 15, 1987, p. 93.

Voors, Mary R., review of *Cowboy Feng's Space Bar and Grille, Voice of Youth Advocates,* June, 1990.

Winnett, Scott, review of *The Gypsy, Locus,* September, 1992, p. 37.

■ For More Information See

PERIODICALS

Analog: Science Fiction/Science Fact, September, 1987, p. 159; December, 1992, p. 161; June, 1993, p. 160.

Booklist, February 15, 1986, p. 851; April 1, 1987, p. 1180; March, 1988, p. 1098; November 1, 1990, p. 504; August, 1991, pp. 2108, 2110; June 15, 1992, p. 1811; March 1, 1994, pp. 1185, 1188; March 15, 1997, p. 1231; September 15, 1998.

Bookwatch, June, 1993, p. 2.

Kirkus Reviews, March 1, 1987, p. 338; September 1, 1991, p. 1121; May 15, 1992, p. 641; February 15, 1994, p. 179.

Kliatt, April, 1990, p. 22; November, 1993, p. 14; July, 1994, p. 13.

Library Journal, September 15, 1991, p. 117; February 15, 1993, p. 196; November 15, 1998, p. 95.

Locus, July, 1991, p. 33; October, 1991, p. 44; July, 1992, p. 47; April, 1993, p. 46; August, 1993, p. 44; March, 1994, p. 35; April, 1994, p. 47; May, 1994, p. 47.

Magazine of Fantasy and Science Fiction, December, 1987, p. 35.

Publishers Weekly, March 4, 1983, p. 97; June 1, 1984, p. 63; November 22, 1985, p. 50; March 27, 1987, p. 36; February 14, 1994, p. 83; January 27, 1997, p. 77; October 19, 1998, p. 60.

Science Fiction Chronicle, December, 1987, p. 46; July, 1990, p. 37; June, 1992, p. 33; December, 1992, p. 38; February, 1994, p. 28; June, 1994, p. 39.

Voice of Youth Advocates, December, 1990, p. 269; April, 1991, p. 10; April, 1992, p. 40; December, 1992, p. 320; February, 1993, p. 345; August, 1994, p. 154.

ON-LINE

The Dream Café, Steven K. Brust Web site, located at http://www.dreamcafe.com.

Albert Camus

Personal

Born November 7, 1913, in Mondovi, Algeria; died January 4, 1960, in an automobile accident near Paris, France; son of Lucien (a farm laborer) and Catherine (a charwoman; maiden name, Sintes) Camus; married Simone Hie, 1933 (divorced); married Francine Faure, 1940; children: (second marriage) Jean (son) and Catherine (twins). *Education:* University of Algiers, diplome d'etudes superieures, 1936. *Religion:* "Atheistic humanist."

Career

Novelist, essayist, and playwright. Worked as meteorologist, stockbroker's agent, and civil servant; actor, writer, and producer of stage productions with Theatre du travail (later named Theatre de l'equipe), 1935-38; journalist with *Alger-Republican,* 1938-40; teacher in Oran, Algeria, 1940-42; journalist in Paris, France, 1942-45; Editions Gallimard, reader, 1943-60, director of Espoir collection; *Combat* (daily newspaper), co-founder, 1945, editor, 1945-47. Staff member of *Paris Soir,* 1938. Founder of Committee to Aid the Victims of Totalitarian States. *Military service:* Member of the French resistance movement.

Awards, Honors

Medal of the Liberation; Prix de la critique, 1947, for *La Peste;* Nobel Prize for literature, 1957; Prix algerian du roman.

Writings

NOVELS

L'Etranger, Gallimard, 1942, translation by Stuart Gilbert published as *The Stranger,* Knopf, 1946, reprinted U.S. edition, Vintage Books, 1972, translation by Matthew Ward published under the same title, Knopf, 1988,(published in England as *The Outsider,* Hamish Hamilton, 1946).

La Peste, Gallimard, 1947, translation by Gilbert published as *The Plague,* Knopf, 1948, reprinted, Vintage Books, 1972.

La Chute, Gallimard, 1956, translation by Justin O'Brien published as *The Fall,* Knopf, 1957.

Le Premier Homme, Gallimard, 1994, translated as *The First Man,* Knopf, 1995.

PLAYS

Le Malentendu [and] *Caligula* (former, three-act, first produced at Theatre des Mathurins, May, 1944; latter, four-act, first produced at Theatre Hebertot in 1945), Gallimard, 1944, translation by Gilbert published as *Caligula* [and] *Cross Purpose* (former produced in New York City, February 10, 1960), New Directions, 1947 (also see below).

L'Etat de siege (first produced in 1948), Gallimard, 1948, translation published as *State of Siege* in *Caligula and Three Other Plays* (also see below).

Les Justes (first produced at Theatre Hebertot, December, 1949), Gallimard, 1950, translation by Elizabeth Sprigge and Philip Warner published as *The Just Assassins*, Microfilm, 1957, published in *Caligula and Three Other Plays* (also see below).

La Devotion a la croix (title means *Devotion to the Cross*; adaptation of the work by Calderon de la Barca), Gallimard, 1953.

Les Esprits (title means *The Wits*; adaptation of the work by Pierre de Larivey), Gallimard, 1953.

Un Cas interessant (title means *An Interesting Case*; adaptation of the work by Dino Buzatti; first produced at Theatre La Bruyere, May, 1955), L'Avant-scene, 1955.

Requiem pour une nonne (adaptation of the novel *Requiem for a Nun*, by William Faulkner; first produced at Theatre des Mathurins, October, 1956), Gallimard,1956.

Caligula and Three Other Plays (also contains *State of Siege, Cross Purpose,* and *The Just Assassins*), translated by Gilbert, Knopf, 1958.

Les Possedes (adaptation of the novel *The Possessed*, by Fyodor Dostoyevsky; first produced at Theatre Antoine, February, 1955), Gallimard, 1959, translation by O'Brien published as *The Possessed: A Modern Dramatization of Dostoevsky's Novel*, Knopf, 1964.

Also author of unfinished play "Don Juan."

ESSAYS

L'Envers et l'endroit (title means "Inside and Out"), Charlot Alger, 1937.

Le Mythe de Sisyphe, Gallimard, 1942, translation by O'Brien published as *The Myth of Sisyphus and Other Essays*, Knopf, 1955.

Lettres a un ami allemand, Gallimard, 1945.

Noces (title means *Nuptials*), Charlot Alger, 1945.

L'Existence, Gallimard, 1945.

Le Minotaur; ou, La Halte d'Oran (title means *The Minotaur; or, Stopping at Oran*), Charlot Alger, 1950.

Actuelles I: Chroniques, 1944-1948 (title means *Now I: Chronicles, 1944-1948*), Gallimard, 1950.

L'Homme revolte, Gallimard, 1951, translation by Anthony Bower published as *The Rebel: An Essay on Man in Revolt*, Knopf, 1954, revised edition, 1956.

Actuelles II: Chroniques, 1948-1953 (title means *Now II: Chronicles, 1948-1953*), Gallimard, 1953.

L'Ete (title means *Summer*), Gallimard, 1954.

(With Arthur Koestler) *Reflexions sur la peine capitale* (contains "Reflexions sur la potence," by Koestler, and "Reflexions sur la guillotine," by Camus; translation of latter published separately as *Reflections on the Guillotine: An Essay on Capital Punishment*; also see below), Calman-Levy, 1957.

Actuelles III: Chronique algerienne, 1939-1958 (title means *Now III: Algerian Chronicle, 1939-1958*), Gallimard, 1958.

Discours de suede, Gallimard, 1958, translation by O'Brien published as *Speech of Acceptance Upon the Award of the Nobel Prize for Literature, Delivered in Stockholm on the Tenth of December, 1957*, Knopf, 1958.

Reflections on the Guillotine: An Essay on Capital Punishment, translation by Richard Howard, Fridtjof-Karla Publications, 1960.

Neither Victims nor Executioners, translated from the French by Dwight Macdonald, Liberation, 1960.

Resistance, Rebellion, and Death, translated from the French by O'Brien, Knopf, 1961.

Meditations sur le theatre et la vie, P. Alberts, 1961.

Theatre, recrits, nouvelles, Gallimard, 1962.

Essais, Gallimard, 1965.

Lyrical and Critical Essays, edited by Philip Thody, translated from the French by Ellen Conroy Kennedy, Knopf, 1968.

Between Hell and Reason: Essays from the Resistance Newspaper "Combat," 1944-1947, translated from the French and edited by Alexandre de Gramont, University Press of New England, 1991.

OTHER

L'Exil et le royaume (short stories; contains "Le Renegat," "Jonas," "La Femme adultere," "Les Muets," " L'Hote," and "La Pierre qui pousse"), Gallimard, 1957, translation by O'Brien published as *Exile and the Kingdom*, Hamish Hamilton, 1960.

Carnets: Mai 1935-fevrier 1942, Gallimard, 1962, translation published as *Notebooks: Volume I, 1935-1942*, Knopf, 1963 (published in England as *Carnets: 1935-1942*, Hamish Hamilton, 1963).

Lettre a Bernanos, Minard, 1963.

Carnets: Janvier 1942-mars 1951, Gallimard, 1964, translation by O'Brien published as *Notebooks: 1942-1951*, Modern Library, 1970.

La Mort heureuse, Gallimard, 1971, translation by Jean Sarocchi published as *A Happy Death*, Vintage Books, 1973.

Le Premier Camus, suivi de Ecrits de jeunesse d'Albert Camus, Gallimard, 1973, translation by Kennedy published as *Youthful Writings*, Knopf, 1976.

Fragments d'un Combat: 1938-1940, Alger Republicain, Le Soir Republicain (articles), two volumes, edited by Jacqueline Levi Valensi and Andrea Abbou, Gallimard, 1978.

Journaux de voyage, edited by Roger Quillot, Gallimard, 1978, translation by Hugh Levick published as *American Journals,* Paragon House, 1987.

Albert Camus, Jean Grenier: Correspondance: 1932-1960 (letters), edited by Marguerite Dobrenn, Gallimard, 1981.

Carnets: Mars 1951-decembre 1959, Gallimard, 1989.

Author of prefaces to many works. Contributor to *Combat* (under pseudonyms Bauchart and Albert Mathe, and under joint pseudonym Saetone), to *Alger-Republican, Soir-Republican, L'Express,* and many other newspapers and magazines.

COLLECTED WORKS

Oeuvres completes d'Albert Camus, five volumes, Club de l'Honnete Homme, 1983.

■ Sidelights

Literary scholars place Albert Camus as North Africa's first writer of consequence. A *pied-nort,* or French citizen born in Algeria while it was still a colony of France, Camus emerged from a decidedly tough, underprivileged background to become one of the leading writers of the twentieth century. Trained in philosophy, Camus wrote several acclaimed plays, essays, and short stories, but is best remembered for his two novels: *The Stranger* and *The Plague.*

Often erringly grouped with other French writers of his generation known as the Existentialists, Camus rejected literary labels and strove to write about humankind's struggles against itself, and how an individual might free him- or herself from constraining social, political, or religious dogma. Throughout his works, he attempted to portray the inherent worth of the individual, and explored, via both fiction and essays, the idea that in the end, life is absurd—but that humankind wishes it to be rational. In order to rise above the folly of existence, Camus theorized, one must first wholly come to terms with that absurdity and sense of hopelessness. As a writer, he consistently created protagonists who achieved an inner peace only when they had completely rejected the material world and all of its laws. Political ideologies were, to Camus,

Franz Kafka's work and Greek mythology largely influenced this 1942 collection of existentialist essays, which did not appear in the United States until 1955.

divisive and futile. As he wrote in his *Notebooks,* "the revolutionary spirit lies in man's protest against the human condition."

Camus, who lived in France during much of his adult life, was feted both there and on the international literary scene. Though his reputation rose quickly, it also declined when he became the subject of lengthy, contentious diatribes in the French press, some of them penned by leading French writers who had once been his friends; many of them were harshly critical of Camus's political ideologies after he achieved success. Camus died in an automobile accident in 1960, three years after he was awarded the Nobel Prize for literature. Since his death, critics have reassessed his body of work and deem him one of the major literary figures of the century.

Humble Beginnings

Camus grew up in an impoverished, though not unpleasant, milieu, and his feeling of solidarity with the working poor and socially disadvantaged would infuse his works with a genuinely sympathetic moral attitude. Born in 1913, Camus was the younger of two sons born to Lucien and Catherine Camus when they were still living in the Algerian city of Mondovi. At the time, the large North African country was a colony of France, and the ease of life on its coastal cities had lured many Europeans there. Throughout its history, however, Algeria had also attracted other Mediterranean powers. It had been a colony of the Roman Empire at one time, while later Arab and Turkish conquerors had given it a distinctly Islamic culture. In Algiers, the capital to which Lucien Camus returned his young family shortly after the birth of Albert, a growing Algerian nationalist movement was beginning to emerge as a result of the cultural and economic discrimination against the Muslim populace, who endured various forms of discrimination because of French rule.

French males living in Algeria were still eligible for military service, and when France entered World War I in 1914, Lucien left his wife and two young sons to enter the army. He died that same year during the first battle of Marne. The tragedy caused Camus's already reclusive mother to become even more withdrawn. Of Spanish heritage, Catherine Sintes was hard of hearing as well as illiterate, and worked to support her sons as a charwoman. She passed on to Albert, however, a certain Castilian aloofness and sense of pride. The family lived in a small apartment in the working-class area of Algiers, called Belcourt, where Sintes's mother and brother, Etienne, also lived. Its three rooms had no electricity. The rearing of the boys was assumed by the grandmother, who had a strong, forceful personality—much in contrast to her daughter's.

As a child, Camus excelled in both sports and his studies. His fifth-grade teacher, Louis Germain, became the first of several important mentors for the boy, encouraging him to visit the library often and forcing him to put in long hours of study in order to qualify for a scholarship to Algiers's prestigious college-preparatory high school. Germain even convinced the strong-willed grandmother to allow the boy to pursue his studies, though she had strongly urged Camus to instead quit school and enter the workforce in order to begin contributing to the meager income of the household, as his brother had done. Fortunately, Camus received a small government stipend for educational purposes given to the children of France's war casualties.

Camus also had an uncle, Gustave Acault, who supported his ambitions. Acault was a butcher who read extensively, gave the boy money for clothes and books, and even loaned him Andre Gide's 1897 *Les Nourritures terrestres* ("The Fruits of the Earth"), a work that would play a decisive role in shaping the French existentialist movement of Camus's generation. A talented athlete, Camus loved to swim, and also served as goalkeeper for Racing Universitaire Algerois, the local soccer team. But at the age of seventeen, he was diagnosed with tuberculosis, a dangerous and even deadly disease at the time. It forever ended his athletic pursuits, and he would be plagued by a general sickliness and persistent bouts of flu for much of his life.

At the University of Algiers, Camus continued to excel. There, he came to know yet another decisive influence in his life, Jean Grenier, a professor of philosophy. "A peripatetic essayist and decidedly independent thinker who had good connections with the publishing house Gallimard, Grenier was then a man in his early thirties just about to begin a long and mostly underrated writing career," stated *Dictionary of Literary Biography* writer Raymond Gay-Crosier. Grenier encouraged Camus to read classics from Roman and Greek history, aswell of that of later authors like St. Augustine, a fifth-century bishop in Algeria during its late Roman era. "It was Grenier who, from the beginning, made his student reflect on commitment and indifference and who, above all, acted as an exemplary practitioner of productive ambiguity, discreet irony, and noncorrosive skepticism," noted Gay-Crosier. "It is no accident that Grenier's reading list of the late 1920s and early 1930s prefigured by several decades the standard curriculum of the post-World War II generation."

Around 1934, while still a philosophy student at the university, Camus married Simone Hie, who was known as "the Siren of Algiers." The relationship with Hie, a spirited beauty with a drug problem, upset Camus's family, and his uncle Acault refused to support him after the wedding. Fortunately, Hie's mother was an opthamologist who provided the necessary financial assistance to allow Camus to finish his degree by 1936. The

Camuses were an unusual pair, preferring to address one another by the formal *vous,* as one did with strangers, elders, and authority figures in the French language; Hie, however, conducted numerous extramarital affairs that spelled the rather quick end to the union.

A career as a teacher was prohibited for Camus, since candidates for academic jobs were forced to pass grueling examinations barred to those with conditions like tuberculosis. By 1937, he was living with student friends in a house overlooking the Mediterranean, had been expelled from the Communist Party—which Grenier had encouraged him to join—and continued his association with a local theater group, the Theatre du travail ("Work-

Critics compare this 1947 work about a plague that engulfs a previously serene town to the suffering and madness of Hitler's Germany.

ers' Theater"), which he had co-founded in 1935. Camus served as actor, writer, and producer of its stage productions, which drew working-class audiences, and enjoyed one of his more notable failures with an early play that was banned by the Algiers mayor because of its incendiary political themes.

In that same year, 1937, Camus's first book was published. *L'Envers et l'endroit* ("Inside and Out"), was dedicated to Jean Grenier, and contained five essays about the writer's early life in the Belcourt district. "First, poverty has never meant misfortune to me: light spread its riches," Camus wrote. "Even my rebellions have been enlightened by it." Some passages, however, reflect the lingering bewilderment that Camus felt about his mother, whom he adored despite her emotional absence from his life. In "Death in the Soul," he recounts a visit to Prague and a return trip via Italy. "Amour de vivre" ("Love of Life"), another essay, details a journey to Majorca, from where the Sintes family came.

Camus held a number of jobs in Algiers during the late 1930s. He tried to become a civil servant in the local bureaucracy, but was tempermentally ill-suited for the job and summarily dismissed. He found a more promising career as a journalist instead, and in 1938 began a stint as a city-desk reporter for the *Alger-Republicain,* a left-leaning local paper in Algiers. Within a year, however, the paper was virtually out of business due to the censorious tactics of the city's conservative mayor.

Just prior to the outbreak of World War II, Camus and a friend relocated to Paris and joined the staff of *Paris Soir,* one of the city's largest newspapers. Meanwhile, the marriage to Hie was formally ended, and in December of 1940 Camus wed Francine Faure, who was from the Algerian city of Oran. The ceremony took place in Lyons, France, to which the staff of *Paris-Soir* had been evacuated after the invasion of France by German troops earlier that year. Further problems soon forced the couple to return to Algeria, and Camus took a job as a private-school teacher in his wife's hometown. The hot climate was bad for his tuberculosis, however, and the couple managed to obtain a medical pass to return to France in August of 1942. Faure then returned to Algiers, and Camus planned to join her later. However, the Allied invasion of North Africa made his trip impossible, and Camus was forced to remain in France for the duration of the war.

The Stranger

It was during this difficult period that Camus also began to enjoy his first noteworthy successes. In 1942, *L'Etranger* was published by Gallimard in Paris. It appeared in English translation four years later as *The Stranger,* and remained one of Camus's most enduring works for decades; it is the first of the two novels most indelibly associated with his name.

The *L'Etranger* was immediately hailed as the work of a rising young name in French literature. Told in short, simple sentences, the novel is the story of Patrice Meursault, who narrates his tale of decline; its style gives the impression that Meursault is

This 1956 novel about a respectable lawyer whose conscience reveals his downfall was Camus's last novel before his death in 1960.

rather dim of intellect. He leads an unremarkable , uninspired life, and when his mother dies, Meursault finds he feels grief for her passing. He befriends a pimp named Raymond, and after an incident in which the family of an Arab woman threatens Raymond for abusing her, the two men and another couple embark on a beach holiday. There, the men fight with two Arabs who have pursued them, and Raymond suffers a knife wound. Meursault returns to the beach alone, and blinded by sun and the glint of the blade from his opponent's knife, kills one of the Arabs.

Meursault is arrested and jailed for the crime, but refuses to help his lawyer defend him in the trial, though he faces the death penalty. He rejects the pleas of a priest to repent as well, and is resigned to his fate. Through these events, Camus portrays a man who only becomes conscious of life and its meaning after he transgresses, by his own choosing, the border of civilized society. "Above all, Meursault discovers that absurdity, once recognized and defined as the absence of answers to vital questions, can lead to consciousaffirmation of life, to happiness; that death cannot kill the desire for life in this world at this moment," wrote Gay-Crosier in the *Dictionary of Literary Biography* essay.

In France, Camus worked for the publishing house Gallimard for a time as a manuscript reader, and became active in the Resistance movement that worked to sabotage the Nazi occupation of France and help the Allies defeat Germany. He wrote articles for the illegal newspaper of the Resistance, *Combat,* and through the paper came to know Jean-Paul Sartre, Andre Malraux, Simone de Beauvoir, and other notable French writers of his generation. Though most used pseudonyms, it was nevertheless dangerous work, and Camus narrowly escaped detection. *Combat* became an aboveground newspaper just as Allied forces expelled the Germans from Paris in August of 1944, an event that coincided with Camus being named *Combat*'s editor.

The year 1942 also witnessed the publication by Gallimard of Camus's seminal essay, *Le Mythe de Sisyphe,* which first appeared in English translation as *The Myth of Sisyphus* in 1955. In it, Camus describes the plight of Sisyphus, a cursed figure from Greek mythology. The vengeful gods have sentenced him to push a large rock up a mountain, then watch it fall back down again, into eternity. Camus likens this to humankind's penchant for rebellion and recalcitrance, the desire of some to continually buck the system. Sisyphus, despite his labors, comes to find a certain satisfaction in his task.

Throughout his career, Camus would periodically return to the medium of the theater. His first important play, *Le Malentendu*, was produced at Paris's Theatre des Mathurins in May of 1944. The work, translated into English in 1947 for joint publication with another early play of his, *Caligula*, is set at a lonely inn in the countryside of the Czech Republic. Its keeper, Martha,lives with her mother, and to supplement their paltry income, they sometimes kill an occasional guest, rob him, and dispose of the body. When Martha's brother returns after a long absence, they do not recognize him and he becomes their victim as well. Realizing their crime, the two women kill themselves. Here, Camus attempted to show how human beings are linked by mere words, and when communication fails them, these links to one another are, in the end, futile.

Camus's next play, *Caligula*, was first produced at Theatre Hebertot in Paris in September of 1945. Camus based its events upon accounts of the Roman emperor Caius Caesar Germanicus (12-41 CE), who was initially a benevolent, unremarkable leader, but grew increasingly murderous and unreasonable as his reign endured; historians surmise that he may have suffered from a neurological disorder. In the play, the young Caligula is depicted as a just, loving ruler, but becomes cruel and tyrannical after his sister, Drusilla—who was also his lover—dies. Realizing that "men die, and they are not happy," Caligula sets out to free himself from all moral constraints. His nonsensical authoritarian edicts induce a famine, he tortures his political rivals, stages a play starring himself, liberates his slaves and forces the senators to serve him in their stead, and is finally assassinated by a rival. "In *Caligula* the spectator experiences the inevitability with which the pursuit of an absolute degenerates into the exploitation and enslavement of human beings, who have become mere means to the end of the dictator's narcissistic enjoyment of his short-lived capacity to alter the face and facts of the world," observed David R. Ellison in *Understanding Albert Camus.*

Caligula debuted in Paris when revelations of the horrific crimes perpetrated by the Nazi regime were still fresh. Only two characters are willing to speak frankly to the deranged Caligula—Cherea, a political rival, and Scipio, thepoet—and gain his respect. "In these courageous individuals who are unwilling to succumb to the will and vision of their ruler, post-war French audiences could see fictional/theatrical equivalents of those of their countrymen who had joined the Resistance," Ellison remarked.

The Plague

Camus served as editor of the official *Combat*, the leading leftist paper of the postwar era, for two years. During that time, he and his wife became parents to twins born in 1945, and he also traveled to the United States for the first time. In 1947, he left his post at the paper amidst ideological disagreements with its increasingly conservative management, but his second significant novel, *La Peste*, was published by Gallimard that same year and established him firmly in the orbit of France's contemporary literary scene. Translated for English publication a year later as *The Plague*, the work, which Camus wrote largely during the war years, presents itself as the diary of a man in Oran. He recounts the dullness and provincialism of life in this hot, sleepy colonial outpost as the work opens, but begins to note the strange deaths of the city's rat population.

Soon, whatever is killing Oran's rodents also strikes the residents themselves. Only the sharp sense of terror and general municipal panic elicits emotional reactions from the formerly complacent people of Oran. A man named Dr. Rieux works feverishly to find a solution, and at the end of *The Plague* the author of the journal is revealed as the physician himself. An artist and friend of Rieux, Tarrou, as well as a government clerk, a Jesuit priest, and a criminal, all feature prominently in the events of the novel. Like the victims of the Nazi death camps and the civilian population across much of Europe under Nazi occupation during the war, the residents of Oran feel trapped and battle a sense of hopelessness. "The struggle of Oran's citizens against theplague as an agent of absurdity and evil was perceived by the contemporary readers primarily as a thinly disguised allegory of the German occupation," wrote Gay-Crosier in the Dictionary of Literary Biography. "Among the variety of human reactions to oppression two stand out: one can fight the plague with human means, which is what the doctor does, or one can seek recourse in transhuman help, which is what Father Paneloux proposes."

The Plague emerged as a great commercial success for Camus and Gallimard at the time, though it was condemned in some circles as an anti-Christian diatribe. His next major work once again returned him to the theatrical milieu. *L'Etat de siege* was first produced at Paris's Theatre Marigny in October of 1948. The work was translated into English as *State of Siege* and published in a volume with *Caligula* and two other works in 1948. A condemnation of authoritarianism, *State of Siege* takes place in Cadiz, an ancient Spanish port town, where a new leader, King Plague, conducts a reign of terror. Assisted by his secretary, Death, the King creates a list of political enemies who begin to die, one by one, from a mysterious sickness.

Led by Diego, a doctor, the people of Cadiz try to overthrow the King. Death attempts to seduce Diego, but he strikes her, and his plague symptoms suddenly vanish. This event, however, causes more names to be added to list. The King tries to lure Diego into a safe exile, but he refuses. Though many notable names were involved in its first Paris staging, the work was roundly condemned by critics. One succinct reaction has often been cited: "Since I have been going to the theatre, I believe that I have never suffered as much," declared one French writer, Rene Barjavel.

Despite the challenges, Camus regularly wrote dramas and took them through their final process to opening night. He discussed the lure of the stage in a1959 essay for *Le Figaro litteraire* titled "Why I Work in the Theatre," stating that "through the theatre I escape what irks me in my career as a writer." He wrote that while a play of his was in the rehearsal stage, colleagues and acquaintances generally left him alone, and he was pestered with far fewer social invitations. But he also enjoyed the spirit of collaboration and collective effort that a play required. Finally, he described the medium as "a place of truth." Camus wrote, "To be sure, people generally call it a place of illusion. Don't you believe it! It is society, above all, that lives among illusions, and you will certainly find fewer hams on the stage than around town. Take, for example, one of those nonprofessional actors . . . . Put him on the stage, in this exact spot; throw four thousand watts of light on him, and the play will become unbearable."

In another of Camus's works for the stage, the 1949 play *Les Justes,* he once again explored issues of political beliefs in contrast to a sense of responsibility to humankind. Translated into English for 1958 publication as *The Just Assassins,* the work is set in Russia during its Tsarist era, and was loosely based on the memoir of Boris Savinkov, a Russian revolutionary from that time. The focus of the drama rests upon the dilemma of an idealistic poet, Ivan Kaliayev, who falls in with a group of Socialists planning to assassinate Grand Duke Sergei, the uncle of the Tsar. Kaliayev is selected to throw an incendiary device at the Grand Duke's carriage as it passes on the way to the theater. This, it is hoped, will quickly destabilize the detested imperial regime.

When Kaliayev learns that there are children inside the carriage, he balks and does not throw the bomb. Afterward, he argues with a fellow Socialist over the decision, and defends his belief that innocent children should not be harmed in the name of a political goal. A second attempt, however, is a success, andKaliayev is duly uncovered as the perpetrator, taken into custody, and receives a death sentence at his trial. In prison, he refuses to repent for his act, but his lover, Dora, begins to question the justice of murdering the blameless in the name of a greater political good. Dora is also part of the Socialist network, and when the opportunity to carry out another terrorist act appears, she volunteers for it, declaring "It's so much easier to die from one's inner conflicts than to live with them."

L'Homme revolte, the next of Camus's works, returns him again to the novel form. Published in France in 1951 and in English three years later as *The Rebel: An Essay on Man in Revolt*, the work quickly emerged as one of his most important treatises. It also came to be considered one of his most controversial as well, widely viewed as an attack on Marxism. As Camus himself wrote in his the first volume of *Carnets*, or *Notebooks*, "for my own part, I should not have written *L'Homme revolte* if in the forties I had not found myself face to face with men whose acts I did not understand. To put it briefly, I did not understand that men could torture others without ever ceasing to look at them."

The four essays in *The Rebel* center around the dictum from seventeenth-century French philosopher and mathematician Rene Descartes: "I think, therefore I am." But Camus expands this into the idea, "I revolt, therefore we are." In the first of the four pieces, "Metaphysical Revolt," Camus discusses historical figures such as the Marquis de Sade and German philosopher Friedrich Nietzsche, who re-

If you enjoy the works of Albert Camus, you may also want to check out the following:

The works of Franz Kafka, including *The Castle*, 1930, *The Trial*, 1935, and *The Metamorphasis*, 1937.

The works of Jean-Paul Sartre, including *No Exit and Three Other Plays*, 1955.

jected all forms of social constraint in their ideologies. In "Historical Revolt," he writes about state terrorism, but the final essay, "Thought at the Meridian," was the one that brought the most opprobrium upon his name. "In this section he argued that revolutionary ideology based on historical effectiveness, which he associated with NorthernEurope, particularly the Germans, always goes, by its very essence, beyond human and natural limits and turns back on itself, becoming limitless servitude—in opposition to the Mediterranean spirit, 'la pensee solaire' (solar thought), which acknowledges the limits of man and stresses measure and balance between man and nature," explained Gay-Crosier in the *Dictionary of Literary Biography* essay.

Camus's ideas in "Thought at the Meridian"—especially his assertion that communism and fascism were not inherently different—incited a much-publicized rift between himself and those he had befriended in Paris during the war years, when many committed Marxists were working for the French Resistance movement as well. Sartre, de Beauvoir, and Malraux all disagreed strongly with Camus's assertions, and voiced their displeasure at what they felt was his betrayal of the French intellectual left in lengthy newspaper articles. It was the rift with Sartre, however, which was most significant to analysts of French politics and literature at the time. "The break between these two leading French writers touched off literary pyrotechnics vivid even for Paris," wrote the *New York Times*.

The break between Camus and the more committed leftists, led by Sartre, devolved into a lengthy, drawn-out war of words. Sartre, however, emerged in the lead, and the break left Camus disconsolate and feeling scorned by his peers. Then, in 1954 a war for independence erupted in Algeria, led by an indigenous group, the National Liberation Front, or FLN. Many leading French intellectuals sup-

ported the Algerian bid for sovereignty, but France resisted, and several years of deadly conflict ensued in Camus's homeland. Camus, however, refused to take a side in the struggle, and was condemned for this as well. He voiced his opinions on this matter and others in articles he penned for the magazine *L'Express* between 1955 and 1956, and de Beauvoir retaliatedmost infamously for her side with a thinly-disguised portrayal of Camus in her 1955 novel *Les Mandarins*.

Camus's reputation among Europe's literati suffered an even further decline. As Gay-Crosier wrote, "It was fashionable in 'progressive' circles to characterize him as a puppet of capitalism, as a careerist who had sold out his earlier convictions to the bourgeoisie eager to buy his books," the Dictionary of Literary Biography writer declared. To his credit, Camus spoke before a potentially vicious crowd in Algiers in 1956, urging a civilian truce. But his career setbacks and marital difficulties, combined with his always-precarious state of health, brought on a writer's block. He began to adapt the work of others for the stage, enjoying success with a version of William Faulkner's *Requiem for a Nun* in 1956.

Camus's last novel written before his death helped re-establish some of his professional standing, and emerged as yet another of his acclaimed works. *La Chute*, published by Gallimard in 1956 and in English translation the same year as *The Fall*, helped earn him the prestigious Nobel Prize for literature the following year. The plot centers around the voluntary downfall of Jean Baptiste Clamence, once acclaimed as Paris's most formidable of trial lawyers. Told in the form of a monologue by Clamence, the work recounts his former celebrity, his many affairs, and his material wealth—echoing, in many ways, the life that Camus once enjoyed.

Clamence renounces this life, however, realizing that he is suddenly weary of judging others. He recounts a life-changing moment when he saw a woman about to commit suicide by jumping from a bridge, and to his memory of the easy decision to do nothing to stop her Clamence returns time and again in his monologue. Often, he hears a derisive laugh when he crosses the same bridge,and even when he sees his own image in a mirror. He describes himself now as a "judge-penitent," wrestles with questions of right and wrong, and arrives at the belief that perhaps all of humankind is evil.

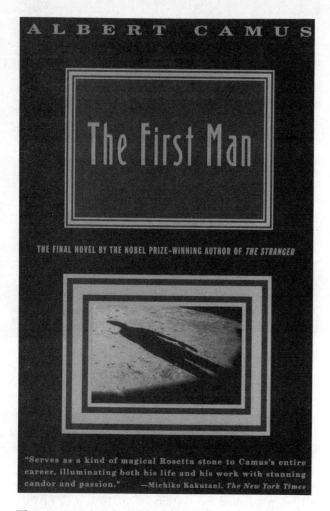

ALBERT CAMUS

The First Man

THE FINAL NOVEL BY THE NOBEL PRIZE-WINNING AUTHOR OF *THE STRANGER*

"Serves as a kind of magical Rosetta stone to Camus's entire career, illuminating both his life and his work with stunning candor and passion."
—Michiko Kakutani, *The New York Times*

The manuscript for this work was among Camus's possessions after his fatal car accident in 1960, but his family did not publish it until 1994.

Clamence finds his way to Amsterdam, where he prefers to drink in a seedy bar frequented by sailors. The Dutch city's network of canals become a metaphor for the war of words he conducts with his own conscience inside his head: the canals are labyrinthine, but symmetrical, and all of Clamence's arguments seem to return him to the same point as well: that he is every bit as guilty as the rest of the human race. In this way, wrote Gay-Crosier in the *Dictionary of Literary Biography*, the former attorney "transforms his rhetorical brilliance, which made him a winning trial lawyer, into dialectical artistry, which borders on exhibitionist sophistry, and involves the reader in a captivating mirror game of delusions."

A critique of *The Fall* by *Commentary* writer Stephen Miller wrote of the relevance of this last novel of Camus's to his own professional burdens. "Some critics have regarded Clamence as a self-portrait, an attempt by Camus to exorcise the burden of his supposed 'sainthood'; others see it as a portrait of Sartre, the man who continually proclaimed his own guilt over belonging to the bourgeoisie," remarked Miller. "But whoever sat for it, this portrait of a twisted hero of our times . . . is Camus's masterpiece."

Accepts Nobel Prize

Camus's standing as a writer received a welcome boost when he was awarded the Nobel Prize in 1957—especially as it came in the midst of the battle over his refusal to publicly take a side in Algeria's war for independence. He dedicated his acceptance speech to Louis Germain, his influential fifth-grade teacher, and in it he attempted to explain his pointof view on political struggles. "The artist fashions himself in that ceaseless oscillation from himself to others," Camus said at the ceremonies, "midway between the beauty he cannot do without and the community from which he cannot tear himself. This is why true artists scorn nothing. They force themselves to understand instead of judging."

At the age of just forty-three, Camus became the youngest recipient of the literary honor after Rudyard Kipling had earned his in 1907. With the prize funds, Camus purchased a farmhouse in Lourmarin, in the French countryside. His collection of short stories, *L'Exil et le royaume*, appeared that same year, and was published in English translation the following year as *Exile and the Kingdom*. Nearly all of the six tales are set in North Africa, and force Camus's characteristic themes of alienation into a tight narrative form. In "The Adulterous Woman," for instance, a French wife, Janine, is unhappily accompanying her sales-representative husband on a business trip that takes them into a remote stretch of desert. Petulant and overwhelmed by the climate, Janine is annoyed by her husband as well, who displays a racist attitude toward their fellow Arab travelers. She comes to feel that her life is as empty as the Sahara, and leaves her sleeping husband in their hotel room in the middle of the night.

"The Renegade," another story from *Exile and the Kingdom*, centers around a former Christian missionary captured and tortured by members of a

Bedouin tribe in a strange city made entirely of salt. His tongue is cut out, and his captors force him to renounce both his god and his ideals. A mysterious voice offers religious salvation. The story was an especial favorite of one reviewer who critiqued the volume. "The virtuosity of these pages is remarkable," stated Victor Brombert about "The Renegade" in *Yale French Studies*. "Nowhere else has Camus revealed himself so accomplished a master of images, sounds and rhythms. The fulgurating whiteness of the landscape, the piercing sunfire of this white hell, the liquefaction of time under the burning refraction of a thousand mirrors—all this is suggested in the hallucinating interior monologues which presses forward as though indeed the only speech left the tongueless narrator were the metaphorical 'tongue' of his feverish brain."

Camus died on January 4, 1960, at the age of forty-six. Michel Gallimard, a friend from his wartime stint at *Combat* and a distant relative of the publishing family, offered him a ride to Lourmarin. Eighty miles outside of Paris, a tire on Gallimard's car blew out, causing the vehicle to spin out of control and hit two trees; Camus died from the impact. With him that day was a partial draft and further notes for a long novel, *Le Premier Homme*, which would examine the role of the French in Algeria through the form of a quasi-autobiography. Faure, his widow, declined to have the work published, but after her death in 1979, Camus's children offered it to Gallimard, who published it in France in 1994. It followed a year later in English translation as *The First Man*.

The First Man recounts the life of the fictional Jacques Cormier, a famous French writer who grew up in a rough section of Algiers. An assessment in the *Chicago Tribune* from Nicholas Delbanco found that though the unfinished manuscript "betrays the haste of its composition throughout, . . . the overwhelming impression is of how well Camus wrote, how natural and unforced was his eloquence."

■ Works Cited

Brombert, Victor, "'The Renegade' or the Terror of the Absolute," *Yale French Studies*, Spring, 1960, pp. 81-84.

Camus, Albert, "Why I Work in the Theatre," *Le Figaro litteraire*, May 16, 1959. Camus, *Carnets*, translated by Philip Thody, Hamilton, 1963, republished as *Notebooks, 1935-1942*, Knopf, 1963.

Camus, excerpt from Nobel Prize acceptance speech, *Short Story Criticism*, Volume 9, Gale, 1992, p. 113.

Delbanco, Nicholas, review of *The First Man*, *Chicago Tribune Books*, September 24, 1995.

Ellison, David R., *Understanding Albert Camus*, University of South Carolina Press, 1990.

Gay-Crosier, Raymond, "Albert Camus," *Dictionary of Literary Biography*, Volume 72: *French Novelists, 1930-1960*, edited by Catharine Savage Brosman, Gale, 1988, pp. 110-135.

■ For More Information See

BOOKS

Anderson, David, *The Tragic Protest*, John Knox, 1969.

Beauclair, Michelle, *In Death's Wake: Mourning in the Works of Albert Camus and Marguerite Duras*, P. Lang (New York City), 1996.

Bloom, Harold, editor, *Albert Camus*, Chelsea House, 1989.

Bree, Germaine, *Camus*, Rutgers University Press, revised edition, 1964.

Bree, *Camus and Sartre: Crisis and Commitment*, Delacorte, 1972.

Bree and Margaret Otis Guiton, *An Age of Fiction: The French Novel From Gide to Camus*, Rutgers University Press, 1968.

Bree, editor, *Camus: A Collection of Critical Essays*, Prentice-Hall, 1962.

Bree, Germaine, and Margaret Guiton, *The French Novel from Gide to Camus*, Harcourt, Brace & World, 1957, pp. 218-33.

Bronner, Stephen Eric, *Albert Camus: The Thinker, the Artist, the Man*, Franklin Watts (New York City), 1996.

Champigny, Robert, *A Pagan Hero: An Interpretation of Meursault in Camus' "The Stranger,"* University of Pennsylvania Press, 1969.

Contemporary Literary Criticism, Gale, Volume 1, 1973, Volume 2, 1974, Volume 4, 1975, Volume 9, 1978, Volume 11, 1979, Volume 14, 1980, Volume 32, 1985, Volume 63, 1991, Volume 69, 1992.

Cruickshank, John, *Albert Camus and the Literature of Revolt*, Galaxy, 1960.

Dictionary of Literary Biography, Volume 72: *French Novelists, 1930-1960*, Gale, 1988.

Drama Criticism, Volume 2, Gale, 1992.

Falk, Eugene H., *Types of Thematic Structure*, University of Chicago Press, 1967, pp. 52-116.

Fitch, Brian T., *The Narcissistic Text: A Reading of Camus's Fiction*, University of Toronto Press, 1982.

Fitch, Brian T., *The Fall: A Matter of Guilt,* Twayne (New York City), 1994.

Frohock, W. M., *Style and Temper: Studies in French Fiction, 1925-1960,* Harvard University Press, 1967, pp. 78-117.

Hanna, Thomas, *The Thought and Art of Albert Camus,* Regnery, 1958.

Jackson, Tommie Lee, *The Existential Fiction of Ayi Kwei Armah, Albert Camus, and Jean-Paul Sartre,* UniversityPress of America (Lanham, MD), 1996.

Kazin, Alfred, *Contemporaries,* Little, Brown, 1962.

Kellogg, Jean Defrees, *Dark Prophets of Hope: Dostoevsky, Sartre, Camus, Faulkner,* Loyola University Press, 1975.

Lazere, Donald, *The Unique Creation of Albert Camus,* Yale University Press, 1973.

Lebesque, Morvan, *Portrait of Camus,* Herder, 1971.

Lottman, Herbert R., *Albert Camus: A Biography,* Doubleday, 1979.

Maquet, Albert, *Albert Camus: The Invincible Summer,* Humanities Press, 1972.

Mauriac, Claude, *The New Literature,* translated from the French by Samuel I. Stone, Braziller, 1959.

McCarthy, Patrick, *Camus: A Critical Study of His Life and Work,* Hamish Hamilton, 1982.

McCarthy, Patrick, *Albert Camus: The Stranger,* Cambridge University Press, 1988.

Merton, Thomas, *The Literary Essays of Thomas Merton,* edited by Patrick Hart, New Directions, 1985, pp. 292-301.

Nadeau, Maurice, *The French Novel Since the War,* translated from the French by A. M. Sheridan-Smith, Methuen, 1967.

O'Brien, Conor Cruise, *Albert Camus of Europe and Africa,* Viking, 1970.

Oxenhandler, Neal, *Looking for Heroes in Postwar France: Albert Camus, Max Jacob, Simone Weil,* University Press of New England (Hanover, NH), 1995.

Panichas, George A., editor, *The Politics of Twentieth-Century Novelists,* Hawthorne, 1971.

Parker, Emmet, *Albert Camus: The Artist in the Arena,* University of Wisconsin Press, 1966.

Peyre, Henri, *French Novelists of Today,* Oxford University Press, 1967.

Podhoretz, Norman, *Doings and Undoings,* Farrar, Straus, 1964.

Pollman, Leo, *Sartre and Camus: Literature of Existence,* Ungar, 1970.

Reck, Rima Drell, *Literature and Responsibility: The French Novelist in the Twentieth Century,* Louisiana State University Press, 1969.

Rhein, Philip H., *The Urge to Live: A Comparative Study of Franz Kafka's "Der Prozess" and Albert Camus' "L'Etranger",* University of North Carolina Press, 1964.

Rhein, *Albert Camus,* Twayne, 1969.

Rizzuto, Anthony, *Camus' Imperial Vision,* Southern Illinois University Press, 1981.

Sartre, Jean-Paul, *Situations I,* Gallimard, 1947.

Scott, Nathan A., Jr., editor, *Forms of Extremity in the Modern Novel,* John Knox, 1965.

Showalter, English, Jr., *Exiles and Strangers: A Reading of Camus's "Exile and the Kingdon,"* Ohio State University Press, 1984.

Sprintzen, David, *Camus: A Critical Examination,* Temple University Press, 1988.

Tarrow, Susan, *Exile from the Kingdom: A Politicals Rereading of Albert Camus,* University of Alabama Press, 1985.

Thody, Philip, *Albert Camus, 1913-1960,* Macmillan, 1962.

Thody, *Albert Camus,* Macmillan, 1989.

Thody, *Albert Camus: A Study of His Work,* Grove Press, 1959.

Ullman, Stephen, *The Image in the Modern French Novel,* Basil Blackwell, 1963, pp. 239-99.

Viallaneix, Paul, *The First Camus: An Introductory Essay and Youthful Writings by Albert Camus,* translated from the French by Ellen Conroy Kennedy, Knopf, 1976.

Willhoite, Fred H., *Beyond Nihilism: Albert Camus's Contribution to Political Thought,* Louisiana State University Press, 1968.

World Literature Criticism, Gale, 1992.

PERIODICALS

American Imago, winter, 1988, p. 359.

American Poetry Review, January-February, 1973.

Contemporary Literature, fall, 1983, pp. 322-48.

Forum for Modern Language Studies, July, 1984, pp. 228-46.

French Review, winter, 1970, pp. 158-67; October, 1986, pp. 30-8.

International Fiction Review, summer, 1980, p. 123.

London Review of Books, September 8, 1994, pp. 6-7.

Paula Danziger

Personal

Born August 18, 1944, in Washington, DC; daughter of Samuel (worked in garment district) and Carolyn (a nurse) Danziger. *Education:* Montclair State College, B.A., 1967, M.A.

Addresses

Home—New York City and Woodstock, NY. *Agent*—Donald C. Farber, 99 Park Ave., New York, NY 10016.

Career

Substitute teacher, Edison, NJ, 1967; Title I teacher, Highland Park, NJ, 1967-1968; junior-high school English teacher, Edison, NJ, 1968-1970; Lincoln Junior High School, West Orange, NJ, English teacher, 1977-1978; full-time writer, 1978—. Worked for the Educational Opportunity Program, Montclair State College, until 1977. Regular appearances on BBC-TV magazine shows, *Going Live!* and *Live and Kicking.*

Awards, Honors

New Jersey Institute of Technology Award, and Young Reader Medal Nomination, California Reading Association, both 1976, Massachusetts Children's Book Award, first runner-up, 1977, winner, 1979, and Nene Award, Hawaii Association of School Librarians and the Hawaii Library Association, 1980, all for *The Cat Ate My Gymsuit;* Children's Books of the Yearcitation, Child Study Association of America, 1978, Massachusetts Children's Book Award, Education Department of Salem State College, 1979, Nene Award, 1980, California Young Reader Medal Nomination, 1981, and Arizona Young Reader Award, 1983, all for *The Pistachio Prescription;* Children's Choice Award, International Reading Association and the Children's Book Council, 1979, for *The Pistachio Prescription,* 1980, for *The Cat Ate My Gymsuit* and *Can You Sue Your Parents for Malpractice?,* 1981, for *There's a Bat in Bunk Five,* and 1983, for *The Divorce Express.*

New Jersey Institute of Technology Award and Books for the Teen Age, New York Public Library, both 1980, and Land of Enchantment Book Award, New Mexico Library Association, 1982, all for *Can You Sue Your Parents for Malpractice?;* Read-a-Thon Author of the Year Award, Multiple Sclerosis Society, and Parents' Choice Award for Literature, Parents' Choice Foundation, both 1982, Woodward

Park School Annual Book Award, 1983, and South Carolina Young Adult Book Award, South Carolina Association of School Librarians, 1985, all for *The Divorce Express*; CRABbery Award, Prince George's County Memorial Library System (MD), 1982, and Young Readers Medal, 1984, both for *There's a Bat in Bunk Five*; Parents' Choice Award for Literature, Bologna International Children's Book Fair exhibitor, and Child Study Association of America's Children's Books of the Year citation, all 1985, all for *It's an Aardvark-Eat-Turtle World*; nomination, New Jersey Garden State Children's Book Awards, 1997, for *Amber Brown Is Not a Crayon*.

■ Writings

FOR CHILDREN

The Cat Ate My Gymsuit, Delacorte, 1974.
The Pistachio Prescription, Delacorte, 1978.
Can You Sue Your Parents for Malpractice?, Delacorte, 1979.
There's a Bat in Bunk Five, Delacorte, 1980.
The Divorce Express, Delacorte, 1982.
It's an Aardvark-Eat-Turtle World, Delacorte, 1985.
This Place Has No Atmosphere, Delacorte, 1986.
Remember Me to Harold Square, Delacorte, 1987.
Everyone Else's Parents Said Yes, Delacorte, 1989.
Make Like a Tree and Leave, Delacorte, 1990.
Earth to Matthew, Delacorte, 1991.
Not for a Billion, Gazillion Dollars, Delacorte, 1992.
Amber Brown Is Not a Crayon, illustrated by Tony Ross, Putnam, 1994.
Thames Doesn't Rhyme with James, Putnam, 1994.
You Can't Eat Your Chicken Pox, Amber Brown, illustrated by Tony Ross, Putnam, 1995.
Amber Brown Goes Fourth, illustrated by Ross, Putnam, 1995.
Amber Brown Wants Extra Credit, illustrated by Ross, Putnam, 1996.
Forever Amber Brown, illustrated by Ross, Putnam, 1996.
Amber Brown Sees Red, illustrated by Ross, Putnam, 1997.
(With Ann M. Martin) *P.S. Longer Letter Later*, Scholastic, 1998.

■ Adaptations

Cheshire has made a filmstrip and cassette from *The Cat Ate My Gymsuit*, 1985; Listening Library has made cassettes of *The Cat Ate My Gymsuit*, *The Pistachio Prescription*, *There's a Bat in Bunk Five*, *Can You Sue Your Parents for Malpractice?*, and *The Divorce Express*, 1985-86.

■ Sidelights

Paula Danziger is a best-selling author of novels for teens and pre-teens who is known for her light and humorous take on the serious problems that beset adolescents, including the break-up of a family, issues of self-esteem and identity, dysfunctional families, new relationships, and political and social issues such as feminism and environmentalism. Sometimes criticized by reviewers and educators for simplistic and cliched versions of teen life, Danziger answers such critics through the voice of her very first teen protagonist, Marcy Lewis, who explains in *The Cat Ate My Gymsuit* that "middle-class kids have problems too."

In YA novels such as *Can You Sue Your Parents for Malpractice?*, *There's a Bat in Bunk Five*, *The Divorce Express*, and *Remember Me to Harold Square*, Danziger has created memorable teenage female protagonists who suffer the usual traumas and indignities of kids of that age, including first rejections and first pimples. More recent novels include two series of books for pre-teens, one featuring eleven-year-old Matthew Martin and another featuring spunky third-grader Amber Brown. Known for her offbeattitles as much as for her snappy one-liner dialogue, Danziger lives well from the sale of her books and is as popular in England—where she resides part of the year—as she is in the United States. Danziger makes frequent visits to schools on both sides of the Atlantic, and is also a regular guest on BBC television shows for children.

A Difficult Childhood

Such success was not a foregone conclusion for Danziger as a child. She did not do exceptionally well in school, and her father went out of his way to make her feel inadequate intellectually. "I grew up in a family which would nowadays be called dysfunctional," she told Chris Powling in a *Books for Keeps* interview. "My parents really cared about their kids . . . which makes it even sadder, I suppose. My father was a very angry man. He never hit my younger brother and me but was emotionally abusive." Early on, Danziger developed a sense of humor to help her get through life. She also determined that she wanted to be a writer and started, as she told Marguerite Feitlowitz in *Authors and Artists for Young Adults*, "mentally recording a lot of information and observations."

In high school Danziger wrote what she called "offbeat features for the school newspaper and a column in the town newspaper." This writing and publishing did a lot to bolster her self-esteem: "Someone was noticing that I wasn't a total idiot," she told Feitlowitz. She also read and re-read J. D. Salinger's *Catcher in the Rye*. "It set me free," she observed. "It made me feel I wasn't alone." Other reading for Danziger at this time included *A Tree Grows in Brooklyn*, *Pride and Prejudice*, *Marjorie Morningstar*, and *Wuthering Heights*.

Danziger attended Montclair State College, and during her university years met a powerful influence in her life, the poet John Ciardi. Baby-sitting for his family, Danziger was introduced to the larger world of professional writing, including the work of e. e. cummings. She borrowed liberally from Ciardi's library, and was also educated by the poet, who "read the poems and explained them, giving me a sense of language structure," Danziger noted to Feitlowitz. Graduating from college in 1967, Danziger began working as a substitute teacher, and then as a full-time English teacher in junior high school. Teaching was not really Danziger's forte—she was strong on connecting with and inspiring her students, but disliked the tedium of correcting papers and disciplining students. After three years of teaching, she returned to university to earn a master's degree, but her studies were brought to an abrupt halt when she was rear-ended in her car one day, suffering severe whiplash. Then, several days later, going to the doctor's for treatment of this injury, she was hit head-on by another car and suffered temporary brain damage.

Writing as Therapy

Recovering from her injuries, Danziger was haunted by nightmares. While undergoing therapy, she began what became her first novel, *A Cat Ate My Gymsuit*. The novel began as part of therapeutic exercises to help Danziger work through her personal problems, and also as a way of communicating with the students she had left behind.

Eleven-year-old Matthew is up to his old tricks in this fourth "Matthew Martin" title.

Drawing heavily on her own family experiences, Danziger created a fictional persona that is the closest to autobiography she has ever written. Thirteen-year-old Marcy Lewis is overweight, out of synch with her parents, and unhappy in a school that stifles creativity. One of her excuses not to dress down for gym is that the "cat ate my gymsuit," and Marcy's protests remain on that level until she gets involved in more meaningful student demonstrations to re-instate a popular English teacher unfairly fired. Though some reviewers came down on Danziger for what was perceived as trite situations, a reviewer for *Journal of Reading* concluded that the book was a "thoroughly enjoyable, tightly written, funny/sad tale of an unglamorous but plucky girl who is imaginative, believable, and worthy of emulation." Dedicated to John Ciardi, the book won a slew of awards as well as a large readership of fans clamoring for more of Danziger's bright and breezy humor.

Danziger's next title, *The Pistachio Prescription*, deals with Cassie's inferiority complex and the crisis brought about by her parents' divorce. Cyrisse Jaffe, writing in *Kliatt*, called the book "lively, believable, and thoroughly readable," while Selma G. Lanes noted in *New York Times Book Review* that "no thoughtful 9- to 13-year-old should let parents see" the novel, as they "may not survive the instant ego deflation of viewing themselves through adolescent eyes." It is, in part, this veryidentification of Danziger with the adolescent protagonists in her novels, the way she takes their side against all-too frequent dullard or

PAULA DANZIGER
AMBER BROWN
GOES FOURTH

What's so great about fourth grade anyway?

SCHOLASTIC

Amber Brown does not think she can make it to fourth grade without a new best friend in this 1995 title from the popular "Amber Brown" series.

insensitive adults, that has won her such a large readership among teens and pre-teens. With publication of her second book, Danziger decided to give up teaching for full-time writing, but as she noted in *English Journal*, "Teaching was and continues to be one of the most important influences on what I do," and a constant source of material for her works.

Focusing on writing books, Danziger has published many more novels, several of which are aimed at the teen audience, for which many commentators believe her best works are produced. Adolescent romance and sexuality, as well as quarreling parents, are at the center of *Can You Sue Your Parents for Malpractice?*, "a fast-moving novel with a title to entice most teenage readers," according to Michele Simpson in *Journal of Reading*. Jane Langton observed in the *New York Times Book Review* that this book "is clever and funny," and that the "chapters rush by in a catapulting present tense."

Marcy Lewis makes a return engagement in *There's a Bat in Bunk Five*, a book that rivals "Judy Blume with her sharp, funny accounts of summer camp," according to Powling in *Books for Keeps*. With *The Divorce Express* and *It's an Aardvark-Eat-Turtle World*, Danziger introduces best friends who become step-sisters when their parents decide to live together. Phoebe narrates the first title, in which she is shuttled back and forth between New York City and Woodstock, New York—both locations where Danziger herself lives.In *The Divorce Express*, Phoebe's friend Rosie—one of Danziger's personal favorites as a character—helps her through the troubled waters of divorce, but in the second book Rosie is the narrator, and the story deals with more than mixing families, for Rosie is a child of a bi-racial marriage and must also cope with that factor. Margery Fisher observed in *Growing Point* that *The Divorce Express* "makes its point in an agreeably relaxed and shrewd manner," and Zena Sutherland concluded in *Bulletin of the Center for Children's Books* that *It's an Aardvark-Eat-Turtle World* "has moments of sweetness to balance some tartness, an honest approach to problems, a lively and natural writing style, and strong, consistent characterization."

With *This Place Has No Atmosphere*, Danziger took dysfunctional parents on the galactic road, and created a twenty-first-century science fiction tale with family problems all too familiar to today's

If you enjoy the works of Paula Danziger, you may also want to check out the following books:

Ilene Cooper, *Star-Spangled Summer*, 1996.
Constance C. Greene, *The Love Letters of J. Timothy Owen*, 1986.
A. C. LeMieux, *The TV Guidance Counselor*, 1993.

teens. *Remember Me to Harold Square* and *Thames Doesn't Rhyme with James* are companion volumes, set in New York and London respectively, that feature Kendra Kayer, her heartthrob Frank Lee, and her pesky little brother, Oscar. Both titles employ scavenger hunts to introduce the reader to cultural sights of each city. Nancy Headley Jones observed in *Voice of Youth Advocates* that *Remember Me to Harold Square* "has all the ingredients to please a young adult market," including sibling rivalry and teen romance. *Publishers Weekly* concluded that in *Thames Doesn't Rhyme with James* "Danziger laces her heroine's first-person narrative with an abundance of verbal sallies, quips and puns."

Creates Popular Series

Danziger abandoned her usual first-person narration for a series of pre-teen books featuring a male protagonist—yet another first for the writer. Four novels deal with the adventures and misadventures of eleven-year-old Matthew: *Everyone Else's Parents Said Yes, Make Like a Tree and Leave, Earth to Matthew,* and *Not for a Billion, Gazillion Dollars.* Written partly in response to the shrinking YA market, Danziger's Matthew books won for her a new and younger audience of readers by adapting the same winning formula employed in her YA titles. Reviewing the first title in the series, *Everyone Else's Parents Said Yes,* a critic commented in *Publishers Weekly* that, with her usual combination of humor and insight, the author's "characters come alive through natural dialogue and universal experiences."

A second series, aimed at even younger readers, features Amber Brown as well as the trademark Danziger attitude. Reviewing *Amber Brown Is Not*

a Crayon, Roger Sutton observed in *Bulletin of the Center for Children's Books* that, while the chapter book was a standard moving-away story, still "Danziger's brisk and empathetic writing brings her the same kind of intuitive connection with kids she's made in books for older readers. . . ." Other titles in the Amber Brown series include *You Can't Eat Your Chicken Pox, Amber Brown, Amber Brown Goes Fourth, Amber Brown Wants Extra Credit, Forever Amber Brown,* and *Amber Brown Sees Red,* books that deal not only with usual school traumas, but also with issues of divorce and blending families. Of *Amber Brown Sees Red,* in which Amber's parents battle for hercustody, Jackie Hechtkopf noted in *School Library Journal* that "real emotion is mixed with comic relief, creating colorful characters in a lively story that will

Two friends, separated by hundreds of miles, exchange problems and support through a series of letters in this 1998 work, cowritten by Paula Danziger and Ann M. Martin.

attract new fans and old ones alike." Taken as a whole, this series of chapter books has been praised for its ability to entice new readers, to make even kids who hate books find that reading can be fun.

Most recently, Danziger has joined forces with Ann M. Martin, author of the "Baby Sitters Club" series, in an epistolary novel entitled *P.S. Longer Letter Later*, which tells of two junior high best friends suddenly separated by hundreds of miles. They have much to write each other about (since telephone calls are too expensive). Elizabeth's affluent parents suffer a reversal of fortune when her father's company is downsized. Tara*Starr (as she signs herself) must cope with her young parents planning for their first "wanted" child. Ron Koertge, writing for *New York Times Book Review*, described *P.S. Longer Letter Later* as a "spirited and readable book with none of the anemia or tendentiousness" associated with much YA writing. He concludes optimistically, "given both authors' propensity for writing series, is it unreasonable to expect a sequel?"

Whether writing for elementary, junior high, or high school students, what counts for Danziger is to communicate directly to her young audience. She related a story to Feitlowitz about a time she was signing books at the American Library Association Convention and how one school librarian toldher she was not going to stand in line for one of Danziger's signed books, but that the kids in her school would kill her if she didn't order them. "And that is what matters to me," Danziger concluded. "That the kids like my books, and that my books touch their lives and make them feel less alone."

■ Works Cited

Review of *The Cat Ate My Gymsuit, Journal of Reading*, January, 1976, pp. 333-35.

Danziger, Paula, *The Cat Ate My Gymsuit*, Delacorte, 1974.

Danziger, Paula, "Facets: Successful Authors Talk about Connections between Teaching and Writing," *English Journal*, November, 1984, pp. 24-27.

Danziger, Paula, in an interview with Marguerite Feitlowitz for *Authors and Artists for Young Adults*, Volume 4, Gale, 1990, pp. 73-80.

Review of *Everyone Else's Parents Said Yes, Publishers Weekly*, September 8, 1989, p. 70.

Fisher, Margery, review of *The Divorce Express, Growing Point*, September, 1986, pp. 4673-74.

Hechtkopf, Jackie, review of *Amber Brown Sees Red, School Library Journal*, July, 1997, p. 61.

Jaffe, Cyrisse, review of *The Pistachio Prescription, Kliatt*, Spring, 1979, p. 6.

Jones, Nancy Headley, review of *Remember Me to Harold Square, Voice of Youth Advocates*, December, 1987, p. 46.

Koertge, Ron, "Please Mr. Postman," *New York Times Book Review*, May 17, 1998, p. 27.

Lanes, Selma G., review of *The Pistachio Prescription, New York Times Book Review*, March 18, 1979, p. 26.

Langton, Jane, review of *Can You Sue Your Parents for Malpractice?, New York Times Book Review*, June 17, 1979, p. 25.

Powling, Chris, "Authorgraph No. 93," *Books for Keeps*, July, 1995, pp. 14-15.

Simpson, Michele, review of *Can You Sue Your Parents for Malpractice?, Journal of Reading*, February, 1980, p. 473.

Sutherland, Zena, review of *It's an Aardvark-Eat-Turtle World, Bulletin of the Center for Children's Books*, June, 1985, pp. 182-83.

Sutton, Roger, review of *Amber Brown Is Not a Crayon, Bulletin of the Center for Children's Books*, June, 1994, pp. 316-17.

Review of *Thames Doesn't Rhyme with James, Publishers Weekly*, September 12, 1994, p. 92.

■ For More Information See

BOOKS

Children's Literature Review, Volume 20, Gale, 1990.

Krull, Kathleen, *Presenting Paula Danziger*, Twayne, 1995.

St. James Guide to Young Adult Writers, St. James Press, 1999.

PERIODICALS

Booklist, June 1 & 15, 1996, pp. 1716-17; November 15, 1996, p. 587; May 15, 1997, p. 1575.

Bulletin of the Center for Children's Books, January, 1987, p. 85; September, 1991, p. 6; October, 1996, p. 54.

Horn Book, January-February, 1988, pp. 62-63; July-August, 1993, pp. 149-50; July-August, 1994, p. 447; January-February, 1997, pp. 54-55.

Junior Bookshelf, August, 1993, pp. 149-50.

Kirkus Reviews, October 1, 1989, p. 1473; July 15, 1995, p. 1022.

Publishers Weekly, June 29, 1990, p. 102; July 27, 1992, p. 63; February 21, 1994, pp. 254-55; February 10, 1995, p. 206.

School Library Journal, September, 1992, p. 250; May, 1994, p. 90; January, 1995, p. 134; February, 1997, p. 75.

Voice of Youth Advocates, October, 1991, pp. 223-24; December, 1992, p. 276; April, 1995, p. 22.*

—Sketch by J. Sydney Jones

Cynthia DeFelice

■ Personal

Born December 28, 1951, in Philadelphia, PA; daughter of William (a psychiatrist) and Ann (an English teacher and homemaker; maiden name, Baldwin) Carter; married Ralph DeFelice (a dentist), February 16, 1974; stepchildren: Michelle, Ralph. *Education:* William Smith College, B.A., 1973; Syracuse University, M.L.S., 1980. *Hobbies and other interests:* Quilt making, dulcimer playing, hiking, backpacking, bird watching, fishing, reading, watching films.

■ Addresses

Office—c/o Farrar, Straus and Giroux, Inc., 19 Union Square West, New York, NY 10003.

■ Career

Storyteller and writer. Worked variously as a barn painter, day-care provider, and advertising layout artist; Newark public schools, Newark, NY, elementary school media specialist, 1980-87. Co-founder of Wild Washerwomen Storytellers, 1980.

■ Member

Authors Guild, Authors League of America, Society of Children's Book Writers and Illustrators, National Storytelling Association, Audubon Society, Nature Conservancy, Wilderness Society, Seneca Lake Pure Waters Association.

■ Awards, Honors

Notable Children's Trade Book for Language Arts, National Council of Teachers of English, and Teacher's Choice Award, International Reading Association, both 1989, both for *The Strange Night Writing of Jessamine Colter;* Best Children's Books of the Year, Library of Congress, BestIllustrated Children's Books of the Year, *New York Times,* and Reading Magic Award, *Parenting,* all 1989, all for *The Dancing Skeleton;* Best Books designation, *School Library Journal,* Notable Children's Book designation, American Library Association, Notable Children's Trade Book in the Field of Social Studies, National Council for the Social Studies-Children's Book Council, and International Reading Association and Children's Book Council Young Adult Choice Award, all 1990, Hodge-Podger Society Award for Fiction, 1992, and Sequoyah and South Carolina children's book awards, all for *Weasel;* Best Book of 1994, New York Public Library, for *Mule Eggs;* listed among Books for the Teen Age, New York Public Library, 1995, for *Lostman's River;* Best Book designation, New York Public Library, 1995, and Anne Izard Storytellers' Choice Award, 1996, for *Three Perfect Peaches;*

South Dakota Prairie Pasque Children's Book Award and Sunshine State Young Reader's Award, both 1995, both for *Devil's Bridge*; Best Book designation, *School Library Journal*, 1996, and Notable Children's Trade Book in the Field of Social Studies designation, 1997, Notable Children's Book designation, American Library Association, Judy Lopez Memorial Award, International Honor Book, Society of School Librarians, Books for the Teen Age selection, New York Public Library, all for *The Apprenticeship of Lucas Whitaker*; Texas Bluebonnet Award, for *The Ghost of Fossil Glen*; New York State Knickerbocker Award, 1998, for body of work; Notable Children's Trade Book in the Field of Social Studies, National Council for the Social Studies-Children's Book Council, for *Nowhere to Call Home*.

■ Writings

JUVENILE NOVELS

Weasel, Macmillan, 1990.
Devil's Bridge, Macmillan, 1992.
The Light on Hogback Hill, Macmillan, 1993.
Lostman's River, Macmillan, 1994.
The Apprenticeship of Lucas Whitaker, Farrar, Straus and Giroux, 1996.
The Ghost of Fossil Glen, Farrar, Straus and Giroux, 1998.
Nowhere to Call Home, Farrar, Straus and Giroux, 1999.
Death at Devil's Bridge, Farrar, Straus and Giroux, 2000.

PICTURE BOOKS

The Strange Night Writing of Jessamine Colter, calligraphy by Leah Palmer Preiss, Macmillan, 1988.
The Dancing Skeleton, illustrated by Robert Andrew Parker, Macmillan, 1989.
When Grampa Kissed His Elbow, illustrated by Karl Swanson, Macmillan, 1992.
Mule Eggs, illustrated by Mike Shenon, Orchard, 1994.
(Reteller with Mary DeMarsh and others) *Three Perfect Peaches: A French Folktale*, illustrated by Irene Trivas, Orchard, 1995.
Casey in the Bath, illustrated by Chris L. Demarest, Farrar, Straus and Giroux, 1996.
Willy's Silly Grandma, illustrated by Shelley Jackson, Orchard, 1997.

Clever Crow, illustrated by S. D. Schindler, Atheneum, 1998.
Cold Feet, illustrated by Robert Andrew Parker, DK Ink, 2000.

■ Sidelights

Cynthia DeFelice combines the oral skills of a storyteller with the technical skills of a writer to create children's stories drawn from the folk tradition, American history, and contemporary society. Her books feature young people thrust into situations that require them to make vital decisions for themselves and to assume responsibilities far beyond their years. In her picture books and novels, DeFelice mixes the elements of suspense, drama, and humor into "crackling good storytelling," as a *Publishers Weekly* reviewer described her efforts. Whether exploring the plight of Native Americans, as in the award-winning *Weasel*, making a past way of life seem vivid and real to twenty-first century readers, or highlighting the endangered ecosystem as she does in *Lostman's River* and *Devil's Bridge*, DeFelice's primary concern is in telling a compelling story, creating the "then-what-happened?" curiosity that keeps readers turning the page. "DeFelice knows how to make history come alive by providing characters who readers will find both realistic and sympathetic," maintained *Voice of Youth Advocates* contributor Cindy Lombardo, recommending titles by DeFelice that showcase epochs from nineteenth-and early twentieth-century American history.

Born in Philadelphia, Pennsylvania, in 1951, DeFelice has credited her mother for instilling a strong storytelling tradition in her. As she once recalled, "my two brothers, my sister, and I would snuggle in Mom's lap while she read to us. She was a great storyteller and had this terrific sense of rhythm and timing. It was in that big, tan chair where we all used to curl up together that I learned to love stories and to feel their magic." Growing up in a Philadelphia suburb, DeFelice recalled her childhood as "pretty idyllic," with time spent either playing with her brothers or curled up in a chair somewhere lost in a good book. Her psychiatrist father was also supportive of his daughter's interests. "You could tell him anything. So my early years were very nourishing."

Graduating from her local high school's honors program, DeFelice enrolled at William Smith College in the town of Geneva, about forty miles southeast of Rochester, New York. She immediately fell in love with the region, and has lived there ever since. After graduating in 1973, she worked briefly as a barn painter; a year later she was married with two young stepchildren. Being a full-time mother became her priority until the children were older; then she enrolled at Syracuse University and earned an advanced degree in library science. Graduating in 1980, DeFelice got a job as a school librarian in Newark, New York. It would be this job that sparked her interest in both storytelling and writing children's books.

Captures Young Imaginations through Storytelling

DeFelice teamed up with music teacher Mary DeMarsh in a storytelling venture called the Wild Washerwomen. DeFelice and her partner began telling stories in schools throughout upstate New York, and after the sessions, intrigued members of their young audience would invariably ask her if those stories were written down somewhere so they could read them. It did not take many such requests to prompt DeFelice to put pen to paper, resulting in a series of entertaining popular picture books and, later, novels for young readers.

Her first book was *The Strange Night Writing of Jessamine Colter,* which was published in 1988. The inspiration for the story came from a nightmare DeFelice had one night. "I dreamed I saw my hand floating through space, come to rest at my desk, and then pen in perfect calligraphy, 'You are going to die tomorrow night at ten o'clock,'" the author recalled. Although the threatened action never materialized, a picture book did. In DeFelice's story, a calligrapher named Jessie likes to write out all the important notices for her small town. Suddenly she discovers that she has the ability to foretell the future through her writing—even her own death. Before she dies, however, she is able to pass on the art of calligraphy and the gift of her strength and love to a young girl named Callie, who has become her apprentice.

The Strange Night Writing of Jessamine Colter was a critical success. A reviewer in Voice of Youth Advocates called it a "simple, loving story," and a *Publishers Weekly* contributor offered a similar opinion, stating, "DeFelice's novella has a wistful mood and a gently unwinding pace. . . . Thoughtful readers . . . will revel in its poetic language." Roger Sutton, writing in the *Bulletin of the Center for Children's Books,* dubbed the story "sentimental in the best sense."

Success with *Night Writing* Sparks Career Change

Encouraged by the success of her first book, DeFelice left library work and embarked on a career as a full-time writer. Her second picture book, *The Dancing Skeleton,* focuses on the difficulties a widow faces when her deceased husband refuses to stay dead; he comes back to dance about when the widow's new suitor—a fiddler—comes courting.

The idea for this 1988 picture book, which is about a woman who can foretell the future through her calligraphy, came to the author in a dream.

Like several of her picture books, *The Dancing Skeleton* is a retelling of a traditional folk tale. "These stories never get old for me," DeFelice recalled. "Even if I tell them a hundred times, I find something new in them, and looking at the faces in the audience is so much fun. The kids are like my editors: I know immediately when something works or doesn't." In the case of *The Dancing Skeleton,* the tale worked. The book gained special praise for its author's technical skills. Ellen D. Warwick wrote in *School Library Journal* that DeFelice's "rhythmic prose captures the vocabulary, tone, the very cadences of the oral tradition."

With two books in as many years to her credit, DeFelice began to branch out as a writer, in part

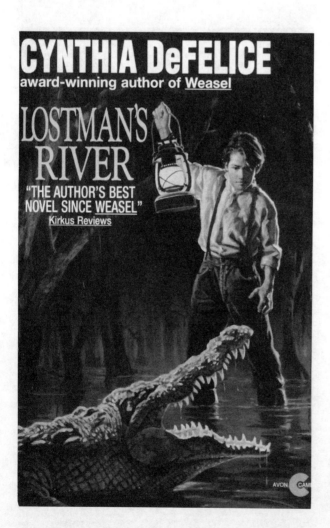

Tyler MacCauley and his family fear that their home and the home of various wildlife will be gone forever when a stranger they trusted misleads them.

as a result of circumstances. "I was home alone one night and heard a knock at the door," the author explained in her interview. "And suddenly I wondered what a couple of kids alone might do if that happened to them. Then I asked myself who those kids in my imagination were and why they were alone. Next, I began wondering who was knocking at their door and why. Suddenly I was involved in a novel without even knowing where it was going. I had to keep writing it to see what was going to happen." Coupling her continued writing with hours of research, DeFelice set her next story in Ohio during the 1830s. Nathan, a member of a pioneering family, wakes one night to learn that a man named Weasel has wounded his father. A former Indian-hunter whose life of hunting and killing has driven him half mad, Weasel now is quick to raise a gun or knife against his own kind. Vowing to avenge his father's attack, young Nathan hunts down Weasel, but when the opportunity to strike arises, the boy realizes that such violence would make him no better than the assailant that he has been hunting.

The story of Nathan's quest for justice was published in 1990 as *Weasel,* a book that received many commendations. Calling DeFelice's rendering of her young protagonist's character "unforgettable," *School Library Journal* contributor Yvonne Frey praised the novel for addressing race relations in a new way, by "turn[ing] the results of hate back on the white race itself." *Weasel* "makes a positive contribution to a world caught up with killing and revenge," reviewer Kathryn Hackler wrote in her *Voice of Youth Advocates* review, while a contributor to *Publishers Weekly* pronounced the novel a "fast-paced" work that "effectively conveys the battle between good and evil."

Creates Award-winning Fiction

Pleased with the critical praise for *Weasel,* DeFelice was encouraged to continue writing novels as well as picture books. Her next effort was 1992's *Devil's Bridge,* a tale that takes place off the East Coast in Martha's Vineyard. Twelve-year-old Ben Daggett hears two men scheming to cheat their way to the ten thousand dollar prize in the annual striped bass fishing derby by injecting an illegally caught fish with mercury to increase its weight. Before he perished in a hurricane the year before, Ben's fisherman father had set the record for the largest bass ever caught, and Ben doesn't want his father's accomplishments overshadowed by anyone's dishonest efforts. Since no one will listen to him when he attempts to divulge the men's scheme, Bendetermines to catch the biggest fish himself. While he manages to hook the winning fish, Ben lets the creature go free at the last minute because he is unwilling to take its life.

In *Devil's Bridge*, DeFelice touches upon Ben's confusion and hurt over the death of his father, as well as several wildlife management and environmental issues, particularly as they relate to the nation's overtaxed fisheries. However, her story never becomes pedantic; as *School Library Journal* contributor Louise L. Sherman attested, *Devil's Bridge* is a "fast paced and involving" adventure yarn featuring what *Booklist* critic Janice Del Negro termed "an appealing main character" in Ben. A *Publishers Weekly* reviewer agreed, calling the novel "more than a straightforward adventure; it is a multi-layered book with feeling." *Devil's Bridge* would later find a sequel in *Death at Devil's Bridge*, which DeFelice published in 2000. In this story Ben—now thirteen—takes a job as first-mate on a fishing boat, only to find himself enmeshed in the illegal drug trade and possibly even murder.

The Light on Hogback Hill, published in 1993, started out as a typical "haunted house" mystery, taking place in the quintessential old, abandoned house on the hill, complete with boarded up windows, creaking doors, and emitting mysterious noises during the night. "But things changed with the writing," DeFelice recalled. In the published version, the author's young protagonists investigate a supposedly haunted house only to find an elderly woman whom they befriend. As DeFelice described it, *The Light on Hogback Hill* is really "a story about the shells we all build around ourselves when we get hurt, and how we can all help each other break through those shells."

Highlights Fascinating—and Grisly—Side of History

The Apprenticeship of Lucas Whitaker, published in 1996, concerns ayoung boy who goes to work for a local physician after his entire family dies of tuberculosis. Once commonly known as called "consumption," tuberculosis was one of the main causes of death prior to the turn of the twentieth century, and it was believed by some that the sickness was passed along by the dead, who acted like vam-

If you enjoy the works of Cynthia DeFelice, you may also want to check out the following books:

Avi, *The Barn*, 1994.
Penelope Farmer, *Thicker than Water*, 1993.
Chelsea Quinn Yarbro, *Laradio's Apprentice*, 1984.

pires in spreading the disease through entire households. DeFelice's historical novel takes place in Connecticut during the mid-1800s, and introduces readers to Lucas, a twelve-year-old who feels responsible for the death of his parents. Working alongside the town doctor allows Lucas to understand that the folk remedy he had failed to perform—digging up the body of the first member of the family to die of consumption, removing the heart, and burning it—could not have saved his family.

Praising DeFelice for her compelling main characters and for illustrating the harsh realities of life in New England farming communities in the nineteenth century, *School Library Journal* contributor Jane Gardner Connor noted that "Readers will experience a period when even a doctor's knowledge was very limited, and . . . will come to realize how fear and desperation can make people willing to try almost anything." In her *Horn Book* review of *The Apprenticeship of Lucas Whitaker*, Elizabeth S. Watson added, "The pace of this fine piece of historical fiction is brisk in spite of a wealth of detail [about] . . . health, hygiene, and witchcraft."

As it was in *The Apprenticeship of Lucas Whitaker*, the loss of both parents is a motivating factor in the life of twelve-year-old Frances Barrow in DeFelice's 1999 novel *Nowhere to Call Home*. When her father loses his Philadelphia-based business—as well as everything else—during the stock market crash of 1929, he commits suicide, leaving his daughter an orphan. Left with nothing, Frances decides to cut her hair, disguise herself as a boy, and strike out for herself by "riding the rails" westward as a train-jumping hobo,rather than going to live with an aunt she has never met. Noting that "The dialogue rings true," *Voice of Youth Advocates* critic Cindy Lombardo added that the story's "fast pace . . . will keep readers turning pages until the poignant resolution." While the story takes place in the past century, Margaret A. Bush noted in *Horn Book* that DeFelice bridges the gap between her young protagonist and modern-day readers. "The story is a good adventure," Bush maintained, "presenting readers with insights into homelessness quite relevant to our own time."

DeFelice returned to the here-and-now, but with a supernatural twist, in her 1998 novel *The Ghost of Fossil Glen*. Readers are introduced to Allie Nichols, an eleven-year-old who enjoys roaming remote areas near her home in search of fossils. One day she hears a ghostly whisper, and soon becomes haunted by the voice of a girl who was murdered in that area four years earlier. Even though her friends question her sanity, Allie is determined to help the spirit, and ultimately helps bring justice to the now-departed Lucy in a story that possesses "unusual warmth" and "vivid characterizations," according to a *Kirkus* reviewer. Praising *The Ghost of Fossil Glen* as a "beautifully crafted thriller," *Booklist* contributor Lauren Peterson added that DeFelice has skillfully crafted an "expertly paced, dynamic page-turner that never gives readers the chance to become distracted or lose interest."

Writing for Picture Book Set Provides Balance

While continuing to entertain young adult readers with her novels, DeFelice continues to add picture books to her bibliography, although she is quick to explain that the two genres require a different approach. "I enjoy doing both kinds of books, both novels and picture books," she once explained. "But with picture books, every word has to count. It is more like writing poetry."

Mule Eggs, DeFelice's 1994 effort, is the story of a city slicker named Patrick. Deciding to become a farmer, he buys a farm and, in addition to the challenges posed by life in the country, has to contend with a local practical joker. In her retelling of the French folktale *Three Perfect Peaches*, three brothers compete among themselves to deliver the most perfect peaches and thus win the hand of the king's daughter. In 1997's *Willy's Silly Grandma* a grandmother's folk cures prove not to be as silly as people thought. "It's grandma's turn this time," DeFelice quipped, referring to her 1992 book *When Grampa Kissed His Elbow*, an "unusual but charming intergenerational story," according to *Booklist* contributor Karen Hutt. Still another picture book,

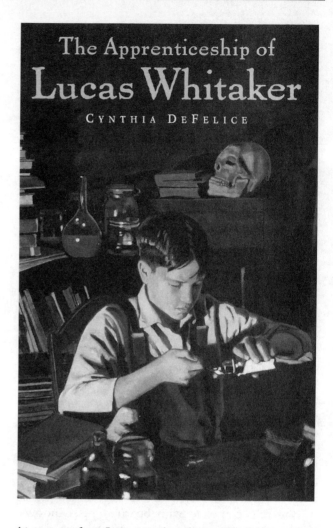

At age twelve, Lucas carries the guilt of not curing his mother of tuberculosis in this 1996 novel.

1998's *Clever Crow*, features a battle of wits involving a young girl named Emma who becomes frustrated when a crow begins to steal small, shiny objects from around her home. When even the house keys find their way into Crow's nest, Emma hatches a plan to trick the feathered thief . . . until Crow outsmarts her. Praising the story as a "sprightly takeoff on Aesop's fable 'The Fox and the Grapes,'" a *Publishers Weekly* contributor commended DeFelice for her "jaunty tone" and energetic rhymes.

Whether creating picture books or novels, DeFelice has the same basic goals. "I want to write a story to entertain, to engage the minds, hearts, and senses of young readers," she once stated. "I really think that kids are the most challenging audience to write for. They demand a satisfying story. They will not sit through something that does not please them."

DeFelice balances her time alone writing with visits to young readers. "It helps to be working with kids," she explained. "I still do storytelling at schools and it is instant feedback for me. They help me to hone my story and my language." Still, the bulk of her time is spent writing, and her focus remains straightforward: "I want my readers to come away from my books with amemory worth having, something that will enrich their lives and something that they might not otherwise have the chance to experience. But I don't like to tie up all the loose ends. I respect my readers and figure they will become part of the process if I don't answer all the questions for them. After all, life isn't like that. We can't know everything in real life. Why should we expect to in fiction?"

■ Works Cited

Bush, Margaret A., review of *Nowhere to Call Home, Horn Book,* March-April, 1999, p. 207.

Review of *Clever Crow, Publishers Weekly,* May 4, 1998, p. 211.

Connor, Jane Gardner, review of *The Apprenticeship of Lucas Whitaker, School Library Journal,* August, 1996, p. 142.

Del Negro, Janice, review of *Devil's Bridge, Booklist,* December 1, 1992, p. 669.

Review of *Devil's Bridge, Publishers Weekly,* September 7, 1992, pp. 96-97.

Frey, Yvonne, review of *Weasel, School Library Journal,* May, 1990, pp. 103-4.

Hackler, Kathryn, review of *Weasel, Voice of Youth Advocates,* June, 1990, pp. 101-2.

Hutt, Karen, review of *When Grampa Kissed His Elbow, Booklist,* March 15, 1992, pp. 1386-87.

Lombardo, Cindy, review of *Nowhere to Call Home, Voice of Youth Advocates,* October, 1999, p. 256.

Peterson, Lauren, review of *The Ghost of Fossil Glen, Booklist,* March 15, 1998, p. 1243.

Sherman, Louise L., review of *Devil's Bridge, School Library Journal,* November, 1992, pp. 88-89.

Review of *The Strange Night Writing of Jessamine Colter, Publishers Weekly,* August 12, 1988, pp. 460-461.

Review of *The Strange Night Writing of Jessamine Colter, Voice of Youth Advocates,* April, 1989, p. 26.

Sutton, Roger, review of *The Strange Night Writing of Jessamine Colter, Bulletin of the Center for Children's Books,* September, 1988, p. 5.

Warwick, Ellen D., review of *The Dancing Skeleton, School Library Journal,* September, 1989, p. 239.

Watson, Elizabeth S., review of *The Dancing Skeleton, Horn Book,* January-February, 1990, pp. 75-76.

Watson, Elizabeth S., review of *The Apprenticeship of Lucas Whitaker, Horn Book,* January-February, 1997, p. 55.

Review of *Weasel, Publishers Weekly,* April 27, 1990, p. 62.

■ For More Information See

PERIODICALS

Bulletin of the Center for Children's Books, November, 1992, pp. 70-71; December, 1993, p. 79; June, 1994, p. 317; October, 1996, pp. 54-55; March, 1998, p. 240.

Horn Book, March-April, 1994; January-February, 1997, p. 55.

Kirkus Reviews, July 15, 1988, p. 1055; November 1, 1992, p. 1374.

Publishers Weekly, April 26, 1999, p. 84.

School Library Journal, August, 1992, p. 134; July, 1998, pp. 92-93; April, 1999, p. 113.

Stephen R. Donaldson

■ Personal

Born May 13, 1947, in Cleveland, OH; son of James R. (an orthopedic surgeon and medical missionary) and Mary Ruth (a prosthetist and occupational therapist; maiden name, Reeder) Donaldson; first marriage ended in divorce; married Stephanie, 1980. *Education:* College of Wooster, B.A., 1968; Kent State University, M.A., 1971.

■ Addresses

Office—41 Broadway, New York, NY 10003.

■ Career

Writer. Akron City Hospital, Akron, OH, assistant dispatcher, 1968-70; Kent State University, Kent, OH, teaching fellow, 1971; Tapp-Gentz Associates, West Chester, PA, acquisitions editor, 1973-74; Ghost Ranch Writers Workshops, NM, instructor, 1973-77; University of New Mexico, teaching assistant in literature after 1982.

■ Member

International Association for the Fantastic in the Arts, United States Karate Alliance, American Contract Bridge League, Duke City Bridge Club.

■ Awards, Honors

British Fantasy Award, 1978, for *The Chronicles of Thomas Covenant: The Unbeliever*; John W. Campbell Award, World Science Fiction Convention, 1979, for best new writer; Balrog awards for best novel, 1981, for *The Wounded Land,* and 1983, and for best collection, 1985, for *Daughter of Regals and Other Tales*; Saturn Award for best fantasy novel, 1983; Book of the Year awards, Science Fiction Book Club, 1987, for *The Mirror of Her Dreams,* and 1988, for *A Man Rides Through.*

■ Writings

FANTASY

The Chronicles of Thomas Covenant: The Unbeliever (Science Fiction Book Club selection), Holt (New York City), 1977, Volume I: *Lord Foul's Bane,* Volume II: *The Illearth War,* Volume III: *The Power That Preserves.*

The Second Chronicles of Thomas Covenant: The Unbeliever, Ballantine (New York City), Volume I: *The Wounded Land,* 1980, Volume II: *The One Tree,* 1982, Volume III: *White Gold Wielder,* 1983.

Gilden-Fire, Underwood-Miller (San Francisco, CA), 1982.

Daughter of Regals and Other Tales (includes the novella *Gilden-Fire*), Del Rey, 1984.

Mordant's Need, Ballantine, Volume I: *The Mirror of Her Dreams*, 1986, Volume II: *A Man Rides Through*, 1987.

(Editor) *Strange Dreams: Unforgettable Fantasy Stories*, Bantam (New York City), 1993.

"THE GAP CYCLE" SERIES; SCIENCE FICTION

The Gap into Conflict: The Real Story, Bantam, 1990.

The Gap into Vision: Forbidden Knowledge, Bantam, 1991.

The Gap into Power: A Dark and Hungry God Arises, Bantam, 1992.

The Gap into Madness: Chaos and Order, Bantam, 1994.

The Gap into Ruin: This Day All Gods Die, Bantam, 1996.

UNDER PSEUDONYM REED STEPHENS

The Man Who Killed His Brother, Ballantine, 1980.
The Man Who Risked His Partner, Ballantine, 1984.
The Man Who Tried to Get Away, Ballantine, 1990.

OTHER

(Contributor) Judy-Lynn del Rey, editor, *Stellar #4*, Ballantine, 1978.

(Contributor) Terry Carr, *The Year's Best Fantasy*, Berkley Publishing (New York City), 1979.

Reave the Just and Other Tales, Bantam/Spectra (New York), 1999.

Also contributor to science fiction magazines; both "Thomas Covenant" series have been translated for publication in other languages; author's papers are housed in the Department of Special Collections of the Kent State University Libraries.

■ Adaptations

White Gold Wielder is available as a recording from Camden, 1983.

■ Sidelights

Stephen R. Donaldson is the author of a number of lengthy, complexly plotted sagas in the science-fiction/fantasy genre that have earned him both critical praise and a devoted readership. Yet he struggled for many years as a writer, unable even to find a publisher who would work with him, before his books landed on the bestseller lists. Donaldson is perhaps best known for his *The Chronicles of Thomas Covenant: The Unbeliever*, which appeared in 1977. It sold millions, and was likened to the one of the most famous trilogies in fantasy fiction, J.R.R. Tolkien's *Lord of the Rings*.

Like all of Donaldson's subsequent novels, the "Thomas Covenant" story drew readers into a plot in which forces of good and evil battled to destroy one another; always, the author's anti-hero protagonists struggle with ethical dilemmas that echo eternal religious themes while cruelty and violence run amok. "The moral import of his fantasies is their very heart and soul," remarked fellow fantasy writer Brian Stableford in an essay about Donaldson for the *St. James Guide to Fantasy Writers*. "[F]ew other writers in the genre are capable of reaching such a terrible pitch of indignation and horror at the contemplation of the human capacity for abusing others."

In a Foreign Land

Born in Cleveland, Ohio, in 1947, Donaldson was the son of Presbyterian missionaries, and at the age of three he left the Midwest with his parents to settle permanently in India. In the city of Miraj, Donaldson's orthopedic surgeon father treated victims of leprosy who had lost their extremities; his mother worked at the same hospital as a prosthetist and occupational therapist.

The exotic Asian locale, meanwhile, offered the young Donaldson the kind of adventures most children only read about in books; on one occasion, he was kept home from school because a deadly tiger was on the prowl. "India is both a mysterious and exotic place," Donaldson told Robert Dahlin in a *Publishers Weekly* interview. "And a very grim place of human misery. I grew up with wild physical beauty, strange cultural evidence of magical or spiritual events. There was a snake charmer on every corner."

A bookworm who devoured whatever English-language titles were available to him in Miraj, Donaldson became enamored with fantasy and adventure literature at an early age, reading everything from the "Hardy Boys" mystery series to the African escapade tales of Joseph Conrad; the

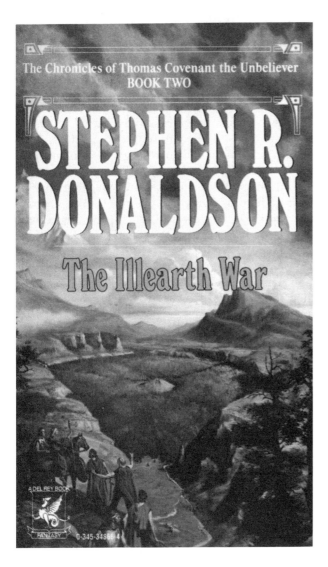

High Lord Elena desperately requests Covenant to use his magic ring against the evil powers of the Illearth Stone in this 1977 installment of "The Chronicles of Thomas Covenant" series.

Chronicles of Narnia by C.S. Lewis was also a particular favorite. Returning to Ohio at the age of sixteen, Donaldson enrolled at its College of Wooster, a small, private liberal-arts school. There, he learned that his years in India did not seem to count for much: "In my wing of the dorm, we had five National Merit scholars, fiveprofessional musicians and a guy who had already written eight novels," he told *People* writer John Neary in 1982. "I was the only person who didn't have something immense to offer the world." One Sunday, Donaldson attended church services, contemplating his future, and found a solution. "Something in my mind

leapt the gap between being addicted to reading stories and wanting to write them," he explained to Neary.

After graduating in 1968, Donaldson went on to study English at Kent State University, earning his master's degree three years later. The following year, he sat in a church pew once again, listening to his father tell a congregation about the years in India and his work treating sufferers of leprosy. A chronic infectious disease that once brought on devastating physical disfigurement, leprosy was so feared in the past that its victims were often sent to die in special colonies on remote islands, to which only religious missionaries would venture as aid workers. In more modern times, the disease has proved treatable, but on that day in church, Donaldson's father was discussing the psychological trauma that leprosy sufferers still experienced. Donaldson began to think about writing a novel with a protagonist, a contemporary husband and father, who contracts the disease. From this came the Thomas Covenant character, hero of the first six of Donaldson's novels.

The Thomas Covenant Stories

In the fall of 1972, Donaldson began writing the first novel in the fantasy series. Married and living in New England, he worked for a Pennsylvania publisher for a year, but spent the next four years involved in the Covenant project. His wife, a social worker, supported him both financially and emotionally, but he became dejected as his pile of rejection slips from publishers grew. The industry professionals who critiqued Donaldson's submissions voiced doubts about the potential appeal of the titlecharacter: Thomas Covenant is a successful novelist devastated by the diagnosis of leprosy; a head injury lands him in another universe where, instead of social ostracism, he is hailed as a messiah-like savior sent to keep Lord Foul from destroying The Land, as the fictional world is known.

Fully aware of the folly of his situation, Donaldson even lied to neighbors about what he did for a living. "I just immersed myself in my work," he told Dahlin in a *Publishers Weekly* interview. "It's difficult to find words to describe how bad I felt." He collected a total of 47 rejection slips from American publishers before trying, one more time, to interest Ballantine, publishers of the wildly popular fantasy novels from English medieval scholar

J.R.R. Tolkien (1892-1973), *The Hobbit* and *The Lord of the Rings*. Donaldson once admitted that his perseverance was curious. As he once told Jean W. Ross, "good writers usually aren't that unlucky; bad writers usually don't try that hard."

But at Ballantine the second time around, Donaldson's manuscript luckily landed on the desk of famed editor Lester del Rey, who believed it held promise. Del Rey worked intensely with the neophyte author to edit the lengthy saga for publication. Published in 1977, the three-volume *Chronicles of Thomas Covenant: The Unbeliever*, appeared in

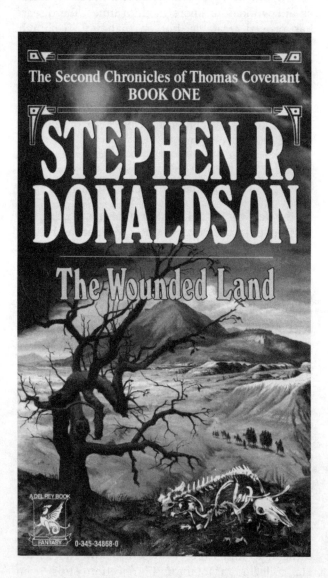

Some four thousand years after Covenant saved the Land, Evil returns stronger than ever to test Covenant and his magical white gold.

hardcover as a Science Fiction Book Club selection, an unusual achievement in the fantasy-fiction genre for a first-time author, but one that spoke highly of del Rey's belief in Donaldson's saga.

Lord Foul's Bane, the first book in *The Chronicles of Thomas Covenant*, introduces the afflicted, unhappy writer and his sudden transcendence into another realm. Soon after Covenant regains consciousness and realizes he is in a puzzling new world called The Land, he is mistaken for one of its mythicalheroes, Berke Halfhand. He also encounters Lord Foul, a powerful, destructive figure who is determined to ruin The Land and kill off its populace by unleashing environmental toxins. Though he was an outcast in his previous life, Covenant is hailed by denizens of The Land as their long-awaited savior, the hero with the power to foil Lord Foul.

In the first volume, Donaldson creates a complex, intricate realm with a long history, highly stratified social organization, and series of alliances and enmities among its many life forms. The narrative and cast are expanded across the other two volumes, *The Illearth War* and *The Power That Preserves*. Covenant discovers early on that he possesses magical powers, but the realization does not heighten his sense of self-esteem to any degree. He emerges as an anti-hero, an unlikely messiah uncomfortable with his role, an embittered man still plagued by the cynicism and pessimism that marked his earthly existence. He begins to call himself "the Unbeliever," and at times even doubts that the fantastical adventures are occurring outside of his own imagination. In the end, he is offered choice between the two worlds.

"The real surprise of the tale," wrote John Calvin Batchelor in a review of the trilogy for the *Village Voice*, "comes not when Foul is unexpectedly undone, but rather when Covenant is returned by the Creator to Earth to die of an allergic reaction." Other assessments were positive, though some faulted the first-time author's ornate prose style—a criticism that would follow Donaldson throughout his career. A *Publishers Weekly* review declared that the work possesses "riches and excitements a plenty for the fantasy minded," while Judith Yamomoto declared that the trilogy "shows promise and makes absorbing reading" in her *Library Journal* review.

The Covenant series quickly reached the two-million sales mark in paperback,was translated into several other languages, and earned Donaldson comparisons to Tolkien. In the United Kingdom, the three-part series won the British Science Fiction Society's top award for 1978. A surge in popularity in the works of Tolkien—related to the posthumous publication in 1977 of his *Silmarillion* manuscript—coincided with Donaldson's debut as an author, and the two authors seemed to share a readership. When asked about the influence of Tolkien upon his work, Donaldson told Ross that "there are obviously many details in *Covenant* which purportedly show the influence of Tolkien. But almost without exception those details were consciously chosen because what I could gain by them was

worth the risk that my readers might think I was imitating Tolkien."

Despite the professional and financial rewards that Donaldson had finally achieved, success also brought unexpected changes to his life. As he explained to Dahlin in the *Publishers Weekly* interview, his wife had become "so used to taking care of me that when she didn't have to anymore, she saw me going away from her"; their marriage ended in divorce. Eager to immerse himself in writing another series—he had spent the years between 1972 and 1976 creating the Covenant trilogy—Donaldson was instead cajoled by Lester del Rey to write a second trilogy. The author was initially reluctant to do so, but then began to think that perhaps there were more complex moral issues left unexplored in the first series, whose battles between good and evil were conducted in a physical arena with a great deal of violent, bloody action.

The Second Chronicles of Thomas Covenant: The Unbeliever, which began with the publication of *The Wounded Land* in 1980, returns Covenant to The Land a few millennia later; Lord Foul has been resurrected and again threatens it. Accompanying Covenant this time is Dr. Linden Avery, a female physician plagued by a guilty conscience related to the untimely death of her parents. In the second volume, 1982's *The One Tree*, the pair set out on a granite ship to an island called the One Tree Land; a delegation of giants and Elohim, considered holders of "Earth Power," come along. Here Covenant and Linden fall in love, adding a romantic twist to the series and centering some of the plot development around issues of love and trust, as Donaldson wanted to do for this second series. Throughout this novel and Volume III, *White Gold Wielder*, which appeared in 1983, Covenant suffers from a poison venom that Lord Foul used against him. Once again, the reluctant hero utilizes his powers to save The Land, which has been afflicted with a Foul-induced plague.

Reviews for this second Covenant trilogy were mixed. "As one burrows deeper into the inflated text it soon becomes apparent that the rules, not to mention the standards, of good fiction are violated repeatedly on every page," decreed Timothy Robert Sullivan in a *Washington Post Book World* review of *White Gold Wielder*. Still, the second trilogy was equally popular among Donaldson's fans. As Stableford noted in the *St. James Guide to Fantasy Writers* essay, both series "demonstrated that vast

In this first book from the "Mordant" series, Terisa Morgan travels to a strange land through one of the mirrors in her apartment.

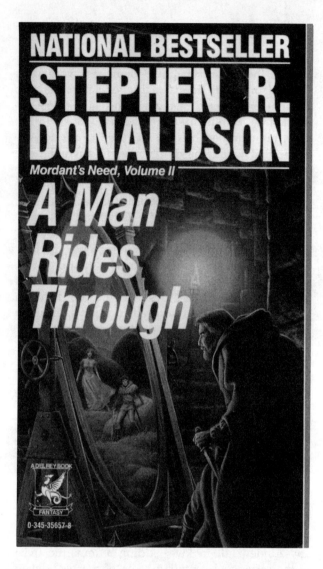

NATIONAL BESTSELLER
STEPHEN R. DONALDSON
Mordant's Need, Volume II
A Man Rides Through

Terisa Morgan discovers she has magic powers in Mordant and uses them to help save the kingdom in this 1987 sequel to *The Mirror of Her Dreams*.

numbers of readers were not only prepared to immerse themselves in the plight of a man with a particularly horrible disease, but were avid to do so . . . . They were enthusiastic to participate in his quest, which was explicitly stated to be a hard battle against his own unbelief, primarily directed against an enemy which personified the determination of others to despise him."

Writing Fantasy Literature with a Purpose

By now Donaldson had spent over a decade writing draft upon draft of his fantastical, allegorical

tales, which drew heavily upon religious themes in their explorations of timeless moral quandaries. As he told Ross, "Science fiction and fantasy try to answer the question 'What does it mean to be human?' by altering the context (the world) in order to test real conceptionsof humanness against alien definitions of reality or alien conceptions of humanness against normal or familiar ones. Science fiction, in fact, takes an explicitly speculative approach to the great theme of literature. Fantasy, on the other hand, does the same thing by delving explicitly into the human imagination. (I don't mean to be confusing about this. Imagination is, of course, the tool of all creative vision. In fantasy, imagination is the subject as well as the tool.) It follows—naturally—that I consider science fiction and fantasy (but especially fantasy) to be the fundamental form of literature. Lacking the imaginative immediacy of fantasy (or the rational rigor of science fiction), 'mainstream fiction' is a bastardized art form, 'a genre apart.'"

During the early 1980s, Donaldson concentrated on two other series of fantasy novels. The first volume of *Mordant's Need*, titled *The Mirror of Her Dreams*, was published by Ballantine in 1986. His unlikely hero this time is a heroine, Terisa Morgan. A wealthy New Yorker with a conflicted relationship with her parents, Terisa possesses a great deal of material wealth but little self-esteem. She is so insecure that inside her home is a room completely walled in mirrors, to prove to herself her very existence. An *Alice in Wonderland*-type encounter with a unusual mirror transports her to the land of Mordant. Her emissary is Geraden, an inept sorcerer who was attempting to follow an edict to bring a strong male warrior to help Mordant through a particularly trying time of political instability.

The denizens of Mordant exhibit disbelief when the bumbling Geraden presents Terisa, a meek and anxious young woman, as their savior. King Joyse, ruler of the tenuously united kingdom, seems dismissive of her as well, though many in Mordant think that the monarch might be suffering from dementia. In the second and concluding volume of the saga, *A Man Rides Through*, the king continues tobe obsessed with playing a game called hopboard, similar to chess, while his empire disintegrates. Terisa, finding herself in the middle of political battle, realizes that in Mordant she possesses special powers that can indeed help its people. A romance develops between she and Geraden, King

Joyse is not at all deranged, and the army of High King Festten is defeated; Mordant rejoices.

Susan Shwartz, reviewing the first volume of the *Mordant* series for the *New York Times,* wrote favorably of Donaldson's maturation as a writer. The 1986 tome, Shwartz noted, "demonstrates steady growth. Thought he has replaced the tortuous, almost impenetrable, language that proved such heavy going in the *Chronicles* with the leaner, suppler prose of his novellas, Mr. Donaldson still focuses on outcasts."

Adventures in Space

Donaldson, who retreated to New Mexico to write after his flush with success, spent the latter half of the 1980s working on a third saga, *The Gap into Conflict.* The first volume of this space opera, *The Real Story,* was published by Bantam in 1990. A trio of characters—a villain, a victim, and a rescuer—are introduced, but over the course of the series they often exchange roles as plot and character developments warrant. Nick Succorso and Angus Thermopyle are space pirates who despise one another; Morn Hyland is a female law-enforcement official for the United Mining Companies. Thermopyle kidnaps Hyland, setting in motion a series of space chases, unlikely alliances, and fantastical inventions. An evil force called Amnion hopes to achieve complete control over the galaxy. A review of this first volume by Faren C. Miller in *Locus* compared Donaldson's effort to the seventeenth-century dramas of the English stage. "Like those early masters, he esteems nothing better than villainy writ so large, and so charged with anguish, it calls for pity as wellas horror," Miller observed.

In the second volume in the series, *The Gap into Vision: Forbidden Knowledge,* Morn and Nick must flee to one of the galaxy's forbidden zones. Amnion and its agents remain determined to take over the realm. The plot reveals that Morn is haunted by a terrible secret—she once suffered from something called "Gap Sickness," which caused her to wreck a vessel that belonged to her family. A more ominous secret is also disclosed: Morn is expecting a child, the result of a liaison with Angus.

In the 1992 entrant to the series, *The Gap into Power: A Dark and Hungry God Arises,* Nick—less of a hero than before—considers trading Morn to Amnion;

meanwhile, Angus has been brainwashed and is now a far more honorable person. Both men arrive at a trading post, Billingate, with plans to sabotage it. A *Publishers Weekly* review of this volume found Donaldson's plot beyond intricate, and conceded that "through it all runs Donaldson's trademark sadism, betrayal, amorality and purposeless cruelty."

The plot of the Donaldson's fourth volume, 1994's *The Gap into Madness: Chaos and Order,* takes the reader further into Amnion's devious plan to mutate Earth's inhabitants into a race of aliens. Both

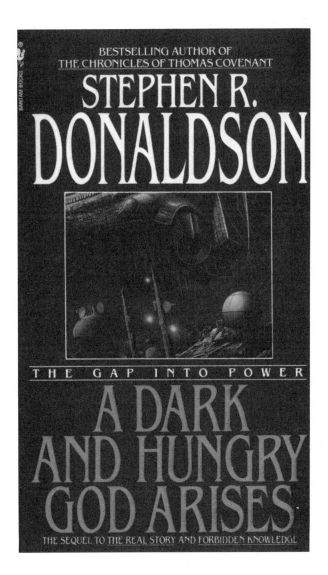

In Donaldson's third book of the "Gap Cycle" series, Nick and Angus plan to sabotage the Billingate trading post.

the United Mining Police and agents of Amnion are desperately trying to locate people whose blood contains antibodies that will become the basis for a drug to prevent the alienization. Morn's son, Davies, begins to take on a more integral role in the action, while Nick and a scientist have develop the immunity drug. Aliens from Amnion pursue a space ship with Davies aboard, but UMC personnel are also on the trail in an attempt to rescue Morn.

In the concluding volume, *The Gap into Ruin: This Day All Gods Die,* Donaldsonties up the complex story and its related subplots. A showdown in Earth's orbit takes place between Morn's forces and an Amnion faction. A review of the final novel in the series from *Publishers Weekly* termed it "a crowd-pleasing story told on a grand scale, SF adventure with a genuinely galactic feel."

If you enjoy the works of Steven R. Donaldson, you may also want to check out the following books:

Lois McMaster Bujold, *The Warrior's Apprentice,* 1986.
Brian Daley, *Fall of the White Ship Avatar,* 1987.
Vernor Vinge, *A Fire upon the Deep,* 1992.

Delves Into Other Genres

Donaldson has also written several other shorter works, as well as a few detective novels. In 1984, a volume of stories titled *Daughters of Regals and Other Tales* was issued by the Del Rey imprint. Included in it was *Gilden-Fire,* an outtake from the second volume of the first Thomas Covenant series, *The Illearth War,* that had to be excised because of length and plot considerations. *Daughters of Regals* also contained several unusual shorter works from the writer, such as "Animal Lover," the tale of a scientist with plans to create an army of genetically modified, weapons-proficient creatures.

Another story in the collection, "The Conqueror Worm," tracks the speedy disintegration of an already-faltering marriage when an enormous centipede appears in the home; Donaldson has said that his story was perhaps the most difficult writing experience of his career. A *Publishers Weekly* assessment of the volume compared *Daughters of Regals* to the work of Donaldson's Thomas Covenant series, and concluded that overall, the pieces "demonstrate that his intense style and offbeat approach can be quite effective in other realms."

Under the pseudonym "Reed Stephens," Donaldson has also written a series of detective novels. The first, *The Man Who Killed His Brother,* was issued by Ballantine in 1980, and introduces another unlikely hero, Mick Axbrewder. A heavy drinker nicknamed "Brew," Mick is approached by his ex-wife, Ginny, a private investigator. Brew's 13-year-old niece has vanished, and Ginny and others fear that a serial killer is at work. A *Publishers Weekly* reviewobserved that while the plot of this amateur detective story offers no surprises, the author "fits the pieces together neatly."

In the second Reed Stephens book, 1984's *The Man Who Risked His Partner,* a sobered Brew and a devastated Ginny—who has lost her hand in an accident—again join forces when a banker hires them, fearing he is the target of a local organized crime ring. *The Man Who Tried to Get Away,* a third in the series, appeared in 1990.

Donaldson is also the author of the 1998 collection, *Reave the Just and Other Tales,* his first since 1984's *Daughters of Regals.* The work contains a number of short stories and novellas, many of them previously published in anthologies or magazines, and garnered its creator the customary critical plaudits. Writing for *Booklist,* Roberta Johnson noted that though a few of the stories were characteristically bleak, like Donaldson's longer works, the tales in *Reave the Just* were "more often exciting, moving and even comic."

The writer may return to his Thomas Covenant hero for one final trilogy. As he once told Ross, "I do have some ideas I like for a new large fantasy. But I have trouble dealing with all the expectation surrounding such a project—other people's as well as my own. My publishers (and maybe my readers) expect me to change the clothes and the names and a few other details and serve up *Covenant* again," Donaldson said. "I, on the other hand, expect myself to do both 'totally different' and 'better' than *Covenant.* This exerts a lot of pressure (it's one of the problems that comes with success) and I still have to learn to deal with it."

■ Works Cited

Batchelor, John Calvin, "Tolkien Again: Lord Foul and Friends Infest a Morbid but Moneyed Land," *Village Voice,* October 10, 1977, pp. 79-80.

Review of *The Chronicles of Thomas Covenant, Publishers Weekly,* August 15, 1977, p. 56.

Dahlin, Robert, interview with Stephen R. Donaldson, *Publishers Weekly,* June 27, 1980.

Review of *Daughters of Regals, Publishers Weekly,* March 2, 1984, p. 86.

Review of *The Gap into Power: A Dark and Hungry God Arises, Publishers Weekly,* September 28, 1992.

Review of *The Gap into Ruin: This Day All Gods Die, Publishers Weekly,* March 4, 1996, p. 58.

Johnson, Roberta, review of *Reave the Just and Other Tales, Booklist,* December 1, 1998, p. 655.

Review of *The Man Who Killed His Brother, Publishers Weekly,* October 31, 1980, p. 83.

Miller, Faren C., review of *The Gap into Conflict: The Real Story, Locus,* December, 1990, p. 17.

Neary, John, "Both Sales and Sagas Are Fantastic for Stephen Donaldson and His Leper Hero," *People,* July 26, 1982, p. 58.

Shwartz, Susan, review of *Mirror of Her Dreams, New York Times,* November 30, 1986, section 7.

Stableford, Brian, "Stephen R. Donaldson" *St. James Guide to Fantasy Writers,* first edition, edited by David Pringle, St. James Press, 1996.

Sullivan, Timothy Robert, review of *White Gold Wielder, Washington Post Book World,* June 26, 1983, p. 10.

Yamomoto, Judith, review of *The Chronicles of Thomas Covenant, Library Journal,* October 15, 1977.

■ For More Information See

BOOKS

Contemporary Literary Criticism, Volume 46, Gale, 1988.

PERIODICALS

Booklist, April 15, 1994, p. 1484.

Fantasy Review, November, 1986, p. 28.

Galileo, January, 1978.

Kirkus Reviews, February 15, 1996, p. 265.

Locus, June, 1994, p. 27.

Los Angeles Times, January 29, 1978.

Los Angeles Times Book Review, May 1, 1983.

Magazine of Fantasy and Science Fiction, February, 1979.

Montreal Star, December 13, 1977.

New York Times Book Review, February 18, 1979; August 14, 1983.

Publishers Weekly, February 19, 1982, p. 62; November 16, 1990, p. 48; May 3, 1991, p. 66.

San Francisco Examiner, October 5, 1977.

Science Fiction and Fantasy Book Review, May, 1982; November, 1983, p. 24-25.

Science Fiction Review, September/October, 1978; November, 1982; May 1983.

Voice of Youth Advocates, June, 1988, p. 95; June, 1993, p. 100-1.

Washington Post, August 12, 1980; August 21, 1980.

Washington Post Book World, December 11, 1977; November 23, 1986, p. 9.*

Sylvia Louise Engdahl

■ Personal

Born November 24, 1933, in Los Angeles, CA; daughter of Amandus J. (a real estate salesman) and Mildred Allen (a Little Theater director and writer under her maiden name, Butler) Engdahl. *Education:* Attended Pomona College, 1950, Reed College, 1951, University of Oregon, 1951-52, University of California at Santa Barbara, B.A., 1955; graduate study at Portland State University, 1955-57 and 1978-80. *Religion:* Episcopalian. *Hobbies and other interests:* On-line communication via her World Wide Web site at http://www.sylviaengdahl.com.

■ Addresses

E-mail—sle@sylviaengdahl.com.

■ Career

Elementary teacher in Portland, OR, 1955-56; System Development Corp. (computer programming for SAGE Air Defense System), 1957-67, began as programmer, became computer systems specialist, working in Lexington, MA, Madison, WI, Tacoma, WA, and Santa Monica, CA; freelance writer, 1968-80; self-employed developer and vendor of software for home computers, 1981-85; Connected Education, Inc., White Plains, NY, on-line staff, 1985-97.

■ Awards, Honors

Notable book citation from American Library Association, honor list citation from *Horn Book Magazine,* and Newbery Honor Book Award, 1971, all for *Enchantress from the Stars;* Christopher Award, 1973, for *This Star Shall Abide;* Phoenix Award, 1990, for *Enchantress from the Stars. Enchantress from the Stars* was a Junior Literary Guild selection.

■ Writings

FICTION

Journey between Worlds (novel), illustrated by James and Ruth McCrea, Atheneum, 1970.

Enchantress from the Stars (novel), illustrated by Rodney Shackell, Atheneum, 1970, Gollancz, 1974, new edition with jacket by Leo and Diane Dillon, Walker, 2001.

The Far Side of Evil (novel), illustrated by Richard Cuffari, Atheneum, 1971, Gollancz, 1975.

This Star Shall Abide (first novel in a trilogy), illustrated by Richard Cuffari, Atheneum, 1972, published in England as *Heritage of the Star*, Gollancz, 1973.

Beyond the Tomorrow Mountains (second novel in a trilogy), illustrated by Richard Cuffari, Atheneum, 1973.

(Editor with Rick Roberson) *Universe Ahead: Stories of the Future*, illustrated by Richard Cuffari, Atheneum, 1975.

(Editor) *Anywhere, Anywhen: Stories of Tomorrow*, Atheneum, 1976.

The Doors of the Universe (third novel in a trilogy), Atheneum, 1981.

Children of the Star (contains *This Star Shall Abide*, *Beyond the Tomorrow Mountains*, and *The Doors of the Universe*), Meisha Merlin, 2000.

NONFICTION FOR YOUNG READERS

The Planet-Girded Suns: Man's View of Other Solar Systems, illustrated by Richard Cuffari, Atheneum, 1974.

(With Rick Roberson) *The Subnuclear Zoo: New Discoveries in High Energy Physics*, Atheneum, 1977.

(With Rick Roberson) *Tool for Tomorrow: New Knowledge about Genes*, Atheneum, 1979.

Our World Is Earth (picture book), illustrated by Don Sibley, Atheneum, 1979.

■ Sidelights

Oregon-based computer programmer-turned-author Sylvia Louise Engdahl produced ten books in the years between 1971 and 1981—six science fiction novels, three nonfiction books for teenage readers, and a picture book for children—but since then her literary voice has fallen silent. Engdahl's reputation as a writer rests mainly on the strength of her fiction, particularly her first novel, the Newbery Honor Book *Enchantress of the Stars*, and a science fiction trilogy that includes *This Star Shall Abide*, *Beyond the Tomorrow Mountains*, and *The Doors of the Universe*, recently republished as adult science fiction under the omnibus title *Children of the Star*.

Engdahl's writing is difficult to categorize. That is one of the reasons her books are not as widely known as they might be otherwise. Some readers regard Engdahl's vivid tales of future worlds and extraterrestrial civilizations as science fiction. Oth-

ers—including the author herself—tend to view her books more as novels of ideas for readers without special interest in the SF genre. "Though people in the children's literature field usually describe me as a science fiction author, that's not quite accurate according to how people in the science fiction field look at it," Engdahl explained in a speech at the June 1990 conference of the Children's Literature Association in San Diego, California, published on-line at http://www.sylviaengdahl.com. "In terms of publishing and reviewing categories, my books weren't initially issued in that field, and while some of them—especially the 'Star' trilogy—are enjoyed by adult SF fans, I have always tried to make them intelligible to a general audience."

It seems clear that there are undeniable elements of both genres in Engdahl's work. At her Web site she explains, "I write about space and other worlds because I believe that expansion into space is essential to human survival, and that how people feel about the universe beyond Earth is therefore becoming more and more crucial."

The picture of Engdahl that emerges from her own writings and from the few media interviews that are available is one of a woman who is uncomfortable with many aspects of the literary world, and with the demands of writing for the mass market. Engdahl's approach to writing is as dispassionate as it is cerebral. She is rarely able to imagine story events, a problem she has found a barrier to the ongoing creation of fiction. In a 1988 essay for the *Something about the Author Autobiography Series* (*SAAS*) she wrote, "To me, a story's plot incidents are not what matter; they were what I always found hardest to think of, and such action scenes as I managed to put in (usually long after the first draft of the rest) were a real struggle to write. The ideas in the story, plus the thoughts and feelings of the characters, were what inspired me, and in most cases these could be absorbed only by introspective older teens." Engdahl remains convinced that stories about future worlds appeal to young adults, who are concerned about the problems besetting our world today.

Growing Up in the Company of Adults

Engdahl was born in Los Angeles, California, in 1933, in the lean years of the Great Depression.

Her mother was a former English teacher and Little Theater director who hailed from New England; her father, a Swedish immigrant, scratched out a living as a salesman. The couple's marriage was not a happy one. Engdahl was an only child who grew up in the company of adults, mainly her mother (whose own mother lived with the family during most of Engdahl's youth). Writing in her *SAAS* essay, the author described herself as a loner and something of a free-thinker who was at odds with her peers and schoolteachers. "I never had anything in common with other children and didn't enjoy playing with them," she confided. "I was bored by school. What I learned, I learned at home from my mother and from reading; school was mainly hours to live through, punctuated by moments of fierce anger at teachers who wanted me to participate in active games." Engdahl went on to add, "I was never openly rebellious except in refusing to play ball games and to socialize with my peers; certainly I never told teachers or classmates that my views on most subjects didn't match those of society. But my inner convictions were always my own."

As a girl, Engdahl aspired to become a teacher. However, she later realized that even then she had been ill-suited for the classroom. "During my early teens I organized summer arts-and-crafts classes through which I earned some spending money. What I . . . enjoyed was planning and being in charge, not the actual contact with children," she recalled in *SAAS*. At the same time, Engdahl was bored with her own schooling. It was not until she was twelve and in ninth grade that she received the first lesson that captured her attention and fired her imagination: a science lesson on astronomy. "One day the teacher read aloud a short description of what it might be like to travel in space, and for some reason it excited me in a way nothing else ever had," Engdahl stated in her autobiographical essay for *SAAS*. "I had not read any science fiction, and had never talked to anyone who knew of it; and of course this was in 1946, before space travel was widely discussed. Yet I went home that day and began drawing pictures of rockets on the way to Mars. . . . From then on I read whatever I could find about space, though I did not care for much of the science fiction I encountered. I was interested in what space travel and colonization of other planets might actually be like, not in wild adventure tales or stories designed to be as exotic and far-removed from real life as possible."

> *"I write about space and other worlds because I believe that expansion into space is essential to human survival, and that how people feel about the universe beyond Earth is therefore becoming more and more crucial."*
>
> —Sylvia Louise Engdahl

At that time, Engdahl had no aspirations to write. Despite her lack of rapport with children, she pressed ahead with her plan to become a teacher. Followingher 1950 graduation from high school, Engdahl began studies at Pomona College, a small school in Claremont, California. However, she felt out of place there, disliked dormitory life, and longed to leave Southern California. For those reasons, Engdahl transferred to Reed College in Portland, Oregon, for the spring term. But she was no happier there. That fall, Engdahl began attending the University of Oregon in Eugene, where her mother was studying for a Master of Arts degree in drama. The two resumed living together.

While Engdahl was content in Oregon, she knew that she would have to transfer to another school to get her teaching certificate. Thus, when her mother finished her own degree and moved temporarily back to California, Engdahl went with her, enrolling at the University of California at Santa Barbara. Upon graduation from UCSB, she took a job teaching the fourth grade at a school in Portland, Oregon. "My temperamental unfitness for the job became all too apparent. It was a disaster," Engdahl recalled in *SAAS*. As a result, she was asked to resign after her first year on the job.

Thrilled by the First Satellite Launchings

Engdahl was faced with the prospect of being unemployed, and she had no real career plans. In the fall of 1956, she began taking night courses toward a Master of Education degree, in the vague hope that this might enable her to become a school counselor. Uninspired by her course work, in her spare time Engdahl began musing about space and interplanetary travel. By this time, the so-called "space race" between the United States and the former Soviet Union was underway. Engdahl was thrilled by the first satellite launchings, for she believed that only a focus on space could bring peace to the world, and had long before—accurately, as it happened—predicted that a spaceship would land on the moon before 1972. Engdahl began putting some of her own ideas about space on paper. "Partial drafts of the stories that ultimately became my novels were all written then—and I haven't had an idea for a real story since!" she quipped in her SAAS essay.

None of the short stories that Engdahl sent to various SF magazines were accepted for publication, so the author put them in a drawer and forgot about them. Still puzzling over what to do with herself, one day Engdahl applied on impulse for a job with the SAGE Air Defense System computer programming project, which was being developed for the United States government by the Rand Corporation. "I was twenty-three years old with no other prospect of employment, and though I had little idea what computer programming was, it sounded interesting," Engdahl wrote in SAAS. At the time, computers were massive devices that filled whole rooms and had to be programmed by specially punched cardboard cards. "I found programming easy and loved it right from the start," Engdahl wrote. "How strange it seemed to be paid a salary for attending a class much more interesting than any I'd had in college!"

Engdahl's work with SAGE took her to various parts of the country in the following ten years, and she eventually became a computer systems specialist. However, by 1967 she found the long hours and travel physically exhausting, and welcomed the opportunity to quit her job and serve as full-time companion to her aging mother—a situation that would give her time for writing. They again moved to Oregon, a state both women loved. Engdahl's mother, by this time in her 70s, was writing books for young people under her maiden name—Mildred Allen Butler—and this inspired Engdahl to try writing for the YA audience. She began work on the first of several novels about communication between species of higher intelligence and about the ethical and moral implications of space travel and space colonization.

Engdahl's first effort was the novel *Journey between Worlds*, which was aimedspecifically at teenage girls. "I wanted very much to make teenage girls aware of how important the colonization of space

is to mankind's future," the author explained in SAAS. While that manuscript was initially rejected by several publishers, the author's second novel, *Enchantress from the Stars,* was accepted for publication by Atheneum. That book involved three peoples at different levels of technological advancement, without revealing which should be viewed as our own. Writing in the *St. James Guide to Young Adult Writers,* Claudia Nelson noted: "In [this novel] Engdahl foregrounds concerns that extend throughout her works: the importance of empathy, intelligence, and moral courage; the individual's role in effecting change; and the need to approach problems on a symbolic as well as a literal level and to combine the mundane with the spiritual."

Enchantress from the Stars is set on Andrecia, a primitive planet still in the village-and-myth stage. When Andrecia is threatened by colonists from a more advanced planet, agents from an organization called the Anthropological Service of the Interplanetary Federation attempt to thwart the plans. These agents—a young anthropology student named Elana, her father, and a young man named Evrek who is Elana's betrothed—come from a wondrous interstellar civilization in which the inhabitants communicate using extrasensory perception, move objects by psychokinesis, and believe completely in the primary importance of psychic development.

Enchantress from the Stars was among the first young adult science fiction novels to feature a female protagonist. It deals with some serious philosophical and moral themes, one of which is the need for people to respect others. This complex story was well received by most critics, and it won several prestigious awards, including the Newbery Honor Book Award and the 1990 Phoenix Award of the Children's Literature Association, given "from the perspective of time" to a book considered worthy of special recognition. Ursula K. LeGuin, writing in the *New York Times Book Review,* hailed *Enchantress from the Stars* as "an original and charming exercise of one of fiction's finest prerogatives, getting into other skins and seeing through (literally) alien eyes." A reviewer for the *Times Literary Supplement* described *Enchantress from the Stars* as being "full of drama and suspense, and . . . very well written." *Horn Book* critic Ruth Hill Viguers wrote that the novel "is completely absorbing and should have a wider appeal than much science fiction."

On the heels of the success of *Enchantress from the Stars*, Atheneum published Engdahl's first novel, *Journey between Worlds*. That book is a coming-of-age story about a young woman named Melinda Ashley, who moves from Oregon to Mars. There she finds love and fulfillment. Nelson pointed out that "Melinda's quest is predominantly framed in the terms of the teen romance . . . [and this] directs the story toward a different audience than that addressed by Engdahl's more characteristic works." Other reviewers who noted this were divided in their assessments of *Journey between Worlds*. *Library Journal* contributor Elizabeth Haynes felt that this novel was "not up to the level of her first one." She added, "Told entirely in the first person, this story is long on self-analysis and short on action." Meanwhile, reviewer Zena Sutherland of the *Bulletin of the Center for Children's Books* found more to like about the book. "The love story occasionally falters," she wrote, "but the descriptions of the world of the future and of the flight through space are convincing, the characterization is capable if not subtle, and the writing style is competent." A review in *Horn Book* was more enthusiastic: "Deftly blending scientific possibility, suspense, and youthful emotion in the first-person narrative, the author has projected a plausible picture of the post-twentieth-century world—a world where pioneers on Mars and envisioned as a continuationof the endless chain of settlers who have been moving to new frontiers ever since the human race began."

The Far Side of Evil, which appeared in early 1971, is a sequel to *Enchantress from the Stars,* although because it is less suitable for pre-teen readers, Engdahl has since regretted connecting the two so closely. Elana, the heroine from the earlier book, is dispatched on a mission to the planet Toris—which is a thinly disguised version of Earth as it was in the 1950s—to observe the inhabitants' use of nuclear technology and lack of progress toward space exploration. As a result of the actions of another Anthropological Service agent, Elana is faced with jail, torture, possible death, and getting involved in the planet's affairs, a forbidden practice for agents. Haynes, again writing in *Library Journal*, stated that although *The Far Side of Evil* is "slow-moving at times," it "should nevertheless appeal to thoughtful SF fans." Pamela Bragg of *Publishers Weekly* expressed a similar opinion in *Publishers Weekly*, writing that Engdahl "has a direct, forceful style of writing that sparks the reader's imagination, but taken as a whole, it

is a long, over-extended story filled with too many philosophical undertones." Sarah Hayes of the Times Literary Supplement, on the other hand, wrote: "[G]ripping psychological science fiction . . . the relationship between the heroine and her sophisticated, unbrutish interrogator is beautifully balanced and adds another dimension to a story which is already multi-faceted."

Trilogy for Older Readers

Engdahl next embarked on what would eventually develop into her signature trilogy: *This Star Shall Abide, Beyond the Tomorrow Mountains,* and *The Doors of the Universe*. In these novels, which were directed to older readers than her earlier ones, a rebellious young man named Noren fights for his endangered people, descendants of space travelers who had escaped theiroriginal planet before its sun went supernova. All three books are set on a metal-poor planet that is inhospitable and cannot support the technology the original travelers had developed on their home planet. "The trilogy is an extended meditation on the need for total commitment to an ideal, for willingness to challenge assumptions, and for change," Nelson wrote.

All three books in Engdahl's trilogy were generally well received by reviewers and readers alike, and *This Star Shall Abide* won the Christopher Award for "affirmation of the highest values of the human spirit." Assessing that novel, a reviewer for the *Bulletin of the Center for Children's Books* wrote, "The concept of the culture is imaginatively and convincingly detailed, the story line moves with brisk momentum, and the characters have solidity." *Horn Book* reviewer Paul Heins praised *This Star Shall Abide* for "its dramatization of the crucial meeting of science, man, and the universe." The same reviewer lauded *Beyond the Tomorrow Mountains* for having "genuine metaphysical significance," but he noted that "it is not a compelling story." A critic for the *Bulletin of the Center for Children's Books* echoed those sentiments, writing that "the writing style is often heavy and therefore the book moves slowly." Other reviewers expressed contrary opinions. For example, Margaret Chatham, writing in *School Library Journal*, wrote that *The Doors of the Universe* "is a long book filled with discussions of moral dilemmas, but it still holds interest, especially if the earlier books have been read." *Voice of Youth Advocates*

If you enjoy the works of Sylvia Louise Engdahl, you may also want to check out the following books:

David Brin, *Brightness Reef*, 1995.
Octavia E. Butler, *Parable of the Sower*, 1983.
Gene Wolfe, "The Book of the New Sun" tetralogy, 1980-87.

critic Mary K. Chelton wrote that the novel is "an exquisite story of the lonely quest for knowledge and the burden of unsought leadership."

Engdahl feels that the second and third volumes of the trilogy failed to reach the majority of the people apt to enjoy them because most librarians judged, and shelved, them alongside books for younger readers than their intendedaudience of mature high school students. The trilogy's recent new edition was issued by an SF/fantasy specialty press as adult science fiction. Of this edition, reviewer Roz Spafford wrote, "[The novels were first] marketed as young adult books, but there is nothing juvenile about them. . . . Engdahl tells an important and pertinent story, a parable about the ethical uses of mythology . . . [T]hese novels . . . read quickly; the writing is plain and direct, the only lyricism in the stunning liturgical language she invents."

Nonfiction Books

In her other work, Sylvia Engdahl has also undertaken the challenge of writing nonfiction books for young readers about physics, genetics, and astronomy. However, her main focus remains on space exploration, which she continues to maintain should be a high priority for the human race, and she hopes to instill that conviction in thoughtful young people. "It frightens me when I hear people say we should solve the problems on Earth before we devote money and effort to leaving it," she noted in *SAAS*. "I do not believe they *can* be solved as long as our species is confined to a single planet. The natural course of evolution is for all successful species to expand to new ecological niches, and space is the one awaiting us. Attempts to postpone that destiny can lead only to disaster, for us and for all other life here on our home world."

In recent years, Sylvia Engdahl has devoted more time to computer-related activity than to writing. After a financially unsuccessful try at designing software for home computer use, she became involved in creating a computer-network educational system as an on-line staff member of Connected Education, a New York-based organization that offered credits for graduate-level courses from the New School for Social Research. Through that organization, she taught on-line Media Studies courses in science fiction as an aspect of Space Agemythology, a topic about which she expects to eventually publish adult nonfiction. Engdahl presently does Web design and desktop publishing work—mostly as a volunteer for the public library and other nonprofit organizations—from her small house in Eugene, Oregon, a place from which she seldom ventures far. The Internet is Engdahl's link to the wider world.

Recently, there has been revived interest in Engdahl's novels, fueled by the enthusiasm of her adult fans on the Internet who remember them from their teen years. Her trilogy is now available in paperback, and a new hardcover edition of *Enchantress from the Stars*, with a jacket by Leo and Diane Dillon, the Caldecott-winning illustrators of children's fantasy, is scheduled for 2001 publication. She hopes to get her other novels back into print also, although as yet she has no plot ideas for new ones. Despite that, Engdahl says she still would like to write more fiction sometime in the future. "I have always been an observer of this planet more than a participant in its affairs," she noted. "All writers are good observers; the difference between me and most others is that I tend to observe in terms of long-range things, like the evolution of space-faring species, rather than nearby specific ones."

■ Works Cited

Review of *Beyond the Tomorrow Mountains, Bulletin of the Center for Children's Books*, June, 1973, p. 153.

Bragg, Pamela, review of *The Far Side of Evil, Publishers Weekly*, May 31, 1971, p. 135.

Chatham, Margaret, review of *The Doors of the Universe, School Library Journal*, April 1981, p. 138.

Chelton, Mary K., review of *The Doors of the Universe, Voice of Youth Advocates*, June 1981, p. 37.

Review of *Enchantress from the Stars, Times Literary Supplement,* September 20,1974, p. 1006.

Engdahl, Sylvia Louise, entry in *Something about the Author Autobiography Series,* Volume 5, Gale, 1987.

Engdahl, Sylvia Louise, excerpts from a speech published at her Web site, located at http://www.sylviaengdahl.com (March 30, 2000).

Hayes, Sarah, review of *The Far Side of Evil, Times Literary Supplement,* September 19, 1975.

Haynes, Elizabeth, review of *The Far Side of Evil, Library Journal,* April 1971, p. 1514.

Haynes, Elizabeth, review of *Journey between Worlds, Library Journal,* October 15, 1970, p. 3636.

Heins, Paul, review of *Beyond the Tomorrow Mountains, Horn Book,* June, 1973, p. 276.

Heins, Paul, review of *The Star Shall Abide, Horn Book,* June 1972, p. 274.

Review of *Journey Between Worlds, Horn Book,* April, 1970, p. 481.

LeGuin, Ursula K., review of *Enchantress from the Stars, New York Times Book Review,* March 5, 1970, p. 22.

St. James Guide to Young Adult Writers, St. James, 1999, pp. 266-68.

Review of *This Star Shall Abide, Bulletin of the Center for Children's Books,* February, 1973, p. 89.

Spafford, Roz, review of *Children of the Star, San Jose Mercury News,* June 4, 2000.

Sutherland, Zena, review of *Journey between Worlds, Bulletin of the Center for Children's Books,* January, 1971, p. 72.

Viguers, Ruth Hill, "Stories for Older Boys and Girls," *Horn Book,* April, 1970, pp. 165-66.

■ For More Information See

BOOKS

Children's Literature Review, Volume 2, Gale, 1976.

The Phoenix Award of the Children's Literature Association 1990-1994, Scarecrow Press, 1996.

PERIODICALS

Booklist, May 15, 1971, p. 798.
Bulletin of the Center for Children's Books, June, 1973.
Horn Book, October, 1970; February, 1975.
Kirkus Reviews, February 15, 1973.
Times Literary Supplement, September 20, 1974.

ON-LINE

Sylvia Louise Engdahl's Web site is located at http://www.sylviaengdahl.com.

—*Sketch by Ken Cuthbertson*

David Fincher

■ Personal

Born in 1963, in Colorado; raised in San Rafael, CA; son of Jack Fincher (a writer and bureau chief for *Life* magazine) and his wife, a mental health nurse; married Donya Fiorentino (a photographer), divorced; children: one daughter.

■ Addresses

Office—Propaganda Films, 940 North Mansfield Ave., Los Angeles, CA 90038. *Agent*—Creative Artists Agency, 9830 Wilshire Blvd., Beverly Hills, CA 90212.

■ Career

Film director. Korty Films (animation studio), Hollywood, CA, film loader; Industrial Light and Magic, Hollywood, camera operator and crew member, c. 1981-84; filmed television commercials for various organizations and products, including the American Cancer Society and Nike athletic equipment; director of music videos for such artists as Madonna, Paula Abdul, Don Henley, George Michael, Michael Jackson, Aerosmith, the Wallflowers, and the Rolling Stones; co-founder (with others), Propaganda Films, 1986.

■ Credits

FILM WORK

Special photographic effects, *Twice upon a Time* (animated), Warner Bros., 1983.

Assistant cameraman in miniature and optical effects unit, *Return of the Jedi,* Twentieth Century-Fox, 1983.

Matte photography, *Indiana Jones and the Temple of Doom,* Paramount, 1984.

The Blue Iguana, Paramount, 1988.

Director, *Alien 3,* Twentieth Century-Fox, 1992.

Director, *Seven* (also known as *Se7en*), New Line Cinema, 1995.

Director, *The Game,* Polygram, 1997.

Director, *Fight Club,* Twentieth Century-Fox, 1999.

Director second unit, *Star Wars: Episode I—The Phantom Menace,* Twentieth Century-Fox, 1999.

■ Sidelights

Film director David Fincher began his career in Hollywood as a special effects man working for director George Lucas. Eighteen and fresh out of high school when he joined the Lucas team for 1983's *Return of the Jedi,* Fincher has since forged a path through the film industry maze to become one of the most influential directors at the turn of the

David Fincher's first feature film, 1992's *Alien3*, stars Sigourney Weaver as space traveler Ripley.

twenty-first century. With films such as *Seven, The Game,* and *Fight Club* to his credit, Fincher is known for an unorthodox style that eschews advance planning in favor of just winging it. Taking place in gritty urban settings awash in rain-soaked pavements dimly lit by sputtering neon lights, his films are known for their frenetic violence, desolation, decay, and bloodshed, sometimes even death.

Fincher, whose films are far more popular with the movie-going public than with the film critic establishment, has been described by *Entertainment Weekly* reviewer David Hochman as possessing both "an unflinching eye for dark, elegantly eerie images" and a "notorious reluctance to compromise on subject matter." Fincher has also been labeled by another *Entertainment Weekly* writer as "the man who [with *Seven* and *The Game*] made moral ambiguity and psychological dubiety into a marketable cinematic style." The director's own explanation of

his peculiar cinematic style is that he is "always interested in movies that scar."

Off to Soaring Start with *Star Wars*

Born in Colorado in 1963, Fincher and his parents soon moved to California, where he attended school in Marin County. A film buff at an early age, he knew he wanted to be a film director from the time he was eight years old. Growing up in San Rafael just a few doors from *Star Wars* director George Lucas was for Fincher like living near God. It also gave him a definite edge when he decided to go into films as a high school grad; rejecting a four-year sentence at film school, he instead took a job loading camera film for Korty Films, then went down the street to neighbor Lucas. By 1983, he was working for Lucas's special effects company, Industrial Light and Magic.

During the four years he spent learning his craft at Industrial Light, Fincher was involved in the animated feature *Twice upon a Time,* worked as assistant cameraman and optical effects person for *Return of the Jedi,* and produced matte photography for the 1984 hit *Indiana Jones and the Temple of Doom.* Fincher was just twenty four in 1987, when he left Lucas' employ to direct television commercials, his first being a anti-smoking ad for the American Cancer Society. From commercials, it was a short step to music videos. Noted for his edgy style and sense of innovation, Fincher's ads for Nike, Coca Cola, and Levi's feature dark, high-action visuals and a driving soundtrack, giving them a distinct, cutting-edge style that has since become much imitated. Particularly noteworthy were his Super Bowl spots for Honda, which broke new ground in auto advertising, dispensing with the traditional chrome shots and creating a scenario positing a sinister character in hot pursuit of a couple driving Honda's latest sports coupe.

Fincher's music videos capture the same offbeat energy as his commercials, particularly those for Madonna's "Vogue," Aerosmith's "Janie's Got a Gun," the Rolling Stones' "Love Is Strong," and former Eagle Don Henley's "End of Innocence." While audiences may relish the videos' evocative qualities, Fincher remains far more dispassionate. "I just make these things and try to live them down," he admitted to David Wild in a 1996 *Rolling Stone* interview. "It's just creating a context for understanding a song. These are not windows into somebody's soul. For me, this is my film school, and quite honestly, I'm embarrassed by a lot of my work."

Morgan Freeman and Brad Pitt are detectives on the hunt for a serial killer in David Fincher's 1995 thriller *Seven.*

Wrestles with Unwieldy Alien

Fincher's first feature film was *Alien 3,* which he directed for Twentieth Century-Fox in 1992. This third installment of the space epic franchise that began in 1979 starred Sigourney Weaver as veteran space traveler Ripley. The plot of *Alien 3* finds Ripley stranded on a maximum-security penal space colony-gone-New Age, unwittingly and unfortunately towing along yet another predatory ancestor of the original Alien creature. With no weapons around—it was, after all, a penal colony—the task for all is to find a way to kill the Alien before it kills them.

While praising Fincher as "a gifted image maker," *New Yorker* critic Terrence Rafferty contended that in *Alien 3* the music video director "doesn't seem to have the skill to make even the simplest action sequence coherent, or the patience to give the audience the narrative information it needs. . . . [Viewers are] trapped in these elaborate sets and have no better idea where [they] are than the monster does." A *Time* reviewer, while pointing out that "a lot of good, serious work" had gone into the film's production, faulted the script as much as its direction, noting that the screenwriter "neglects to develop the kind of human relationships any movie needs to draw us into its web." Noting that director Fincher is "strong on atmosphere and angst, lousy on kinetics and point-by-point story mechanics," *New Statesman* reviewer Anne Billson added that because of its "atmosphere and angst," *Alien 3* "has a faircrack at being another Hollywood art

Michael Douglas plays Nicholas Van Orton, a rich but unhappy investment banker who receives a puzzling and unsettling birthday gift in David Fincher's third feature film, *The Game,* released in 1997.

movie at which visuals take precedence over storytelling."

Although *Alien 3* eventually netted a profit for the studio, its lengthy production phase, coupled with the fact that it received tepid reviews, did not encourage Fincher to abandon his successful stint as a commercial director in favor of working in the motion picture industry. Faulting the Fox studio for destroying the film's continuity during the final editing cycle, Fincher turned his back on Hollywood feature films, and happily returned to the familiar. The rock group the Wallflowers appreciated his reappearance behind the videocam in 1993 when Fincher agreed to devote three months to directing their "Sixth Avenue Heartache" piece. The music video format meshes perfectly with Fincher's by-the-seat-of-your-pants style; as he explained to *Rolling Stone* contributor Wild, "That's really how music videos come about. You say, 'Here's my idea,' and somebody goes, 'OK, get on the plane.'"

Fincher continued shooting music videos until he was approached by New Line Cinema to direct a moody thriller called *Seven*. Fincher agreed, and his willingness to do so won the film one of its two main stars. According to *Los Angeles Magazine*, Brad Pitt, who plays opposite Morgan Freeman in the film, signed on just for the chance to work with Fincher.

As *Entertainment Weekly* contributor Ty Burr noted, little in Fincher's music video style could prepare viewers for "the oppressive nihilism of his movies." However commonalties existed, namely a "love of posturing and a near-complete lack of humor," according to Burr, who maintained that, like *Alien 3, Seven* continued the trend. More "joyless" than Fincher's previous effort, *Seven* is the story of a serial killer whose closely timed murderous attacks, while at first appearing random, really represent a punishment for each of the seven deadly sins: gluttony, sloth, pride, greed, and so on. Against what Burr described as "an underlit murk," in "a squalid, unnamed city where the rain never stops," Pitt plays a brash young detective, with Morgan Freeman as a disillusioned older cop whose instinct for solving crimes keeps the two officers hot on the twitching tail of the deranged, but brilliant, killer. Gwyneth Paltrow and Kevin Spacey round out the stellar cast. Dubbing the film a "heebiejeebies thriller, the kind people will go to for a good, cathartic creep-out," reviewer Owen Gleiberman added in *Entertainment Weekly* that *Seven*'s title se-

quence is "a small masterpiece of dementia," while its director's unwillingness to present anything more than minimal "clinical carnage" forces the audience to "re-create the details of the killings in our heads," a "canny" maneuver in a film that "works to keep the audience off balance, sifting through the darkness for clues and portents." Quipping that Freeman and Pitt "get more use out of their flashlights than any sleuths since the Hardy Boys," *Newsweek* critic David Ansen called *Seven* a "mighty solemn thriller" filmed in "proper *noir* style—a style so chic, studied and murky it resembles a cross between a Nike commercial and a bad Polish art film."

The Game Reestablishes Reputation

The year 1997 saw the release of Fincher's third feature, *The Game,* a Polygram film starring Michael Douglas and Sean Penn. Cast as Nicholas Van Orton, a self-absorbed investment banker with scads of dough, Douglas still finds there are things that money cannot buy. Fortunately, little brother Conrad (played by Penn)—who hasn't quite made it into the big time—forks over enough of his hard-earned cash to give the man who has everything a unique birthday gift: an adventure from a mysterious company called Consumer Recreation Services. The streets of San Francisco become a maze of intrigue as Van Orten suddenly finds himself propelled into a world of people and situations he cannot control, "a nightmare world where all certainties turn into enigmas, the rules turn into riddles and paranoia is the only logical response to events," in the words of *Newsweek* reviewer Ansen. Praising Fincher as "a master of atmosphere, creating in *The Game* a claustrophobic, darkly burnished world of ominous signs and portents," Ansen concluded that "the rational side of my brain can pick this movie apart. . . . [but] The movie-mad side . . . had a hell of a good time."

The Game reestablished Fincher's his reputation as "a hot commodity" in Hollywood, silencing rumors that the popularity of *Seven* was a fluke. However, as a director who operates on instinct, and who views each new project as another session of "film school," Fincher was still reported to exhibit the need for "affirmation of what he's doing" on the set, according to David Hochman of *Entertainment Weekly. Game* star Douglas reflected the attitude of some actors who have worked with Fincher, telling Hochman: "David can be relentless, but in the best possible way. He doesn't stop. He's constantly trying to do things in new ways, and he doesn't stop until things are done right." As quoted by Nancy Griffin in the *Los Angeles Magazine*, Douglas also noted of his experience under Fincher's direction: "I am constantly amazed by his vision. I've only worked with two other directors with that kind of depth: Milos Forman and Paul Verhoeven. David is the most talented person of his generation."

Founder of Propaganda

Praised for embedding stunning visual images within his films—critics have voiced special praise for the title sequences in *Seven* and *Fight Club*, as well as the suicide scene in *Alien 3*—Fincher has also been criticized for his position as co-founder of Propaganda Films, an association of directors that includes Michael Bay (*The Rock*), Simon West

(*Con Air*), and Antoine Fuqua (*The Replacement Killers*). *The Game* would be the first film produced by Propaganda, a training ground for young directors that provided what *Premiere* contributor Maximillian Potter described as: "a working laboratory, a budget, and some advice so that its young guns get the opportunity to learn, as Fuqua says, 'on somebody else's dime.'" By 1997, Propaganda—which would soon after be acquired by Polygram—could boast forty-five directors whom among them claimed credit for eighty television commercials and 124 MTV rock videos.

A five-minute celluloid sales pitch is one thing; a full-length motion picture quite another, note critics of the Propaganda-fueled "new Hollywood." Several have questioned whether the path to the director's chair has been re-routed in the best direction. While the traditional road to directorial stardom has been through a festival such as Sundance,

In 1999's *Fight Club*, a white-collar worker played by Edward Norton meets charismatic Tyler Durden, played by Brad Pitt, and together they form an underground organization that promotes fighting as therapy.

after reaping accolades for an independent film made on a shoestring, Propaganda directors are counseled along a clearly defined path stretching from music videos to commercials to motion pictures. However, as Maximillian Potter noted, there is a downside to this systematic nurturing of technical expertise. While fledgling Propaganda directors "arrive at a studio's door with technical experience few independent directors can match, [w]hether they also bring stories worth telling" is debatable. "They're not concerned with having a voice," *New York Times* film critic Janet Maslin was quoted as saying in *Premiere*. "They haven't just undermined film narrative, they've demolished it." Fast action is of equivalent value as emotional substance in the Propaganda view, which appeals to a generation raised on the visual rather than intellectual stimulus of the thirty-minute television sitcom.

Created under the aegis of the increasingly successful Propaganda, Fincher's 1999 film *Fight Club* received a decidedly mixed critical reception. That controversial effort, starring Brad Pitt, Edward Norton, and Helena Bonham Carter, was based on a novel by Oregon mechanic Chuck Palahniuk. The directorviewed the film as a social satire along the same lines as the 1967 film *The Graduate*—it's a tale of maturity," he told *Guardian* interviewer Andrew Pulver. However, others saw it differently; *New Yorker* critic David Denby went so far as to label the work "a fascist rhapsody posing as a metaphor of liberation," and its director as "both art-conscious and morally unconscious."

In *Fight Club*, a pair of thirty-something men get a reality check amid the consumer-oriented ennui of the twenty-first century via the visceral experience of hand-to-hand combat. The narrator, played by Norton, is a yuppie middle-management type who leads an empty life as an automobile insurance accident investigator. His boredom drives him to find solace in catalogue shopping and loitering around twelve-step support groups in search of true emotion—and a cure for his own insomnia. Norton meets Pitt's character, the charismatic Tyler Durden, on his way back from a business trip, just about the time his secure world starts to fall apart. The two link up, become roommates, and soon found fight club, a subterranean retreat "where ordinary guys can come and beat the crap out of each other in bare-knuckle, no-holds-barred combat," according to *Time* reviewer Richard Schickel. Soon the film "lurches from satire into fantasy,"

If you enjoy the works of David Fincher, you may also want to check out the following films:

A Clockwork Orange, a Stanley Kubrick masterpiece, 1971.

The three other films in the "Alien" series: *Alien*, 1979, *Aliens*, 1986, and *Alien: Resurrection*, 1997.

Cape Fear, directed by Martin Scorcese, 1991.

Schickel continued, as Durden plants fight clubs around the country and transforms them into paramilitary bases from which to launch an effort to destroy the nation's credit-card empire.

Planned for July 1999 release, the shadow of the tragic shootings at Columbine High School prompted studio execs to hold off because of the film's apparent glorification of violence. Richard Schickel of *Time* concluded that *Fight Club* broaches "*American Beauty*—Susan Faludi territory, that illiberal, impious, inarticulate fringe that threatens the smug American center with an anger that cannot explain itself, can act out its frustrations only in inexplicable violence." In a related take on the film, *Maclean's* critic Brian D. Johnsonnoted that *Fight Club* "is a movie about men . . . seeking their inner warrior." Like *American Beauty,* in this "uglier, bloodier" film "a guy with his brain on fire rebels against conformity, tells his boss to shove it and discovers the meaning of muscle." Placing *Fight Club* in a slightly broader social perspective, Andrew Pulver of the *Guardian* opined that the film "taps into a virulent skein of rage that's been dominating American protest politics for years, the dehumanizing effect of an all-pervading corporate culture."

Hones Ability to Tell a Story

Since *Fight Club*, Fincher has returned to his roots, working as second unit director for the 1999 blockbuster *Star Wars: Episode I—The Phantom Menace*. He continues to approach each of his films as a new chance to perfect a simple task: telling a story. "I don't purport for a second to know what a film should be, what entertainment should be, how much it should teach, how much it should titillate," Fincher explained to an *Entertainment Weekly* interview to promote *Fight Club*. The director later expanded upon his craft in a discussion with *Rolling Stone* contributor Fred Schruers saying, "My attitude is: Take the camera out of the box and work as hard as you can to tell your story as simply as possible. You know, the best analogy for moviemaking is you're doing a watercolor from three blocks away through a telescope, with 40 people holding the brush, and you have a walkie-talkie."

Fincher believes that a movie must do more than simply entertain its audience; it must involve viewers in its detached reality, getting them to navigate the story line within its own laws, and be drawn into the unfolding drama at the same pace the characters traverse the film's fictional world. "You're dealing with the most plastic medium there is," he explained to Andrew Pulver. "Now there are computers that can make anything look real . . . so you have to be very careful about what you show an audience. I think the first rule of cinema is that a movie has to teach an audience how to watch it. That's what the first act is, showing the audience the things they have to take seriously, the characterization and technique, laying the groundwork for point of view, and how you will or won't betray it."

■ Works Cited

Review of *Alien 3, Time*, June 1, 1992, p. 87.

Ansen, David, review of *Seven, Newsweek*, October 2, 1995, p. 85.

Ansen, David, "Michael Douglas Is Trapped in a Nightmare 'Game'," *Newsweek*, September 22, 1997, p. 84.

Billson, Anne, "Back into the Closet," *New Statesman*, August 21, 1992, p. 35.

"Blood, Sweat & Fears" (interview), *Entertainment Weekly*, October 15, 1999, pp. 24-26.

Burr, Ty, "Gloom with a View," *Entertainment Weekly*, March 29, 1996, pp. 71-72.

Denby, Denby, "Boys Will Be Boys," *New Yorker*, October 18, 1999, pp. 254-55.

Gleiberman, Owen, review of *Seven, Entertainment Weekly*, September 29, 1995, p. 36.

Griffin, Nancy, and Holly Sorensen, "40 under 40," *Los Angeles Magazine*, March, 1997, p. 66-90.

Hochman, David, "Game Boy," *Entertainment Weekly*, September 19, 1997, pp. 32-33.

Johnson, Brian D., "Bare-knuckled Knockout," *Maclean's*, October 25, 1999, p. 86.

"Outcasts of the Universe," review of *Alien 3, Time*, June 1, 1992, p. 87.

Potter, Maximillian, "Do These Men Represent the Future of Hollywood Filmmaking . . . .", *Premiere*, February, 1998, pp. 68-73.

Pulver, Andrew, "Fight the Good Fight," *Guardian*, October 29, 1999.

Rafferty, Terrence, review of *Alien 3, New Yorker*, June 1, 1992, pp. 61-62.

Schickel, Richard, "Conditional Knockout: *Fight Club* Packs a Visual Punch . . . .," *Time*, October 11, 1999, p. 83.

Schruers, Fred, "Rebel Director David Fincher's Bizarro Game," *Rolling Stone*, April 3, 1997, pp. 52-53.

Wild, David, "Hollywood Director David Fincher Returns to Video," *Rolling Stone*, October 17, 1996.

■ For More Information See

PERIODICALS

Entertainment Weekly, January 23, 1998, pp. 64-65.

Los Angeles Times, September 9, 1997.

National Review, October 13, 1997, p. 76.

New Republic, November 8, 1999, p. 64.

New York Times, August 31, 1997, pp. 9H, 14H.

Shoot, March 17, 1995, p. 17.

Time, September 25, 1995, p. 68.*

Erik Christian Haugaard

■ Personal

Born April 13, 1923, in Frederiksberg, Denmark; came to the United States in March, 1940; son of Gotfred Hans Christian (a professor of biochemistry) and Karen (Pedersen) Haugaard; married Myrna Seld (a writer), December 23, 1949 (died, 1981); married Masako Taira (a professor; died, 1996), 1987; children: (first marriage) Mikka Anja, Mark. *Education:* Attended Black Mountain College, 1941-42, and New School for Social Research, 1947-48. *Hobbies and other interests:* Reading the Icelandic sagas.

■ Addresses

Home—Toad Hall, Ballydehob, County Cork, Ireland.

■ Career

Author of children's books, drama, and poetry. Worked as a farm laborer in Fyn, Denmark, 1938-40, and later as a sheep herder in Wyoming and Montana. *Military service:* Royal Canadian Air Force, 1943-45; became flight sergeant; received War Service Medal from Christian X of Denmark.

■ Awards, Honors

John Golden Fund fellowship, 1958, for *The Heroes;* honorable mention, *New York Herald Tribune* Children's Spring Book Festival, 1962, for *Hakon of Rogen's Saga,* and 1967, for *The Little Fishes;* American Library Association (ALA) Notable Book Awards citation, 1963, for *Hakon of Rogen's Saga,* 1965, for *A Slave's Tale,* and 1971, for *The Untold Tale; Boston Globe-Horn Book* Award, 1967, Jane Addams Children's Book Award, 1968, and Danish Cultural Minister's Prize, 1970, all for *The Little Fishes;* ALA Best Books for Young Adults citation, 1980, for *Chase Me! Catch Nobody!;* Phoenix Award, 1988, for *The Rider and His Horse.*

■ Writings

FICTION

Hakon of Rogen's Saga, Houghton, 1963.
A Slave's Tale (sequel to *Hakon of Rogen's Saga*), Houghton, 1965.
Orphans of the Wind, Houghton, 1966.
The Little Fishes, illustrated by Milton Johnson, Houghton, 1967.
The Rider and His Horse, Houghton, 1968.
The Untold Tale, Houghton, 1971.
A Messenger for Parliament, Houghton, 1976.

Cromwell's Boy, Houghton, 1978.

Chase Me! Catch Nobody!, Houghton, 1980.

Leif the Unlucky, Houghton, 1982.

A Boy's Will, illustrated by Troy Howell, Rinehardt, 1983.

The Samurai's Tale, Houghton, 1984.

Prince Boghole, illustrated by Julie Downing, Macmillan, 1987.

Princess Horrid, illustrated by Diane Dawson Hearne, Macmillan, 1990.

The Boy and the Samurai, Houghton, 1991.

The Story of Yuriwaka, Rinehart, 1991.

The Death of Mr. Angel, Rinehart, 1992.

Under the Black Flag, Rinehart, 1993.

The Revenge of the Forty-seven Samurai, Houghton, 1994.

TRANSLATOR

Complete Fairy Tales and Stories of Hans Christian Andersen, Doubleday, 1973.

Hans Christian Andersen: His Classical Fairy Tales, illustrated by Michael Foreman, Doubleday, 1978.

Hans Christian Andersen, *The Emperor's Nightingale,* Schocken Books, 1979.

Hans Christian Andersen: The Complete Fairy Tales & Stories, Doubleday, 1983.

OTHER

Twenty-five Poems, Squire Press, 1957.

The Heroes (play), first produced in Antioch, OH, 1958.

Portrait of a Poet: Hans Christian Andersen (pamphlet), Library of Congress, 1974.

Also author of unpublished adult novel, "The Last Heathen"; author of plays *The President Regrets* and *An Honest Man*. Translator of Eskimo poetry, collected by Knud Rasmussen, for *American Scandinavian Review*.

■ **Work in Progress**

A novel, tentatively titled *Mary's History*.

■ **Sidelights**

Danish author Erik Christian Haugaard has written a number of acclaimed works for young adults that transport readers back to a time and place in history that placed upon children burdens nearly unimaginable to the contemporary North American adolescent. Religious strife, World War II, and feudal Japan are just some of the settings Haugaard has explored in his books, which usually feature a child whose hardships are made all the worse due to the loss of parents or other guardians. "Despite its variety, his work is readily identifiable, not only for its consistently high quality but for certain common themes," wrote Caroline C. Hunt in the *St. James Guide to Children's Writers*. "In almost every Haugaard novel, a boy comes of age at a time of turmoil and stress. Usually, he is uprooted from his own home and seeks (and often finds) a father figure or mentor who helps him to cope with nightmarish conditions: war, ethnic strife, loss of family, often hunger, andalways danger."

Critics have praised Haugaard, who writes in English, for the richness of period detail that his novels possess, the result of his extensive research. He admits to a wanderlust that plagued him even as a young child growing up in Denmark, but as with many of his protagonists, Haugaard found his own pleasant, easygoing world shattered by political fortune. After daydreaming for years about sailing the open seas, as a teenager he made it on board the last ship out of free Denmark before the country was invaded by Nazi Germany. He spent much of his early adulthood traveling the world before finally settling into a remote corner of Ireland. But even in his seventies Haugaard still immerses himself in other cultures and considers himself a citizen not of one country, but of the world. Haugaard's protagonists reflect his indomitable faith that youth can prevail despite frequent encounters with adult betrayal, persecution, and death.

A Childhood in Denmark

Haugaard was born in Denmark in 1923 into an educated, well-to-do urban family. His parents possessed somewhat of a leftist outlook—both were members of Denmark's Radical Party, and his mother had been the first woman in the country to ride a motorbike; she also studied engineering in college. Haugaard, whose father was a respected scientist, grew up in Copenhagen with an older brother and another one seven years his junior in a permissive household that encouraged creative pursuits. He remembers his hometown along Baltic Sea as a quaint port city still mired in the airs of the previous century.

Cromwell's Boy
Erik Christian Haugaard

In this 1978 sequel to *A Message for Parliament*, Oliver becomes a spy for Cromwell's army during the English Civil War.

The author also recalls a deep dislike of school from the start; for some years, his only friend there was the sole other student from an affluent family, and their teacher favored them at the expense of the others. She was particularly unkind to a pair of orphans in the class. "Still I am grateful to her; inadvertently she taught me how repulsive snobbery is," Haugaard wrote in the *Something about the Author Autobiography Series* (SAAS) Haugaard exhibited a literary imagination at an early age; he concocted stories even before he could read, which he called "self" stories to distinguish them from the ones his parents read aloud to him from books, and after crossing the literacy threshold himself he spent hours late into the night reading in bed with a flashlight. By his early teen years, he was delving into the European classics in his parents' extensive library.

Haugaard entered preparatory school at the age of twelve, but he likened this institution to a prison. He was an indifferent student who dreamed of running away and finding a place on an outgoing ship. In 1936, he and his class visited Germany on a class trip, a setting that became the basis for his 1980 young adult novel, *Chase Me, Catch Nobody!* Many Germans had enthusiastically embraced the rise to power of the Nazi Party by this point, and Haugaard's class was a microcosm of pan-European reaction to fascist politics: one clique of boys loved Nazi culture and even bought insignia as souvenirs; another group was uninterested in all political matters; but a third set, to which Haugaard belonged, was repelled by the thuggishness of the Nazi culture. In *Chase Me, Catch Nobody!*, the personal morality and political loyalties of a young Danish student are tested when he is asked to smuggle documents for the anti-Nazi side.

Haugaard's desire for adventure even extended to a plan to run away and fight for the anti-fascist International Brigade in the Spanish Civil War when he was fourteen. He and a friend fled, but they were caught and sent home before they even crossed the Danish border. Finally, Haugaard's parents consented to his longtime desire to leave school. This was an unusual circumstance for a family of his background, and it was generally viewed by others as a portent of failure. Since he had often expressed a wish to become a farmer, in 1938 his parents arranged for him to work a six-month stint on an asparagus farm on the Danish island of Fyn.

The work was physically demanding, and he and the other workers were treated with contempt by the owner. He slept in a room near the stable's hayloft, where mice and rats scurried at night, and the food was meager. "My master bought meat for us from a travelling butcher who was arrested for selling meat from animals that had died of sickness," Haugaard remembered in *SAAS*. In November, he returned to Copenhagen and began studying English at the home of an English military officer, whom Haugaard later learned was likely Britain's chief of intelligence in Denmark. The man told him that he would fight in a war before he was twenty-one, a remark at which the young Haugaard, just fifteen, scoffed.

Haugaard spent another stint as a farm hand in 1939, but in a much more pleasant, egalitarian workplace. This period of his life was "very useful to me as an author of historical novels," he later wrote in *SAAS*. "The difference between life on a farm then and a hundred or even two hundred years earlier was not so very great." In the late summer of 1939, his parents and youngest brother sailed for the United States after his father had obtained a professional fellowship; Germany invaded Poland and Britain declared war a few days later. The parents sent for Haugaard and his older brother, who arrived in New York just days before Denmark was invaded by Nazi Germany.

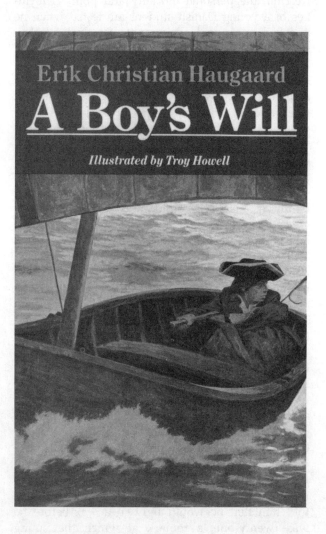

Set in the late eighteenth century, Haugaard's 1983 historical novel illustrates the deep tension between Catholics and Protestants in Ireland—tension that still exists today.

Living in a New Country

Haugaard found living with his parents in a new country a difficult situation. He disliked the borough of Queens, where they lived, and felt trapped as a refugee, unable to return to his former life indefinitely. He worked on a Cape Cod farm, and then it was arranged that he would go to California, where he could live with a friend of his parents and attend high school. He took a bus cross-country, which he liked very much, and when the school year ended he bought a bike and a tent and went off by himself. Riding for a hundred miles a day at times, Haugaard threaded through northern California, the Pacific Northwest, and into Idaho and Montana.

After receiving word from his parents about a progressive North Carolina college, he hitchhiked back to Boston and entered Black Mountain College in 1941. Here, Haugaard thrived, since the emphasis was not on results, but enrichment. He later remarked that the year there changed his life; he wrote poetry and even a play in his second language, in which he was now fluent.

During a stint in Cambridge, Massachusetts, Haugaard worked as a translator for a professor, and one evening was invited to a dinner party where he likely drank too much and told another guest that he wished to fight for Denmark. The guest turned out to be a Canadian Air Force officer, and Haugaard left for Toronto shortly afterward for basic training to become a fighter-plane pilot. He failed his courses there and became an air gunner instead. "Of all the things I have been a failure at, I think I mind least being such a hopeless soldier," he wrote in *SAAS*.

A Writing Career Begins

After the war, Haugaard spent time in New York City, traveled through Mexico, and continued to write fiction. He also returned to Copenhagen for a year, and in 1949 returned to New York City to marry his girlfriend, Myrna Seld, a well-connected translator and poet. Soon afterward, they moved to Italy, spending time in Rapallo, then traveling extensively through theMediterranean area on meager funds. In 1957, a book of Haugaard's poetry appeared in print, and the following year an Ohio college produced a play he had written, *The Heroes*. He and his wife had settled in Denmark when he began writing his first book, which he planned as a biography of one of Norway's last Viking rulers. He submitted it to a New York publisher, who suggested that he revise the tale for juvenile readers.

Hakon of Rogen's Saga was published in the United States in 1963 and was met with admiring critical reception. His debut, declared Ruth Hill Viguers in her essay on Haugaard for *A Critical History of Children's Literature*, "introduced one of the most important writers of the sixties to the United States." Though the work possessed features of the saga, an epic poem form common to early Scandinavian literature, it was actually an original story

Shortly after his first wife died, Haugaard moved to Japan and produced this novel about an orphaned Japanese boy adopted by nobility and taught to be a samurai.

about an orphaned boy whose birthright is a remote island off the coast of Norway called Rogen. Haugaard set the work at the close of Norway's Viking era and the beginning of Christian rule, as the eleven-year-old orphaned Hakon fights his uncle for control of Rogen.

Haugaard wrote a sequel to *Hakon of Rogen's Saga* titled *A Slave's Tale*, which was published in 1965. Helga, a slave girl who befriended Hakon in the first book, stows away on a ship that carries Hakon and another former slave to Brittany. On the way, they encounter war, a new religion, and extreme danger. Many of the passengers do not survive. Pairing Haugaard's second book with his first, Viguers noted that "although the action is violent, brutal, and tragic, the stories are moving and often beautiful." Other reviewers lavished similar accolades upon his work. "The events are so absorbing, the emotions aroused so powerful that we hardly notice the skill with which the historical background is drawn, but it is splendidly imagined and convincing," opined Margaret Sherwood Libby in *Book Week—The Sunday Herald Tribune*.

Haugaard ventured into far different historical territory with his 1966 novel for children, *Orphans of the Wind*. Much of the action takes place on a ship bound for the Carolina coast at the time of the American Civil War. The orphan boy Jim fulfilled Haugaard's childhood fantasy of signing on to an ocean-going vessel as a helper, but Jim learns that the ship carries a cache of arms bound for the Confederate Army. The crew assumes that the ship's Bible-quoting carpenter is merely a religious fanatic, but as a foe of slavery the carpenter is opposed to the Confederate cause and sets fire to the ship.

Jim and some other mates barely survive the conflagration, and they make it to land, where they successfully avoid being conscripted by the Confederate Army of the secessionist South. When they arrive at the Northern border, they join the Union army instead. In the end, Jim realizes that he and his fellow shipmates were not "orphans of the wind," but rather "brothers of the earth." Polly Burroughs, writing in the *New York Times Book Review*, called it "a powerful, absorbing tale with a finely honed plot and distinctive literary style." Viguers, in her assessment of *Orphans of the Wind*, praised Haugaard, noting that a story from his pen "leaves a residue of wisdom and compassion in the hearts of his readers. He accomplishes what is expected of the best novelists—a reflection of life that throws light upon humanity and the needs and desires of the human spirit."

Little Fishes Based on Real Life

Some of the Italians Haugaard met during the time he spent in Italy in the late 1940s became the basis for his next work, 1967's *The Little Fishes.* Its protagonist is a little boy named Guido, whose life is one of extreme hardship because of Italy's role in World War II and the presence of Nazi German occupation forces. Guido, who lives in cave near the city of Naples, also takes care of two other orphaned children, Anna and her little brother.Haugaard said in *SAAS* that this particular book "is special to me, for everything that happens in the book had really taken place." He and his wife met a woman who had indeed lived in a cave during the war—the book is dedicated to her—and Guido was inspired by a street urchin, whose name they never learned, to whom the Haugaards used to provide clothing and other incidentals. As Haugaard told *Language Arts* interviewers Shelton L. Root Jr. and M. Jean Greenlaw, he and his wife knew that the boy usually sold the items for money, but he chastised him one day after he had given the boy a pair of warm winter boots. When he saw him the next day, the boy was still in his sneakers, despite the snow. Haugaard recalled the boy then asked him to wait in the marketplace, which Haugaard did, and "about twenty minutes later, he returned with a five-year-old boy who was wearing the boots tied to his legs to keep them on, for they were too big for him. 'My brother,' he announced. 'I take good care of him.'"

The narrative action in *The Little Fishes* centers around the children's decision to journey to nearby Cassino, where they know there is a monastery that will shelter them. Fighting along the way between the Germans and the Allied armies forces them underground. "There is nothing grand or heroic about Haugaard's version of the war, in which survival at any cost is the constant issue," wrote Hunt in *St. James Guide to Children's Writers,* and the writer himself reiterated that the events of the book were culled from first-person accounts. "The cave in the mountains between the Allied and German lines did exist, and in dirt and squalor a hundred people were hidden there," Haugaard wrote in *SAAS. The Little Fishes* won Haugaard a slew of enthusiastic critical remarks, such as *New York Times Book Review* critic Bruce Wilkinson's assessment of it as "an absorbing, dramatic tale. . . . Here is war in one of its most tragic aspects—the backwash of battle, and the terrors and the trauma it inflicts on the young."

More Tales of War

A trip to Israel that Haugaard made became the basis for his 1968 young adult work, *The Rider and His Horse.* Set in the year A.D. 70 in Judea, the book once again illustrates Haugaard's theme of how political events force youngsters—especially those left defenseless without parents or protectors—into situations that test their mettle as both survivors and sympathizers to the plight of others. David, the hero, is the son of a wealthy merchant from Phoenicia who longs for adventure. He unexpectedly finds it on a journey in which he is taken prisoner by Roman forces. Judea was then a Roman colony and site of a bitter conflict between the conquerors, the Samaritans, and Jews like David.

"He is suddenly, by chance, thrown into a completely different world where strange values are taken for granted, and he is a total nobody," Haugaard wrote in *SAAS,* in which he likened the story to his own dilemma upon dropping out of school in 1938 and arriving in Fyn as an utterly inexperienced farmhand. In the end, David makes his way to King Herod's famous sea fortress, Masada, as it prepares for its legendary showdown with the Romans. *School Librarian* reviewer P. Robertson called *The Rider and His Horse* "a fine but very demanding book. . . . By showing the qualities which ensured their survival as a nation, he provides insight into the fierce nationalism of modern Israel."

Haugaard's 1971 novel for younger readers, *The Untold Tale,* returned to Scandinavia and its historic traumas. The story of Denmark's war with Sweden in the mid-1600s is told through the eyes of a poor farm boy, Dag, who is left an orphan by the war and starvation. He ambitiously plans a trek to see the king and ask for help; along the way he meets a series of adults, but none enter into the role of protector or mentor for Dag, as is common in nearly allof Haugaard's other novels. As a result, Dag does not survive, and the work has been termed the author's most deeply pessimistic effort. Nancy Berkowitz, reviewing *The Untold Tale* in *Li-*

This 1991 novel set in sixteenth-century Japan features an orphaned boy, Saru, whose hard-learned lessons of survival aid him and the samurai against a strong warlord.

brary Journal, called it "a moving experience for any reader," however. "The landscapes and events are recorded with the precision of a camera in poetic, saga-style prose," Berkowitz noted.

Haugaard, his wife, and their two children continued to live in Denmark for some years, but moved to England when their daughter entered Cambridge University. From there, they traveled to Ireland one day and spied "an old warehouse standing in the sea," as Haugaard described it in SAAS. "I turned to my wife and said, 'Why is something like that never for sale?' Well it was and two weeks later I had bought it." The new setting yielded a fresh set of historical inspiration for him to research, and a

pair of tales set in Britain during a time of great civil strife was the result. In the 1640s, a conservative Puritan member of Parliament, Oliver Cromwell, went to battle with the king of England and deposed him; Cromwell's forces then entered Ireland and dealt with its populace most brutally. Haugaard's 1976 book, *A Messenger for Parliament*, relates the events of the era through Oliver Cutter, a young, motherless boy whose father abandons him to join Cromwell's army.

Cutter reveals the events of his life as an old man living in Boston. The first book recounts his conscription into the Cromwell camp while working for a printer in Oxford, a city still loyal to the crown. His employer secretly prints a seditionary newspaper, and Cutter and a friend, Easy Jack, are selected to deliver a letter to Cromwell in nearby Cambridge. On the way, Jack is killed, and Oliver barely escapes; his completion of the mission sets up the sequel, *Cromwell's Boy*. In this 1978 novel, the Lord Protector enlists Oliver as a spy, which gives him an eyewitness involvement to a great deal of grisly action. This latter book was praised by critics for its historic flavor. Most reviewers commended Haugaard for convincingly portraying the tension of the times, as well as the sundry historical oddity, such as the travelling dentist who pulls bad teeth in the town square. "A style enriched with aphorisms and details enhances the color and atmosphere of the story without diminishing tension," wrote Virginia Haviland in *Horn Book*, "although the book may demand an audience of superior young readers."

Haugaard's next book for young readers was *Chase Me! Catch Nobody!* Published in 1980, the novel draws upon his class trip to Germany forty-three years before. His doppelganger is Erik, described by William Blackburn in *The World of Children's Books* as "proud and clumsy, caustic and confused," and edgy with the constraints of authority. On the trip, a shadowy figure hands Erik a cache of falsified passports to smuggle back to Denmark, and when the teen sees the same man arrested by the brutal Nazi internal police, he vows to carry out the mission, knowing it will save lives. "Nuances of Danish and German social class and political humor permeate the story," noted Jack Forman in *School Library Journal*. Erik's friend Nikolai and even a teacher are drawn into the action, which intensifies when Erik meets a Jewish girl—who calls herself Nobody—and decides to take her with him. From this comes the pun of the book's title.

The serious dangers presented in *Chase Me! Catch Nobody!* are lightened by some humor: the pranks of his classmates, for instance, and Erik's brave decision to sacrifice himself to the water when the rowboat on which he and the others must flee starts to sink—but he realizes that the water is only three feet deep. Haugaard's "story is consistently entertaining without ever ceasing to convey a sense of the complexity of human experience," opined Blackburn. "This deft combination of serious theme and fast-paced adventure deserves—and richly repays—both our interest and our gratitude." Zena Sutherland,reviewing the work in *Bulletin of the Center for Children's Books,* praised the way in which Haugaard portrays Erik's sudden encounter with maturity and personal conviction as he grasps the full horror of political injustice—"an impressive (and credible) display of courage and initiative," stated Sutherland.

Norway's abandoned colony on the vast Arctic island of Greenland was the basis for Haugaard's 1982 novel for young adults, *Leif the Unlucky.* Founded in the tenth century, the colony dwindled to a few hundred despairing residents by the time of the book's action in the 1400s. Its title character is a teen who attempts to rally the dispirited population, who believe they exist at the very end of the world and worry about the increasingly colder climate. Realizing that they are losing a battle with nature and the encroaching ice, they dream of a ship to take them back home. Leif's heroic teens are challenged by a vicious rival gang. Hazel Rochman, reviewing the novel for *School Library Journal,* criticized the author for being "unable to depict Leif and his friends in much depth: the dialogue is stilted and the relationships are unconvincing." But Rochman did grant that *Leif the Unlucky*'s best attribute lay instead in its description of "a natural landscape of beauty and terror. . . [Haugaard] captures the malaise of the dying community with its ruined and abandoned farms."

Another work that Haugaard set in the Irish past, *A Boy's Will,* was published the following year. Here, the vicious struggles between the Protestant and Roman Catholic factions land its protagonist, the orphan Patrick, with a grandfather who deeply resents the interfaith union that brought him into the world. His grandfather even despises Patrick's name, an homage to the Roman Catholic patron saint of Ireland. The work takes place in the 1770s, and Patrick overhears his grandfather discussing an act of sabotage by the Britishthat will cripple the fleet hiding offshore, a passel of ships about to set sail to North America to help the colonies in their struggle for independence from the British crown. Patrick takes a boat out by himself to deliver a warning, knowing he will never be able to return. "The action is vividly described, observed a *Publishers Weekly* critic, "right up to the bittersweet close."

Experiences in Japan Influence Haugaard

When Haugaard's younger child went off to college, he decided to expand his horizons and apply for a fellowship in Japan. Shortly after learning that he and his wife would be spending the next year in the country at the invitation of the Japan Foundation, his wife was diagnosed with cancer. He nursed her at their home in Ireland, where she died in 1981. Less than a month later, Haugaard left by himself for Japan. He described the journey there as undertaken with some degree of apprehension—he had rarely been separated from his wife during their marriage, and he was embarking on a long extended stay to a land whose language he did not speak. The reception his Japanese hosts gave him, however, stilled any qualms, and he was treated as an honored guest, provided with a translation staff and installed in a villa near a Shinto temple.

Haugaard's time near Kofu, where he lived, inspired his next series of books for children. In particular, he became interested in a sixteenth-century leader in the area, whose palace and fortress ruins were nearby. After thoroughly delving into the country's history and culture during its feudal era, he wrote *The Samurai's Tale,* published in 1984. In it, an orphaned boy finds refuge from the turmoil of the times—in which warring lords have disrupted the economy and stability of the region—at the home of a noble family, who adopt him and instruct him in the art of the samurai warrior.

After a pair of illustrated books for younger readers, Haugaard returned to the subject of feudal Japan with his 1991 book, *The Boy and the Samurai.* Again, the tale is set in sixteenth-century Japan and features a young boy in reduced circumstances. Saru, whose name means "monkey," is a beggar child with neither parents nor home; a little stray cat is his sole companion. Once again, his personal safety is threatened by the skirmishes carried out by the lords of the area, and he even witnesses one bloodbath. Saru comes to abhor the samurai culture, since it has caused his own life to be so unstable, and takes refuge one winter at a small shrine. There he meets a helpful Buddhist priest, Jogen, who becomes a much-needed friend and mentor to Saru. When he overhears a conversation between Murakami Harutomo—the now-grown samurai who had been adopted in *The Samurai's Tale*—he re-evaluates his feelings and decides to save Harutomo's beloved wife, who has been kidnapped by a rival. "Haugaard writes with quiet skill and his mastery of the complex political scene is apparent," declared Kathleen Beck in *Voice of Youth Advocates*. Beck also praised the author's ability to portray "the autumnal mood of resignation" in Japanese art and society as the feudal period

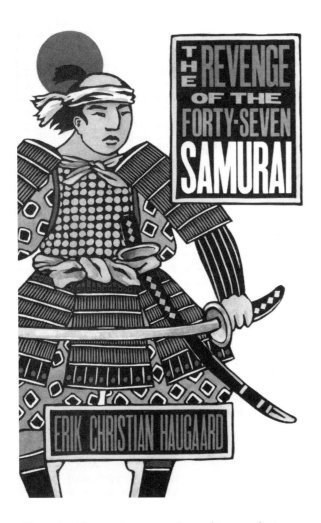

When the Shogun become rulers of Japan, forty-seven samurai decide to avenge them with the help of Jiro, a lowly servant boy turned spy, in this 1994 historical novel.

came to terms with its own demise. A *Publishers Weekly* reviewer called *The Boy and the Samurai* "a vivid look at an unusual place and time" and praised Haugaard's creation of a believable character for Western readers, as well as his decidedly unfamiliar adventures in a far-off land and place.

Switches to a Contemporary Setting

After his 1991 book, *The Story of Yuriwaka*, a retelling of a Japanese folk tale, Haugaard tackled an equally distant setting for his next young-adult novel, *The Death of Mr. Angel*. Published in 1992, it was the only work of his at that time to be set in the contemporary United States. Its hero is Dick Shaw, a lonely teen who lives in a small town. Shaw's notebooks, found in a motel room after he has run away from home, relate the story of hisdisillusionment with his family and community. He rails against the lack of spiritual awareness and cultural barrenness he sees around him; like another famous literary teen hero disillusioned with society, Holden Caufield in the J. D. Salinger novel *The Catcher in the Rye*, Shaw is also from a well-to-do family. Yet here Haugaard mercilessly portrays Shaw's parents, townsfolk, and peers as shallow. When the town's only like-minded soul, the English teacher of the title, is murdered, Dick knows who the culprit is. His striving, ambitious father, however, forces him to remain silent on the matter, which affirms his decision to run away. "A harsh view of human nature and the convoluted emotional ties that link families together, this is a book that will give readers much to think about," wrote Stephanie Zvirin in *Booklist*.

Haugaard's next work was the 1993 tale *Under the Black Flag*. Set in the seventeenth century, the novel's lead figure is William Bernard, the teenage son of a Jamaica plantation owner. William is sent off to school in England, but his ship is seized by the infamous pirate Blackbeard. At first he is able to hide his affluent background, but then a fellow captive betrays him and the pirates decide to hold him for ransom. He befriends another teen on the ship, a slave, and together they escape. *Under the Black Flag* depicts, through the impressionable William's eyes, the harsh and ferocious nature of the pirateers' world, which is far from the swashbuckling one that most boys like himself had imagined. There is also much detail about such ships, their riggings and sails, and how they maneuver though the seas and fierce storms. Laura B. Warren commended Haugaard in a *Kliatt* article for fashioning "a tight plot . . . [I]t is with reluctance that the reader sees the book come to a close."

A Return to Japan

In his next book, Haugaard returns to Japan's past with a reworking ofthe tale of its Chushingura incident, which is still commemorated generations later. *The Revenge of the Forty-seven Samurai*, published in 1994, reaches back to eighteenth-century Japan for this true story about a group of ronin—samurais who have been left without a master to serve. The story is narrated by a servant, Jiro, in the household of Lord Asano, an honorable leader. Asano's rival is the malicious Lord Kira, who besmirches Asano's name, causing the latter to commit ritual suicide, as was customary among such men. A band of Asano's many samurai—now ronin—then devote themselves to avenging their lord's death. One warrior, Oishi, confides in Jiro and enlists his help to carry out their devious plan.

By using Jiro as the voice relating this tale, *The Revenge of the Forty-seven Samurai* is able to examine the situation from a balanced perspective. Jiro, for example, considers the samurai brave men, but questions their harsh code of vengeance; he also wonders what will become of him should their plan succeed, for the ronin must die then, too. As the story nears a conclusion, Jiro learns a secret about his own heritage, which helps him to unlock the key to his own future. "This is excellent, authentic historical fiction that brings [the end of Japan's feudal era] to vivid life," asserted Katharine Kan in *Voice of Youth Advocates*. Other critics found praise for the objective perspective that the work presents through Jiro. His confusion "allows Haugaard to explore ethical implications . . . while he refrains from judging their actions," observed Elizabeth Bush in a review in *Bulletin of the Center for Children's Books*. The period and place are also well-executed aspects of the book, noted *Booklist* contributor Janice Del Negro, adding that "the fabric of daily life, woven so carefully into the tale, is easily absorbed."

Haugaard married again in 1987, taking as his wife a professor who was one of his interpreters in Japan. He and Masako Taira divided their time between ToadHall in Ireland—what he named his Irish warehouse—and a home in Tokyo, until her death in 1996. Haugaard still enjoys remarkable

If you enjoy the works of Erik Christian Haugaard, you may also want to check out the following books:

Kara Dalkey, *The Heavenward Path*, 1998.
Geraldine McCaughrean, *The Pirate's Son*, 1998.
Lensey Namioka, *Island of Ogres*, 1989.

success in his craft, but, as he wrote in *SAAS*, "my idea of richness is not sports cars or swimming pools, but to be able always to say to oneself as one wakes up in the morning: 'What should I do today?'" With their historical settings but timeless messages, his books have endured in popularity with young readers and critics alike over the years, and will likely persist in that accomplishment in the future. Lois R. Kuznets wrote about Haugaard's body of work in a 1980 critique published in *Children's Literature in Education*, reflecting upon the durability of his themes: "While showing children themselves as coping with—and developing in spite of—great cruelty and suffering, Haugaard gives all children both hope for the future and identification with the oppressed."

■ Works Cited

Beck, Kathleen, review of *The Boy and the Samurai, Voice of Youth Advocates*, June, 1991, p. 96.

Berkowitz, Nancy, review of *The Untold Tale, Library Journal*, September, 1971, pp. 127-28.

Blackburn, William, review of *Chase Me! Catch Nobody!, The World of Children's Books*, Volume 6, 1981, p. 70.

Review of *The Boy and the Samurai, Publishers Weekly*, February 8, 1991, p. 58.

Review of *A Boy's Will, Publishers Weekly*, October 21, 1983, p. 67.

Burroughs, Polly, review of *Orphans of the Wind, New York Times Book Review*, July 31, 1966, p. 18.

Bush, Elizabeth, review of *The Revenge of the Forty-seven Samurai, Bulletin of the Center for Children's Books*, May, 1995, p. 309.

Del Negro, Janice, review of *The Revenge of the Forty-seven Samurai, Booklist*, May 15, 1995, p. 1641.

Forman, Jack, review of *Chase Me! Catch Nobody!, School Library Journal*, April, 1980, p. 124.

Haugaard, Erik Christian, essay in *Something about the Author Autobiography Series,* Gale, Volume 12, 1991, pp. 141-56.

Haviland, Virginia, review of *Cromwell's Boy, Horn Book,* December, 1978, p. 644.

Hunt, Caroline C., "Erik Haugaard," *St. James Guide to Children's Writers,* fifth edition, St. James, 1999, pp. 484-85.

Kan, Katharine, review of *The Revenge of the Forty-seven Samurai, Voice of Youth Advocates,* August, 1995, p. 159.

Kuznets, Lois R., "Other People's Children: Erik Haugaard's 'Untold Tales,'" *Children's Literature in Education,* summer, 1980, pp. 62-68.

Libby, Margaret Sherwood, review of *A Slave's Tale, Book Week—The Sunday Herald Tribune,* May 30, 1965, p. 15.

Meigs, Cornelia, editor, *A Critical History of Children's Literature,* Macmillan, 1969.

Robertson, P., review of *The Rider and His Horse, School Librarian,* March, 1970, p. 80.

Rochman, Hazel, review of *Leif the Unlucky, School Library Journal,* March, 1982, p. 158.

Root, Shelton L. Jr., and M. Jean Greenlaw, "Profile: An Interview with Erik Christian Haugaard," *Language Arts,* May, 1979, pp. 549-61.

Sutherland, Zena, review of *Chase Me! Catch Nobody!, Bulletin of the Center for Children's Books,* June, 1980, p. 191.

Review of *Under the Black Flag, Publishers Weekly,* November 23, 1992, p. 63.

Warren, Laura B., review of *Under the Black Flag, Kliatt,* July, 1994, pp. 8-9.

Wilkinson, Bruce, review of *Little Fishes, New York Times Book Review,* May 7, 1967, p. 14.

Zvirin, Stephanie, review of *The Death of Mr. Angel, Booklist,* January 15, 1993, p. 889.

■ For More Information See

BOOKS

Children's Literature Review, Gale, Volume 11, 1986.

Crouch, Marcus, *The Nesbit Tradition: The Children's Novel in England, 1945-1970,* Ernest Benn Limited, 1972.

PERIODICALS

Horn Book, February, 1968, p. 14.

Los Angeles Times Book Review, March 6, 1994, p. 8.

Publishers Weekly, November 22, 1993, p. 64.

School Library Journal, April, 1992, p. 119; April, 1995, p. 153.

—*Sketch by Carol Brennan*

Guy Gavriel Kay

■ Personal

Born November 7, 1954, in Weyburn, Saskatchewan, Canada; son of Samuel Kopple (a surgeon) and Sybil (an artist; maiden name, Birstein) Kay; married Laura Beth Cohen (a marketing consultant), July 15, 1984; children: two sons. *Education:* University of Manitoba, B.A., 1975; University of Toronto, LL.B., 1978.

■ Addresses

Home—Toronto, Ontario, Canada.

■ Career

Worked as editorial consultant on posthumous book by J. R. R. Tolkien, *The Silmarillion*, 1974-75; practiced law, 1981-82; Canadian Broadcasting Corporation (CBC-Radio), Toronto, Ontario, writer and producer in drama department, 1982-89; writer.

■ Member

Association of Canadian Television and Radio Artists, Law Society of Upper Canada.

■ Awards, Honors

Scales of Justice Award for best media treatment of a legal issue, Canadian Law Reform Commission, 1985, for *Second Time Around*; Casper Award for best speculative fiction novel in Canada, 1986, for *The Wandering Fire*; Casper Award, 1987; World Fantasy Award nominee and Aurora Award, 1991, both for *Tigana*.

■ Writings

"THE FIONAVAR TAPESTRY"

The Summer Tree, McClelland & Stewart, 1984, Arbor House, 1985.
The Wandering Fire, Arbor House, 1986.
The Darkest Road, Arbor House, 1986.

"THE SARANTINE MOSAIC"

Sailing to Sarantium: Book One of The Sarantine Mosaic, HarperPrism, 1999.
Lord of Emperors: Book Two of The Sarantine Mosaic, HarperPrism, 2000.

FANTASY NOVELS

Tigana, Viking, 1990.
A Song for Arbonne, Crown, 1992.
The Lions of Al-Rassan, Viking, 1995.

OTHER

(Editor with Christopher Tolkien) J. R. R. Tolkien, *The Silmarillion*, Houghton, 1977.

Also author of radio drama *Second Time Around*.

■ Sidelights

The fantasy novels of Canadian writer Guy Gavriel Kay have become bestsellers and have won critical acclaim for their appealing protagonists, lively pacing, and deft interweaving of complex plot lines. Best known for "The Fionavar Tapestry" trilogy from the mid-1980s, Kay has progressed from the pure fantasy genre into works of fiction that mine the treasures of medieval European history for inspiration. "Guy Kay creates complex psychological characters and a rich sense of ambience, place and time,"declared *Washington Post Book World* writer John H. Riskind, who has also hailed Kay's novels as being "resonant and powerful, almost impossible to put down, satisfying the reader on multiple levels."

Kay was born in a small town in the prairie province of Saskatchewan in 1954, and he grew up in nearby Winnipeg, Manitoba. His father was a surgeon, and his mother an artist. Kay went on to pursue a degree in philosophy from the University of Manitoba, but his education was interrupted by a fortuitous opportunity. Through a connection to the family of the woman who had become the second wife of famed British novelist J. R. R. Tolkien, Kay was introduced to Tolkien's son, Christopher. A medievalist by profession, Tolkien had gained a cult following with his 1937 fantasy novel *The Hobbit,* and continued the story about the mythological Middle Earth kingdom with a trilogy of books in the 1960s known as *The Lord of the Rings.* Tolkien left behind a cache of other fantasy writings when he died in 1973, and Kay, a devoted enthusiast of the Tolkien books, was invited by the son to England to help assemble the materials for publication. The result was *The Silmarillion,* published in 1977 to great success; Kay and Christopher Tolkien were listed as joint editors. "The public didn't have any idea who I was, except for the dyed-in-the-wool Tolkien junkies," Kay told *Maclean's* writer Ann Jansen in 1992. "But the industry did, because *The Silmarillion* was a monstrous success."

Kay went on to earn a law degree from the University of Toronto in 1978, but practiced only briefly. Instead, he found an opportune way to merge his literary ambitions with his training, taking a job with the Canadian Broadcasting Corporation in 1982 as a writer and producer of radio and television dramas. Kay was particularly associated with the television series *The Scales of Justice,* which dramatized landmark cases in Canadian history, for seven years.

Fionavar

However, the publication of *The Silmarillion* incited a spate of fantasy novels, and Kay was dismayed by the second-rate imitators of Tolkien and the other masters of the genre that he found on bookstore and library shelves. Thus he went to work on writing his own series, "The Fionavar Tapestry." Its first installment, *The Summer Tree,* was published in 1984, and like all of Kay's books it became a tremendous commercial success. The novel introduced five University of Toronto students who find themselves suddenly immersed in an entirely different realm—that of Fionavar—and must fight to save both it and themselves.

As *The Summer Tree* opens, the students have been invited to a Celtic studies conference by a reclusive academic named Lorenzo Marcus, but Marcus is actually an ambassador from Fionavar who has been charged with the task of bringing representatives from other universes back to Fionavar for a royal jubilee. Thus the students find themselves in a meta-world that possesses characteristics of many other worlds and mythologies; Fionavar is the "Weaver's World" where all of these other belief systems—Celtic tenets, Norse legends, matriarchal practices—find common ground. A magical Tapestry of Life is the repository for the answers as to how and why all these philosophies are interrelated.

Each of the five Toronto characters has distinctive strengths and weaknesses, which find a way to interweave on Fionavar as well: Dave's self-esteem has been damaged by a father who favors his brother over him; Paul's girlfriend died in an accident; Kevin is handsome and well-liked, but realizes his world is shallow; Jennifer's heart has been saddened by the end of a relationship; and Kim is a loner. As *The Summer Tree* gets underway, the students learn that Fionavar is in grave

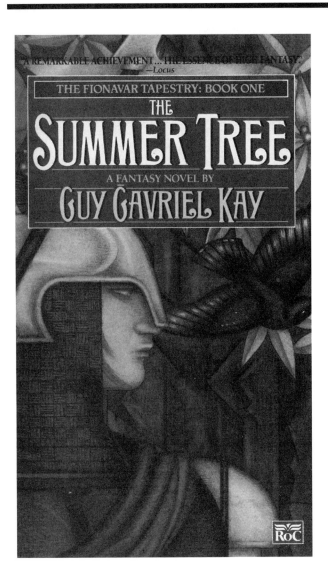

The lives of five university students are changed forever when they meet a man who is actually a wizard in this 1984 fantasy.

danger: the malevolent Rakoth Maugrim, imprisoned for athousand years, has escaped, and plans to abscond with the Tapestry of Life. The group of five ally with an exiled prince to save Fionavar, and find that they each possess a special power. In the end, one has sacrificed his life, and Jennifer has been sexually assaulted by Rakoth.

Booklist reviewer Sally Estes found *The Summer Tree* "an ambitious undertaking that succeeds in itself and as a precursor of what is to come." Though the work did invoke some comparisons to Tolkien's books, in her essay for the *St. James Guide to Fantasy Writers* Maureen Speller called

Kay "among the foremost modern fantasy writers on the strength of the *Fionavar Tapestry*." Speller noted that while Kay's books and Tolkien's classic cycle shared some similarities, the former "nevertheless set a new standard in what could be achieved in original fantasy writing."

The second installment of the Fionavar trilogy, *The Wandering Fire*, was published in 1986. Here the students return to Fionavar a year later, and Jennifer is carrying Rakoth's child, which is not expected to survive. A perpetual winter has descended upon Fionovar, the curse of a wicked magician who has allied with Rakoth. However,

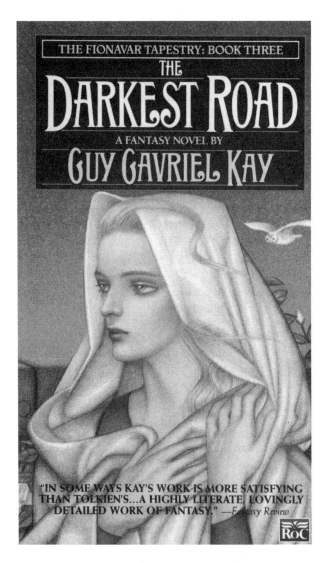

In the final book of the "Fionavar Tapestry" trilogy, Darien, the child born of Darkness and Light, becomes a crucial link to Fionavar's destiny.

the students have brought with them representatives from the Arthurian legends to assist them in saving the Tapestry of Life. Jennifer emerges as the Arthurian female Guinevere, and a cabal of virtuous deities help the students shatter the magic cauldron and end the winter on Fionavar. Another student, Kevin, loses his life—sacrificed to the Mother Goddess on Midsummer's Eve—but like Paul, he remains a guiding spirit in the plot. *Booklist* reviewer Estes termed *The Wandering Fire* "a most satisfying sequel" and a book "rich in mythological lore."

Critics also commended Kay for creating a believable cast of innocents who, like readers, were utterly new to the strange universe of Fionavar. Kay's deftand full delineation of each character is considered one of the trilogy's primary strengths, and his convincing description of a complex world won additional praise. Kay concluded the trilogy with another book published in 1986, *The Darkest Road.* As it opens, spring has finally arrived, but the rains bring disease. Kim persuades a nation of giants known as the Paraiko to take their side, and the armies of good arrive at Rakoth's fortress to do battle.

"Even the prose weighs a ton," noted a *Kirkus Reviews* assessment of *The Darkest Road*, commenting upon the very intricate layer of plot, action, and cast created by Kay, "a density that's often impenetrable." Jennifer's son Darien, feeling that the pro-Fionavar forces have rejected him because of his mixed heritage, steals a dagger with magical properties and heads off, ostensibly, to fight for Rakoth's side. Darien becomes "the random thread in the Weaver's story, the one who can control many destinies by his choice," explained Penny Blubaugh in *Voice of Youth Advocates.* "Like Tolkien, Kay recognizes that there must be sacrifice as well as a happy ending and the Fionavar trilogy is more successful than most modern fantasies for acknowledging this," observed Speller in *St. James Guide to Fantasy Writers.*

The Fionavar books were a success for Kay both in English and in foreign-language editions. By 1989 he had quit his job with the CBC, but later said that his years writing radio and television drama, especially for *The Scales of Justice,* helped give his works their gripping pace so often cited by critics. "I proudly acknowledge my sense of the operatic and theatrical," he told Ann Jansen of *Maclean's.* "I want to give the readers that page-

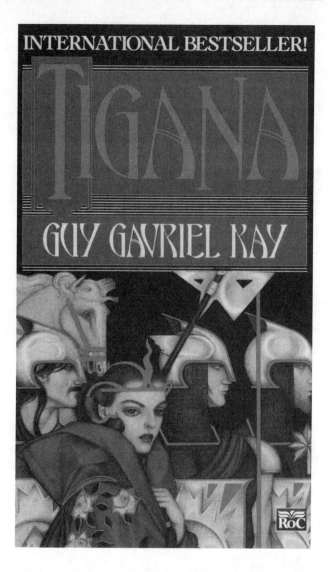

Magic and myth fill the pages of this 1990 novel about the land of Tigana—a once free world now ruled by the tyrant king Brandin.

turning energy." As a writer, Kay has been fortunate enough to be able to ensconce himself in a psychically rich part of the world to inspire his prose. He traveled to Crete and New Zealand to write two of the Fionavar books, and then arrived in Tuscany to research and write his next project, *Tigana,* which waspublished in 1990. Here he created another fantasy world, but one which bears some resemblance to Renaissance Italy.

Tigana is threatened by sorcerer-king Brandin, who battles to erase from history the very word "Tigana." The Mediterranean realm was once a powerful and noble kingdom, but Brandin's beloved son died in a battle against it, and he has made its destruction his revenge. After erasing its borders, he has been able to cast a spell that renders the very word Tigana unhearable. A few surviving Tiganans band together to fight him, and their lost prince, Alessan, and a troubadour named Devin also join the cause. The courtesan Dianora becomes a spy in Brandin's camp, and achieves in the end what bloodshed could not. Reviewing the novel for *Voice of Youth Advocates,* Edith S. Tyson termed *Tigana* an even more intricate creation than the Fionavar trilogy. "This well crafted, fully realized mega-fantasy is designed to appeal to the fans of Tolkien and Donaldson," Tyson wrote. "It is not for casual readers or for the faint of heart."

Other reviewers found problems with Kay's post-Fionavar effort, and commented that the characters did not emerge as the well-rounded personalities who saved Fionavar. The troubadours, outlaws, exiles, and magicians who made up the large cast of *Tigana* were faulted for being too attractive and heroic. Some critics also found that the intersection of an array of mythologies and worlds was confusing. "There is a sense that this novel was intended to be much more closely related to the Fionavar trilogy than it is now," assessed Speller in the *St. James Guide to Fantasy Writers.*

Medieval Sagas

Kay set his next book in the Mediterranean world as well. The 1992 fantasy, *A Song for Arbonne,* takes place in a medieval Europe where Christianity never took hold. Arbonne is in Provence, a place in modern times that is part of the south of France; here, a more progressive outlook on gender issues fostered the rise of the troubadour in the twelfth century. These wandering poets/ musicians sang verse, in a dialect called *langue d'oc,* about romantic love, nature, and war. In Kay's novel, the most famous among them is Bertran of Arbonne. In contrast, the disintegrating patriarchal kingdom of Gorhaut to the north is ruled by the brutal, corrupt King Ademar. Blaise, an honorable young man from Ademar's court, flees this world to Arbonne, where he becomes a mercenary soldier in the war ignited by his own father against Arbonne and its heretical system that worships a female deity. Blaise eventually challenges Ademar for the throne.

If you enjoy the works of Guy Gavriel Kay, you may also want to check out the following books:

Steven R. Brust, *Brokedown Palace,* 1986.
Katherine Kurtz, *Deryni Rising,* 1970.
Diana L. Paxson, *The White Raven,* 1988.

The liberal climate and revolutionary rethinking of masculine and feminine behaviors in Provence and the Languedoc region—before they became an actual part of France—came to a repressive close with the events surrounding the Albigensian Crusade. Kay's novel, however, has a more positive ending. As the author explained to Ann Jansen of *Maclean's,* "I'm basing my works on a period, but I'm not writing *about* that period. I reinterpret it in order to allow for some reflection on how we didn't have to end up where we are today," Kay stressed.

A Song for Arbonne was published to positive reviews. "This panoramic, absorbing novel beautifully creates an alternate version of the medieval world," a *Publishers Weekly* reviewer wrote. Candace Smith of *Booklist* described it as a "lush, lengthy medieval saga" with a "compelling narrative." However, a later assessment in the *St. James Guide to Fantasy Writers* faulted *A Song for Arbonne* for its scope. "The novel is strong on background flavor, and many of its characters are as attractive as those in *Tigana,* but the plot might easily have been accomplished in half the pages," Speller remarked.

Kay's next novel also tackled a historically significant epoch, though here he created a complex series of nations and alliances under entirely fictitious names. However, many critics remarked that *The Lions of Al-Rassan* (1995) was entirely reminiscent of a period of Spanish medieval history, when Christians, Moors, and Jews enjoyed a tenuous but culturally rich coexistence. The novel is set on a peninsular land called Esperana, ruled by Asharites who had come from desert lands. As the story opens, this once powerful group's hold on the conquered land is waning. Esperana has disintegrated into rival city-kingdoms, and a holy war against the imperialist Jaddites seems imminent. The Jaddites are led by Rodrigo Belmonte, and two other characters who play crucial roles:

a female physician and a poet-courtier. The novel comes to an emotionally wrenching conclusion. Margaret Miles, writing in *Voice of Youth Advocates,* called Kay's sixth book "yet another monumentally impressive historical novel." His heroes and the wide cast of other figures, Miles noted, "come vividly to life, set in the matrix of an equally vivid and complex society and involved in a plot as intricate and subtle as the characters themselves."

Kay began another trilogy with his 1999 novel, *Sailing to Sarantium: Book One of The Sarantine Mosaic.* Again, the Mediterranean landscape pro-

vides the backdrop. The book's protagonist is a mosaic artisan living in Rome at the time of the Visigoths in the sixth century. The Roman Empire has fallen, but the center of power has shifted eastward to Sarantium—an ersatz Byzantine empire. The artist, Caius Crispin, has been invited to Sarantium's capital to work on a massive mosaic project for its famous church. Since Crispin has recently lost his entire family in a plague, he accepts the mission. Before he departs the queen learns of his plans, however, and she sends with him a secret message to deliver to Sarantium's brutal emperor. Along the way, Crispin rescues a prostitute, and once in Sarantium, becomes embroiled in political and religious discord. "*Sarantium* also harbors intriguing elements of magic, adding the chiaroscuro of pagan blood-worship and alchemic transmutation to this tale about a people terrified of darkness and night," observed John Burns, writing in *Quill & Quire.* A *Publishers Weekly* review remarked that "Kay is at his best when describing the intertwining of art and religion or explicating the ancient craft of mosaic work." In 2000 Kay published the second book in the trilogy, *Lord of Emperors.*

Kay told *Locus,* "The aspect of fantasy I'm most interested in now is the most difficult to explain. I'm beginning to see fantasy as a way of looking at history, as an antidote to what they call 'faction'—fiction using real people, real lives, and embedding them in narrative." He added, "In *Sailing to Sarantium* and *Lord of Emperors,* the reign of Justinian and Theodora, with Count Belisarius and the eunuch Narses, is clearly my source, but I'm saying right from the beginning that this is not even *pretending* to know what the real people were like. It's a fantasy on themes."

Kay has said that his novels usually take him nearly a year to research, and another to write. Creating entirely fictional characters, who participate in actual historic events and sometimes even alter their outcome, has allowed his creativity to flourish. "I lack the utter autonomy some writers have," Kay told *Maclean's.* "I don't want to write on the back of a real person. That smacks of hubris."

"Elegant, sweeping, and colorful...one of those books you wish would never end."
—*San Francisco Chronicle*

GUY GAVRIEL KAY

A SONG FOR ARBONNE

RoC

Kay's 1992 fantasy features a young man who leaves his native Gorhaut to settle in Arbonne—a place he must eventually defend against Gorhaut.

■ Works Cited

Blubaugh, Penny, review of *The Darkest Road, Voice of Youth Advocates,* April, 1987, p. 38.

Burns, John, review of *Sailing to Sarantium, Quill & Quire*, October, 1998, p. 35.

Review of *The Darkest Road, Kirkus Reviews*, October 1, 1986, p. 1475.

Estes, Sally, review of *The Summer Tree, Booklist*, September 1, 1985, p. 4.

Estes, Sally, review of *The Wandering Fire, Booklist*, May 15, 1986, p. 1361.

"Guy Gavriel Kay: Lord of Fantasy," *Locus*, May, 2000, pp. 6-7, 63-64.

Jansen, Ann, "Castles in the Air: Guy Gavriel Kay Mixes History and Fantasy," *Maclean's*, December 14, 1992.

Miles, Margaret, review of *The Lions of Al-Rassan, Voice of Youth Advocates*, October, 1995, p. 234.

"Playing Fast and Fun with Past Events," *Maclean's*, October 26, 1998, p. 82.

Riskind, John H., review of *The Lions of Al-Rassan, Washington Post Book World*, July 28, 1996, p. 8.

Review of *Sailing to Sarantium, Publishers Weekly*, February 8, 1999, p. 199.

Smith, Candace, review of *A Song for Arbonne, Booklist*, January 15, 1993, p. 878.

Review of *A Song for Arbonne, Publishers Weekly*, November 23, 1992, pp. 56-57.

Speller, Maureen, "Guy Gavriel Kay," *St. James Guide to Fantasy Writers*, St. James Press, 1996, pp. 318-19.

Tyson, Edith S., review of *Tigana, Voice of Youth Advocates*, April, 1991, p. 44.

■ For More Information See

PERIODICALS

Booklist, January 1, 1999, p. 842; March 15, 2000, p. 1335.

Fantasy Review, January, 1985; December, 1986.

Globe and Mail (Toronto), February 9, 1985; June 28, 1986; September 8, 1990.

Kirkus Reviews, May 15, 1986, p. 752.

Library Journal, October 15, 1985, p. 104; November 15, 1986, p. 112; August, 1990, p. 147; December, 1998, p. 161.

Locus, June, 1990; September, 1992; November, 1992.

Maclean's, March 23, 1987; July 1, 1995.

Magazine of Fantasy and Science Fiction, December, 1995.

New Statesman, November 28, 1986.

Publishers Weekly, May 16, 1986, pp. 72-73; October 10, 1986, p. 81.

Quill & Quire, May, 1995, p. 33.

Voice of Youth Advocates, December, 1986, p. 237.

ON-LINE

Guy Gavriel Kay's authorized Web site is located at http://www.brightweavings.com.*

Harry Mazer

■ Personal

Born May 31, 1925, in New York, NY; son of Sam (a dressmaker) and Rose (a dressmaker; maiden name, Lazevnick) Mazer; married Norma Fox (a novelist), February 12, 1950; children: Anne, Joseph, Susan, Gina. *Education:* Union College, B.A., 1948; Syracuse University, M.A., 1960.

■ Addresses

Agent—Marilyn Marlow, Curtis Brown Ltd., 10 Astor Pl., New York, NY 10003.

■ Career

New York Central Railroad, brake man and switchtender, 1950-55; New York Construction, Syracuse, sheet metal worker, 1957-59; Central Square School, Central Square, NY, English teacher, 1959-60; Aerofin Corp., Syracuse, welder, 1960-63; full-time writer, 1963—. *Military service:* U.S. Army Air Force, 1943-45; became sergeant; received Purple Heart and Air Medal with four bronze oak leaf clusters.

■ Member

Authors Guild, Authors League of America, Society of Children's Book Writers and Illustrators, American Civil Liberties Union.

■ Awards, Honors

Best of the Best Books list, American Library Association (ALA), 1970-73, for *Snow Bound; Kirkus* Choice list, 1974, for *The Dollar Man;* Best Books for Young Adults, ALA, 1977, and Children's Choice, International Reading Association-Children's Book Council, 1978, both for *The Solid Gold Kid;* Best Books for Young Adults, ALA, and Dorothy Canfield Fisher Children's Book Award nomination, Vermont Congress of Parents and Teachers-Vermont Department of Libraries, both 1979, both for *The War on Villa Street;* Best Books, *New York Times,* 1979, Books for the Teen Age, New York Public Library, 1980, Best Books for Young Adults, ALA, 1981, and Best of the Best Books list, ALA, 1970-83, all for *The Last Mission; Booklist* Contemporary Classics list, 1984, and "Preis der Lesseratten" (West Germany), both for *Snow Bound;* Arizona Young Readers Award nomination, Arizona State Library Association, 1985, for *The Island*

Keeper: A Tale of Courage and Survival; Best Books for Young Adults, ALA, 1986, for *I Love You, Stupid!;* Books for the Teen Age, New York Public Library, 1986, and International Reading Association-Children's Book Council Young Adult Choice list, 1987, both for *Hey, Kid! Does She Love Me?;* Best Books for Young Adults, ALA, 1987, Iowa Teen Award Master list, Iowa Educational Media Association, 1988, and West Australian Young Reader's Book Award, Australian Library and Information Association, 1989, all for *When the Phone Rang;* Best Books for Young Adults, ALA, Books for Reluctant Young Adult Readers, ALA, 1988, and Books for the Teen Age, New York Public Library, 1988, all for *The Girl of His Dreams;* Books for the Teen Age, New York Public Library, 1989, for *Heartbeat;* Books for Reluctant Young AdultReaders, ALA, 1989, for *City Light;* Quick Picks for Reluctant Young Adult Readers, ALA, 1998, for *Twelve Shots: Outstanding Stories about Guns;* Best Books, *School Library Journal,* 1998, and Fanfare list, *Horn Book,* 1999, both for *The Wild Kid.*

■ Writings

NOVELS; FOR YOUNG ADULTS

Guy Lenny, Delacorte, 1971.

Snow Bound, Delacorte, 1973.

The Dollar Man, Delacorte, 1974.

The War on Villa Street, Delacorte, 1978.

The Last Mission, Delacorte, 1979.

The Island Keeper: A Tale of Courage and Survival, Delacorte, 1981.

I Love You, Stupid!, Crowell, 1981.

Hey, Kid! Does She Love Me?, Crowell, 1984.

When the Phone Rang, Scholastic, 1985.

Cave under the City, Crowell, 1986.

The Girl of His Dreams, Crowell, 1987.

City Light, Scholastic, 1988.

Someone's Mother Is Missing, Delacorte, 1990.

Who Is Eddie Leonard?, Delacorte, 1993.

(Editor) *Twelve Shots: Outstanding Short Stories about Guns,* Delacorte, 1997.

The Dog in the Freezer: Three Novellas, Simon & Schuster, 1997.

The Wild Kid, Simon & Schuster, 1998.

WITH NORMA FOX MAZER

The Solid Gold Kid, Delacorte, 1977.

Heartbeat, Bantam, 1989.

Bright Days, Stupid Nights, Bantam, 1992.

■ Adaptations

Snow Bound was produced as a National Broadcasting Company (NBC) "After School Special" in 1978. *Snow Bound* and *The Last Mission* were recorded on audio cassette by Listening Library, 1985.

■ Sidelights

In addition to being part of a writing family that includes wife Norma Fox Mazer and daughter Anne Mazer, novelist Harry Mazer has received critical acclaim for his many young adult novels—including *The Island Keeper, Cave under the City,* and *Who Is Eddie Leonard?*—which illustrate the values of perseverance, self-esteem, and inner fortitude. Noting that, "despite their predicaments, Mazer's protagonists usually emerge morally victorious," *Twentieth-Century Young Adult Writers* contributor Mary Lystad cited as Mazer's strength his depiction of the "emotional turmoil, the humor and pain" of adolescence. "His characters are resilient and strong," Lystad continued. "His endings emphasize compassion, understanding, resourcefulness, and honesty."

"A dream is made by real effort," Mazer once explained in an essay in *Something about the Author Autobiography Series (SAAS).* Mazer was in his mid-thirties when he and his wife began to write every day; they wrote for the "women's true confessions" market, using the money to support the family. "My writing dismayed me," the author revealed; "I had dark moments when I wondered why I was going on with this. . . . I wrote a lot about my feelings, interpreting my dreams, trying to keep myself together."

In 1971 Mazer's "real effort" resulted in *Guy Lenny,* his first novel, and since then, many of his novels have been translated into German, French, Finnish, and Danish. Kenneth L. Donelson asserted in *Voice of Youth Advocates* that "Mazer writes about young people caught in the midst of moral crises, often of their own making. Searching for a way out, they discover themselves, or rather they learn that the first step in extricating themselves from their physical and moral dilemmas is self-discovery. Intensely moral as Mazer's books are," continued Donelson, "they present young people thinking and talking and acting believably," a characteristic that accounts for Mazer's continued popularity among readers and critics alike.

A story of raw survival by Harry Mazer

After fifteen-year-old Tony Laporte steals his family's car and picks up hitchhiker Cindy Reichert, they must fight for their lives in this 1973 adventure.

The son of hard-working Polish-Jewish immigrants, Mazer grew up in an apartment building in the Bronx, New York. The building was part of a two-block complex called the Coops, and Mazer recalled in *SAAS* that "you could feel the optimistic spirit that built these houses—in the centralcourtyards with their gardens and fountains, in the library, the gymnasium, and the kindergarten. The Coops were special, an island, a community, a village in a great city built on a shared dream of cooperation and social justice." Mazer shared the bedroom of the two-room apartment with his brother, while his parents slept in the living room, which also served

as a dining room and kitchen. The halls and the stairs were Mazer's playground, and he grew up between two worlds—the park and the street—both of which he would later use in his novels. "The park was mine, so big it was limitless," recalled Mazer. The many games that the street offered, such as marbles and chalk-drawing, also appealed to Mazer, as did the huge fires built in empty lots after dark.

Lack of money was always a problem for Mazer during these years. While he did not retain many memories of his school days, he remembered reading *The Gingerbread Man* and *Little Black Sambo*, for reading was among his favorite pastimes. "I read and ate," he noted, recalling memories of lying on the couch with his nose in a book and "a pile of apple cores on the floor." Mazer read everything from series books and adventure stories to the collected works of Charles Dickens. "Two of my all-time favorite books were *Robinson Crusoe*, the story of a man alone on a desert island, and *Tarzan of the Apes*," stated Mazer in *SAAS*.

Changes loomed large in Mazer's life when he entered his high-school years. Questions about his future occupied his mind; jobs were scarce at the time,and many employers wouldn't hire Jews. If he had been a dutiful son, Mazer later reflected, he would have become a teacher; "but I was in rebellion. I was impatient. I wanted to be great, famous. . . . My secret desire was to be a writer, but I knew nothing about how to make it happen. I had the idea that if I could only write it down, if I could only put all my feelings into words, I would finally figure everything out (whatever everything was)." Mazer took the competitive exam for the Bronx High School of Science and got in, but the courses that most interested him were English and history, and the questions concerning his future still lingered.

Going to War

World War II was on Mazer's mind also. At age seventeen he qualified to join the Army Air Force Cadets, but had to wait until he was eighteen to serve. "I prayed that the war didn't end before I got in," Mazer remembered in his *SAAS* essay. While he waited, he started attending college classes, only to quit after less than a week. The army finally called him, and Mazer served for two and a half years. Starting out as an airplane mechanic, he volunteered for aerial gunnery school, training as a ball-turret and waist gunner. After training, Mazer was assigned to a crew on a B-17 bomber. In December of 1944 the young crew headed for Europe and flew their first mission two months later. Their last mission was flown in April when the plane was shot down over Czechoslovakia; only Mazer and one other crew member survived. "I remember thinking afterward that there had to be a reason why I had survived," recalled Mazer. "I didn't think it was God. It was chance. Luck. But why me? Chance can't be denied as a

Jack Raab, a Jewish fifteen-year-old who lies about his age to get into the military during World War II, learns the reality of war when he is sent to a German POW camp in this 1979 novel.

factor in life, but I clung to the thought that there was a reason for my survival."

Mazer was discharged from the army in October of 1945, and days later began attending classes at a liberal arts college. He began writing, but his work "was too serious and self-conscious. I turned each word over in my head before I allowed it out into the open. . . . I wrote, but I was full of doubt, my standards were miles higher than my abilities. I suffered over what I wrote and didn't write any more than I had to." Graduating with a liberal arts degree, Mazer took a blue-collar job while struggling to define himself as a writer. A three-month course in welding resulted in a job in an auto-body shop. "I was dramatizing myself," Mazer later admitted, "imagining myself a leader of the downtrodden, pointing the way to the future. . . . I was idealistic. I was unrealistic. Most of all I was avoiding the real issues of my life. I didn't have the belief or the nerve to say I was a writer, to begin writing and let everything else take care of itself."

Politics also interested Mazer during this period; it was while working on a campaign that he met Norma Fox for the second time. He had met her two years earlier when she was fifteen and he was twenty-one, but it was the second meeting that started their on-again, off-again romance. A year later Norma began college, but Mazer pressed her to get married. "Norma said yes, we'd get married, then she said no," Mazer remembered. "When she was with me it was yes, but when she went back to school it was no again." The couple finally married and settled in a tiny apartment in New York City, but soon moved back upstate to Schenectady, and then to Utica, finally settling in Syracuse. Mazer worked at various jobs, doing welding, sheet metal work, and track work for the railroad. "I was moody and didn't talk and I wasn't nice to be around," he recalled of these years. "I didn't know what was bothering me. I only knew I had to get out, move, walk off the mood. I'd walk along the railroad tracks and pick wild asparagus or I'd go to Three Rivers, where I'd sit under a tree and watch birds. I thought if I could only write down what I was feeling—if only I could put thought to paper—I'd know what I ought to do. But I didn't know how to start."

Dives into Writing Career

After ten years of factory work, Mazer became a teacher. It was at this point that he and Norma talked, discovered that they both longed to be writers, and began writing every day. Mazer lost his teaching job and returned to factory work, taking paperbacks with him, trying to understand how a story worked. The insurance money from an accident finally enabled him to quit his job and begin writing full-time; the couple were soon writing two confession stories a week. "These stories demanded that I develop a character, a plot, action that rose to a climax, and a satisfying ending. And I had to do it every week, week after week. It was a demanding school. I was being forced to write to stay out of the factory," Mazer wrote in *SAAS*. He also

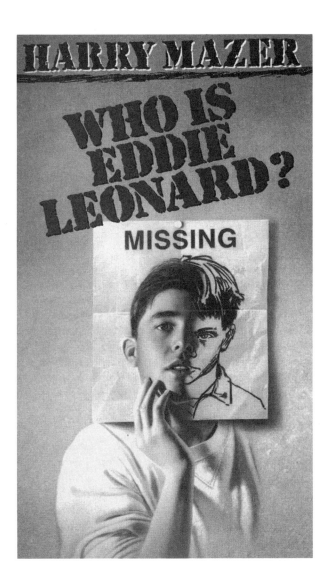

Published in 1993, this moving novel features fifteen-year-old Eddie Leonard who needs to find out the truth about himself and his real parents.

tried other forms of writing, including televisionscripts and pieces for literary magazines. The Mazers' agent finally suggested they try the children's field.

A piece in a "Dear Abby" column gave Mazer the idea for his first children's book. The column was about a boy who was concerned about an older girl he liked. She was going with someone else who was no good for her, and the boy wanted to know how he could break them up. "It was the germ that started my first book, *Guy Lenny*," Mazer revealed in his essay. *Guy Lenny* is the story of a boy whose parents are divorced, a subject that children's books of the time did not deal with. His mother has left him, and he is living with his father when she returns to claim him. "It's a children's story because it's about a boy and is told from his point of view," explains Mazer in *SAAS*; "it's also an adult story because it's about growing up and having to live with some of the hard, intractable things of life. And that's what made it a young-adult book, a new category of fiction that was still to be named." Norma's novel *I, Trissy* had just been accepted for publication; Mazer sent his book off reluctantly, expecting the worst. "There is no moment to equal the moment when your first book is taken," Mazer claimed, recalling the call from his agent saying that his book had found a publisher.

Many of Mazer's novels use characters from earlier books, and father-and-son relationships appear again and again. "I've gone about the work of writing like a bird building a nest each year with the bits of thread andpaper I snatch up in the street, but also from the scraps of memory I weave together in book after book," the novelist noted in *SAAS*. "I didn't have a plan, there was no agenda, no burning purpose, no passion about injustice," he continues. "There was passion, but it was a passion for the characters, for the world they lived in."

A *Publishers Weekly* contributor maintained that Mazer "creates credible characters . . . and incorporates splashes of humor while maintaining the established mood and tone." In the novel *The Girl of His Dreams*, for example, Mazer relates the romance of Willis and Sophie, two ordinary young adults, with "a credibility apart from [the book's] fairy-tale ending," in the opinion of Marianne Gingher in the *Los Angeles Times*. Willis is a factory worker and dedicated runner who has a clear vi-

Each story in Mazer's 1997 collection of novellas centers on dogs and their owners.

sion of exactly what the girl of his dreams should be like. Sophie does not fit this image, and their relationship develops slowly and awkwardly. "No run-of-the-mill, boy meets girl story here," stated Libby K. White in *School Library Journal*, adding that the novel "is romantic without being either mushy or explicitly sexual. Willis and Sophie are attractive characters who will interest and involve readers."

Snow Bound is another tale of two mismatched teens who are caught unprepared for a New York blizzard and must cooperate to survive. Tony is a spoiled rich kid who sets out to get revenge on his parents for not letting him keep a stray dog. He steals his mother's car and takes off in the middle of a snowstorm, picking up hitchhiker Cindy along

the way. Besides getting lost, Tony wrecks the car in a desolate area, and he and Cindy must save themselves from the cold and a pack of wild dogs. "The relationship that develops between the two of them is sensitively handled, never foolishly romanticized, and will probably be an easy thing for young readers to identify with," maintains Tom Heffernan in *Children's Literature*. *New York Times Book Review* contributor Cathleen Burns Elmer concluded that "the final measure of the book's capacity to enthrall lies in the *mature* reader's willingness to suspend disbelief. 'Snow Bound' is a crackling tale; Mazer tells it with vigor and authority."

Uses Wartime Experiences

Highly praised by critics, *The Last Mission*, based in part on Mazer's own experiences in World War II, "represents an amazing leap in writing, far surpassing anything [the author] had written before," according to Donelson. Jewish fifteen-year-old Jack Raab is so desperate to fight against Hitler that he borrows his older brother's identification to enlist in the Army Air Forces. Jack is trained as a gunner, and he and his fellow crew members fly more than twenty missions out of England before being hit by enemy fire. Jack bails out and is the only one to survive—but ends up a German prisoner of war. While war stories are common, Donelson maintained that *The Last Mission* "conveys better than any other young adult novel, and better than most adult novels, the feeling of war and the desolation it leaves behind. . . . This book is a remarkable achievement, both for its theme and its portrait of a young man who searches and acts and finds the search futile and the actions incoherent." Paxton Davis asserted in the *New York Times Book Review*: "Mazer is a prize-winning writer for young people."

The main character in *I Love You, Stupid!* is faced with more typical adolescent problems. A senior in high school, Marcus wants to be a writer and is obsessed with sex. *School Library Journal* contributor Kay Webb O'Connell pointed out that Marcus's erotic dreams include almost every young female he meets—everyone but Wendy, a girl he knew in grade school. Marcus even goes so far as to babysit for a young divorced woman, hoping she'll become his lover. Wendy and Marcus finally make love, but Marcus, looking for a reason to do it every day, drives Wendy away. By the end of the book, they are back together, and Marcus realizes the importance of friendship and love. "It takes most of the book to get them together, but it's better that way; Marcus and Wendy are friends who become lovers," observed O'Connell, concluding that "they're honest and humorous; their conversations and adventures are fresh and funny."

Who Is Eddie Leonard? introduces readers to the fifteen-year-old title character, who lives with an eccentric elderly woman he calls "Grandmother." When she dies, he is left alone, feeling that he must belong somewhere. A poster of a missing child named Jason Diaz changes everything for Eddie. Seeing the resemblance between himself and the missing boy, and calculating that Jason would now also be fifteen years old, Eddie huntsdown the boy's family and introduces himself as their missing son. Now divorced and having given up their son as lost forever, Jason's parents are skeptical, and the missing boy's sister, Miller, is happy as an only child. Eddie becomes involved in this new family, and when the truth about his birth is finally discovered, he must suffer further loss. "Mazer has written a book teens will respond to," maintained *Voice of Youth Advocates* contributor Ruth E. Dishnow, "a story about the often painful search for self-identity." While *School Library Journal* reviewer Lucinda Snyder Whitehurst felt that Mazer's terse, detached style makes *Who Is Eddie Leonard?* more a "series of strong character studies" than a cohesive story, Chris Sherman had praise for the novel, writing in *Booklist* that Mazer's is "an emotionally charged story that readers will not be able to put down."

The Wild Kid finds twelve-year-old Sammy, who has Down's Syndrome, building a reputation as a no-good kid. Leaving the house without permission, Sammy gets his bike stolen and becomes lost in the woods outside of town while following the thief. In the forest he meets Kevin, a teen on the run. First Kevin's prisoner, Sammy gradually becomes the wild teen's friend, and Kevin ultimately helps the younger boy find his way home. Mazer's story was praised by several reviewers for its positive portrayal of a child with Down's Syndrome. *School Library Journal* contributor Carol A. Edwards asserted: "Vividly and with a fast pace, Mazer describes Sammy's world, his awful predicament, his magnificent spirit, and his incredible determination." Edwards concluded that *The Wild Kid* is "for anyone lookingfor an adventure, a survival story on many levels, or a compelling read."

Stories with Urban Settings

Other novels by Mazer include *The War on Villa Street,* about a boy's attempts to find stability in a family where his father's alcoholism and his mother's passivity mean constant upheaval and relocation. Ultimately his own passivity and sense of shame at his father's abuse cause the boy to fight back, building his own self-confidence in the process. *The War on Villa Street* was called "a moving, fast-paced story that once more proves Mazer's understanding of adolescence" by *School Library Journal* contributor Robert Unsworth. Also set in an urban area, *Cave under the City* takes place during the Great Depression, as two brothers find themselves parentless after their father's departure in search of work and their mother's subsequent col-

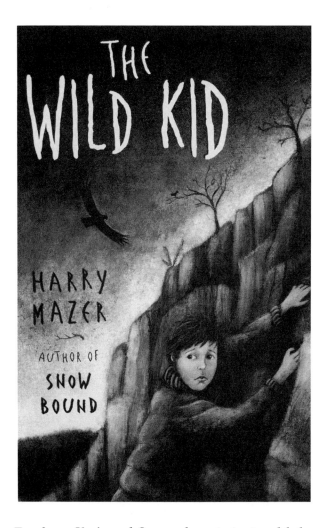

Two boys, Kevin and Sammy, learn to trust and help each other in this 1998 tale about the meaning of friendship.

If you enjoy the works of Harry Mazer, you may also want to check out the following books:

Marion Dane Bauer, *Face to Face*, 1991.
Gary L. Blackwood, *Wild Timothy*, 1987.
Gary Paulsen, *The River*, 1991.

lapse and hospitalization. When social workers attempt to separate the boys, they flee and live among New York City's homeless population until their father returns. *School Library Journal* contributor Christine Behrmann noted that *Cave under the City* contains "resonances of the plight of today's homeless."

In addition to novel-length books and a few collaborative efforts with his wife, Mazer has also written *The Dog in the Freezer*, a collection of three novellas. Focusing on dogs, the boys who own them, and the fathers who rule the family home, each of the stories has a slightly quirky perspective. In "My Life as a Boy," the family dog trades places with his human master for a day, while "Puppy Love" weaves a teen boy's summer crush on a pretty dog trainer with his growing affection for the puppy he adopted as a way of gaining the young woman's attention. "The Dog in the Freezer" finds a boy struggling to figure out how to bury a neighbor's dead dog rather than leave it lying on the street. While of the opinion that Mazer is more adept at longer fiction, a *Kirkus Reviews* contributor praised *The Dog in the Freezer* as "an interesting departure."

Drawing on his personal concerns about modern society, Mazer served as editor of *Twelve Shots: Outstanding Short Stories about Guns*, which was released in 1997. Inviting a dozen authors to write stories concerning "not the politics of the gun, not the heated arguments or the polemics, but the way guns are present in people's lives," Mazer assembles works by such well-known children's authors as Walter Dean Myers, Chris Lynch, Frederick Busch, and Rita Williams-Garcia, as well as contributing his own short story, based on his novel *The Last Mission*. While the stories included range from serious commentary on the devastation wrought by gun-related violence in modern society to humorous folk-like tales, Mazer's own anti-gun slant is made clear. "Destruction clearly outweighs redemption in the bulk of these stories," Elizabeth Bush commented in the *Bulletin of the Center for Children's Books*, "with manipulative power, paranoia, or profound despair generally behind the trigger." Including statistics about guns and other helpful information, *Twelve Shots* is "timely and thought provoking" as well as "an excellent springboard for discussion," according to *Booklist* contributor Helen Rosenberg.

From his novels to his shorter works of fiction, Mazer's writing has been characterized by reviewers as containing a belief in the essential goodness of people, particularly young people. As *Horn Book* reviewer Margaret A. Bush observed, Mazer's "characters are down to earth, very ordinary people who are flawed, inept, good. Their eccentricities, loneliness, and dreams are lightly touched with humor." In his *SAAS* essay, Mazer concluded: "I think underlying all my writing has always been the belief that beneath the surface of our differences there is a current, a dark stream that connects all of us, readers and writers, parents and children, the young and the old. Despite the erosion of time the child in us never dies. The search for love never ends, the need for connection, the desire to know who we are, and the need to find someone of our own to love. How else do I keep writing for young readers?"

■ Works Cited

Behrmann, Christine, review of *Cave under the City*, *School Library Journal*, December, 1986, pp. 105-06.

Bush, Elizabeth, review of *Twelve Shots: Outstanding Short Stories about Guns*, *Bulletin of the Center for Children's Books*, October, 1997, p. 61.

Bush, Margaret A., review of *The Girl of His Dreams*, *Horn Book*, March-April, 1988, pp. 209-10.

Davis, Paxton, review of *The Last Mission*, *New York Times Book Review*, December 2, 1979, p. 41.

Dishnow, Ruth E., review of *Who Is Eddie Leonard?*, *Voice of Youth Advocates*, April, 1994, p. 29.

Review of *The Dog in the Freezer: Three Novellas*, *Kirkus Reviews*, March 15, 1997, p. 466.

Review of *The Dog in the Freezer: Three Novellas*, *Publishers Weekly*, February 10, 1997, p. 84.

Donelson, Kenneth L., "Searchers and Doers: Heroes in Five Harry Mazer Novels," *Voice of Youth Advocates*, February, 1983, pp. 19-21.

Edwards, Carol A., review of *The Wild Kid, School Library Journal*, October, 1998, p. 140.

Elmer, Cathleen Burns, review of *Snow Bound, New York Times Book Review*, August 12, 1973, p. 8.

Gingher, Marianne, "A Boy Who Runs Meets a Girl Anxious to Catch Up," *Los Angeles Times*, March 12, 1988.

Heffernan, Tom, review of *Snow Bound, Children's Literature*, edited by Francelia Butler, Volume 4, Temple University Press, 1975, p. 206.

Lystad, Mary, *Twentieth-Century Young Adult Writers*, St. James Press, 1994, pp. 429-31.

Mazer, Harry, essay in *Something about the Author Autobiography Series*, Volume 11, Gale, 1991, pp. 223-40.

O'Connell, Kay Webb, review of *I Love You, Stupid!, School Library Journal*, October, 1981, p. 152.

Rosenberg, Helen, review of *Twelve Shots: Outstanding Short Stories about Guns, Booklist*, August, 1997.

Sherman, Chris, review of *Who Is Eddie Leonard?, Booklist*, November 15, 1993, p 615.

Unsworth, Robert, review of *The War on Villa Street, School Library Journal*, December, 1978, p. 62.

White, Libby K., review of *The Girl of His Dreams, School Library Journal*, January, 1988, pp. 86-87.

Whitehurst, Lucinda Snyder, review of *Who Is Eddie Leonard?, School Library Journal*, November, 1993, p. 125.

■ For More Information See

BOOKS

Children's Literature Review, Volume 16, Gale, 1989, pp. 125-33.

Nilsen, Alleen Pace, and Kenneth L. Donelson, *Literature for Today's Young Adults*, Scott, Foresman, 1985.

Reed, Arthea J. S., *Presenting Harry Mazer*, Twayne, 1996.

PERIODICALS

Booklist, March 15, 1997, p. 1236.

Bulletin of the Center for Children's Books, November, 1997, p. 109.

Kirkus Reviews, July 1, 1997, p. 1033.

Publishers Weekly, August 10, 1990, p. 446.

Voice of Youth Advocates, August, 1997, p. 190.

Norma Fox Mazer

■ Personal

Born May 15, 1931, in New York, NY; daughter of Michael and Jean (Garlen) Fox; married Harry Mazer (a novelist), February 12, 1950; children: Anne, Joseph, Susan, Gina. *Education:* Attended Antioch College, 1949-50, and Syracuse University, 1957-59. *Politics:* "I believe in people—despise institutions while accepting their necessity." *Religion:* "Jewish by birth, pantheistic by nature." *Hobbies and other interests:* Reading, racquetball, gardening.

■ Addresses

Agent—Elaine Markson, 44 Greenwich Avenue, New York, NY 10012; Abner Stein, 10 Roland Gardens, London SW7 3PH, England.

■ Career

Writer, 1964—. Has worked as a secretary at a radio station, punch press operator, waitress, and cashier.

■ Awards, Honors

National Book Award nomination, 1973, for *A Figure of Speech;* Lewis Carroll Shelf Award, University of Wisconsin, 1975, for *Saturday, the Twelfth of October;* Christopher Award, *New York Times* Outstanding Books of the Year, Best Books, *School Library Journal,* Best Books for Young Adults, American Library Association (ALA), Notable Book, ALA, and Lewis CarrollShelf Award, all 1976, all for *Dear Bill, Remember Me? and Other Stories;* Best Books for Young Adults, ALA, 1977, Children's Choice, Children's Book Council-International Reading Association, 1978, and 100 Best of the Best Books, ALA, 1993, all for *The Solid Gold Kid;* Best Books for Young Adults, ALA, 1979, Best Books, *School Library Journal,* 1979, and Best of the Best Books list, ALA, 1970-83, all for *Up in Seth's Room;* Austrian Children's Books list of honor and German Children's Literature prize, both 1982, both for *Mrs. Fish, Ape, and Me, the Dump Queen;* Edgar Award, Mystery Writers of America, 1982, and California Young Readers Medal, California Reading Association, 1985, both for *Taking Terri Mueller;* Best Books for Young Adults, ALA, 1983, for *Someone to Love;* Best Books for Young Adults, ALA, *New York Times* Outstanding Books of the Year list, and Books for the Teen Age, New York Public Library, all 1984, all for *Downtown;* Iowa Teen Award, Iowa Educational Media Association, 1985-86, for *When We First Met;* Children's Choice, Children's Book Council-

International Reading Association, 1986, for *A, My Name Is Ami;* Newbery Honor Book, Best Books, *School Library Journal,* Notable Book, ALA, Best Books for Young Adults, ALA, Children's Choice, Canadian Children's Books Council, *Horn Book* Fanfare selection, and Association of Booksellers for Children Choice, all 1988, all for *After the Rain;* Best Books for Young Adults, ALA, 1989, Iowa Teen Award, 1991, and One Hundred Best of the Best Books, 1968-93, ALA, all for *Silver;* Children's Choice, Children's Book Council-International Reading Association, German Literature Prize, and Books for the Teen Age, New York Public Library, all 1989, all for *Heartbeat;* Books for the TeenAge, New York Public Library, 1989, for *Silver* and *Heartbeat* and 1990, for *Waltzing on Water: Poetry by Women* and *Babyface;* Pick of the Lists, American Booksellers Association, 1990, for *Babyface, Bright Days, Stupid Nights, Out of Control,* and *Missing Pieces;* Best Books for Young Adults, ALA, 1994, for *Out of Control;* Best Books, *School Library Journal,* Editor's Choice, *Booklist,* both 1997, Best Books for Young Adults, ALA, 1998, all for *When She Was Good.*

■ Writings

NOVELS; FOR YOUNG ADULTS

I, Trissy, Delacorte, 1971.
A Figure of Speech (also see below), Delacorte, 1973.
Saturday, the Twelfth of October, Delacorte, 1975.
Dear Bill, Remember Me? and Other Stories, Delacorte, 1976.
Up in Seth's Room, Delacorte, 1979.
Mrs. Fish, Ape, and Me, the Dump Queen, Dutton, 1980, reissued as *Crazy Fish,* Morrow, 1998.
Taking Terri Mueller, Avon, 1981.
When We First Met (sequel to *A Figure of Speech;* also see below) Four Winds, 1982.
Summer Girls, Love Boys, and Other Short Stories, Delacorte, 1982.
Someone to Love, Delacorte, 1983.
(With Axel Daimler) *When We First Met* (screenplay based on novel of sametitle), Learning Corporation of America, 1984.
Downtown, Morrow, 1984.
Supergirl (novelization), Warner, 1984.
A, My Name Is Ami, Scholastic, 1986.
Three Sisters, Scholastic, 1986.
B, My Name Is Bunny, Scholastic, 1987.
After the Rain, Morrow, 1987.
Silver, Morrow, 1988.

C, My Name Is Cal, Scholastic, 1990.
Babyface, Morrow, 1990.
D, My Name Is Danita, Scholastic, 1991.
E, My Name Is Emily, Scholastic, 1991.
Out of Control, Morrow, 1993.
Missing Pieces, Morrow, 1995.
When She Was Good, Arthur A. Levine, 1997.
Good Night, Maman, Harcourt, 1999.

WITH HARRY MAZER

The Solid Gold Kid, Delacorte, 1977.
Heartbeat, Bantam, 1989.
Bright Days, Stupid Nights, Bantam, 1992.

OTHER

(Editor with Margery Lewis) *Waltzing on Water: Poetry by Women,* Dell, 1989.
(Editor with Jacqueline Woodson) *Just a Writer's Thing: A Collection of Prose and Poetry from the National Book Foundation's 1995 Summer Writing Camp,* National Book Foundation, 1996.

Contributor to anthologies, including *Sixteen: Short Stories by Outstanding Writers for Young Adults,* edited by Donald R. Gallo, Delacorte, 1984; *Short Takes: A Short Story Collection for Young Readers,* edited by Elizabeth Segal, Lothrop, 1986; *Visions: Nineteen Short Stories by Outstanding Writers for Young Adults,* edited by Donald R. Gallo, Delacorte, 1987; *Hot Flashes: Women Writers on the Change of Life,* edited by Lynne Taetzsch, Faber and Faber, 1995; *Night Terrors: Stories of Shadow and Substance,* edited by Lois Duncan, Simon & Schuster, 1996; *When I Was Your Age: Original Stories about Growing Up,* edited by Amy Ehrlich, Candlewick, 1996; *Stay True: Short Stories for Strong Girls,* edited by Marilyn Singer, Scholastic, 1998; *Places I Never Meant to Be: Original Stories By Censored Writers,* edited by Judy Blume, Simon & Schuster, 1999. Also contributor of stories and articles to magazines, including *Jack and Jill, Ingenue, Calling All Girls, Child Life, Boys and Girls, Redbook, English Journal, Voice of Youth Advocates, Signal, Top of the News,* and *ALAN Review.*

■ Adaptations

When We First Met was made into a movie for HBO in 1984. Mazer'snovels recorded on audio cassette and released by Listening Library include *Taking Terri Mueller,* 1986, *Dear Bill, Remember Me? and Other Stories,* 1987, and *After the Rain,* 1988.

■ Sidelights

Norma Fox Mazer has garnered numerous awards, as well as high praise from critics, for novels like *Silver, After the Rain,* and *Saturday, the Twelfth of October* that depict teenagers in everyday situations, experiencing common problems. "At her best," observed Suzanne Freeman in the *Washington Post Book World,* "Mazer can cut right to the bone of teenage troubles and then show us how the wounds will heal. . . . What's apparent throughout all of this is that Mazer has taken great care to get to know the world she writes about. She delves into the very heart of it with a sure and practiced hand." It took many years of discipline for Mazer to become such a writer, and even longer for her to consider herself one; it wasn't until she was writing her 1976 novel *Dear Bill, Remember Me? and Other Stories* that Mazer actually believed she was a real author. In an essay in *Something about the Author Autobiography Series* (SAAS), she recalled that "during the months I spent working on [*Dear Bill*], I somehow lost time, I began to believe fearlessly in the endless vitality of that mysterious source from which my imagination is constantly replenished."

Mazer grew up in Glens Falls, New York, the middle daughter in a family of three girls. Her father was a route driver, delivering such things as milk and bread, and the family lived in a succession of various apartments and houses. "The year we lived on Ridge Street, when I was eight," stated Mazer in her autobiographical essay, "I learned to ride a two-wheeler, changed my name (briefly, because I kept forgetting I'd changed it) to the more glamorous Diane, made up triplet brothers in the Navy to impress my new girlfriend, and was caught stealing." School, reading, and boys were her childhood loves, and it was in a new apartment on First Street that she may have realized the possibilities of her imagination: "A girlfriend and I are playing near . . . wooden steps. I have forgotten the game, although I made it up, but not her words. 'Norma Fox! What an imagination!' And perhaps it was precisely then that I realized that my imagination had some other function than to torment me with witches in doorknobs and lurking figures in the shadows of the stairs."

During Mazer's teen years, her family started calling her the "Cold One," as she began to live more and more in her own world. Feeling like an outsider, Mazer admitted in *SAAS* that "were I to be asked to use one word to describe myself then and for years afterward, it would be—eyes. There's a picture of me around thirteen, sitting in a high-backed leather chair, looking out of the corner of my eyes, looking around, watching, a little frightened smile on my face. Along about then, it struck me, a bone-aching truth, that grown-ups—adults, these powerful mysterious people—were allplay-acting; they weren't, in fact, any older, any more grown-up than I was."

Writing Takes Hold

A job with the school newspaper gave Mazer her first opportunity to write for publication, and writing soon became the focus of her years in school. "But I wanted to write more than newspaper articles. There was a longing in me, vague, . . . but real, almost an ache," the novelist recalled. When she was fifteen, Mazer met her future husband, Harry Mazer, for the first time. He was a friend of her older sister, and at the age of twenty-one, he seemed ancient to Mazer. Two years later, they met again, and a much more confident Mazer was determined that Harry should fall in love with her. Harry thought that Mazer was too young, though, and she had to work at making him notice her— the couple fell in and out of love and quarreled many times before finally getting married.

During the early part of their marriage, the Mazers worked at "boring" jobs and tried to learn how to cook. Three children soon became part of the family, and Mazer took on the role of Mommy. "I had almost forgotten Norma," she remembered. "One day, looking around at the houseful of kids and listening to the never ending cries of Mommy! Mom! Mama!, it occurred to me that the day I'd been both putting off and waiting for—the day when I was all grown up—had arrived without my noticing. Indeed, it must have been here for quite a while. And that famous question 'What are you goingto do when you grow up?' had not gone away." A serious talk with her husband followed, and both Mazers revealed a desire to be a writer. They decided that if they were really serious about writing, they had to do at least a little every day. So, for three years, the Mazers spent an hour at the end of each day writing. Money from an insurance settlement finally enabled them to write full-time. "It was mildly terrifying," revealed Mazer in her autobiographical essay. "I had some days when

I sat in front of the typewriter and shook because I couldn't think of what to write next."

To support the family, the Mazers wrote for the "women's true confessions" market. These stories were presented as first-person confessions of women who had made serious mistakes in their lives, but were actually the work of professional writers. During the following years, the Mazers each wrote one of these 5,000-8,000 word stories every week, leaving little time to devote to the writing of novels. In 1970 Mazer managed to find the time to write the novel *I, Trissy,* and it was published the following year. *A Figure of Speech* came two years later and received a National Book Award nomination. "I remember meeting a member of the National Book Award committee some time after *A*

Despite her abusive, dysfunctional family, Em Thurkill finds the courage and determination to move forward in this 1997 work.

Figure of Speech had received a . . . nomination and hearing him say to me, '. . .and you just came out of nowhere.' I laughed. My 'nowhere' had been the ten years I'd spent writing full time and learning the craft."

YA Novels Draw Praise

Mazer has been particularly noted for her young adult novels, some ofwhich she has written with her husband. *Taking Terri Mueller,* for example, earned her an Edgar Award from the Mystery Writers of America, although she had not intended it as a mystery. The book follows Terri Mueller and her father as they wander from town to town, never staying in one place for more than a year. Although Terri is happy with her father, she is old enough to wonder why he will never talk about her mother, who supposedly died ten years before; an overheard discussion leads Terri to discover that she had been kidnapped by her father after a bitter custody battle. "Skillfully handling the deeply emotional situation, the author portrays Terri's conflicting feelings as well as the feelings of both her parents," remarked a *Horn Book* reviewer, who added: "The unfolding and the solution of the mystery are effectively worked; filled with tension and with strong characterization . . . we believe in just about everything Terri does, because Mazer's writing makes us willing to believe. She wins us completely with this finely wrought and moving book."

In the novel *Babyface,* Mazer handles another parent/daughter relationship that is threatened by secrets. Toni Chessmore believes she has perfect parents and an ideal best friend. During the summer of Toni's fourteenth year, though, her opinions begin to change when her father has a heart attack and she goes to stay with her sister in New York. Toni learns shocking secrets about her parents' past, and has a hard time dealing with them when she returns home. A *Publishers Weekly* contributor felt that "Toni's inner growth and increasing awareness . . . are realisticallyportrayed," and that "Mazer offers a thorough, sensitive exploration of parent/teen relationships."

In both *A Figure of Speech* and *After the Rain,* Mazer deals with the relationship between a young girl and her grandfather. Jenny, the granddaughter in *A Figure of Speech,* feels like an outsider in her own family. The only one she relates to is her grandpa, who lives in an apartment in the basement, neglected by the rest of the family. When Jenny's older brother returns home with a young wife and wants to move into Grandpa's apartment, the family decides to put Grandpa in a nursing home. Grandpa runs away, and Jenny goes with him, sharing the last days of his life. "The fine definition of all characters, the plausibility of the situations and the variety of insights into motivation make [the novel] almost too good to be true," Tom Heffernan asserted in *Children's Literature. A Figure of Speech* was followed by the sequel *When We First Met* in 1982.

Family relationships are also the focus of Mazer's *Missing Pieces*. Raised by her mother with help from her elderly aunt Zis after her father abandoned the family over a decade before, fourteen-year-old Jessie Wells wishes she had a "normal" family, and this wish has become almost an obsession. During the process of trying to get her mom to talk about the reasons for her dad's disappearance and then attempting to relocate him, Jessie gains a new understanding of family structure, using this newknowledge to help balance relationships among her friends. "Between snappy dialogue and tangy insights, Mazer thoughtfully explores issues of loyalty, compassion and forgiveness," noted a *Publishers Weekly* contributor.

In *After the Rain* Rachel's grandfather, Izzy, has cancer, so Rachel begins to go with him on his long afternoon walks. Izzy's crusty exterior has often prevented his family from getting close to him. Rachel is the youngest member of her family, half the age of her older brother, and her parents embarrass her and seem incredibly old. During the walks with her grandfather, Rachel comes to know and love him before he dies. When he is gone, she is able to deal with the death and loss, and even teach her parents a few things. A *Kirkus Reviews* contributor asserted that *After the Rain* is "beautifully and sensitively written, sounding the basic chords of the pleasures and pains of family relationships."

Growing up in a single-parent family is given an unpleasant twist in *When She Was Good*, which was published in 1997. Em Thurkill's mother died years ago, and her stepmother doesn't want to deal with her husband's children by his first marriage. When older sister Pamela moves out on her own, Em follows her, and becomes captive to Pamela's controlling personality, drastic mood swings, and daily outbursts of violent temper. After four years, Pamela's unexpected death leaves seventeen-year-old Em on her own, with no one to tell her what to do. Beginning her story after Pamela's death, as a newly liberated Em looks back at the unfortunate circumstancesthat brought her to this point and her sometimes self-destructive attempts to deal with the emotional void in her life, Mazer "conveys both the emotional poverty such daily abuse incurs and

---

"I love stories. I'm convinced that everyone does, and whether we recognize it or not, each of us tells stories. A day doesn't pass when we don't put our lives into story."

---Norma Fox Mazer

---

the victim's need for some sort of interior solution or healing in addition to the cessation of abuse," according to Deborah Stevenson of the *Bulletin of the Center for Children's Books*. "Using language at once fierce and unpretentious, Mazer captures . . . not only Em's vulnerability and inner struggle but also Pam's quirky madness," added Stephanie Zvirin in *Booklist*, concluding that *When She Was Good* is a "believably rendered testament to the resiliency of the human spirit."

Published in 1993, Mazer's *Out of Control* features a male protagonist named Rollo Wingate, whose friendship with the wrong crowd brings him into a situation bordering on the tragic. Rollo becomes a tagalong member of a group of three high-school juniors who dub themselves the Lethal Threesome. The trio corner fellow student Valerie Michon in a deserted part of the school and grope her. Eventually discovered and reprimanded, Rollo is uncertain why his actions so disgust his father and upset the school administration, and can't fathom why his attempt at an apology is rejected by a traumatized Valerie. In the opinion of *Voice of Youth Advocates* reviewer Kevin Kenny, *Out of Control* "is an exemplary exploration of an essentially random act of violence which by today's jaded standards might be written off by too many. . . . This is a work of real strength, a book in which every character, every facet of plot, suggests credibility andprovokes introspection." Echoing Kenny's praise

If you enjoy the works of Norma Fox Mazer, you may also want to check out the following books:

Janine Boissard, *Cecile: A Novel,* 1988.
Kaye Gibbons, *Ellen Foster,* 1987.
Paul Zindel, *The Pigman,* 1968.

in *Booklist,* Janice Del Negro praised the novel as "deal[ing] directly and realistically with the complexities of sexual harassment."

Books for Other Audiences

Less intense in plot than most of her YA novels are the books in the growing series that includes *A, My Name Is Ami* and *B, My Name Is Bunny.* Written for a slightly younger, less emotionally sophisticated audience, the books touch upon the everyday problems and situations encountered by average American teens. In *D, My Name Is Danita,* for example, Mazer's thirteen-year-old protagonist finds her image of the perfect family destroyed when she runs into a previously unknown half-brother at the mall. Other problems also enter the mix, including boy trouble, ups and downs with her best friend Laredo, and the antics of a younger sibling. In *E, My Name Is Emily,* the boy trouble cheerfully encouraged by the title character is offset by Emily's mother's interest in a man Emily can't stand, in a novel that *School Library Journal* contributor Susan Oliver called "an entertaining step up from those ever-present series books."

Along with her novels, Mazer has also written several short-story collections. The eight short stories in *Dear Bill, Remember Me? and Other Stories* deal with young girls going through a period of crisis. In "Up on Fong Mountain," Jessie strives to be accepted as something other than an extension of her boyfriend. Eighteen-year-old Louise in "Guess WhoseFriendly Hands" knows she's dying of cancer, and merely wishes that her mother and sister would accept it as she has. The stories in this collection "are clearly broadcast on a young teenager's wavelength, with the signal unobtrusively amplified as in good YA novels," contended a *Kirkus Reviews* contributor. The stories in Mazer's second collection, *Summer Girls, Love Boys, and Other Short Stories,* are connected by the setting of Greene Street.

In "Do You Really Think It's Fair?," Sarah tells about the death of her younger sister and questions the existence of justice. Another story, "Amelia Earhart, Where Are You When I Need You?," relates the short vacation a young girl spends with her eccentric Aunt Clare. "Each story has a strength and a sharpness of vision that delights and surprises in its maturity," commented Ruth I. Gordon in the *New York Times Book Review.* Gordon added that "Mazer has the skill to reveal the human qualities in both ordinary and extraordinary situations as young people mature."

By the time *Dear Bill, Remember Me? and Other Stories* was published, Mazer had enough successes under her belt, including thirteen years as a freelancer and two published books, to finally consider herself a "real writer." With their children grown, she and her husband purchased an old farmhouse for use as a weekend getaway. "No windows, no plumbing, no heating, no electricity. Even the outhouse had fallen in on itself and was useless. We loved it. It took every cent we had to buy it, but we wanted it too much to care," Mazer recalled in *SAAS.* The farmhouse was eventually fixed up, just in time for the Mazers to discover Canada. They sold the house and bought seventeen acres of woods and scrub on a cliff one hundred feet above a small lake in Canada. Many of Mazer's books involve memories of those summers spent camping. "Each one, in its own way, took me over," she reflected. "I lived in the world I was creating; it became real to me. Sometimes I'm asked about 'writer's block.' I don't have it and I don't fear it. Those years of writing pulp fiction taught me that there are always more words. And writing my own novels taught me that there are things inside me waiting to come out that I hardly know are there."

Mazer pointed out in her autobiographical essay that there is "a kind of mystery" in all of her books: "I write and my readers read to find out the answers to questions, secrets, problems, to be drawn into the deepest mystery of all—someone else's life." Freeman asserted that "in its sharpest moments, Mazer's writing can etch a place in our hearts," and in her *Top of the News* essay, Mazer declared: "I love stories. I'm convinced that everyone does, and whether we recognize it or not, each of us tells stories. A day doesn't pass when we don't put our lives into story. Most often these stories are . . . of the moment. They are the recognition, the highlighting of . . . our daily lives. . . . In my own life, it seems that events are never finished until I've either told them or written them."

■ Works Cited

Review of *After the Rain, Kirkus Reviews,* May 1, 1987, p. 723.

Review of *Babyface, Publishers Weekly,* July 27, 1990, p. 235.

Review of *Dear Bill, Remember Me?, Kirkus Reviews,* October 1, 1976, pp. 1101-02.

Del Negro, Janice, review of *Out of Control, Booklist,* June 1-15, 1993, p. 1804.

Freeman, Suzanne, "The Truth about the Teens," *Washington Post Book World,* April 10, 1983, p. 10.

Gordon, Ruth I., review of *Summer Girls, Love Boys, and Other Short Stories, New York Times Book Review,* March 13, 1983, p. 29.

Heffernan, Tom, review of *A Figure of Speech, Children's Literature,* No. 4, edited by Francelia Butler, Temple University Press, 1975, pp. 206-207.

Kenny, Kevin, review of *Out of Control, Voice of Youth Advocates,* August, 1993, p. 154.

Mazer, Norma Fox, "Growing up with Stories," *Top of the News,* winter, 1985, pp. 157-167.

Mazer, Norma Fox, essay in *Something about the Author Autobiography Series,* Volume 1, Gale, 1986, pp. 185-202.

Review of *Missing Pieces, Publishers Weekly,* June 12, 1995, p. 62.

Oliver, Susan, review of *E, My Name Is Emily, School Library Journal,* November, 1991, p. 120.

Stevenson, Deborah, review of *When She Was Good, Bulletin of the Center for Children's Books,* October, 1997, p. 61.

Review of *Taking Terri Mueller, Horn Book,* April, 1983, pp. 172-73.

Zvirin, Stephanie, review of *When She Was Good, Booklist,* September 1,1997, p. 118.

■ For More Information See

BOOKS

Children's Literature Review, Volume 23, Gale, 1991, pp. 214-34.

Holtze, Sally Holmes, *Presenting Norma Fox Mazer,* Twayne, 1987.

Holtze, Sally Homes, editor, *Fifth Book of Junior Authors and Illustrators,* H. W. Wilson, 1983, pp. 204-6.

PERIODICALS

Booklist, September 15, 1990, p. 157; October 15, 1990, p. 437.

Bulletin of the Center for Children's Books, May, 1991, p. 223; May, 1992, p. 232; April, 1993, p. 259; December, 1999, pp. 141-42.

Kirkus Reviews, April 1, 1995, p. 472.

Publishers Weekly, September 16, 1996, p. 85; July 21, 1997, p. 202.

School Library Journal, March, 1991, p. 193; July, 1992, p. 90.

Voice of Youth Advocates, June, 1987, p. 80; August, 1992, p. 168.

Colleen McCullough

■ Personal

Born c. 1938 in Wellington, New South Wales, Australia; married Ric Robinson (a housepainter), April 13, 1984. *Education:* Attended University of Sydney. *Hobbies and other interests:* Photography, music, chess, embroidery, painting, and cooking.

■ Addresses

Home—Norfolk Island, Australia.

■ Career

Worked as a teacher, a library worker, and a bus driver in Australia's Outback; journalist; Yale University, School of Internal Medicine, New Haven, Connecticut, associate in research neurology department, 1967-76; writer, 1976-.

■ Awards, Honors

D. Litt., Macquarie University, Sydney, 1993.

■ Writings

NOVELS

Tim, Harper, 1974.
The Thorn Birds, Harper, 1977.
An Indecent Obsession, Harper, 1981.
A Creed for the Third Millennium, Harper, 1985.
The Ladies of Missalonghi, Harper, 1987.
The First Man in Rome, Morrow, 1990.
The Grass Crown, Morrow, 1991.
Fortune's Favorites, Morrow, 1993.
Caesar's Women, Morrow, 1996.
Caesar: Let the Dice Fly, Morrow, 1997.
The Song of Troy, Orion (London), 1998.

OTHER

An Australian Cookbook, Harper, 1982.

Contributor to magazines.

■ Adaptations

Tim was released as a film starring Piper Laurie and Mel Gibson, directed and produced by Michael Pate, in 1979. *The Thorn Birds* was broadcast as a ten-hour miniseries on ABC-TV in March, 1983, starring Rachel Ward and Richard Chamberlain.

■ Sidelights

Colleen McCullough's 1977 novel, *The Thorn Birds*, became an international publishing sensation as its sales climbed past the seven-million mark. This saga of three generations in an Irish Catholic family in Australia seemed to pique interest in the history and culture of the continent, as witnessed by a spate of books and films set "Down Under" that entered into the annals of pop culture in the years following *The Thorn Birds*'s success. Yet McCullough has enjoyed only intermittent critical approval for her fiction throughout her career, and was never able to match the tremendous success of the 900-plus-page blockbuster. Her books often clock in at several hundred pages, and in interviews, McCullough comes across as equally loquacious in person. "I think there are two kinds of writers: those who write because they can't talk and those who write because they talk so much nobody listens to them," she told *Writer's Digest* interviewer Kay Cassill in 1980. "I belong to the second group."

McCullough was born in the late 1930s in Wellington, a large city in the Australian state of New South Wales. Her father was a relatively recent Irish immigrant to the continent, while her mother came from neighboring New Zealand. As a child, McCullough lived with her family for a time in the Outback, Australia's rough, arid region, but spent most of her formative years in the large city of Sydney. A voracious reader from an early age, she excelled in academic pursuits, especially the sciences, and pinned her hopes upon becoming a doctor.

At Holy Cross College, and from there the University of Sydney, McCullough continued to earn good grades, but her career plans were dashed when she discovered she suffered from an allergic reaction to soap, which made scrubbing for surgery impossible. As a young woman, she worked as a teacher, librarian, bus driver in the Outback, and journalist, but eventually settled into a career niche as a researcher in neurophysiology in Sydney. She was hired by Yale University School of Internal Medicine in 1967 for similar work, and relocated to Connecticut that same year.

Gets the Writing Bug

It was in New England that McCullough first began to write with a purpose. She once said she had written several dozen novels, but threw them all away. As she entered her thirties and remained single, however, McCullough began to fear a retirement marred by penury. Hoping to build a nest egg, she decided to write a work of fiction in her spare time that would provide some easy income to invest. At the time—in the early 1970s—Erich Segal's tearjerker novel *Love Story* had remained on the bestseller lists for some time, and was made into an equally successful feature film. McCullough thoughtthe sentimental romantic story about two Ivy League students—one of whom dies tragically after both overcome the opposition of family to marry—was overly maudlin, but she interviewed several of her bright student assistants at Yale about why they had all liked it. She then sat down at her typewriter, determined to write a work that would pull similar heartstrings.

McCullough submitted chapters to publishers, with no response. As she told Cassill in the interview for *Writer's Digest*, "I'd been going the ethical route, sending the manuscript out unsolicited, unagented, waiting months for a printed rejection slip. The parcel would come back completely untouched. You could tell it hadn't even been unwrapped, let alone read." Knowing she might have better luck if she found an agent to champion her work to the industry, McCullough set about trying to interest one in her fiction. Making a tuna dish one day for a friend, she chanced upon the name of an agent named "Fishbein" on the papers that were sitting on her kitchen table, and decided to sent it there. She devoted a good deal of energy to writing a lengthy, entertaining missive to Frieda Fishbein, with the assumption that "if I'm as good as I think I am—if I'm a writer—I should be able to persuade an agent to at least read my manuscript simply by writing one a persuasive letter," as McCullough recalled in the Writer's Digest interview.

Fishbein indeed liked the Australian's style, and interested New York publishing giant Harper & Row into publishing *Tim*, McCullough's first novel, in 1974. The story of relationship between a tough, older woman and a gentle, handsome young man who is slightly developmentally disabled, the title character was based in part on some of the patients at Yale Medical School that McCullough had known. The novel begins when Mary Horton, a mining-company executive, hires Tim to do odd jobs around her house. As the unlikely romance progresses, the lonely, sometimes insensitive Mary comes to learn much from her paramour, and when she learns that Tim has a possibly precarious future ahead of him—his parents are aging—she realizes that marriage would enrich both their lives.

Tim earned McCullough respectable reviews, and sold well. It was made into a 1981 film starring Mel Gibson, a relatively unknown Australian actor at the time. Having earned $50,000 from it, McCullough—still working at Yale—decided to write a book three times in length with the assumption that it would bring in $150,000. In her head, she had already developed the rough outline for a generational saga set in Australia before she had penned *Tim*. To create it, McCullough came home every night from work and wrote several thousand words. At one point, she had to wear elbow-length evening gloves to keep the skin on her chafed forearms intact. A year later, she turned a thousand pages over to Harper & Row.

A Huge Success

Published in the spring of 1977 and backed by a generous advance-publicity budget from Harper's marketing executives, who believed in the work immensely, *The Thorn Birds* was an immediate bestseller. The work follows the lives and sorrows of three women in the Cleary family, but is centered around the lovely Meggie, the only girl born to Fiona and Paddy Cleary, and sister to eight boys. Set in Australia, the story begins in 1915 when Meggie, who possesses the arresting combination of grey eyes and red hair, is a little girl who relocates with her family to a remote part of Australia. Her father has taken a job as manager of a sheep station, Drogheda, that belongs to a wealthy relative. The Cleary family's strong Irish Catholic heritage, the rigors of sheep farming, and the harsh, trying climate of the Australian countryside—torrential rainy seasons are halted by years of devastating draught—all feature prominently in *The Thorn Birds*'s events.

Largely ignored by her overworked mother, the young Meggie develops an innocent crush on the kind, handsome priest who has sent to the desolate area as punishment for offending his superior. The attraction, however, between Meggie and Father Ralph de Bricassart is a mutual one, and Meggie emerges as a stunning teenager whose blundering attempt to kiss the celibate priest results in

his abrupt departure. When the hated Cleary matriarch dies, she leaves the sheep station not to the hardworking Paddy and his sons, but to the Roman Catholic Church, and Father Ralph becomes its agent. The legacy advances Father Ralph's career in the diocese, and he keeps the Clearys at Drogheda to manage it.

The frustrated Meggie, realizing her limited options, weds a brutish stockman, Luke, with whom she has a daughter. Themes of female hardship and sacrifice dominate *The Thorn Birds*, whose title refers to a bird that impales itself but continues to sing delightfully as it dies. "Don't you see?" Meggie asks Father Ralph at one point in the novel. "We create our own thorns, and never

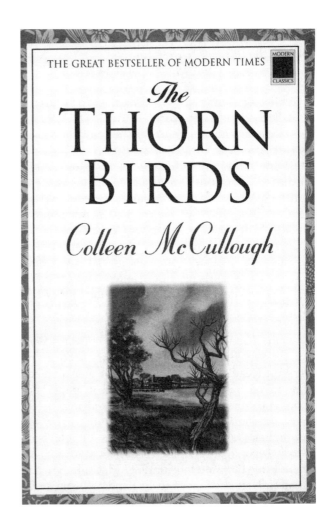

This 1977 instant bestseller that follows the lives of three generations of Cleary women made McCullough a household name.

stop to count the cost. All we can do is suffer the pain, and tell ourselves it was well worth it." When Father Ralph surprises Meggie one day while her husband is away cutting sugar cane for the season, they have a brief affair on a remote island, and Meggie conceives a child. She realizes that it will be the only part of her beloved priest that she will ever possess.

As Father Ralph advances to the post of cardinal, and spends much of his life in Rome, Meggie and Luke's daughter Justine becomes a famous stage actress in London. The son, however, exhibits the same stolid, pious qualities of his biological father, and drifts toward the priesthood himself—a career choice that breaks Meggie's heart once again. But soon after Dane's ordination, he drowns in Greece. The work concludes in 1969 with this tragedy—an event mined from McCullough's own life, for her brother had drowned off the island ofCrete. "That's how death with the young happens," McCullough said in the *Writer's Digest* interview. "You get a phone call and your whole world falls apart."

A publishing sensation, *The Thorn Birds* became a bestseller around the world, earned McCullough comparisons with Margaret Mitchell and her great saga of American history, *Gone with the Wind,* and was widely reviewed. "*The Thorn Birds* offers big, simplified emotions, startling coincidences and thumping hammer blows of fate," declared Walter Clemons in a *Newsweek* review, and many literary-establishment critics were far less kind. Christopher Lehmann-Haupt, however, of the *New York Times* described the plot developments in *The Thorn Birds* as wholly unsurprising, but granted that "predictability is inevitable in gold old-fashioned story-telling."

When the paperback rights for *The Thorn Birds* were sold for $1.9 million, it set an industry record and earned McCullough a tidy sum for her pension plan. Seven million copies were sold in paperback alone, and when the book was adapted into a ten-hour television drama in 1983, it captured the second-highest ratings for a miniseries in television history, second only to 1977's *Roots* broadcast. After quitting the Yale job in 1976, McCullough had actually planned to move to England to begin training as a nurse the following year, but her name appeared in newspaper headlines when the paperback rights were sold, and she suddenly found herself a household name—which, she felt, would preclude her chances of success as a caregiver. As

In 1983 *The Thorn Birds* was adapted into a ten-hour television drama starring Rachel Ward as Meggie and Richard Chamberlain as Father Ralph de Bricassart.

she told Sybil Steinberg in a *Publishers Weekly* interview, "when I became rich and famous, life became very complicated. It was unsafe for me to live on my own on any major landmass; you become prey to all sorts of nuts and bolts in the community."

McCullough applied for and received permission from the Australian governmentto settle on one of its South Pacific Ocean possessions called Norfolk Island. Here, she was able to devote herself to writing full-time, but ironically, never again achieved the spectacular success of *The Thorn Birds*, which she had written under such difficult circumstances. "I resented bitterly having to go to work at the medical school," during the period when she was writing her saga, McCullough told Cassill in *Writer's Digest.* "I resented leaving the book. I think had I not had to leave it it would have been far better. Going to a job when you're writing means you have to keep shifting gears. I can do it, but I don't like it."

Harper published McCullough's eagerly-anticipated next book, *An Indecent Obsession*, in 1981. A South Pacific romance that takes place as World War II is drawing to a close, the focus of the novel is Sister Honour Langtry, a dedicated, kindhearted Australian nurse at a military hospital in the tropics. Langtry's special Ward X houses veterans suffering from nervous collapse brought on by the rigors of fighting in the jungle. Some suffer psychosomatic illnesses, while other may be genuinely disturbed. The individual stories of the men, some of whom also fear returning to civilian life because of permanent physical disabilities, become part of the narrative, but Langtry's romantic involvement with two of her patients is the main focus of the novel.

Langtry is tentatively engaged to one patient, Neil, an officer who believes he erred in the line of duty and now suffers tremendous guilt over the needless deaths of his men. A new patient, Michael Wilson, arrives on the ward with no apparent disability, but the papers accompanying him reveal that he nearly killed a man in a fight who had made a sexual overture toward him. Luce, a devious, devastatingly handsome patient, stirs up trouble on the ward, which already feels betrayed, on the whole, by Honour's attraction to Michael. "Sexual jealousy and domination turn to murder and disfigurement", wrote *LosAngeles Times Book Review* writer Kirsten Grimstad.

Reviewing the work for the *Washington Post Book World*, William A. Nolen asserted that "*An Indecent Obsession* is never boring. Colleen McCullough has created fully drawn and believable characters, and she keeps her plot moving along nicely." In a *New York Times Book Review* assessment, the critic Joanne Greenberg opined that perhaps McCullough's prim, self-sacrificing heroine was a bit too perfect to win readers' sympathies, but conceded that the author had managed to make her appealing, "a vibrant enough character" nonetheless. Greenberg also commended the author for giving "an immediate sense of time and place to her portrayal of Ward X, and her attention to detail makes one feel the discomfort of the sweltering tropical nights as well as appreciate the awesome beauty of the sea, the torrential rains and the sunsets."

It would be four years before McCullough published another novel, characteristic of the long process of writing and rewriting that she forced herself to undergo. *A Creed for the Third Millennium*, published in 1985, was a major departure from her two previous novels in both setting, theme, and protagonist. The work takes place in the United States, a crumbling former superpower, in the year 2032 CE. Large-scale environmental disaster looms as scientists assert that another ice age is imminent. Every aspect of society is dominated by a pervasive government bureaucracy, and when the suicide rate begins to climb, the White House decides to present a messiah-like figure who might reassure people and help maintain social order. A computer-database query leads them to Dr. Joshua Christian, a physician with Department of the Environment.

Christian steps easily into his role as an author, then spokesperson, then cult-like leader, but the number of his enemies grows correspondingly with hispopularity. Several characters are clear biblical parallels—his greatest foe, for instance, is a colleague, Dr. Judith Carriol, whose name mimics Judas Iscariot, the apostle who betrayed Christ to the Romans. After the doctor leads a massive march on Washington, he commits suicide himself. Andrew M. Greeley, in a *Washington Post Book World* review that stressed the book's clear religious themes, called the novel "an embarrassing failure, despite McCullough's unquestioned skills as a storyteller," but declared that "the blame for her failure many be less attributable to her than to Jesus. He is as maddeningly difficult to categorize as He ever was."

One of the shortest of McCullough's books, *The Ladies of Missalonghi*, provided her fans with another historical romance in just under 200 pages. Published in 1987, the novel recounts the tale of Missy Wright, a beautiful but poor young woman in Australia in the early years of the twentieth century. In order to win a marriage proposal from her handsome, wealthy, but mysterious suitor, Missy pretends to suffer from an incurable disease.

Roman Saga

The Ladies of Missalonghi would be the last of McCullough's works published before the first volume in a lengthy, six-part series set in ancient Rome appeared. She had hoped to write such a saga for nearly thirty years: her enchantment with Imperial Rome, its fascinating leaders, and their tragic-heroic missteps dated back to her college years when she and her friends delved into the classics as a break from their dry science courses. After *The Thorn Birds* was finished, McCullough took a break and began re-reading Cicero, Pliny, and the *Commentaries* of Julius Caesar. The books easily rekindled her fascination with this world. "Reading Cicero's letters as he wavers between loyalty to Pompey and the temptation to turn to Caesar, and his glancing references to Cleopatra—whom he loathed—I suddenly saw a world that I wantedto enter as a novelist, desperately," she told Steinberg in a *Publishers Weekly* interview.

For the first time in her career, McCullough paid a researcher to help her, which cost her more than $100,000 over a three-year period. Her assistant began sending extensive materials to McCullough's Norfolk Island home, and where she wrote two millions words of nonfiction—"a

monograph of each of the major characters," as she explained to *Publishers Weekly*. "Next . . . I made a chronological list of every single thing that happened. I did all of that before I started writing the first volume," she told Steinberg. She also created an outline for a planned five books, each projected to swell to nearly a thousand pages in this chronicle of the long decline of the Roman Republic. But her longtime publisher, Harper, was wary about the project, so McCullough signed with Morrow instead.

The first volume of the *Masters of Rome* saga, *The First Man in Rome*, appeared in 1990. It centers upon Gaius Marius and his conflicted relationship with his aristocratic brother-in-law, Lucius Cornelius Sulla. A newcomer to Rome from the provinces, Marius is clever and rises quickly, sometimes with Sulla's help, over the eleven-year period of this first volume. A profusion of details about life

Tim, McCullough's first novel, was made into a film in 1979, starring newcomer Mel Gibson as Tim (right) and Piper Laurie as Mary Horton.

in ancient Rome, from feasts to footwear, provides added insight. The work earned Mc-Cullough several laudatory reviews—for the first time in her career. Don G. Campbell, writing in the *Los Angeles Times Book Review,* asserted that *The First Man in Rome* "is an absolutely absorbing story—not simply of the military and political intrigues that went into the final days of the Republic but also of what it was like to live, love and survive at this pivotal point in our civilization."

Rita Mae Brown, writing in the *Washington Post Book World,* described thecentral characters as "well conceived but burdened with dialogue not only un-Roman but nearly unreadable . . . . What a pity, because the narrative sweeps along as does the force of history." Yet Brown also gave praise to McCullough's chronicle of the problematic marital union between Sulla and the daughter of a caesar. "Love in its various guises fascinates McCullough, which is a good thing because it appears to fascinate the rest of us as well," stated Brown. "The rise of Sulla . . . and the fall of his wife, Julilla, again show this author at her best." A review from James Idema of *Chicago Tribune Books* called it "both entertaining and compelling" as a tale, and asserted further that "persevering readers will want to pursue the next book to discover the fate of Marius, the title character—and the novelist renders the volatile political and social fabric of ancient Rome convincingly."

The Grass Crown, the second in the *Masters of Rome* series and published in 1991, tracks Sulla's political rise. Like all of the books in the series—the five grew to a projected six—the tome contained an extensive glossary and maps drawn by Mc-Cullough herself. A review from Fred Mench in the academic journal *Classical World* assessed the book's fitness as supplementary reading material for college courses, though it faulted some historical errors in this and its predecessor. "But McCullough tells the stories well and creates interesting characters—some witty, brave, warm, some evil and cruel, some you like and some you hate . . . . Much of the material is, of course, fiction, not verifiable history, but it may help that period come alive for students who otherwise find Drusus dull or the Social war unintelligible," Mench concluded.

The third installment, *Fortune's Favorites,* appeared in 1993. This volume chronicles Sulla's final years and the emerging new leadership

---

If you enjoy the works of Colleen McCullough, you may also want to check out the following books:

Lois Battle, *The Past Is Another Country,* 1992.
Linda Lael Miller, *The Legacy,* 1994.
Barbara Wood, *The Dreaming,* 1992.

---

cadre in Rome. The actual intrigues perpetrated by military commanders, senators, and others genuine figures such as Pompey the Great, Spartacus, Crassus, and Julius Caesar figure prominently here. Norma Jean Richey, writing in *World Literature Today,* termed the book "a joy to read both for its marvelous narrative and for its presentation of truly extraordinary details" *Washington Post Book World* reviewer Judith Tarr declared that "McCullough has found her stride" in this third installment. "The clunking and clanking of style and characterization in the earlier novels have smoothed perceptibly," Tarr stated. "The dialogue moves more quickly, and the speeches are much less wooden. The characters are still a bit transparent around the edges, but now, more often than not, they seem to come closer to living, breathing humanity."

One of the goals for McCullough with her *Masters of Rome* series was to show the role of women in Rome's history in a more detailed scope. The action in *Caesar's Women,* published in 1996, takes place across ten years in the life of this most famous of Roman leaders, and here McCullough is able to provide a closer look at the many women in Caesar's life and their impact upon events and decisions. They include Aurelia, his brilliant mother, his second wife Pompeia—whom he detested—and his beloved daughter, Julia. The rivalry between Caesar and Marcus Tullius Cicero, an orator, philosopher, and senator, also takes shape here, and in turn shapes Rome's fall. "With great brio . . . McCullough captures the driven, passionate soul of ancient Rome," stated a *Publishers Weekly* review.

The 1997 installment of McCullough's *Masters of Rome* was titled *Caesar: Let the Dice Fly.* The work begins in 54 B.C., and follows Caesar across his impressive expansion of the Roman Empire into the rest of Europe. The decisive act of crossing the Rubicon, the conquests of Germania and Britannia, and a power dispute with Pompey, his son-in-law, provide the bulk of the action.

"McCullough's legion of readers now dwarfs Caesar's own considerable army,"remarked a *Publishers Weekly* review.

McCullough had one more *Masters of Rome* book to complete, but the film rights to *The First Man in Rome,* the series debut, had been sold by the mid-1990s. She still lives on the 13-square-mile Norfolk Island, and is one of 2,700 residents. Many of her neighbors are descendants of the crew of the infamous *H.M.S. Bounty,* whose sailors mutinied in 1789 and set their captain, Bligh, on a small boat that survived a 3,600-mile drift to Indonesia. The past is very much a part of McCullough's present, evidenced by her long involvement in the immense Roman saga, and she does not hesitate to view her future, and her legacy, in similarly pragmatic terms. Proud of her achievements as a writer, McCullough dismisses the snipes of the more bookish critics of her work. "Only time tells," she told Cassill in the *Writer's Digest* interview back in 1980. "If it lasts, it's good literature. If it dies, it's just another book. Very often the books the critics like today are gone tomorrow . . . .I don't have any children, so my books had better live forever. You put so much of yourself into a novel, you want everyone to go on reading it long after you're gone."

■ **Works Cited**

Brown, Rita Mae, "Friends, Romans and Countrymen," *Washington Post Book World,* November 4, 1990, p. 6.

Review of *Caesar: Let the Dice Fly, Publishers Weekly,* October 13, 1997, p. 55.

Review of *Caesar's Women, Publishers Weekly,* October 16, 1995, p. 42.

Campbell, Don G., "McCullough's Roman a Clef," *Los Angeles Times Book Review,* October 28, 1990.

Cassill, Kay, "Confessions of a Chain Smoker," *Writer's Digest,* March, 1980, p. 35, and "The Thorned Words of Colleen McCullough," pp. 32.

Clemons, Walter, "Bed of Thorns," *Newsweek,* April 25, 1977, pp. 93, 96-97.

Greeley, Andrew M., "Brave New World," *Washington Post Book World,* April 28, 1985, p. 4.

Greenberg, Joanne, review of *An Indecent Obsession, New York Times Book Review,* October 25, 1981.

Grimstad, Kirsten, "A Microuniverse in a Mental Ward," *Los Angeles Times Book Review,* October 25, 1981, pp. 12-13.

Idema, James, "Vast Roman Saga: Colleen McCullough Tackles Marius and Sulla," *Chicago Tribune Books,* October 7, 1990, p. 3.

Lehmann-Haupt, Christopher, "The Song Is Familiar," *New York Times,* May 2, 1977, p. 31.

Mench, Fred, review of *The First Man in Rome* and *The Grass Crown, Classical World,* July, 1993.

Nolen, William A., review of *An Indecent Obsession, Washington Post Book World,* October 11, 1981.

Richey, Norma Jean, review of *Fortune's Favorites, World Literature Today,* Summer, 1994, p. 632.

Steinberg, Sybil, "Colleen McCullough: The Indefatigable Author Has Embarked on a Five-Volume Series Set in Ancient Rome," *Publishers Weekly,* September 14, 1990, pp. 109-10.

Tarr, Judith, "On the Way to the Forum," *Washington Post Book World,* November 21, 1993, p. 4.

■ **For More Information See**

PERIODICALS

America, August 10, 1974.

Atlantic Monthly, June, 1977.

Booklist, November 1, 1995, pp. 434-35; September 15, 1997, p. 181.

Chicago Tribune Book World, October 11, 1981.

Commonweal, July 22, 1977, pp. 473-75.

Los Angeles Times Book Review, July 21, 1985.

New York Times, March 25, 1979; September 17, 1981; October 29, 1981, p. C24; March 26, 1983; March 27, 1983.

New York Times Book Review, April 21, 1974; May 8, 1977; October 25, 1981; November 15, 1981; April 26, 1987, p. 15; November 4, 1990, p. 19; October 6, 1991, p. 13.

People, May 7, 1984; May 11, 1987, p. 18; January 29, 1996, p. 90.

Publishers Weekly, March 7, 1977; February 22, 1980; February 18, 1984; August 9, 1991, p. 43.

Time, May 9, 1977; May 20, 1985.

Times (London), November 30, 1981.

Times Literary Supplement, October 7, 1977; December 11, 1981.

Tribune Books (Chicago), October 31, 1993, p. 3.

Village Voice, March 28, 1977.

Washington Post, April 24, 1977; November 26, 1981; March 27, 1983.

Washington Post Book World, January 20, 1985.*

Gordon Parks

◼ Personal

Born November 30, 1912, in Fort Scott, KS; son of Andrew Jackson (a dirt farmer) and Sarah (Ross) Parks; married Sally Alvis, 1933 (divorced, 1961); married Elizabeth Campbell, 1962 (divorced, 1973); married Genevieve Young (a book editor), August 26, 1973; children: (first marriage) Gordon Jr. (deceased), Toni Brouillaud, David; (second marriage) Leslie. *Politics:* Democrat. *Religion:* Methodist.

◼ Addresses

Home—860 United Nations Plaza, New York, NY 10017. *Agent*—(film) Ben Benjamin, Creative Management Associates, 9255 Sunset Blvd., Los Angeles, CA 90069.

◼ Career

Photographer, writer, film director, songwriter, and composer. Held various jobs until 1937; freelance fashion photographer in Minneapolis, MN, 1937-42; photographer with Farm Security Administration, 1942-43, Office of War Information, 1944, and Standard Oil Co. of New Jersey, 1945-48; *Life* magazine, New York City, photojournalist, 1948-72; film director, 1968—; *Essence* magazine, New York City, editorial director, 1970-73. President, Winger Enterprises, Inc. Composer of concertos and sonatas performed by symphony orchestras in the United States and Europe. Director of motion pictures, including *Shaft,* MGM, 1971; *Shaft's Big Score,* MGM, 1972; *The Super Cops,* MGM, 1974; and *Leadbelly,* MGM, 1976.

◼ Member

Directors Guild of America (member of national board, 1973-74), Authors Guild (member of board, 1973-74), Authors League of America, Newspaper Guild, Black Academy of Arts and Letters (fellow), American Federation of Television and Radio Artists, American Society of Magazine Photographers (former board member), American Society of Composers, Authors, and Publishers, American Federation of Television and Radio Artists, National Association for the Advancement of Colored People, Directors Guild of New York (council member), Urban League, Players Club (New York City), Kappa Alpha Mu.

◼ Awards, Honors

Rosenwald Foundation fellow, 1942; Frederic W. Brehm award, 1952; two Mass Media Awards,

National Conference of Christians and Jews, 1964, for outstanding contributions to better human relations; Carr Van Anda Journalism Award, University of Miami, 1964, Ohio University, 1970; named photographer-writer who has done the most to promote understanding among nations of the world in an international vote conducted by makers of Nikon cameras, 1967; honorary A.F.D., Maryland Institute of Fine Arts, 1968; Litt. D., Kansas State University, 1970; Carr Van Anda Journalism Award, Ohio University, 1970; Spingarn Medal, National Association for the Advancement of Colored People, 1972; Georgia Children's Book award, 1972, for *J. T.*; H.H.D., St. Olaf College, 1973, Rutgers University, 1980, and Pratt Institute, 1981; Christopher Award, 1980, for *Flavio*; President's Fellow award, Rhode Island School of Design, 1984; National Medal of Arts, 1988; World Press Photo award, 1988; Artist of Merit, Josef Sudek Medal, 1989. Additional awards include Photographer of the Year, Association of Magazine Photographers; awards from Syracuse University School of Journalism, 1963, Philadelphia Museum of Art, 1964, Art Directors Club, 1964, and University of Miami, Coral Gables, 1964; honorary degrees from Fairfield University and Boston University, both 1969, Macalaster College and Colby College, both 1974, Lincoln University, 1975, Columbia College, 1977, Suffolk University, 1982, Kansas City Art Institute, 1984, Art Center and College of Design, 1986, Hamline University, 1987, American International College and Savannah College of Art and Design, both 1988, University of Bradford (England) and Rochester Institute of Technology, both 1989, Parsons School of Design, 1991, Manhattanville College and College of New Rochele, both 1992, Skidmore College, 1993, and Montclair State University, 1994. Stockton School, East Orange, NJ, was renamed Gordon Parks Academy in honor of Parks, 1998.

■ Writings

NONFICTION

Flash Photography, [New York City], 1947.

Camera Portraits: The Techniques and Principles of Documentary Portraiture, F. Watts, 1948.

A Choice of Weapons (autobiography), Harper, 1966.

(And photographer) *A Poet and His Camera* (poems), Viking, 1968.

(Photographer) Jane Wagner, *J. T.* (for children), Van Nostrand, 1969.

(And photographer) *Born Black* (essays), Lippincott, 1971.

(And photographer) *Whispers of Intimate Things* (poems), Viking, 1971.

(And photographer) *In Love* (poems), Lippincott, 1971.

(And photographer) *Moments without Proper Names* (retrospective exhibition of photographs with verse), Viking, 1975, Secker & Warburg (London), 1975.

Flavio, Norton, 1978.

To Smile in Autumn: A Memoir, Norton, 1979.

Voices in the Mirror: An Autobiography, Doubleday, 1990.

Arias in Silence, Bulfinch Press, 1994.

Glimpses toward Infinity, Bulfinch Press, 1996.

(Photographer) *Half Past Autumn: A Retrospective* (with introduction by Philip Brookman), Bulfinch Press, 1997.

A Star for Noon, Bulfinch Press, 2000.

Contributor to *Show, Vogue, Venture*, and other magazines.

OTHER

(And director) *Flavio* (screenplay), Electra Studios, 1961.

The Learning Tree (autobiographical novel), Harper, 1963.

Shannon (novel), Little, Brown, 1981.

Half Past Autumn (television documentary), HBO, 2000.

Author of television documentaries produced by National Educational Television, including *Mean Streets*. Author of *Martin* (ballet), 1990.

■ Adaptations

The Learning Tree was directed by Parks and filmed by Warner Brothers-Seven Arts in 1968. Selections from *The Learning Tree* and *A Choice of Weapons*, read by the author, were recorded on audiocassette, both by Scholastic Records, both 1970.

■ Sidelights

The life of Gordon Parks is a study in self-reliance and determination. Moreover, it has served as a blueprint for many people on how to over-

"Black Muslim Rally, New York, 1963," is among the many documentary photos from Gordon Parks's illustrious career that appear in his 1997 memoir, *Half Past Autumn: A Retrospective.*

come racial, social, and economic barriers within America. From a childhood characterized by poverty, Parks seemed to be following a typical downhill path by dropping out of high school at age sixteen after the death of his mother. However, Parks would have no part of failure; he fended for himself on the streets until he discovered something that ignited his passion. That something was a camera, and since 1937 Parks's talent as a photographer has allowed him to channel his abundant creative gifts and energy into creating a life that reads like a quintessential American success story. That Parks is also an African American makes his life story particularly inspiring to young men and women of color. In 1988, in recognition of his many achievements, President George Bush awarded the multitalented Parks the National Medal of Arts.

Poet, novelist, composer, photojournalist: Parks has found success in several creative arenas. However, particularly notable is his position as the first African American ever to be signed as a director to a major Hollywood film studio. His directorial debut, *The Learning Tree,* filmed in 1968, was based on his own childhood in Fort Scott, Kansas, where Parks was raised in abject poverty. Typical of the multi-talented Parks, not only did he write the autobiographical novel upon which the film was based, but he also penned the screenplay adaptation, composed the soundtrack, and directed and produced the film.

Born in Fort Scott in 1912, Parks was the youngest of fifteen children born to sharecropper Andrew Jackson and his wife, Sarah. After the death of his mother in 1928, Parks was sent by his father to live with one of his older, married sisters. The stock market crashed a year later, signaling the start of the Great Depression, and Parks soon found himself out of high school and on the streets of St. Paul, Minnesota, evicted from his sister's home by his brother-in-law and forced to live by his wits. Odd jobs like waiting tables, playing basketball, mopping floors, and playing piano kept the young man from starvation, but it was a stint with the Civilian Conservation Corps (CCC) in 1933 that allowed Parks to get his feet squarely under him. Married to Sally Alvis that same year, Parks and his wife eventually had three children.

After his year with the CCC, Parks supported his growing family by working as a porter and waiter on passenger trains run by the Northern Pacific Railroad. It would be the glossy magazines left behind by patrons of the train's dining car that first gave Parks the idea of becoming a photographer. There he saw the work of men and women such as Ben Shahn, Jack Delano, Dorthea Lange, and Walker Evans bringing to view the nation's underclass, a world of poverty that Parks knew so well. In 1935 he spent $7.50 of his hard-earned cash on a camera and began to develop basic photographic skills by taking pictures of Minneapolis's black neighborhoods. Soon, a local store owner took notice of his work and exhibited the young man's photographs documenting the lives of urban blacks.

A move to Chicago further expanded Parks's opportunities. His talents as a documentary photographer eventually earned him a Julius Rosenwald Foundation fellowship, and in 1942 he went to work for the Washington, D.C.-based Farm Security Administration (FSA). With the outbreak of World War II, the FSA was dissolved, and Parks was given the job of correspondent for the newly formed Office of War Information (OWI), where he developed his writing skills. When a well-earned chance to go overseas with the all-black 332nd Fighter Group was denied him, Parks left the OWI. Working briefly with the Standard Oil Photography Project, Parks travelled throughout the United States between 1944 and 1946, shooting such pictures as "Dinner Time at Mr. Hercules Brown's Home, Somerville, Maine," "Car Loaded

with Furniture on Highway," and "Grease Plant Worker, Pittsburgh, Pennsylvania." Once his work for Standard Oil was completed, Parks moved his family to Harlem to renew his search for work as a freelance photographer.

Camera Becomes Mirror of African American Society

Self-taught in photography, Parks had learned the stylistic ropes as a fashion photographer while living in Minneapolis, and his innate artistic sense made him a success at selling photos to major periodicals, including *Vogue* and *Life*. In 1946 he wrote his first book, *Flash Photography*, the editing

Parks directed this 1971 box-office smash film *Shaft*, which stars Richard Roundtree as a New York City private eye.

of which was an arduous experience for the fastidious Parks. A freelance job profiling Harlem gang leader Red Jackson endeared him to the editors at *Life* magazine, and Parks was invited to join that magazine's staff in 1948. As with many of his accomplishments, Parks was the first black to receive such a job opportunity. He would spend more than two decades on staff at the prestigious magazine before ending his career there in 1972 at the age of sixty. The many photographs by Parks, appearing not only in the pages of *Life* but in other magazines as well, chronicled the mid-twentieth-century development of the African American consciousness. Among his many photo-documentaries were stories on civil rights leaders Martin Luther King Jr., Eldridge Cleaver, and Malcolm X, the Black Panthers, urban crime, and segregation in the South. "As passionate as he is peace-seeking despite all the hurt he has endured, Parks, in his words as well as in his actions, has become a pioneer as both an artist and a defender of the human spirit," concluded *Booklist* critic John Brosnahan in a review of Parks' *Voices in the Mirror: An Autobiography*.

While working as a photojournalist for *Life,* Parks also turned his attention to several other pursuits, among them film directing, writing, and music composition. Although such pursuits served as outlets for his burgeoning creativity, they also reflected another, more personal need that had its roots in his childhood. "It was a desperate search for security within a society that held me inferior simply because I was black," Parks was quoted as saying in *Black Literature Criticism*. "It was a constant inner rebellion against failure." While sports activities or hobbies like photography were indulged in by most young people, in order for Parks to do such things as a teen they had to make money. "In my fright, I set up all sorts of hypothetical tragedies for myself, then I would contemplate an alternative to offset whatever tragedy I felt might strike," he recalled of his youthful efforts at coping with the ever-present fear of ending up on the streets. "For instance, I would imagine I had lost my legs in an accident. Then, just as quickly I would daydream myself into a situation whereby I would play music or perhaps compose for a living. Or if I lost my sight or hearing I could learn Braille and somehow survive by writing. . . . with all the tragic possibilities considered, and all the alternatives accounted for, I could push on with a little less fear."

Parks's moving photograph "Child and Doll, North Carolina," circa 1980.

Writing as a Way to Reflect upon the Past

While "writer" was one of Parks' alternative means of survival, it was also an excellent channel for self-expression, and much of his published work has focused on his own life story. His first novel, 1963's *The Learning Tree*, parallels Parks' own childhood, as teen protagonist Newt Winger grows to manhood in 1920s Kansas despite being beset by economic and personal tragedies similar to those endured by Parks. The author's "unabashed nostalgia for what was good there, blended with sharp recollections of staggering violence and fear, makes [*The Learning Tree*] an immensely readable, sometimes unsettling book," noted a *Time* reviewer.

After the success of *The Learning Tree*, Parks would continue to trace his life story in such books as *A Choice of Weapons*, *Voices in the Mirror*, and *To Smile in Autumn*. Published in 1966, *A Choice of Weapons* focuses on Parks' decade on the street after his mother died. Recalling the legacy of a woman "who placed love, dignity, and hard work over hatred," Parks writes what *Saturday Review* contributor Edwin M. Yoder Jr. described as "an excellent introduction to what it must have been like to be black and ambitious—and poor—in the America of [the 1930s], when nearly every door

was sealed to Negroes." While covering the same events that Parks had fictionalized in *The Learning Tree*, *A Choice of Weapons* "has greater impact because Parks documents his life with no embellishments. . . . The dashed hopes and hard-won victories are presented in a forthright manner," according to *Dictionary of Literary Biography* essayist Jane Ball.

Voices in the Mirror, published in 1990, focuses on Parks' traumatic adolescence, as he enters into his teen years with an ambition to live the American

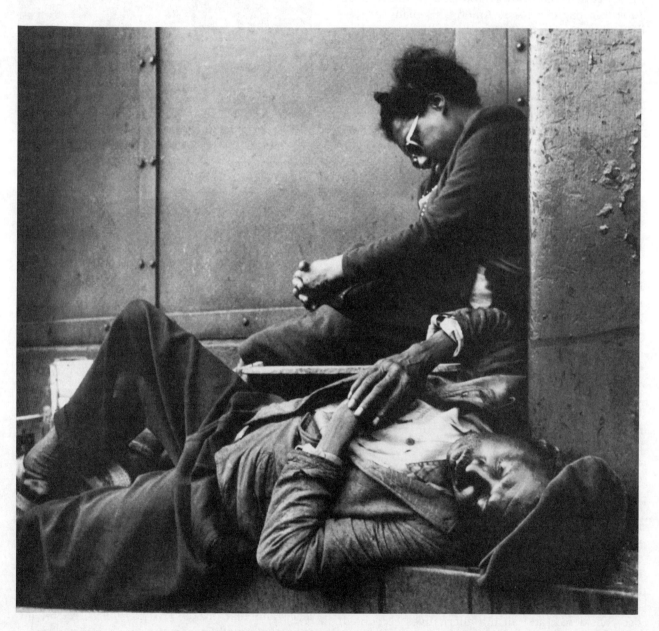

Many of Park's photographs, like this one titled "Homeless Couple," documented the lives of the urban poor, particularly African Americans.

dream only to have that dream put seemingly out of reach by racism, poverty, and, ultimately, the death of his mother. Following Parks during his efforts to make a living on his own and establish himself in his chosen vocation, the book also serves as a tribute to Parks's family and to those men and women who fought for racial equality in the early years of the civil rights movement. His career drew him into encounters with such notable individuals as Malcolm X, Winston Churchill, and Dwight D. Eisenhower, all of whom make an appearance in *Voices in the Mirror*. The volume "underscores a belief in dignity and the difference one man can create," according to *School Library Journal* contributor Mike Printz. A *Publishers Weekly* reviewer declared that Parks's "exhilarating, inspirational autobiography . . . provides a searing view of what it's like to be black in America."

Reflecting on a Successful Life

To Smile in Autumn covers the years 1943 through 1979, the period during which Parks rose to success, first in the magazine industry and then in films. Interspersing prose, letters, journal entries, photographs, and poems, Parks creates a patchwork of his adult life, positioning his professional successes alongside his personal ups and downs: three marriages, children, the tragic death of his oldest son, Gordon Parks Jr., in a plane crash, and his many friendships. Among his successes as director is the 1971 box-office smash *Shaft*, which Parks directed. Other films benefiting from Parks' involvement include *The Super Cops, Leadbelly,* and a film version of his novel *The Learning Tree*. *To Smile in Autumn* also follows the author's still-photography career, both as a documentary photographer recording dead Harlem gang leaders and as a fashion photographer shooting stylish portraits of heiress and designer jeans purveyor Gloria Vanderbilt. Throughout the book, Parks reflects upon his personal quandary: how to reconcile his personalsuccess with the limitations imposed upon an African American working within a white, elitist power structure. Ultimately, however, *To Smile in Autumn* is a book about success. As Mel Watkins noted in a review for the *New York Times Book Review,* it "is about the triumph of achievement, the abundance and glamour of a productive life . . . dotted with memories of Mr. Parks's casual and intimate brushes with the rich and famous."

If you enjoy the works of Gordon Parks, you may also want to check out the following:

The soft sculptures and story quilts of Faith Ringgold.
The murals of Diego Rivera.
Cotton Comes to Harlem, a film written and directed by Ossie Davis, 1970.

Parks' talent as a photographer is documented in *Half Past Autumn: A Retrospective*, a volume designed to accompany a 1997 traveling exhibit of his work organized by the Corcoran Gallery in Washington, D.C. Covering the period from 1949 through the late 1990s, the volume includes over three hundred examples of Parks' work. Interestingly, *New York Times Book Review* contributor Andy Grundberg maintained that Parks' talent and longevity actually served as his "undoing." Successful at such a wide variety of photographic approaches—everything from documentary and photojournalism to travel, fashion, and portrait photography—Parks lost his individuality, his "own eye," according to Grundberg. "What saved him from becoming an invisible man," the critic maintained, was his black heritage and his experiences of poverty, both of which give to Parks' photographs of the urban poor "the power of personal conviction."

In addition to his other talents, Parks has published several volumes of poetry, and has illustrated *J. T.,* a children's book by Jane Wagner that documents a young inner-city boy's realization that an injured animal is worth more than a stolen radio. Most well known among his photo essays is *Flavio*. Based on Parks' 1961 *Life* piece about a Brazilian family living in destitution, *Flavio* follows a young Brazilian boy's rescue from a Rio de Janeiro slum, as Flavio Da Silva is taken to the United States and treated for malnutrition. In a volume that a *Publishers Weekly* contributor characterized as "both poignant and depressing," the boy makes the choice to return to his family in his native country and resume a life of hardship.

As Parks' career began to slow in the late twentieth century, many retrospectives of his work have been organized, a testament to the energy and creativity of an individual many would characterize as one of the few, true, twentieth-century Renaissance men. "The remarkable thing about [Gordon Parks]," museum curator Michael Kan was quoted as telling David Lyman in the *Detroit News & Free Press*, "is that he fits the image of everything any man aspires to be. He's the prototypical adventurer: He goes to places that nobody else goes to and is able to come out with something that speaks to the essence of these experiences."

Remarking on the many outlets his creativity has found over the years, Parks credits two qualities as central to his personal success: curiosity and a strong will to survive. "I'm a little amazed that I've done all this," he told Lyman in reflecting on his life from the perspective of being eighty-six years old. "But it's not as monumental as it appears to be. It's just doing things, you know. I think a lot of people could do a lot of things if they just tried." And channeling this curiosity and energy into an autobiographical mode has served Parks—and society—well. "I go on attempting to reveal my experiences, each time in a different way, through a different medium," he once added, "hoping that, in some small way, they might make a dent—some mark—on our times. If only I could feel that a photograph, a piece of music or a film of mine could help put an end to hatred, poverty, bigotry, or war, the pain of those early years would have been worthwhile."

■ Works Cited

Ball, Jane, "Gordon Parks," in *Dictionary of Literary Biography*, Volume 33: *Afro-American Fiction Writers after 1955*, Gale (Detroit), 1984, pp. 203-8.

Black Literature Criticism, Volume 3, Gale (Detroit), 1992.

Brosnahan, John, review of *Voices in the Mirror: An Autobiography*, *Booklist*, November 1, 1990, p. 494.

Review of *Flavio*, *Publishers Weekly*, January 2, 1978, pp. 56-57.

Grundberg, Andy, review of *Half Past Autumn*, *New York Times Book Review*, February 23, 1997, p. 16.

Review of *The Learning Tree*, *Time*, September 6, 1963.

Lyman, David, "Hunger to Know People, not a Need for Fame, Drives Gordon Parks' Career," *Detroit News & Free Press*, February 4, 1999.

Printz, Mike, review of *Voices in the Mirror: An Autobiography*, *School Library Journal*, February, 1991, p. 107.

Review of *Voices in the Mirror: An Autobiography*, *Publishers Weekly*, October 12, 1990, p. 52.

Watkins, Mel, "Renaissance Photographer," *New York Times Book Review*, December 23, 1979, p. 7.

Yoder, Edwin M., Jr., "No Catch for the Hawk," *Saturday Review*, February 12, 1966, p. 40.

■ For More Information See

BOOKS

Berry, S. L., *Gordon Parks*, Chelsea House, 1991.

Bush, Martin H., *The Photographs of Gordon Parks*, Edwin A. Ulrich Museum of Art (Wichita, KS), 1983.

Donloe, Darlene, *Gordon Parks*, Melrose Square (Los Angeles, CA), 1993.

Harnan, Terry, *Gordon Parks: Black Photographer and Film Maker*, illustrated by Russell Hoover, Garrard, 1972.

Roslansky, John D., editor, *Creativity*, North-Holland Publishing, 1970.

Turk, Midge, *Gordon Parks*, illustrated by Herbert Danska, Crowell, 1971.

PERIODICALS

American Visions, February-March, 1993, pp. 14-19.

Booklist, August 19, 1997, p. 1845; February 15, 1999, p. 1025.

Kirkus Reviews, October 1, 1979, pp. 1193-94.

Library Journal, January, 1992; June 15, 1997, p. 64; February 1, 1998, p. 83.

Life, October, 1994, pp. 26-29; September, 1997, pp. 94-99.

New York Times Book Review, December 9, 1990, p. 19; March 10, 1996, p. 16; December 7, 1997, p. 38.

Publishers Weekly, October 12, 1990 p. 52.

School Library Journal, March, 1980, p. 149; February, 1991, p. 107.

Smithsonian, April, 1989, pp. 66-75.

USA Today (magazine), September, 1998, p. 46.

Washington Post Book World, November 18, 1990, p. 4.

J.D. Salinger

■ Personal

Born Jerome David Salinger, January 1, 1919, in New York, NY; son of Sol (an importer) and Miriam (Jillich) Salinger; married wife Sylvia (a physician), September, 1945 (divorced, 1947); married Claire Douglas, February 17, 1955 (divorced, October, 1967); children: (second marriage) Margaret Ann, Matthew. *Education:* Graduated from Valley Forge Military Academy, 1936; attended New York University, Ursinus College, and Columbia University (where he studied with Whit Burnett).

■ Addresses

Home—Cornish, NH. *Agent*—Harold Ober Associates, Inc., 425 Madison Ave., New York, NY 10017.

■ Career

Writer. Worked as an entertainer on the Swedish liner *M.S. Kungsholm* in the Caribbean, 1941. *Mili-*tary service: U.S. Army, 1942-46; served in Europe; became staff sergeant; awarded five battle stars.

■ Writings

The Catcher in the Rye (novel), Little, Brown, 1951.
Nine Stories, Little, Brown, 1953, published in England as *For Esme—With Love and Squalor, and Other Stories*, Hamish Hamilton, 1953.
Franny and Zooey (two stories; "Franny" first published in *New Yorker*, January 29, 1955, "Zooey" in *New Yorker*, May 4, 1957), Little, Brown, 1961.
Raise High the Roof Beam, Carpenters; and Seymour: An Introduction (stories; "Raise High the Roof Beam, Carpenters" first published in *New Yorker*, November 19, 1955, " Seymour," in *New Yorker*, June 6, 1959), Little, Brown, 1963.
Hapworth 16, 1924, Orchises Press, 1997.

Contributor to periodicals, including *Harper's, Story, Collier's, Saturday Evening Post, Cosmopolitan,* and *Esquire.* Collections of Salinger's correspondence are housed at the Harry Ransom Humanities Research Center, University of Texas at Austin, and at the Firestone Library, Princeton University.

■ Adaptations

"Uncle Wiggily in Connecticut" (published in *Nine Stories*) was made into the motion picture *My Foolish Heart*, 1950.

■ Sidelights

J. D. Salinger remains well known for a single novel: *The Catcher in the Rye*, which was hailed as "brilliant" upon its publication in 1951. While several of the short short stories Salinger also wrote and published in popular magazines during the 1950s were eventually collected in book form, it remains *Catcher in the Rye* that has kept his name a familiar one, particularly among the many young readers who have found in the novel's teen protagonist, Holden Caulfield, an attitude of rebellion against the world of "phoniness" that serves as a model for their own rejection of adult values and mores.

While Salinger's novel reaches teen readers on one level, it also holds an appeal to adult readers who are aware of its complexity. The subject of considerable critical scrutiny in the years since its publication, *The Catcher in the Rye* has earned comparisons to *The Adventures of Huckleberry Finn* by American humorist Mark Twain, as well as to F. Scott Fitzgerald's *The Great Gatsby*. Remarking on the coming-of-age themes that Salinger consistently explored throughout his brief publishing career, novelist Norman Mailer remarked in his *Advertisements for Myself* that Salinger was "the greatest mind to ever stay in prep school."

Salinger was born in New York City in 1919, the product of mixed parentage: his father was Jewish and his mother was Scotch-Irish. Along with an older sister, he grew up in fashionable areas of Upper Manhattan, eventually moving to a home within a block from the Metropolitan Museum of Art. In 1932, when Salinger was thirteen, his father enrolled him at Manhattan's McBurney School. Unfortunately, Salinger's absence at every school function except meals, as well as his status as a loner, made his first year less than successful, and he flunked out. In response, two years later he found himself at Valley Forge Military Academy near Wayne, Pennsylvania. Attending Valley Forge for two years, Salinger impressed his fellow students with his sharp, sarcastic wit, his tendency to break the rules whenever possible, and his talent as a writer. During his second year he became editor of the school's yearbook, and for graduation penned for the school a poetic tribute that would later be treasured by the Valley Forge staff and set to music for annual performances. Salinger graduated from Valley Forge in 1936, but his school experience there would haunt

him, becoming the foundation for *Catcher in the Rye*.

From Valley Forge to Columbia

After graduating from Valley Forge, Salinger enrolled at New York University for the 1936 summer session, then abandoned academics in favor of a tour of Austria and Poland. The intent of his father was that he learn the family ham and cheese importing business. However, the political situation in Europe rapidly deteriorated in 1938 with the German invasion of Austria, causing Salinger to return stateside, whereupon he enrolled in Ursinus College at Collegeville, Pennsylvania. At Ursinus he made a mark for himself, both through his sophisticated European-influenced dress and his declaration to fellow students that he would one day write the Great American Novel. Although he resumed his writing and contributed humorous vignettes and movie reviews to the school's weekly newspaper, Salinger felt that the Ursinus English department did little to support his literary development. Although intelligent, he grew impatient with the by-the-book learning offered by academia, and he left Ursinus after only one semester, thus putting an end to his efforts to earn a four-year degree.

Despite his aversion to formal education, in 1939 Salinger enrolled in an evening class offered by Columbia University, a short-story writing class taught by veteran writer and *Story* magazine founder/editor Whit Burnett. Burnett made a lasting impression on the young writer, and *Story* ended up publishing Salinger's first story, "The Young Folks," in the spring of 1940. Encouraged by the twenty-five dollar sale to *Story*, Salinger expended an increasing amount of time on his writing; within a year he boasted sales of stories to several popular magazines. Appearing in the pages of such slick publications as *Colliers'*, *Saturday Evening Post*, *Good Housekeeping*, *Cosmopolitan*, *New Yorker*, and *Esquire*, Salinger's early stories were characterized by *Dictionary of Literary Biography* essayist Warren French as "very short, highly colloquial, sentimental, yet heavily ironic tales" modeled on those of writer O. Henry. "Many of them are the very popular 'short, short stories' with a surprise ending that could be printed on a single page," French added.

When the United States entered World War II, Salinger volunteered for military service but was initially rejected because of a mild heart complaint. In the spring of 1942, however, he was reclassified and drafted into the army where he served until the end of the war. After being stationed at several U.S. training centers, Salinger flew overseas in 1944 to train with the Counter-Intelligence Corps. He landed with the 4th Division in Normandy on D-Day, only six hours after the first allied assault for the liberation of France. Although he never rose above the rank of sergeant, Salinger participated in five European campaigns and was responsible for ferreting out former Gestapo by interviewing German prisoners in their native language, thanks to his travels in Europe. He also experienced some of the heaviest fighting of the war and was at one time hospitalized for combat-related stress.

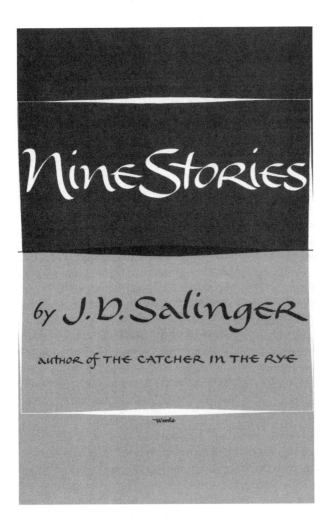

Many of the stories in this postmodernist short story collection feature characters trying to make sense of a changed world during and after World War II.

Despite his military responsibilities, Salinger also continued to write, sending home stories about his experiences in the Army Signal Corps on a portable typewriter he carried throughout Europe in his jeep. Interestingly, he would later refuse to republish any of these early stories and went so far as to file a lawsuit to prevent distribution of a pirated edition of his uncollected early pieces that appeared in 1974. In an interview with Lacey Fosburgh for the *New York Times,* Salinger expressed outrage over the theft of his copyrighted property and his annoyance at the continued invasion of his privacy. Denying that he wished to hide anything, the author insisted rather that he wanted his apprentice work "to die a perfectly natural death."

After World War II Salinger remained in Europe, working as a civilian. He married a French woman named Sylvia, but was divorced within two years. By that time Salinger had returned to the United States. Now back home and living in his parents' house, Salinger continued to write stories for magazine publication, notable among them "Slight Rebellion off Madison," which appeared in the *New Yorker* in December, 1946. Not only was "Slight Rebellion" his first sale to the prestigious *New Yorker,* but it also marked the first appearance of Holden Caulfield, who would be the main character in *Catcher in the Rye.*

New Influences Mark *Nine Stories*

By the mid-1940s Salinger appeared to be taking a more serious slant to his fiction writing. Between 1946 and 1951 he published seven stories in the *New Yorker,* which made him one of the magazine's top contributors. The *New Yorker's* editors liked Salinger's work because it fit in with their market: the young, sophisticated, and well-educated upper-middle-class men and women enjoying the nation's renewed prosperity following World War II. The mid-1940s also marked the beginning of Salinger's interest in Zen Buddhism, evidenced by his attendance at the Rama Krishna-Vivekananda Center in New York City. Zen-influenced themes—among them, counselling the abandonment of material values and the relinquishment of personal ego as a way to attain enlightenment of one's soul—would begin to show themselves in his fiction by the early1950s, notably in the short story "Teddy," published in the *New Yorker.*

The short stories Salinger penned during the late 1940s and early 1950s exhibit not only more serious, Eastern influence, but also reflect tendencies that literary critics would later dub Post-Modernist. In the years following World War II, writers and artists reacted to the dismal realities of a world in which entire human populations had almost been exterminated through the efforts of other human populations. It was also a world over which the threat of nuclear destruction now hung. Within this growing Cold War mentality, the creative arts began to reflect the same sense of despair, paranoia, and irrationality that pervaded society as a whole. The postmodern sensibility can be seen in the literary works of not only Salinger, but also Saul Bellow, Norman Mailer, Kurt Vonnegut, and Thomas Pynchon. In 1953 a number of Salinger's postmodernist works would be collected in *Nine Stories.*

While Salinger's postwar stories are not completely hopeless in their outlook, the bulk of those collected in *Nine Stories* demonstrate the seemingly insoluble dilemma people face in coming to terms with the "hell on earth" that has been either self-created in their own minds or imposed by the hostile conditions of contemporary life. Children are frequently cast as victims of the adult world, as in "Teddy," where the spiritually sophisticated young protagonist is killed in an empty pool; and "Down at the Dinghy," which tells of four-year-old Lionel's initiation into the world of bigotry and hatred. Other stories in the collection focus upon the problems encountered by adults, who are either portrayed as helpless against the complex emotional entanglements of modern life or as corrupted exploiters of others. In the story "Pretty Mouth and Green My Eyes," for instance, an attorney tries to comfort a co-worker calling late at night for guidance because he suspects his absent wife of infidelity. As the attorney calmly and rationally explains away the caller's fears, he is all the while laying in bed next to the very woman under discussion.

Another characteristic of Salinger's *Nine Stories,* as well as much of his fiction, is the quest for honest human emotional contact. Searching for unconditional love as a counter to life's travails is illustrated in "For Esme—With Love and Squalor." Considered by critics to be one of Salinger's most expertly crafted pieces of short fiction, the story is also celebrated for its effective depiction of the World War II experience. "For Esme" compiles the experiences of writer/narrator Sergeant X while in Devon, England, shortly before D-Day, and involves an upper-class teen whom the narrator meets in a tearoom. The narrator, suffering from battle fatigue, is struck by the thirteen-year-old Esme's innocence, as well as her beauty and friendliness, and he promises to write a story for her about "squalor." Almost a year later, while Sergeant X lies in a German hospital recovering from combat-provoked insomnia, haunted by lingering images of Nazi atrocities, he receives a battered package from Esme. Along with a letter reminding him of his promise to write a story about "squalor" and containing her best wishes on his recovery, Esme encloses her dead father's broken watch as a gift. Reading her letter and cheered by her genuine affection, the writer/narrator can now sleep. An invitation to Esme's wedding six years later coincides with his full recovery and his completion of the story.

The Catcher in the Rye

Salinger once said that he thought his fiction writing would be confined to short stories only. However, he later went on to write *The Catcher in the Rye.* The product of ten years' work, Salinger's magnum opus is considered by many to be the most sensitive portrait of a boy's coming-of-age produced during the twentieth century. Few other books have had as great an impact on a generation—so much so that its main character, sixteen-year-old Holden Caulfield, would enter the popular mythology of mid-twentieth-century U.S. culture alongside such figures as Mark Twain's Huck Finn. As critic Malcolm Bradbury noted in his *What Is a Novel?*, *The Catcher in the Rye* describes "the point [in human experience] at which the child becomes adult and at which an innocent and hopeful love, a desire to protect life, becomes a profound human problem."

A few days before Pencey Prep school lets out for Christmas break, Holden is informed that he is being expelled for bad grades. An intelligent young man, his failure in school is partly the result of the fact that he is haunted by the death of his younger brother, Allie. Holden idealizes the innocence of childhood that Allie embodied, and he resists the hypocritical adult world his education is forcing him to accept. While he is determined to escape adulthood by moving west and living a pastoral existence in a log cabin, Holden's first step is impulsively taken in the opposite direction: home to New York where he plans to say goodbye to his ten-year-old sister, Phoebe. During a three-day odyssey in the city he participates in a series of humorous adventures that, while appearing haphazard, *Dictionary of Literary Biography* essayist French noted are actually "akin to the archetypal night journey as rite of passage into maturity." A promising date with a young women goes awry, after which a night of drinking with a former schoolmate illustrates for Holden that his preconceptions about the trappings of "adulthood"—particularly adult sexuality—are perhaps ill-founded.

In typical teen fashion, narrator Holden is unaware of his own lack of maturity, and Salinger continually places Holden in situations wherein the boy's weaknesses are exposed. Despite revealing his protagonist's hypocrisy and weaknesses, the author also allows readers to bond with the teen due to Holden's caring, sensitivity, and intelligence. Unable to deal effectively within the strictures of the adult world presented to him, Holden lashes out at whatever he cannot cope with as "phoniness," and dismisses those adults successfully surviving in the trap of society as mere "victims." While Holden tries to deceive a host of "phonies"—the parent of a teen friend, a pair of nuns, a prostitute—his dishonesty is inspired by a desperate need for human connection and to find one person with whom he can truly communicate. Much of Holden's sympathetic appeal for readers lies in his loneliness and misguided attempts to navigate the confusing landscape of adulthood. His ultimate realization—that childhood innocence cannot last forever—is brought home to him through his sister, Phoebe, the person who until now he has most idealized. His epiphany comes as he watches her reach for the brass ring during a carousel ride. "The thing with kids is, if they want to grab for the gold ring, you have to let them do it, and not say anything," Holden finally admits to the reader. "If they fall off, they fall off, but it's bad if you say anything to them." The choice of how to function within the adult arena—whether to accept the prevailing value system and strive for material gain or not—is one that each person must make and for which each person ultimately takes responsibility.

As Ron Evans explained in the *St. James Guide to Young Adult Writers*, *The Catcher in the Rye* is "an often hilarious parody of the classical heroic od-

yssey. The hero separates from a previously intolerable existence, finds in himself new integrity and self-confidence, and returns to hishomeland with the quality of leadership." In Salinger's novel, Holden's quest takes him to New York, and ultimately to his parents' home, where he arrives with a new knowledge of society and his place within it.

"I keep picturing all these kids playing some game in this big field of rye and all. Thousands of little kids, and nobody's around—nobody big, I mean—except me. And I'm standing on the edge of some crazy cliff. What I have to do, I have to catch everybody if they start to go over the cliff—I mean if they're running and they don't look where they're going I have to come out from somewhere and catch them. That's all I'd do all day. I'd just be the catcher in the rye and all."

—from *The Catcher in the Rye*

While Salinger's childhood—particularly his memories of Valley Forge Military Academy—provided the model for Holden and his experiences at the fictitious Pencey Prep in *The Catcher in the Rye*, parallels between the novelist and his fictional alter-ego are not as significant as readers might at first assume. While both boys grew up in upper-class Manhattan households, Holden has strong relationships with four siblings, while Salinger had a distant relationship with his older sister. Holden's father led a colorful life as a lawyer and a producer of Broadway shows; Salinger's father was a nose-to-the-grindstone businessman. Instead of being shy and short of friends at school like Holden, Salinger has been remembered by his former schoolmates as gregarious, mischievous, and welcoming the company of others. Most importantly, Holden Caulfield is a post-war teen, a creation of the Post-Modern sensibility; Salinger grew up in a far more optimistic, humanistic era.

Appeal to Youth Makes Novel Controversial

The Catcher in the Rye has been the subject of extensive controversy since its publication in 1951, partly because of the obscene language Salinger uses in the novel, and partly because of the rebellious attitude of its protagonist/narrator. Banned in Australia and South Africa when it attracted young readers in droves, the book was also condemned by the Nevada-based National Organization for Decent Literature in 1956. During the 1960s *Catcher* was removed from public school shelves in three states, and even as late as the 1970s, after the novel had lost enough of its incendiary effect to be placed on the required reading list in high schools and colleges across the United States, small-town libraries could still be found shelving *Catcher in the Rye* in the "restricted reading" section.

Part of the controversy for critics has been the intention of the novel's author. Is Holden an "unreliable narrator" expressing a viewpoint the author knows to be flawed, or does he actually serve as a voice for Salinger? Maintaining that the novel's author "sees the world in terms of allies and enemies," Mary McCarthy viewed the book negatively in an essay for *Harper's. The Catcher in the Rye*, she wrote, "is based on a scheme of exclusiveness." Salinger divides his characters "into those who belong to the club and those who don't." Whether the novelist ultimately sides with Holden "remains dubious," since "The only 'good' person Holden meets is his little sister—himself in miniature." McCarthy found Salinger's position to be surreptitiously elitist. "There is something false and sentimental here," she concluded. "Holden is supposed to be an outsider in his school, in the middle-class world, but he is really an insider with the track all to himself." In *Ramparts*, critic Robert O. Bowen agreed, blasting *Catcher in the Rye* as "catty, snide and bigoted in the most thorough sense" due to Holden/Salinger's repeated indulgence in "caste snobbery" through judgements made against people lacking in the bourgeois manners and economic trappings valued by an upper-class, prep-school elite.

Other criticisms were leveled against Salinger for fomenting a rebellious attitude among his teen readers. Interestingly, although the novel's protagonist does indeed rebel against adult society, he does not want to overturn society's established value system. Rather, what Holden insists upon isthat traditional, nonmaterialistic values be restored from the perversion suffered during the post-war economic boom to their original idealistic basis. As reviewer Hugh Maclean argued in

College English, Catcher in the Rye is in many ways a conservative work that expresses the increasing difficulty of preserving moral integrity in a world prone to destroying its most treasured values. If such is the case, there has probably not been any other work of traditional values more misunderstood and actively persecuted than *The Catcher in the Rye.*

Publication of *The Catcher in the Rye* catapulted its author to international prominence, but such notoriety was not something that Salinger seems to have sought—or welcomed. Against the recurring waves of critical examination that delved into his personal mores, attitudes, and integrity, thirty-four-year-old Salinger withdrew to a small home in

Both of these short stories, which first appeared in the *New Yorker*, focus on the two youngest members of the Glass family, Franny and Zooey.

Cornish, New Hampshire, on New Year's Day, 1953. Although he welcomed local visitors—particularly groups of local teens with whom he would spend hours talking to and entertaining with music—Salinger avoided the press and the general public with increasing vigor over the ensuing years. In 1955 he married again, this time wedding British-born Radcliffe College student Claire Douglas, whom he had met two years earlier and with whom he would have two children—Margaret Ann and Matthew—before the couple ultimately divorced in 1967. Claire Salinger would go on to become a Jungian psychologist.

In addition to avoiding the press, Salinger avoided any chance of repeating his large-scale success by concentrating exclusively on the short story form, working sometimes in story cycles that shared themes and characters. The tenets of Zen, which the author increasingly embraced during the 1950s, began to show themselves most clearly in his largest story cycle, the Glass family saga.

Glass Family Saga

While *The Catcher in the Rye* became a favorite of adolescent readers during the late 1950s and early 1960s, critical response to the young novelist was slow in coming; it was not until the novel was supported by the 1953 appearance of *Nine Stories* that Salinger's works began to attract serious critical attention. During the 1950s his literary profile was further enhanced by the gradual unfolding of the Glass family saga in the pages of the *New Yorker*. The Glass family of New York—retired vaudeville performers Les and Bessie Glass, and their children Seymour, Buddy, Boo Boo, twins Walt and Waker, Zooey, and the youngest, Franny—are profiled in six short stories: "A Perfect Day for Bananafish," "Franny," "Zooey," "Raise High the Roof Beam, Carpenters," "Seymour: An Introduction," and "Hapworth 16, 1924," all of which have since been republished in book form.

Published in the late 1940s, "A Perfect Day for Bananafish" is the first story to feature Seymour Glass, eldest of the Glass children and a tragic figure who haunts the entire saga. "Bananafish" examines Seymour's life, particularly the spiritual quest that was the young man's central preoccupation, and recounts his unhappy end. "Bananafish" also introduces themes that would

become central to the Glass family saga: the conflict between those in search of spiritual meaning and those in search of material wealth; the loss of childhood innocence; and the search for genuine, unconditional love.

Although "Bananafish" ends shockingly—Seymour calmly sits down opposite his sleeping wife and blows out his brains—it does not depend on sensationalism to achieve its impact. Rather, the ending is not surprising, given the ambivalence created by Salinger toward his troubled protagonist, a man who seems both innocent and threatening, highly spiritual yet somehow perverse. Although Seymour actually appears only in "A Perfect Day for Bananafish," the influence he holds over his younger siblings makes him the pivotal character in all the Glass stories.

First published in 1955, "Franny" is considered the most conventional story of the cycle. In it the youngest of Seymour's sisters, a student in college, suffers an emotional and physical breakdown while attempting to reconcile her need for spiritual balance with her sexual dependency on Luke, her crude and insensitive boyfriend. Franny's crisis continues in the companion story, 1957's "Zooey," in which her older, television-actor brother reminds her of the example set by Seymour, who aided Zooey in learning to accept the worldly nature of religious experience. The constant introspection characteristic of the Glass siblings as each of them attempts to integrate the spiritual standards set by their older brother into their flawed lives serves as the central conflict within Salinger's saga.

1955's "Raise High the Roof Beam, Carpenters" and 1959's "Seymour: An Introduction" were published together in book form in 1963. Again, both stories revolve around Seymour, and both are narrated by his younger brother and budding writer Buddy Glass, a character Salinger once identified as his alter-ego. In "Raise High the Roof Beam, Carpenters" Buddy recalls Seymour's wedding to fiance Muriel Fedder in 1942, when the bride and groom bowed out in favor of eloping. While Seymour is not physically present, he is revealed through Buddy's record of the conversations of annoyed wedding guests. Reflecting on these overheard conversations, Buddy begins to understand a facet of Seymour's character: that his older brother will not allow himself to be compromised by others' opinions of him.

Raise High the Roof Beam, Carpenters

and

Seymour
an Introduction

J. D. Salinger

Buddy Glass narrates a pair of stories that focus on his older brother, Seymour Glass, in this 1963 publication.

After Seymour's suicide, Buddy pens "Seymour: An Introduction" as a way to enable the "general reader" to understand the saintly nature of his dead brother. A rambling and disjointed narrative, "Seymour" often reveals more about Buddy than it does about its purported subject. As an experimental work of fiction, "Seymour: An Introduction" has often been viewed as less than successful, and was dismissed by many critics. Its lack of focus marked a change in Salinger's style, a change that preceded his decision to end his public career as a writer.

Salinger's last piece of published fiction is "Hapworth 16, 1924," a novella-length story published in the New Yorker in 1965. The final installment in the Glass family saga, "Hapworth" consists of a thirty-thousand-word letter purportedly written by seven-year-old Seymour to his family describing his and five-year-old Buddy's experiences at summer camp. The letter contains such well-wrought prose and intimations of sexual sophistication and erudition that readers cannot accept it for what Salinger presents it as—the work of a young child, even one as bright as Seymour. However, as French contends, the disparity between what is plausible and what appears on the page only underscores the "heart-rending evocations of an exquisitely sensitive young person trapped in a situation for which he can find no physical or metaphysical justification." In this sense, "Hepworth" is valuable as a means to explain the Glass saga's mournful undercurrents, which can be sensed even beneath the often humorous surface narratives.

According to critic Eberhard Alsen in his *Salinger's Glass Stories as a Composite Novel*, the best way to grasp the long and complex Glass family saga is to consider all the stories together as a complete unit. Alsen asserted that in this light the work can be read as a kind of *Kunstler-Roman*, or novel about the growth of an artist's aesthetic sensibility. Three major themes appear in the Glass cycle, said Alsen: 1) a concern over the lack of spiritual values in modern society; 2) the development of the character Buddy as a writer; and 3) Seymour's quest for spiritual enlightenment. These themes are familiar to readers of Salinger's other short fiction, and shadows of them are woven throughout *The Catcher in the Rye* as well.

Continued Critical Interest

With the appearance of the Glass family saga in book form during the 1960s, critics reevaluated the work as a literary "whole." While the 1960 publication of *Franny and Zooey* became a literary event, it also ushered in some harsh criticism as overarching themes were revealed. Many reviewers now faulted the Glass family members for being smug, snobbish, and self-absorbed. Reviewing the work in an appraisal included in his *Contemporaries*, Alfred Kazin accused Salinger of appealing to a "vast public" of readers "released by our society to think of themselves as endlessly sensitive, spiritually alone, gifted, and whose suffering lies in the narrowing of their consciousness to themselves." The attack on the preoccupation with self that characterizes the Glass family saga was continued by John Updike in his review of *Franny and Zooey* in the *New York Times Book Review.* The novelist-critic pointed to Salinger's apparent loss of artistic objectivity, commenting that the author "loves the Glasses more than God loves them. . . . Their invention has become a hermitage for him. He loves them to the detriment of artistic moderation . . . [and] never rests from circling his creations, patting them fondly, slyly applauding." In doing so, Updike contended, Salinger "robs the reader of the initiative upon which love must be given." However, other critics viewed Salinger's purpose differently, Evans noting that while "sometimes criticized for otherworldly elitism, Salinger's narratives give young adults a perspective for fashioning a spirituality in an age of anti-spiritual consumerism."

Despite negative reviews of *Franny and Zooey,* the book was a popular success. However, reader interest began to erode with the appearance of the final Glass stories in the mid-1960s. Aiding to this evaporation of public interest was Salinger's refusal to participate in the debate over his work, as well as his decision to discontinue publishing after the appearance of "Hapworth 16, 1924" in June of 1965.

While Salinger's appeal to young readers waned during the early 1970s due to both his lack of concern for political or social reform and as a result of the passivity and escapism evidenced by his main protagonists, his works continued to be analyzed and discussed by critics, particularly as interest in oriental philosophies resurfaced in the early 1980s. According to essayist Warren French, this resurgence of interest occurred to a writer "who has deeply enough absorbed . . . traditional wisdom from the East to be able to use it artfully in shaping legends that enable readers to appreciate through familiar icons the meaning of esoteric doctrines. Like the Phoenix of Eastern mythology," added French, "Salinger has risen from the ashes of his own *timely*reputation to assume what may prove a timeless one."

A Victim of His Own Success

In the years since his final story was published in the *New Yorker,* Salinger has grown increasingly protective of his privacy, fending off autograph-seekers, the press, biographers, and most other public contact. While rumors continued to surface

If you enjoy the works of J. D. Salinger, you may also want to check out the following books:

Brock Cole, *The Facts Speak for Themselves,* 1997.
Sarah Dessen, *That Summer,* 1996.
Rob Thomas, *Rats Saw God,* 1996.

about one author or another being Salinger writing under a pen name, every rumor has, in turn, been shown to be false. In 1981 Salinger's son Matthew garnered some publicity when he began to appear on stage as an actor, but he refused to divulge any information about his famous father, telling *People Weekly* interviewer Paul Corkery, "I won't let people try to get at my father . . . through me. I know how much he does not want public attention. . . . He is a wonderful father and I respect him." Despite the renewed interest in his work that surfaced in the 1980s, Salinger remained firm in his desire for privacy. In 1987 he was forced to file legal papers to prevent publication of a comprehensive study of his life and work by biographer Ian Hamilton. The following year an extensively revised version of Hamilton's work was published as *In Search of J. D. Salinger.*

A fence was eventually constructed around Salinger's New England home, solidifying the writer's desire to remove himself from public scrutiny. It is a position from which he has not wavered since. Even after a fire damaged parts of the Salinger home in the fall of 1992, none but necessary personnel were allowed inside the compound. In a studio he constructed from concrete blocks, he is now reported to write for his own pleasure, sometimes spending as much as fifteen hours a day on his prose.

In one of the rare opportunities he presented to interviewers, he was asked about his craft. Salinger responded that he considered writing a hard life, although the rewards could be great. Among the writers he listed among his major influences were Franz Kafka, Marcel Proust, Arthur Rimbaud, Emily Bronte, Henry James, William Blake, and Leo Tolstoy. Interestingly, each of them reflects a time, and a society, that has long since vanished.

■ Works Cited

Alsen, Eberhard, *Salinger's Glass Stories as a Composite Novel*, Whitston (Troy, NY), 1983.

Bowen, Robert O., "The Salinger Syndrome: Charity against Whom?," *Ramparts*, May, 1962, pp. 47-66.

Bradbury, Malcolm, *What Is a Novel?*, Edward Arnold, 1969, p. 67.

Corkery, Paul, "Solitude May Be Bliss for Author J. D. Salinger, but to Son Matt, All the World's a Stage," *People Weekly*, October 31, 1983.

Dictionary of Literary Biography, Volume 2: *American Novelists since World War II, First Series*, Gale, 1978, pp. 434-444.

Dictionary of Literary Biography, Volume 173: *American Novelist since World War II, Fifth Series*, Gale, 1996, pp. 235-248.

Fosburgh, Lacey, "J. D. Salinger Speaks about His Silence," *New York Times*, November 3, 1974, pp. 1, 69.

Kazin, Alfred, *Contemporaries*, Atlantic Monthly Press, 1962.

Mailer, Norman, *Advertisements for Myself*, Putnam, 1959, pp. 467-468.

Maclean, Hugh, review of *Catcher in the Rye*, *College English*, March, 1954, pp. 315-325.

McCarthy, Mary, "J. D. Salinger's Closed Circuit," *Harper's*, October, 1962, pp. 46-48.

St. James Guide to Young Adult Writers, St. James, 1999, pp. 736-738.

Updike, John, "Anxious Days for the Glass Family," *New York Times Book Review*, September 17, 1961, pp. 1, 52.

■ For More Information See

BOOKS

Belcher, W. F., and J. W. Lee, editors, *J. D. Salinger and the Critics*, Wadsworth, 1962.

Bloom, Harold, editor, *J. D. Salinger: Modern Critical Views*, Chelsea House, 1987.

Carpenter, Humphrey, *Secret Gardens: A Study of the Golden Age of Children's Literature*, Houghton, 1985.

Children's Literature Review, Volume 18, Gale, 1989.

Concise Dictionary of American Literary Biography: The New Consciousness, 1941-1968, Gale, 1987, pp. 448-458.

Contemporary Literary Criticism, Gale, Volume 1, 1973; Volume 3, 1975; Volume 8, 1978; Volume 12, 1980; Volume 55, 1989; Volume 56, 1989.

Dictionary of Literary Biography, Gale, Volume 102: *American Short-Story Writers, 1910-1945*, 1991, pp. 258-265.

Donelson, Kenneth L., and Alleen Pace Nilsen, *Literature for Today's Young Adults*, Scott, Foresman, 1980.

Engel, Steven, *Readings on The Catcher in the Rye*, Greenhaven Press, 1998.

Filler, Louis, editor, *Seasoned "Authors" for a New Season: The Search for Standards in Popular Writing*, Bowling Green University Popular Press, 1980.

French, Warren, *J. D. Salinger, Revisited*, Twayne, 1988.

Geismar, Maxwell, *American Moderns: From Rebellion to Conformity*, Hill & Wang, 1958.

Grunwald, Henry Anatole, editor, *Salinger: A Critical and Personal Portrait*, Harper, 1962.

Gwynn, Frederick L., and Joseph L. Blotner, *The Fiction of J. D. Salinger*, Pittsburgh University Press, 1958.

Hamilton, Ian, *In Search of J. D. Salinger*, Random House, 1988.

Hamilton, Kenneth, *J. D. Salinger: A Critical Essay*, Eerdmans, 1967.

Hassan, Ihab, *Radical Innocence: Studies in the Contemporary American Novel*, Princeton University Press, 1961.

Holzman, Robert S., and Gary L. Perkins, *J. D. Salinger's "The Catcher in the Rye,"* Research & Education Association, 1995.

Laser, Marvin, and Norman Fruman, editors, *Studies in J. D. Salinger*, Odyssey, 1963.

Lundquist, James, *J. D. Salinger*, Ungar, 1979.

Marsden, Malcolm M., editor, *"If You Really Want to Know": A Catcher Casebook*, Scott, Foresman, 1963.

Maynard, Joyce, *At Home in the World: A Memoir*, Picador USA, 1998.

Miller, James E., Jr., *J. D. Salinger*, Minnesota University Press, 1965.

Rosen, Gerald, *Zen in the Art of J. D. Salinger*, Creative Arts, 1977.

Schulz, Max F., *Radical Sophistication: Studies in Contemporary Jewish-American Novelists*, Ohio University Press, 1969, pp. 198-217.

Short Story Criticism, Gale, Volume 2, 1989, pp. 288-320, Volume 28, 1999, pp. 220-339.

Something about the Author, Volume 67, Gale, 1992.

Simonson, Harold P., and E. P. Hager, editors, *"Catcher in the Rye": Clamor vs. Criticism*, Heath, 1963.

Sublette, Jack R., *J. D. Salinger: An Annotated Bibliography, 1938-1981*, Garland, 1984.

Weinberg, Helen, *The New Novel in America: The Kafkan Mode in Contemporary American Fiction,* Cornell University Press, 1970.

PERIODICALS

America, January 26, 1963.

American Quarterly, winter, 1977, pp. 547-562.

American Literature, November, 1968, pp. 352-369.

American Speech, October, 1959, pp. 172-181.

Atlantic, August, 1961, pp. 27-31.

Book Week, September 26, 1965.

Chicago Review, winter, 1958, pp. 3-19.

Chicago Tribune, June 17, 1987.

College English, November, 1956, pp. 76-80; January, 1961, pp. 262-264; December, 1961, pp. 226-229; December, 1965, pp. 248-251.

College Language Association Journal, March, 1963, pp. 170-183.

Commentary, September, 1987, pp. 61-64.

Commonweal, February 23, 1973, pp. 465-469.

Crawdaddy, March, 1975.

Critical Inquiry, autumn, 1976, pp. 15-38.

Criticism, summer, 1967, pp. 275-288.

Critique, spring-summer, 1965.

Dalhousie Review, autumn, 1967, pp. 394-399.

English Journal, March, 1964; April, 1993.

Entertainment Weekly, July 15, 1994, p. 80.

Harper's, February, 1959, pp. 83-90; December, 1962.

Horizon, May, 1962.

Life, November 3, 1961.

London Review, winter, 1969-1970, pp. 34-54.

Los Angeles Times, November 7, 1986.

Mademoiselle, August, 1961.

Mainstream, February, 1959, pp. 2-13.

Modern Fiction Studies, autumn, 1966.

Modern Language Quarterly, December, 1964, pp. 461-472.

Mosaic, fall, 1968, pp. 3-17.

Nation, November 14, 1959, pp. 360-363.

New Republic, October 19, 1959, pp. 19-22; April 28, 1973, pp. 30-32.

Newsweek, May 30, 1961; January 28, 1963; July 30, 1979.

New York Herald Tribune Book Review, July 15, 1951.

New York Post Weekend Magazine, April 30, 1961, p. 5.

New York Times, April 12, 1977, Section 1, p. 3; November 8, 1986; August 4, 1987; October 6, 1987; September 3, 1989.

New York Times Book Review, June 3, 1979.

Partisan Review, fall, 1962, pp. 594-598.

Renascence, summer, 1970, pp. 171-182; spring, 1971, pp. 115-128; spring, 1972, pp. 159-167.

Saturday Review, September 16, 1961; November 4, 1961.

Studies in Short Fiction, spring, 1967, pp. 217-224; spring, 1970, pp. 248-256; winter, 1973, pp. 27-33; winter, 1981, pp. 1-15; summer, 1981, pp. 251-259.

Time, September 15, 1961, pp. 84-90.

Twentieth-Century Literature, October, 1958, pp. 92-99.

Village Voice, August 22, 1974.

Washington Post, November 6, 1986; November 8, 1986; November 19, 1986; December 4, 1986; December 12, 1986; January 30, 1987; February 4, 1987; February 9, 1987; February 13, 1987; May 5, 1987; October 7, 1987; December 6, 1989.

Western Humanities Review, spring, 1956, pp. 129-137; summer, 1963, pp. 271-277.

Western Review, summer, 1957, pp. 261-280.

Wisconsin Studies in Contemporary Literature, winter, 1961, pp. 5-30; winter, 1963, pp. 109-149.*

Tom Shadyac

■ Personal

Surname pronounced "SHAY-dee-ak"; born in Virginia in 1959; son of Richard (an attorney) and Julie Shadyac. *Education:* University of Virginia, B.A. (pre-law), 1980; University of California at Los Angeles, M.A. (film), 1989.

■ Addresses

Agent–United Talent Agency, 9560 Wilshire Blvd., Beverly Hills, CA 90212.

■ Career

Director, writer, and producer. Joke writer for comedian Bob Hope, c. 1983-85; rewrote, directed, and worked on movies-of-the-week for Fox; stand-up comedian at the Improv in Los Angeles. Founder of Shady Acres Productions and 333 Music Group, 1999. Appeared in role of Chris in the film *Jocks,* Crown, 1987; other film credits include: director of *Ace Ventura, Pet Detective,* Warner Bros., 1994, *The Nutty Professor,* Universal, 1996, and *Liar, Liar,* Uni-

versal, 1997; director and executive producer of *Patch Adams,* Universal, 1998; executive producer of *The Nutty Professor II: The Klumps,* Universal, 2000; television work includes production consultant for movie *Working Trash,* syndicated, 1990, and director of movie *Frankenstein: The College Years,* Fox, 1991.

■ Writings

SCREENPLAYS

(With Jack Bernstein and Jim Carrey) *Ace Ventura, Pet Detective,* Warner Bros., 1994.
(With others) *The Nutty Professor* (based on the screenplay by Jerry Lewis and Bill Richmond), Universal, 1996.

■ Sidelights

With his first four major motion pictures grossing close to one hundred million dollars each in box office receipts, director and screenwriter Tom Shadyac would certainly qualify as a hot Hollywood property. Boasting a set of directoral credits that include *Ace Ventura, Pet Detective, Liar, Liar, The Nutty Professor,* and *Patch Adams,* Shadyac has a good sense of what constitutes entertainment for many U.S. moviegoers. As Susan Wloszczyna declared in a *USA Today* review of the film *Liar, Liar,* "Every great filmmaker has a signature, an artistic trademark that immediately lets audience members know they haven't wandered into the wrong multiplex theatre. . . . For Tom Shadyac, it's bathroom humor."

Born in 1959 and raised in upscale Falls Church, Virginia, Shadyac–who is of Lebanese ancestry--proved to be a good student, although he exhibited an unbridled tendency toward hijinks during his high school years. After graduating from J. E. B. Stuart High School with good grades, he planned to follow in the footsteps of both his attorney father and his older brother and prepared for a career in the legal arena. Enrolling at the University of Virginia, Shadyac got enough exposure to the field through his course work to reconsider his choice of a legal career soon after graduating with a major in pre-law. Instead, he decided, he would break with family tradition and pursue a career in the entertainment industry. Recalling

the sense of humor that had helped him survive high school as a short person, Shadyac decided that he would go into acting, maybeeven become a comedian.

Following the Comic Muse to Hollywood

In 1983 Shadyac packed up his belongings and moved to Hollywood; he was twenty-three at the time. Planning to enroll at the University of California—Los Angeles, Shadyac immediately immersed himself in the West Coast film culture, helping friends with their film-school projects, and even getting a gig as a stand-up comic at the Hollywood Improv. In between writing scripts, teaching acting classes, and scoring bit parts in films and television series—he played a surfer in an episode of *Magnum, P.I.*, and had a minor role in the 1987 film *Jocks*—he got the help of an uncle and landed

Jon Capodice (left), Jim Carrey (center), and Sean Young star in Tom Shadyac's directorial debut, *Ace Ventura, Pet Detective*, released in 1994.

a job on the staff of well-known comedian Bob Hope's joke-writing brigade. While penning "bad jokes" for Hope, he also attended to his studies and earned his master's degree in filmmaking in 1989, the same year he served as an actor's coach on the film *War Party*. Shadyac's student production for UCLA was *Tom, Dick, and Harry*, a short film about a talking penis. Exhibiting the same sophomoric humor that had gotten him and his friends into hot water in high school, *Tom, Dick, and Harry* was the project that convinced Shadyac that directing, rather than acting, was where he wanted his life's work to focus. It was also the film that he showed around Hollywood once he completed grad school, the one that first got him noticed.

The subject matter and quality of humor of *Tom, Dick, and Harry* distills Shadyac's basic approach to the motion picture arts: aim to be puerile and popular. Referring to his characteristic use of bathroom humor and other sophomoric hijinks—his *Nutty Professor* is well known for its massive gas attack scene—Shadyac admitted in *USA Today*: "I am known as the orifice director. The director who can make comedy come out of any orifice." While its humorous punch aimed low, it also aimed true, and Shadyac was picked up by the Fox television network to direct a send-up of Mary Shelley's *Frankenstein* story adapted as a television film.

Shadyac Meets Carrey for Career Lift-Off

While *Frankenstein: The College Years,* which aired on the Fox network in 1991, was Shadyac's first effort at directing a commercial film product, 1994's *Ace Ventura, Pet Detective* would be his full-length feature-film directoral debut. Starring Canadian comedian Jim Carrey in his first film role, *Ace Ventura*'s high-energy slapstick content was aimed directly at the high school and college crowd. Fresh from a run on the popular comedy television show *In Living Color,* Carrey pulls out all the stops in his portrayal of the title character, a wacko sleuth specializing in tracking down runaway hounds and missing kitties. His specialized line of detective work is making it pretty hard to keep up with payables until Ventura is hired to track down the person or persons guilty of making off with the Miami Dolphin's water-bound mascot, Snowflake. Playing opposite Carrey is perky Courteney Cox as Melissa, a Miami Dolphins publicist who must fend off an endless barrage of amorous advances from

Ventura—as well as navigate, uninjured, through his menagerie-like apartment—while helping to solve the crime. As the pet-loving gumshoe goes on the trail of the missing dolphin, he becomes entangled in a plot involving Miami quarterback Dan Marino and a mysterious Super Bowl fumble that seems to be connected to a cold-blooded murder.

Shadyac's first-time directoral effort resulted in mixed reviews from critics. *Chicago Sun-Times* stalwart Roger Ebert called *Ace Ventura, Pet Detective* "a long, unfunny slog through an impenetrable plot." In the *Washington Post,* film critic Desson Howe questioned the film's reliance on both the "big strain of homophobic jokes . . . [and] profane and sexual situations that rule out the kiddie audience." However, Howe added that "Carrey is one funny animal." While the screenplay—penned by Shadyac and writer Jack Bernstein—depended heavily upon Carrey's rubber-faced antics for laughs, the film still managed to gross one hundred million dollars in revenue from its worldwide release. As *Variety* critic Steve Gaydos concluded of the box-office gross, "Dumb good times still wield a strong lure for the Saturday night date crowd." Overcoming the mixed critical response to become a box-office bonanza, *Ace Ventura* impressed film industry insiders and gained Shadyac the attention of industry bigwigs such as Steven Spielberg and Michael Eisner. Soon his phone was ringing and comedy scripts were pouring in for his consideration. While 1997's *Liar, Liar* would again reunite the Shadyac-Carrey combo, Shadyac's next film found him rehashing an old film, in typical 1990s Hollywood fashion.

Play It Again, Shadyac

The Nutty Professor, 1996's vehicle for comedian Eddie Murphy, was a remake of a film funnyman Jerry Lewis first released in 1963. In the updated version revised by Shadyac and others, a four-hundred-pound biochemistry professor named Sherman Klump develops a fat-reducing concoction. When he ingests some of it he turns into a svelte ladies' man who immediately makes moves on a fellow scientist, played by Jada Pinkett. In several memorable scenes, Murphy follows in the footsteps of actors Peter Sellers and Alec Guinness as he portrays several relatives of Klump, thus keeping intact the family resemblance and keeping the opportunity for humor ever present. While noting

Tom Shadyac directed the 1996 box-office hit *The Nutty Professor*, which stars comedian Eddie Murphy as Professor Sherman Klump.

that the original film, co-written and directed by Lewis, was characterized by "self-indulgent moments," *Entertainment Weekly* contributor Bruce Fretts praised Shadyac as one of the "real creative forces" in a film that, although displaying "coarse humor,. . . exudes a sweet spirit that Lewis . . . never could have achieved." Praising Murphy's performance in the film, *USA Today* critic Mike Clark dubbed *The Nutty Professor* as, "at long last, an Eddie Murphy movie [that] has its plug in the socket."

As with the previous Carrey-Shadyac collaboration, *Liar, Liar* would boast domestic profits in excess of one hundred million dollars, making it three for three in Shadyac's favor. On the heels of a poorly reviewed performance in *Cable Guy*, Carrey tones down his quirky persona somewhat in playing Fletcher Reede, a workaholic attorney on the fast

track to partner in a law firm. Unfortunately, Reede's career obligations continually sideline his son, Max. Tired of hearing all his dad's excuses for not showing up as promised, Max makes a birthday wish on the five candles his father is not around to watch him blow out. The wish: that Dad would have to tell the truth for twenty-four hours. The result: "all the false promises and compliments that ease our paths through the day, all the little evasions that oil the wheels of social and professional . . . intercourse are suddenly unavailable to Fletcher," explained *Time* critic Richard Schickel. "And remember, he's a lawyer."

Praised by Schickel for direction that retains "enough surrealism . . . to content all but the most exigent Carrey fans," Shadyac serves up "the most conventional movie Jim Carrey has ever made," in the opinion of *Newsweek* contributor Jeff Giles. But *Liar, Liar* also "delivers some perfect laughs," Giles continued. Dubbing it "Ace Ventura, Attorney-at-Law, but with familyvalues," *People Weekly* critic Leah Rozen agreed that *Liar, Liar* is funny "if you like your humor broad."

Undaunted Despite Critical Failure

Continuing in the comic vein, Shadyac's 1998 project involved him in the direction of another major comic talent: Robin Williams. That project was the film *Patch Adams*, based on the book *Gesundheit: Good Health Is a Laughing Matter*. The book's author, Hunter "Patch" Doherty Adams, M.D., is also the movie's lead character, played by Williams, a doctor who regularly ignores medical orthodoxy in his attempts to bring humor and healing into the lives of his patients. From his own stay in a mental hospital as a young man, the film follows Patch as he enrolls in medical school, fights the medical establishment to be allowed to inject the doctor-patient relationship with some compassion and much-needed humor, and showcases his efforts to establish a hospital that can dispense free medical care—and a full dose of levity—to those in need.

Patch Adams caused a stir among critics, several of whom maintained that the film's leading star, Williams, needed some serious intervention himself. Calling the movie "the most slovenly and whorishly sentimental work to become a big hit in [the United States] since 'Love Story' in 1970," *New Yorker* reviewer David Denby added that *Patch Adams* "re-

Jim Carrey appears in another Shadyac film, *Liar, Liar* (1997), along with actress Jennifer Tilly.

duced medical training to a choice between becoming a cold-hearted technician or a clown." A *People Weekly* reviewer agreed, calling the film "blatantly manipulative" and opining that Shadyac directs Williams' "borderline bizarre" character "without a trace of subtlety." And in *Entertainment Weekly* Lisa Schwarzbaum panned *Patch Adams* as "an offensive and deeply false 'inspirational' drama that idiotically indicts the entire medical profession in the service of making one man . . . look like a cockeyed saint."

While critics relentlessly panned the film, Shadyac preferred to listen to the reaction of the audiences attending test screenings, who, he maintained in a *New York Times* by Bernard Weinraub, responded "very strongly." Part of his defensiveness of the film was the result of his family: his father was very active in the St. Jude's hospital for children with cancer, while his mother, who passed away during the filming of *Patch Adams* after a long and debilitating illness, had used humor in the same way Patch does, as a means of helping her family deal with her condition. As the director told Weinraub, "I connected to the material in a very personal way." Shadyac dismissed negative critical reaction to the film by comparing it to the criticism heaped upon Frank Capra's Christmas classic *It's a Wonderful Life* and Steven Spielberg's blockbuster *E.T.*

Despite being raked over the coals by critics, *Patch Adams* grossed 130 million dollars in domestic profits, making the film his most profitable venture yet. On the strength of such consistently solid box-office returns, Shadyac was soon wooed by several film studios, among them Universal, with which he had worked on previous projects. In 1999 the thirty-something director entered into a three-year agreement with Universal Studios to direct and produce not only motion pictures but music as well. Film ideas, as well as new acting and technical talent, would be developed through Shadyac's Shady Acres Productions, while through his music company, 333 Music Group, Shadyac planned to produce soundtrack recordings for his Shady Acres films, as well as sign and promote new instrumental and vocal artists through recordingcontrasts. Universal management seemed enthusiastic about the deal. As C.E.O. Ron Meyer was quoted as saying in *PR Newswire:* "Our incredibly successful creative partnership with Tom has resulted in the highest quality films that are loved by audiences around the world. . . . We're delighted that Tom continues

---

If you enjoy the works of Tom Shadyac, you may also want to check out the following films:

Blazing Saddles, a comic masterpiece by Mel Brooks, 1974.
National Lampoon's Animal House, starring John Belushi, 1978.
The works of Peter and Bobby Farrelly, including *There's Something about Mary,* 1998.

---

to be an important member of the Universal family."

Film Industry Future Fills up Calendar

Shadyac's first project under the long-term deal with Universal was reported to be *Karaoke Knight,* a film starring comedian Ben Stiller. Stiller planned to co-produce the film, which was described in typical film industry fashion by *Hollywood Reporter* contributor Dana Harris as "*Kingpin* set in the world of karaoke." In a sequel to the popular Eddie Murphy vehicle, Universal pegged Shadyac to serve as executive producer for *The Nutty Professor II: The Klumps,* which was released in 2000. Meanwhile, a joint effort between Shadyac's Shady Acres Productions and Twentieth Century-Fox aimed for the production of *Slow Man,* a film about a man whose metabolic rate is so slow that he has scarcely aged since his brain was damaged by shrapnel during the Civil War. Shadyac was slated to direct.

Having had the opportunity to work for a while as an actor and stand-up comic before taking a seat in a director's chair has provided Shadyac a perspective on his craft that continues to serve him well with actors. "A lot of directors get me on the set and, because I have a background in improvising, they just say 'action' and 'cut,'" Eddie Murphy explained in *USA Today* of his experiences working under the former actor. Energetic and unwilling to back down from what he wants, Shadyac understands the momentum of improvisation, and also knows its limitations. "Shadyac pushes you," Murphy maintained. "He wants you to go *too* far."

■ Works Cited

Clark, Mike, review of *The Nutty Professor, USA Today*, December 1, 1998.

Denby, David, review of *Patch Adams, New Yorker*, January 25, 1999, p. 96.

Ebert, Roger, review of *Ace Ventura, Pet Detective, Chicago Sun-Times*, February 4, 1994.

Fretts, Bruce, "Fabulous Beaker Boys," *Entertainment Weekly*, November 8, 1996, pp. 77-79.

Gaydos, Steve, review of *Ace Ventura, Pet Detective, Variety*, February 7, 1994, pp. 40-41.

Giles, Jeff, "When Human Nature Calls, Hang Up," *Newsweek*, March 24, 1997, p. 82.

Harris, Dana, "Shadyac, Uni in Pitch-perfect 'Karaoke' Duet," *Hollywood Reporter*, March 17, 1999, p. 1.

Howe, Desson, review of *Ace Ventura, Pet Detective, Washington Post*, February 4, 1994.

Review of *Patch Adams, People Weekly*, January 11, 1999, p. 35.

Rozen, Leah, review of *Liar, Liar, People Weekly*, March 24, 1997, p. 19.

Schickel, Richard, review of *Liar, Liar, Time*, March 24, 1997, p. 88.

Schwarzbaum, Lisa, "Bad Medicine," *Entertainment Weekly*, January 8, 1999, pp. 47-48.

"Tom Shadyac Enters into Long-Term Motion Picture and Music Agreement," *PR Newswire*, March 4, 1999, p. 9123.

Weinraub, Bernard, "At the Movies: Laughter Medicine," *New York Times*, December 25, 1998, p. E19.

Wloszczyna, Susan, "Tom Shadyac, the Nutty Director," *USA Today*, March 21, 1997, p. D1.

■ For More Information See

PERIODICALS

Christian Science Monitor, April 25, 1997, p. 13.

Hollywood Reporter, July 22, 1999, p. 3.

National Review, February 8, 1999, p. 58.

New Yorker, July 8, 1996, p. 86; March 31, 1997, p. 107.

New York Times, February 5, 1994, p. 12; April 17, 1994, p. H25; April 6, 1997, p. H16.

Time, July 8, 1996, p. 66.

Wall Street Journal, March 21, 1997, p. A17.*

John Updike

Personal

Born March 18, 1932, in Shillington, PA; son of Wesley Russell (a teacher) and Linda Grace (an author; maiden name, Hoyer) Updike; married Mary Entwistle Pennington, June 26, 1953 (divorced, 1977); married Martha Bernhard, September 30, 1977; children: (first marriage) Elizabeth Pennington, David Hoyer, Michael John, Miranda; (second marriage) three stepchildren. *Education:* Harvard University, A.B. (summa cum laude), 1954; attended Ruskin School of Drawing and Fine Art, Oxford, 1954-55. *Politics:* Democrat. *Religion:* Christian.

Addresses

Home—Beverly Farms, MA.

Career

Novelist, critic, short story writer, poet, essayist, and dramatist. *New Yorker* magazine, reporter, 1955-57. Visited the U.S.S.R. as part of a cultural exchange program of the U.S. Department of State, 1964.

Member

American Academy and Institute of Arts and Letters (secretary, chancellor), American Academy of Arts and Sciences.

Awards, Honors

Guggenheim fellowship in poetry, 1959; American Academy and National Institute of Arts and Letters Richard and Hilda Rosenthal Foundation Award, 1960, for *The Poorhouse Fair;* National Book Award in fiction, 1963, and Prix Medicis Etranger, 1966, both for *The Centaur;* O. Henry Award for fiction, 1966, for short story "The Bulgarian Poetess"; Fulbright fellow in Africa, 1972; American Book Award nomination, 1980, for *Too Far to Go: The Maples Stories;* Edward MacDowell Medal for Literature, MacDowell Colony, 1981; Pulitzer Prize for fiction, 1981, American Book Award, 1982, and National Book Critics Circle award for fiction, 1982, all for *Rabbit Is Rich;* National Book Critics Circle award for criticism, 1984, for *Hugging the Shore: Essays and Criticism;* Medal of Honor for Literature, National Arts Club (New York City), 1984; National Book Critics Circle award in fiction nomination, 1986, for *Roger's Version;* PEN/Malamud

Memorial Prize, PEN/Faulkner Award Foundation, 1988, for "excellence in short story writing"; National Medal of Arts, 1989.

National Book Critics Award and Pulitzer Prize, both 1990, both for *Rabbit at Rest*; Premio Scanno, 1991; Howells Medal, American Academy of Arts and Letters, 1995; National Book Foundation Medal, 1998; Thomas Cooper Library Award for Literary Achievement, University of South Carolina.

■ Writings

NOVELS

The Poorhouse Fair (also see below), Knopf, 1959.
Rabbit, Run (also see below), Knopf, 1960.
The Centaur, Knopf, 1963.
Of the Farm, Knopf, 1965.
The Poorhouse Fair [and] *Rabbit, Run*, Modern Library, 1965.
Couples, Knopf, 1968.
Rabbit Redux (also see below), Knopf, 1971.
A Month of Sundays, Knopf, 1975.
Marry Me: A Romance, Knopf, 1976.
The Coup, Knopf, 1978.
Rabbit Is Rich (also see below), Knopf, 1981.
Rabbit Is Rich/Rabbit Redux/Rabbit, Run (also see below), Quality Paperback Book Club, 1981.
The Witches of Eastwick, Knopf, 1984.
Roger's Version, Knopf, 1986.
S., Knopf, 1988.
Rabbit at Rest, Knopf, 1990.
Memories of the Ford Administration, Knopf, 1992.
Brazil, Knopf, 1994.
Rabbit Angstrom: The Four Novels (contains *Rabbit Is Rich, Rabbit Redux, Rabbit, Run*, and *Rabbit at Rest*), Knopf/Everymans, 1995.
In the Beauty of the Lilies, Knopf, 1996.
Toward the End of Time, Knopf, 1997.
Gertrude and Claudius, Knopf, 2000.

POETRY

The Carpentered Hen and Other Tame Creatures (also see below), Harper, 1958, published as *Hoping for a Hoopoe*, Gollancz, 1959.
Telephone Poles and Other Poems (also see below), Knopf, 1963.
Verse: The Carpentered Hen and Other Tame Creatures/ Telephone Poles and Other Poems, Fawcett, 1965.

The Angels (poem; limited edition), King and Queen Press, 1968.
Bath after Sailing (poem; limited edition), Pendulum Press, 1968.
Midpoint and Other Poems, Knopf, 1969.
Seventy Poems, Penguin, 1972.
Six Poems (limited edition), Oliphant Press, 1973.
Cunts (poem; limited edition), Frank Hallman, 1974.
Tossing and Turning, Knopf, 1977.
Sixteen Sonnets (limited edition), Halty Ferguson, 1979.
Five Poems (limited edition), Bits Press, 1980.
Spring Trio (limited edition), Palaemon Press, 1982.
Jester's Dozen (limited edition), Lord John, 1984.
Facing Nature: Poems, Knopf, 1985.
Collected Poems: 1953-1993, Knopf, 1993.
A Helpful Alphabet of Friendly Objects (juvenile poetry; photographs by David Updike), Knopf, 1994.

SHORT STORIES

The Same Door, Knopf, 1959.
Pigeon Feathers and Other Stories, Knopf, 1962.
Olinger Stories: A Selection, Vintage, 1964.
The Music School, Knopf, 1966.
Bech: A Book, Knopf, 1970.
Museums and Women and Other Stories, Knopf, 1972.
Warm Wine: An Idyll (short story; limited edition) Albondocani Press, 1973.
Couples: A Short Story (limited edition), Halty Ferguson, 1976.
From the Journal of a Leper (short story; limited edition), Lord John, 1978.
Too Far to Go: The Maples Stories, Fawcett, 1979, British edition published as *Your Lover Just Called: Stories of Joan and Richard Maple*, Penguin Books, 1980.
Three Illuminations in the Life of an American Author (short story; limited edition), Targ (New York City), 1979.
Problems and Other Stories, Knopf, 1979.
The Chaste Planet (short story; limited edition), Metacom, 1980.
People One Knows: Interviews with Insufficiently Famous Americans (limited edition), Lord John, 1980.
Invasion of the Book Envelopes (short story; limited edition), Ewert, 1981.
Bech Is Back, Knopf, 1982.
The Beloved (short story; limited edition), Lord John, 1982.

Confessions of a Wild Bore (short story; limited edition), Tamazunchale Press, 1984.

More Stately Mansions: A Story (short story; limited edition), Nouveau Press, 1987.

Trust Me: Short Stories, Knopf, 1987.

The Afterlife and Other Stories, Knopf, 1994.

Bech at Bay: A Quasi-Novel, Knopf, 1998.

ESSAYS

Assorted Prose, Knopf, 1965.

On Meeting Authors (limited edition), Wickford 1968.

A Good Place (limited edition), 1973.

Picked-Up Pieces, Knopf, 1975.

Hub Fans Bid Kid Adieu (limited edition), Lord John, 1977.

Talk from the Fifties (limited edition), Lord John, 1979.

Ego and Art in Walt Whitman (limited edition), Targ, 1980.

Hawthorne's Creed (limited edition), Targ, 1981.

Hugging the Shore: Essays and Criticism, Knopf, 1983.

Emersonianism (limited edition), Bits Press, 1984.

Just Looking: Essays on Art, Knopf, 1989.

Odd Jobs: Essays and Criticism, Knopf, 1991.

Concerts at Castle Hill (music criticism, 1961-65; limited edition), Lord John, 1993.

Golf Dreams: Writings on Golf, Knopf, 1996.

More Matter: Essays and Criticism, Knopf, 1999.

AUTHOR OF INTRODUCTION

Henry Green, *Loving, Living, Party Going*, Penguin Books, 1978.

Bruno Schulz, *Sanatorium under the Sign of the Hourglass*, Penguin Books, 1979.

The Art of Mickey Mouse, edited by Craig Yoe and Janet Morra-Yoe, Hyperion, 1991.

Heroes and Anti-Heroes, Random House, 1991.

Henry Green, *Surviving*, Viking, 1993.

Edith Wharton, *The Age of Innocence*, Ballantine, 1996.

Frederic Tuten, *The Adventures of Mao on the Long March*, Marion Boyars, 1997.

Herman Melville, *The Complete Short Fiction*, Knopf, 1997.

OTHER

(Adapter with Warren Chappell) *The Magic Flute* (juvenile fiction; adapted from libretto of same title by Wolfgang Amadeus Mozart), Knopf, 1962.

(Adapter with Warren Chappell) *The Ring* (juvenile fiction; adapted from libretto by Richard Wagner), Knopf, 1964.

A Child's Calendar (juvenile poetry), Knopf, 1965.

Three Texts from Early Ipswich (historical pageant; produced in Ipswich, MA, 1968), 17th Century Day Committee of the Town of Ipswich, 1968.

(Adapter) *Bottom's Dream* (juvenile fiction; adapted from William Shakespeare's play *A Midsummer Night's Dream*), Knopf, 1969.

(Editor) David Levine, *Pens and Needles: Literary Caricatures*, Gambit, 1970.

(Author of words and music with Gunther Schuller) *The Fisherman and His Wife*, first performed at Savoy Theatre in Boston, MA, by the Opera Company of Boston, May, 1970.

(Contributor of translations) Jorge Luis Borges, *Selected Poems: 1923-1967*, edited by Norman Thomas di Giovanni, Delacorte, 1972.

A Good Place: Being a Personal Account of Ipswich, Massachusetts, Aloe Editions, 1973.

Buchanan Dying (play; produced in Lancaster, MA, 1976), Knopf, 1974.

(Author of afterword) Edmund Wilson, *Memoirs of Hecate County*, Nonpareil, 1980.

(Editor with Shannon Ravenel and author of introduction) *The Best American Short Stories: 1984*, Houghton, 1984.

Self-Consciousness: Memoirs, Knopf, 1989.

(Editor with Katrina Kenison) *The Best American Short Stories of the Century*, Houghton, 1999.

Contributor to books, including *Five Boyhoods*, edited by Martin Levin, Doubleday, 1962, and *The First Picture Book: Everyday Things for Babies*, Fotofolio and Whitney Museum of American Arts (New York City), 1991. "Talk of the Town" reporter, *New Yorker*, 1955-57. Contributor of short stories, book reviews, and poems to the *New Yorker*. Contributor of reviews and short stories to numerous periodicals.

Updike's papers are housed in the Houghton Library, Harvard University.

■ Adaptations

Couples was purchased by United Artists in 1969; *Rabbit, Run* was filmed by Warner Bros. in 1970; *Bech: A Book* was adapted for a play entitled, *Bech Takes Pot Luck*, produced in New York at Theatre Guild, 1970; *The Music School* was broadcast by Public Broadcasting System, 1976; *Too Far to Go* was made into a television movie by National Broadcasting Co. in March, 1979, later revised and released for theater distribution by Sea Cliff Productions, 1982; director George Miller's movie *The Witches of Eastwick,* 1987, is loosely based on Updike's novel of the same title; "The Christian Roommates," a short story, was made into a ninety-minute movie for television.

■ Sidelights

"A reader would be hard pressed to name a contemporary author other than John Updike whose work is more in tune with the way most Americans live," wrote Donald J. Greiner in *Dictionary of Literary Biography.* Greiner went on to note in his entry on Updike that the author, essayist, poet, and dramatist "writes about ordinary people leading ordinary lives. Man, wife, home, children job—these mundane concerns have rested at the heart of his art since he published his first book." Updike's fiction plumbs the quotidian, examining the fracture lines of middle-class life in sex and adultery, mortality and loss, religion and sports.

Updike is considered by many to be the master of portraying small town and suburban America and charting the course of family life in the late twentieth century. In award-winning novels such as *The Poorhouse Fair,* the "Rabbit" books, *The Centaur, Couples, In the Beauty of the Lilies,* and a dozen more, Updike has created a cast of memorable characters who chart the progress of America from roughly 1950 to the present. He waxes poetic of the mundane objects and artifacts of daily life; he makes heroic the vacillations and struggles of the Everyman to determine what is morally right in a constantly changing world. As Updike told Jane Howard in a *Life* magazine interview, "Everything can be as interesting as every other thing. . . . An old milk carton is worth a rose. . . . The idea of a hero is aristocratic. Now either nobody is a hero or everybody is. I vote for everyone." In his *John Updike Revisited,* James A. Schiff called Updike "the Vermeer of American authors." Schiff went on to explain that "Updike has created canvases worthy of the seventeenth-century Dutch painter whom he so admired. Whereas others before him satirized the values and aesthetics of middle-class life, Updike has embraced and celebrated this world, revealing its poetic beauty."

Updike won a National Book Award for *The Centaur,* a Pulitzer and a National Book Award for *Rabbit Is Rich,* and another Pulitzer for *Rabbit at Rest.* But this diverse writer has also been honored for other forms, including a National Book Critics Circle Award in criticism for *Hugging the Shore* and an O'Henry Award for the short story "The Bulgarian Poetess," which first presented the character of Henry Bech, the fictional author and Updike alter-ego who is at the center of three short story collections, *Bech: A Book, Bech is Back,* and *Bech at Bay.* Updike's collections of short stories have put him in the role of a modern-day pioneer of the form, and indeed some critics say that his ultimate place on the classics bookshelf may come from the short story rather than his novels. "It is in his short stories that we find Updike's most assured work," noted Jonathan Yardley in the *Washington Post Book World,* "and no doubt it is upon the best of them that his reputation ultimately will rest."

Praised by critics and fellow writers alike, Updike has become a father figure of American letters, anthologized, lionized and adapted for stage and screen. Writing in *Modern Fiction Studies,* the novelist Joyce Carol Oates offered this assessment of Updike's work up to 1975: "Updike has fashioned a body of writing that is as rich, mysterious, and infinitely rewarding as life itself—which in fact, it *is,* finally claiming no intellectual or moral excuse for its being. It is uniquely Updike's, and uniquely American. Updike exiled from America is unthinkable, and America without Updike to record it—unthinkable as well." Little has changed in the more than quarter century since that writing to change such an evaluation.

Pennsylvania Roots, Massachusetts Home

Initially, however, it was the pen or pencil wielded to a different purpose that informed young Updike's life. Growing up in Shillington, Pennsylvania, he wanted to be a cartoonist for Walt Disney or *The New Yorker.* But all of this was far in the future for young Updike, whose father, Wesley R. Updike, taught mathematics at the local junior high school. An only child, Updike lived in a small town for his first thirteen years, and thereafter the family moved to a farm outside of town. It was a lonely existence as an only child on a farm away from friends,

THE NATIONAL BESTSELLER

John Updike

pigeon feathers
and other stories

Seventeen of the nineteen semi-autobiographical stories in this 1962 collection of short stories were first published in the *New Yorker.*

and solitary hours helped to fuel his young imagination. The local Shillington library also became an after-school refuge and his mother's encouragement to write all figured into the mix. Updike's mother, Linda, a homemaker and would-be writer, later published two volumes of stories on her own.

After graduating president and co-valedictorian of the senior class from high school, Updike won a scholarship to Harvard University, where, according to Greiner in *Dictionary of Literary Biography,* his "lifelong commitment to prose style, to the sheer sound of words artfully selected and rhythmically grouped to suggest resonance and tone," was developed. An English major, Updike

still devoted much of his time to cartooning, drawing for the *Harvard Lampoon.* But soon his writings in the publication outstripped his artwork, and he later edited the magazine as well. In 1953 he married Mary E. Pennington, a fine arts major at Radcliffe. Graduating summa cum laude in 1954, Updike won a Knox Fellowship at the Ruskin School of Drawing and Fine Arts in Oxford. While a student in England, he placed his first story with *The New Yorker,* "Friends from Philadelphia." His first child, Elizabeth, was born while the couple was still abroad; and then returning from England in 1955, he took a position with *The New Yorker* magazine, writing for the "Talk of the Town" column. This staff job lasted two years. In 1957, after the birth of a second child, son David, Updike and his family moved to Ipswich, Massachusetts, where he focused on his fiction.

The move was a decisive one for Updike. Here in a town not so different from Shillington where he had grown up, Updike "found an atmosphere conducive to writing that would allow him to experience firsthand the middle-class, quotidian life that would become the great subject of his work," according to Schiff in *John Updike Revisited.* Updike would remain in Ipswich, an hour north of Boston, until 1974, and he and his family became part of the warp and woof of that small town, taking part in dramatic societies and sports events. In doing so, Updike created something of an anomalous writing persona for himself: while others of his generation were busy either being the lone artist or being caught up in the social whirl of New York, Updike became solidly bourgeois.

Two years of hard work brought Updike a certain overnight celebrity: by 1959 he had published a book of fiction, *The Poorhouse Fair,* one of poetry, *The Carpentered Hen and Other Tame Creatures,* and the short story collection *The Same Door.* That same year his third child, Michael, was born, followed the next year by a fourth, Miranda. During this time, Updike was also writing magazine articles, essays, poems, and short stories—over one hundred of them placed in *The New Yorker* between 1954 and 1959.

With his first novel, *The Poorhouse Fair,* Updike avoided the usual *Bildungsroman* (or coming-of-age) story typical of most first-time novelists. Instead, he focused on the conflicts in an oldfolks

home where the wards, represented by the retired teacher Hook, must battle the forces of conformity and warehousing-to-death as represented
by the administrator Conner. While Conner simply wants to take care of his charges as effi-
ciently as possible, caring for their sustenance
but not their humanity, the elderly themselves
demand more and get it, with the collection of
trinkets and handicrafts they assemble for the
annual fair held by the home. With this early
novel, Updike takes a prescient look at the welfare state and the possible "sterility of a nation
that supplies everything except the right to be
eccentric, individual, and alone," according to
Greiner, who called the book "an admirable first
novel of verbal skill and significant concerns."

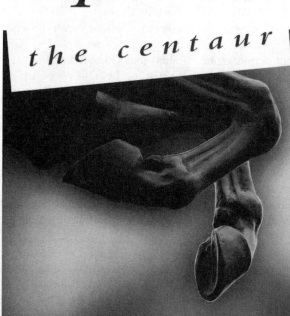

WINNER OF THE NATIONAL BOOK AWARD

John
Updike

the centaur

Updike received the National Book Award in 1963
for this autobiographical story that revolves around
the relationship between a father and son.

Writing in the *New York Times,* Donald Barr
dubbed the book "a work of art," while Fanny
Butcher praised Updike's "brilliant use of words
and . . . subtle observations" in the *Chicago Sunday Tribune.* Updike received the Rosenthal Foundation Award for this first novel, and the critical reception along with modest sales enabled
him to set up a scheduled life as a full-time
writer, working every morning, six days a week,
and turning out about three typed pages per day,
a quota that has created at least one new book
a year since he began writing.

Valentines to Pennsylvania

Most of Updike's early work, written between the
mid 1950s and mid 1960s, was set in fictionalized versions of the Pennsylvania towns with
which he was familiar. His mother once called
them Valentines that her son, living in New England, was sending back to his family in Berks
County. "Marked by their keen and well-estab-
lished sense of place, these writings account for
Updike's Pennsylvania Period," as Schiff commented, "in which the author memorialized his
childhood." Three out of his first four novels, *The
Poorhouse Fair, The Centaur,* and *Of the Farm,* cel-
ebrate family members—his paternal grandfather,
father, and mother respectively. *Rabbit, Run,* published in 1960, is also set in small-town Pennsylvania, though it does not hark back to family.
Additionally, the short story collections *The Same
Door* and *Pigeon Feathers* are semi-autobiographical.

The Centaur is one of Updike's most autobiographical novels, a personal favorite of the
author's, and, according to Schiff, "one of his finest works." The story of a father-son relationship,
the novel features father George Caldwell and
son Peter, reminiscent of Updike himself and his
father, Wesley. Narrated by Peter as a middle-
aged man, a painter living in New York, the book
recounts on one level Peter's high school days
in Olinger, Pennsylvania, and his pain at the
mocking his father—the science teacher—received
at the hands of fellow pupils. On a second level,
the novel retells, according to Greiner, "the Greek
tale of Chiron, the centaur injured in war but
beloved by Zeus, to highlight Caldwell's hero-
ism." Though dying, the father sticks with his
tiresome job, giving of himself. "Updike's style
works its best in *The Centaur* as Peter's reminis-

cence transforms ancient Olympus into modern Olinger via lyrical descriptions of love, uncertainty, and fear," according to Greiner. Reviewing the book in *Modern Fiction Studies*, John B. Vickery commented that "as *The Centaur* subtly and luminously demonstrates, myth and history, the archetypal and the quotidian are inextricably intertwined." *The Centaur* won Updike the National Book Award in 1963.

Another Valentine to Pennsylvania is found in *Of the Farm*, which focuses on a farm family, especially on the wife, Mrs. Robinson, who fears death will take her before she can see her son reach the dream she has fashioned for him to become a poet. The son, Joey, however, resists hismother's dream for him, pursuing instead a career in advertising in New York. The novel is set during one weekend in which Joey comes home with his second wife to seek his mother's blessing for his new union. Greiner called this short novel a "a highly charged . . . psychological thriller."

The "Rabbit" Novels

With his second novel, Updike created one of his most lasting and well-known characters, Harry "Rabbit" Angstrom, one-time high school basketball star who never finds adult life quite so exciting as life on the basketball court. Rabbit, however, tries for excitement, mostly in his sexual pursuits. Four novels make up the "Rabbit" opus: *Rabbit, Run; Rabbit Redux; Rabbit Is Rich;* and *Rabbit at Rest.* Each defines an era, a different decade in the life of Rabbit Angstrom and of America. *Rabbit, Run,* published in 1960, traces the optimism and failed dreams of the 1950s; *Rabbit Redux* (1971) follows the excesses of the 1960s; *Rabbit is Rich* (1981) picks up Rabbit's story at age forty-six and looks at America in the 1970s; and the final volume, *Rabbit at Rest,* came out in 1990, and finds the unlikely hero another decade older but not much wiser.

Rabbit, Run introduces this archetypal American anti-hero, this present-day Babbit, as he attempts to run from his wife, Janice, and his life of selling peelers at a local dime store. This tawdry existence is all a far cry from Rabbit's glory days of high school athletics. Rabbit, who earned his nickname for not only his wily movements on court, but for the look in his eyes and the pecu-

If you enjoy the works of John Updike, you may also want to check out the following books and films:

David James Duncan, *The Brothers K*, 1996.
Anne Rice, *The Witching Hour*, 1990.
Anne Tyler, *Saint Maybe*, 1991.
The Ice Storm, a film starring Christina Ricci, 1997.

liar movement of lips under his nostrils, bobs and weaves between his wife and a part-time prostitute, Ruth, whom he impregnates. Deserted, Janice finds consolation in the bottle which in turn leads to the death of their infant by drowning. In the end, Rabbit does not know what to do. He feels suffocated, lost; everything is second-rate to him now. As such, he is one of the archetypal figures of the 1950s who experiences the gray-flannel syndrome: trapped in a loveless marriage and in a job he despises, he is bored and sexually frustrated. Not even his sexual excesses give him real release.

With *Rabbit Redux,* or restored, the reader returns to Harry's life ten years on, at thirty-six, at the time the United States is experiencing not only the euphoria of the landing on the moon, but also all the dislocations of race riots and the Vietnam War. Back in Brewer, Pennsylvania, and caught up in right wing paranoia, Rabbit is ensnared in the times. A young, wealthy, runaway hippie girl, Jill, moves into Rabbit's home after his wife has left to live with a Greek car salesman. Nelson, Rabbit's son, is taken with Jill, perhaps even having an affair with her. Neighbors are aghast, of course, and while Rabbit is away on an assignation with another woman, Jill is burned to death in a fire seemingly started by objecting neighbors. By the end of the book, Rabbit and Janice have once again reunited.

Rabbit Is Rich picks up the story when Harry Angstrom is forty-six and is riding the wave of affluence brought about by his co-ownership of a Toyota dealership in Brewer. Part of the country club set now, with golf replacing his precious basketball, Rabbit is troubled mostly by his son, Nelson, who drops out of Kent State University and marries a young woman whom he has gotten pregnant. Rabbit is enjoying his cozy new life, but there are now constant struggles with Nelson, whom Janice protects. In this installment, cars are a metaphor; the new Japanese imports particularly holding sway over the older American luxury, gas-guzzling automobiles.

With the fourth volume of the series, *Rabbit at Rest*, Updike views the country in 1990. Rabbit lies near death in semi-retirement in Florida, a victim of his excesses, and still maintains a strained relationship with his businesswoman wife, Janice, and his son, Nelson, who is addicted to cocaine. As with all the novels, Updike blends snapshots of the time as part of the back-story: the AIDS epidemic, the terrorist bombing of Pan Am Flight 103 over Lockerbie, Scotland, the trade war with Japan. The end of the novel, with Rabbit's approaching death, also announced the end of the tetralogy. It was an event important enough to prompt not only book reviews, but also *editorials* in the *New York Times* and the *Washington Post*, as if part of the American fabric had passed. Reviewing *Rabbit at Rest* in the *New York Times*, Michiko Kakutani also summed up the entire series: "Taken together, this quartet of novels has given its readers a wonderfully vivid portrait of . . . Angstrom, a small-town basketball star turned car salesman, and in chronicling the passing parade of Harry's life, the books have also created a Kodachrome sharp picture of American life."

"Rabbit Angstrom is Updike's supreme creation," wrote Schiff in *John Updike Revisited*, "his most natural and memorable character, and the tetralogy that bears his name is the author's commanding achievement." Schiff dubbed the four novels "an epic," further noting, "There are few, if any, characters in American literature with whom we spend more time, and thus, are able to know as fully and as intimately." Schiff also drew attention to the tapestry of America in the last half of the twentieth century, which Updike presents in the novels, from the Cold War to Vietnam, the Iranian hostage crisis and the Reagan years. Greiner, in his *John Updike's Novels*, likened the tetralogy to Anthony Trollope's Barchester chronicles, for "Updike uses his fiction to choreograph the social dance of an age." Likewise, George W. Hunt, writing in *America*, remarked that the novels "become a single epic about a whole generation born in the depths of Depression and surviving into the 1980s."

Despite its subject matter of adultery (considered shocking at its time of publication in 1968), this work remained on bestseller lists for weeks.

But while some see the Rabbit novels as an epic, others find them vapid and the protagonist flat-out boring. Gary Wills commented in the *New York Review of Books* that Rabbit is an implausible and unconvincing character: "Though he is supposed to have been the local star, we hear of no college or semi-pro scouts interested in him. He plays no pick-up ball with young adults—just one pathetic game, in his street clothes, with some unwelcoming teenagers." Wills also takes Harry and Updike to task for the character's interior monologues, thinking in "purple passages," though Rabbit is clearly "not a reader," as well as for "the reactionary dandyism" Rabbit displays in his political conceits. One of Wills's worst criticisms of the books is that they are "profligate with pretty writing," a criticism leveled at Updike by many of his detractors who claim he writes gorgeously about nothing at all. George Will, writing in the *Washington Post,* called Rabbit an "emotionally stunted, intellectually barren, morally repulsive egoist." While writing in the *Wall Street Journal,* Donna Rifkind dubbed Harry Angstrom "an almost entirely antipathetic character."

Countering this perspective, Sven Birkerts, reviewing *Rabbit at Rest* in *Chicago Tribune Books,* noted that the character of Rabbit was "a central paradox, and an indicator of Updike's achievement: that on one level Rabbit is but a shallow and reactionary male of his class and era,but that on another he is a sweet and watchful soul, as deep in his affectionate perceptiveness as the man who made his world." Many critics agree that the weakest of the books is *Rabbit Redux,* while the last two both won critical praise and awards. *Rabbit Is Rich* earned Updike a Pulitzer Prize for fiction, the American Book Award, and the National Book Critics Circle Award for fiction, while *Rabbit at Rest* captured both a Pulitzer and a National Book Critics Circle Award. Reviewing the final book of the quartet, Jonathan Raban commented in the *Washington Post Book World,* "From now on it is going to be hard to read John Updike without seeing all his earlier books as a long rehearsal for the writing of this book. *Rabbit at Rest* is that good." Kakutani also felt that Updike was "working at the full height of his powers," with the fourth novel in the cycle, "reorchestrating the themes that have animated not only his earlier Rabbit novels but his entire oeuvre as well."

Edward Pearce, reviewing *Rabbit at Rest* in the *London Review of Books,* remarked that the books of Updike's tetralogy are composed of the "barest narrative bones," yet it "is the genius of Updike that he can take a weak popular medium and invest it with his own delicate understanding." Pearce concluded that the fourth novel "achieves a certain grandeur. . . . It represents the superb conclusion of a historic labour of writing, a *roman fleuve* undertaken in the age of river pollution. There is no living writer I would as quickly hasten to read." Chilton Williamson, Jr., reviewing *Rabbit at Rest* in *National Review,* called it "not just the best of the Rabbit books . . . it is probably the best of all the author's novels." More superlatives were served up by

Thomas M. Disch in *The Nation.* Noting that Updike's Rabbit books redeem the world they represent by "valorizing its commonplaces," Disch concluded, "For me that makes the Rabbit tetralogy the best large-scale literary work by an American in this century . . ., and Updike the best American writer. Someone has finally written, albeit inadvertently and in the form of a tetralogy, the Great American Novel."

Life after Rabbit

Though perhaps best known for his character Rabbit Angstrom, Updike has created numerous other fictional personas of equal piquancy, if not depth. Schiff and other critics have organized his novels into several categories: marriage novels, including *Couples, Marry Me,* and *The Witches of Eastwick;* homages to Hawthorne with *A Month of Sundays, Roger's Version,* and *S.;* foreign novels, such as *The Coup,* set in Africa, *Brazil,* and the novel published in 2000, *Gertrude and Claudius;* and re-creations of American history as well as projections of America in the near future with *Memories of the Ford Administration, In the Beauty of the Lilies,* and the 1997 title *Toward the End of Time.*

One of Updike's most popular early novels, *Couples* was published in 1968 during the wide-open years of the Sixties, and the book's content, found shocking at the time, reflects that era. Protagonist Piet Hanema and his wife are one of a set of couples who push the envelope of marriage; Piet has affairs with the wives of other men as does his own wife, Angela, with their husbands, but it is his mistress Foxy with whom he finally finds a lasting coupling, leaving his wife and home to build a new life with her. This fifth novel put Updike's picture on the cover of *Time* and made his name synonymous with suburban adultery. Lasting many weeks on the bestseller lists, this novel suffered more at the hands of critics than any other of Updike's novels, being "viewed as an intellectual *Peyton Place,*" according to Schiff.

Something of a departure for Updike is his 1978 novel set in Africa, *The Coup,* the result of a year he spent there in the early 1970s. *The Coup* is set in the fictional state of Kush and is narrated by the dictator of that country, Colonel Ellellou, now retired. John Thompson, writing in the *New*

PULITZER PRIZE WINNER

John Updike

rabbit is rich

This 1981 novel, part of a four-book series which follows the life of Harry "Rabbit" Angstrom, earned Updike his first Pulitzer Prize.

York Review of Books, declared, "There is not a sentence in this book I will not gladly read again for instruction and delight," while Robert Towers noted in the *New York Times Book Review* that Colonel Ellellou "is an extraordinary tour-de-force of a character," and the novel itself is "rich, surprising and often funny."

In 1976 Updike and his first wife were divorced, and the author later married Martha Ruggles Bernhard. They moved first to Georgetown, Massachusetts, and then in 1982 to Beverly Farms, Massachusetts. By this time, Updike was far from living a middle-class lifestyle himself, and much of his fiction reflects that fact. *The Witches of Eastwick* appeared in 1984 and was later loosely

adapted for a movie. As with much of Updike's work, this tale of three suburban, modern-day witches on the loose in Rhode Island drew both praise and rebuke. Writing in the *New York Times Book Review,* Margaret Atwood found the novel to be a "strange and marvelous organism," seeing a metaphor in the fact of the husband-less women freed to cast spells and fly through the air. Atwood went on to laud Updike's "skill and inventiveness of the writing, the accuracy of the detail, the sheer energy of the witches and, above all, the practicality of the charms." Yet Jonathan Yardley, reviewing the novel in the *Washington Post Book World,* said, "Like so much else Updike has written . . . [it is] less a work of art than of artifice." In this novel, Yardley asserted, "Updike is at his most calculatedly puckish and thus least attractive," and the resulting book is "arch, fey, self-indulgent, showy, precious, windy, goatish." Yardley concluded, "That Updike's later work is considered among the literary adornments of the age is a telling comment on the age itself and on those who are setting its 'standards.'"

With the cycle of novels begun in 1975 with *A Month of Sundays,* and continued in 1986 with *Roger's Version* and in 1988 with *S.,* Updike attempted nothing less than a reworking of Nathaniel Hawthorne's *Scarlet Letter.* The first book in the cycle tells of the Rev. Thomas Marshfield, who has been shipped off to a desert retreat after his lecherous attentions to the church organist have been discovered. There he is to write a journal about his spiritual rebirth, but the clergyman has other notions: he knows that both body and soul must be united to function in the world, and his final affair with Ms. Prynne, who is a modern day Hester from *The Scarlet Letter,* lets the reader know that Marshfield has found the proper salvation. Peter S. Prescott, reviewing the novel in *Newsweek,* called it "special" and one that contains much of "Updike's best writing."

This Hawthornian journey continues in *Roger's Version,* a novel about the attempt to prove the existence of God by a computer, and *S.,* told from a woman's point of view through letters to a her husband, children, mother, even her hairdresser and dentist. Greiner called *Roger's Version* Updike's "most intellectually challenging novel," and John Calvin Batchelor, writing in the *Washington Post Book World,* dubbed it a "wonderfully tricky and nakedly sharp-minded" narrative. David Lodge, reviewing the novel in the *New York Times Book Review,* called it "challenging and educative" and concluded that the reader finished it with "renewed respect for one of the most intelligent and resourceful of contemporary novelists."

Updike as Short Story Writer, Poet, and Critic

The same concerns for life in the middle classes found in many of his longer narratives also inform Updike's short stories. Families are often at the center of these tales, as in those collected in *The Same Door* and *Pigeon Feathers,* and such concerns are tinged in *Problems and Other Stories* and *Trust Me* with "irony and the shadow of mortality," according to Greiner. One of his best known early stories, "A & P," appeared in *Pigeon Feathers* and is narrated by nineteen-year-old Sammy, a checker at the local A & P grocery in a New England town who is mesmerized by three teenage summer girls in bathing suits who come into the store. When the store manager of this conservative community upbraids the girls for coming into the store dressed inappropriately, Sammy quits in protest, hoping to gain the girls' attention, but to no avail. Updike's most anthologized tale, "A & P" is "one of the very few Updike stories . . . that ventures into comedy," according to Robert Detweiler in his *John Updike,* "and this comedic quality is achieved through the tempered humor of the clever phrase and through the incongruous action that is meant to hold the slight pathos within its prescribed limits." Ronald E. McFarland, writing in *Studies in Short Fiction* some two decades after the publication of the story, remarked on its continuing popularity, mentioning not only the fact of the age of the protagonist and the use of teenage vernacular, but also "its ambiguity," which is of interest to "literary critics and other serious readers."

Other popular Updike stories are those dealing with the Maple couple, collected in *Too Far to Go,* which was later filmed for television. But some of Updike's best-known collections are those featuring Henry Bech in three volumes, *Bech: A Book, Bech Is Back,* and *Bech at Bay.* Updike returns to this fictional writer at intervals of over a decade, just as he did with Rabbit Angstrom, but with Bech the effect is more humorous than poignant. First introduced in the short story "The

Bulgarian Poetess" from the 1966 collection, *The Music School,* Bech takes center stage with 1970's *Bech: A Book.* "Bech is one of Updike's best creations," noted Anatole Broyard in a *Life* review of that collection. "Lugubrious yet full of hope, toughminded yet tender to the point of panic, depleted yet dizzy with the sheer poetry of things." In seven interrelated episodes, Bech struts through the complexities and difficulties of making books in America. Writing in the *Atlantic Monthly,* L. E. Sissman called the first collection of Bech stories "a good and craftsmanlike and funny book."

Bech returns twelve years later in *Bech Is Back,* a further seven episodes in the life of Updike's

This first work in a three-book series features the timeless and humorous character Henry Bech, a Jewish writer struggling to be published.

alter-ego. Bech overcomes his long-time writer's block and is now writing a new book and has a new wife. Here irony and satire impinge on the straightforward humor, and according to Greiner "the entire book is a delight." Another sixteen years passed before Updike reprised Bech in 1998's *Bech at Bay.* "The five stories that make up this new installment of the saga show an older and grumpier Bech still worrying about his bouts of writer's block and finding ways of getting away from his desk whenever he can," wrote Paul Gray in a *Time* magazine review of the book. According to Gray, this collection "displays the same mordantly comic look at the literary life that enlivened" earlier volumes of the Bech stories. *Booklist* critic Brad Hooper called Bech "a mouthpiece for Updike's often sarcastic, even caustic, insight into writers and the writing life," concluding that "Updike's style is never more jubilantly elaborate than in a Bech book, and his intelligence never more provocatively displayed." Yardley, who has been a severe critic of much of Updike's novel-length work, praised this third collection of Bech stories in the *Washington Post Book World:* "Like other books about Henry Bech, this is modest in size but generous withits rewards. It is a happy reminder, because there is so much evidence to the contrary, that when Updike is good, he is very, very good."

A man of many literary hats, Updike is also well known as a poet, though according to Greiner there is a general misconception about his poetry: because the "comic element is more pronounced in the verse than in the tales," many feel that Updike is essentially a writer of light verse a la Ogden Nash. "This misconception is unfortunate," wrote Greiner, "for his collections of poems show a change in tone and mood from the humor of *The Carpentered Hen and Other Tame Creatures,* through the lyrics of *Telephone Poles* and the autobiographical poems of *Midpoint,* to the meditations on death in *Tossing and Turning* and the celebration of nature in *Facing Nature.* Greiner called *Midpoint* "Updike's most ambitious collection," its title poem a forty-one page analysis of his life to the midpoint at age thirty-five. Reviewing his 1985 collection of poems, *Facing Nature,* Joel Conarroe noted in the *Washington Post Book World* that Updike "has produced one of the year's more appealing books of poetry." Updike's poetry was gathered together in one volume in the 1993 *Collected Poems.*

Updike's efforts in essay and criticism have also earned him wide praise. His 1983 collection, *Hugging the Shore,* won the National Book Critics Circle Award for criticism, a book that "possesses the weight of a new maturity and ambition," according to Michiko Kakutani in a *New York Times* review. Kakutani went on to note, "The presiding emotion in these essays . . . is generosity—a kind of attentive, unmushy generosity, which enables Mr. Updike to illumine the flavor, color and moral vision of a text without ever subjugating it to prejudices of his own." James Atlas, writing in the *London Review of Books,* remarked on a "note of informal authority" that "pervades" *Hugging the Shore,* and enthused, "How heartening it is . . . to have a critic like John Updike." "Especially rewarding," according to Greiner, "are three longish essays on three American giants—Hawthorne, Whitman, and Melville."

Updike's inquisitive mind has led him to write about not only books but art, as in his 1989 collection, *Just Looking,* and musings on golf in 1996's *Golf Dreams,* "a happy combination of fiction and essays about the sport that Updike considers to be the most physically frustrating yet spiritually challenging of all human diversions," according to Greiner. His 1999 collection of essays, *More Matter,* ranges from "the latest biography of F. Scott Fitzgerald and the nature of evil to cars, cartoons and burglar alarms," according to a reviewer in *Publishers Weekly,* and are "bursting with sentiments and observations that defy ideology or neat categorization." *Booklist* critic Brad Hooper felt that this fiftieth book from Updike "is the perfect showcase for his wondrous eloquence."

A Writer Never at Rest

Updike continued to pound away at the keys of his word processor through the 1990s and into new millennium. *Brazil,* published in 1994, employs a sense of magical realism and uses the Tristan and Iseult theme as its narrative frame. As with *The Coup,* it is a novel set outside the confines of small town, middle-class America. And indeed, Updike's fiction increasingly has moved away from that milieu even when set in America. *In the Beauty of the Lilies* is, among other things, a chronicle of the decline of religious faith in American culture. The book focuses on Rev. Clarence Wilmot, a Presbyterian minister who loses his faith and turns instead to sellingencyclopedias. After his death, the novel continues to follow the fortunes of his family for another three generations. Julian Barnes commented in the *New York Times Book Review* that *In the Beauty of the Lilies* is "a novel of accumulated wisdom, with . . . Updike in full control of his subtle, crafty and incessantly observing art." Reviewing the novel in *New Yorker*, George Steiner concluded, "John Updike's genius, his place beside Hawthorne and Nabokov have never been more assured, or chilling."

Updike's 1997 novel, *Toward the End of Time*, is a "companion piece" to *In the Beauty of the Lilies*, according to Greiner. Where *Lilies* looks at America from the beginning of the twentieth century to its close, *Toward the End of Time* looks at the country in 2020, after a nuclear war with China. Ben Turnbull, comfortably upper middle class, looks at the new world in the pages of his journal. "Despite its somber premise . . . the novel mixes fantasy and humor as Updike takes his aging narrator . . . through the ravages of the future," Greiner commented. "There are elements of magic realism in the text," noted Phoebe-Lou Adams in an *Atlantic Monthly* review, "and a few borrowings from science fiction, but futuristic fantasy is the book's basic character." Adams went on to comment, "Altogether, [Ben Turnbull] is a fascinating, amusing, eloquent companion, and one feels genuine regret when the year, his journal, and with them Mr. Updike's novel, come to an end." In *Toward the End of Time*, Updike presents discussions through Turnbull that take the reader into the realms of cosmology, quantum physics and theories of parallel time that are "daring" but also "tough going for a first-time reader," according to William H. Pritchard in the *Wall Street Journal*.

With the turn of the millennium, Updike published his nineteenth novel, *Gertrude and Claudius*, the story of the King and Queen of Denmark before the action of Shakespeare's *Hamlet*. A distinct departure from the author's usual suburban mix, the book still includes large measures of adultery with the incestuous royals of Denmark. While Hooper commented in another *Booklist* review that the book was "one of Updike's lapses, which are occurring with increasing frequency," a reviewer for *Publishers Weekly* found it to be "[p]recisely honed, buoyant with sly with, masterful character analysis and subtly observed his-

torical details." The same writer dubbed the effort a "tour de force by the protean Updike" with a resolution that "is breathtaking."

Updike is, with no debate, most definitely "protean" in his output. While some critics may fault him for purple passages, for beautiful writing about nothing at all, others call him our foremost man of letters. Time will decide who is correct. Meanwhile, Updike keeps on writing. "There's obviously a time when you should hang it up," Updike explained to Michael Rogers in a *Library Journal* interview, "but I don't feel I'm there yet. I still have things I'm trying to do, and I still get pleasure out of the challenge. When I cease to get pleasure out of the challenge or when external indications are that nobody wants to read anything I write, maybe I'll pack it in. But writing is therapy; it's your hobby as well as your profession. It would be hard to give it up."

■ Works Cited

Adams, Phoebe-Lou, review of *Toward the End of Time*, *Atlantic Monthly*, November, 1997, p. 164.

Atlas, James, "Towards the Transhuman," *London Review of Books*, February 2, 1984, pp. 22-23.

Atwood, Margaret, "Wondering What It's Like to Be a Woman," *New York Times Book Review*, May 13, 1984, pp. 1, 40.

Barnes, Julian, "Grand Illusion," *New York Times Book Review*, January 28, 1996, p. 9.

Barr, Donald, review of *The Poorhouse Fair*, *New York Times*, January 11, 1959.

Batchelor, John Calvin, "Hacker and the Heretic," *Washington Post Book World*, August 31, 1986, pp. 1-2.

Birkerts, Sven, "The Inner Rabbit," *Chicago Tribune Books*, September 30, 1990, pp. 1, 4.

Broyard, Anatole, "All the Way with Updike," *Life*, June 18, 1970, p. 12.

Butcher, Fanny, review of *The Poorhouse Fair*, *Chicago Sunday Tribune*, January 11, 1959.

Conarroe, Joel, "Updike, Clampitt, and Merrill: Poets in Their Prime," *Washington Post Book World*, July 28, 1985, pp. 1, 8.

Detweiler, Robert, *John Updike*, Twayne, 1973, pp. 60-79.

Disch, Thomas M., "Rabbit's Run," *The Nation*, December 3, 1990, pp. 688, 690, 692, 694.

Review of *Gertrude and Claudius*, *Publishers Weekly*, January 3, 2000, p. 57.

Gray, Paul, "A Writer's Life," *Time*, November 9, 1998, p. 114.

Greiner, Donald J., *John Updike's Novels*, Ohio University Press, 1984, p. 84.

Greiner, Donald J., "John Updike," *Dictionary of Literary Biography*, Volume 143: *American Novelists Since World War II, Third Series*, Gale, 1994, pp. 250-76.

Hooper, Brad, review of *Bech at Bay, Booklist*, August, 1998, p. 1925.

Hooper, Brad, review of *More Matter, Booklist*, September 15, 1999, p. 235.

Hooper, Brad, review of *Gertrude and Claudius, Booklist*, January 1, 2000, p. 835.

Howard, Jane, interview with John Updike, *Life*, December 4, 1966.

Hunt, George W., "Updike's Rabbit Returns," *America*, November 21, 1981, p. 322.

Kakutani, Michiko, review of *Hugging the Shore, New York Times*, September 13, 1983, p. C14.

Kakutani, Michiko, "Just 30 Years Later, Updike Has a Quartet," *New York Times*, September 25, 1990, pp. C13, C17.

Lodge, David, "Chasing after God and Sex," *New York Times Book Review*, August 31, 1986, pp. 1, 15.

McFarland, Ronald E., "Updike at the Center: Reflections on 'A & P'," *Studies in Short Fiction*, spring-summer, 1983, pp. 95-100.

Review of *More Matter, Publishers Weekly*, August 30, 1999, p. 66.

Oates, Joyce Carol, "Updike's American Comedies," *Modern Fiction Studies*, autumn, 1975.

Pearce, Edward, "Rabbit Resartus," *London Review of Books*, November 8, 1990, pp. 19-20.

Prescott, Peter S., "The Passionate Cleric," *Newsweek*, March 3, 1975, p. 72.

Pritchard, William H., review of *Toward the End of Time, Wall Street Journal*, October 8, 1997, p. A20.

Raban, Jonathan, "Rabbit's Last Run," *Washington Post Book World*, September 30, 1990, pp. 1, 15.

Rifkind, Donna, "The End of the Line for Rabbit Angstrom," *Wall Street Journal*, October 15, 1990, p. A14.

Rogers, Michael, "The Gospel of the Book: *LJ* Talks to John Updike," *Library Journal*, February 15, 1999, pp. 114-16.

Schiff, James A., *John Updike Revisited*, Twayne, 1998, pp. 2, 20, 28-29, 67.

Sissman, L. E., "John Updike: Midpoint and After," *Atlantic Monthly*, August, 1970. Pp. 102-104.

Steiner, George, "Supreme Fiction," *New Yorker*, March 11, 1996, pp. 105-06.

Thompson, John, "Updike le Noir," *New York Review of Books*, December 21, 1978, pp. 3-4.

Towers, Robert, "Updike in Africa," *New York Times Book Review*, December 10, 1978, pp. 1, 55.

Vickery, John B., "'The Centaur': Myth, History, and Narrative," *Modern Fiction Studies*, spring, 1974, pp. 29-43.

Will, George, "Updike, America, Morality," *Washington Post*, October 28, 1990, p. C7.

Williamson, Chilton, Jr., "Harry's End," *National Review*, November 19, 1990, pp. 51-53.

Wills, Gary, review of *Rabbit at Rest, New York Review of Books*, October 25, 1990.

Yardley, Jonathan, "The Sorcery of John Updike," *Washington Post Book World*, May 13, 1984, p. 3.

Yardley, Jonathan, "John Updike: For Better, for Worse," *Washington Post Book World*, May 10, 1987, p. 3.

Yardley, Jonathan, review of *Bech at Bay, Washington Post Book World*, October 18, 1998, p. 3.

■ For More Information See

BOOKS

Aldridge, John W., *Time to Murder and Create: The Contemporary Novel in Crisis*, McKay (New York City), 1966.

Broer, Lawrence R., editor, *Rabbit Tales: Poetry and Politics in John Updike's Rabbit Novels*, University of Alabama Press, 1998.

Burchard, Rachael C., *John Updike: Yea Sayings*, Southern Illinois University Press (Carbondale, IL), 1971.

Concise Dictionary of American Literary Biography: Broadening Views, 1968-1988, Gale (Detroit, MI), 1989.

Contemporary Authors Bibliographical Series, Volume 1, Gale, 1986.

Contemporary Literary Criticism, Gale, Volume 1, 1973; Volume 2, 1974; Volume 3, 1975; Volume 5, 1976; Volume 7, 1977; Volume 9, 1978; Volume 13, 1980; Volume 15, 1980; Volume 23, 1983; Volume 34, 1985; Volume 43, 1987; Volume 70, 1991.

De Bellis, Jack, *John Updike: A Bibliography, 1967-1993*, foreword by John Updike, Greenwood Press (Westport, CT), 1994.

Dictionary of Literary Biography Documentary Series, Volume 3, Gale, 1983.

Dictionary of Literary Biography Yearbook, Gale, 1980, 1981, 1982, 1983, 1997, 1998.

Dictionary of Literary Biography, Gale, Volume 2: *American Novelists since World War II,* 1978, Volume 5: *American Poets since World War II,* 1980.

Greiner, Donald J., *Adultery in the American Novel: Updike, James, Hawthorne,* University of South Carolina Press (Columbia, SC), 1985.

Hunt, George, *John Updike and the Three Great Secret Things,* Eerdmans (Grand Rapids, MI), 1980.

Luscher, Robert M., *John Updike: A Study of the Short Fiction,* Twayne, 1993.

Neary, John, *Something and Nothingness: The Fiction of John Updike & John Fowles,* Southern Illinois University Press, 1992.

Newman, Judie, *John Updike,* St. Martin's (New York City), 1988.

Plath, James, editor, *Conversations with John Updike,* University Press of Mississippi (Jackson), 1994.

Ristoff, Dilvo I., *John Updike's Rabbit at Rest: Appropriating History,* P. Lang, 1998.

Schiff, James A., *Updike's Version: Rewriting the Scarlet Letter,* University of Missouri Press (Columbia), 1992.

Short Story Criticism, Volume 13, Gale, 1993.

Singh, Sukhbir, *The Survivor in Contemporary American Fiction: Saul Bellow, Bernard Malamud, John Updike, Kurt Vonnegut, Jr.,* B. R. Publishing (Delhi), 1991.

Tallent, Elizabeth, *Married Men and Magic Tricks: John Updike's Erotic Heroes,* Creative Arts (Berkeley, CA), 1981.

Thorburn, David, and Howard Eiland, editors, *John Updike: A Collection of Critical Essays,* G. K. Hall (Boston, MA), 1982.

Trachtenberg, Stanley, editor, *New Essays on Rabbit, Run,* Cambridge University Press (Cambridge, England), 1993.

Updike, John, *Self-Consciousness: Memoirs,* Knopf, 1989.

Uphaus, Suzanne Henning, *John Updike,* Ungar (New York City), 1980.

PERIODICALS

Booklist, January 1, 1997, p. 762; August, 1997, p. 1849; January 1, 1999, p. 780; April 1, 1999, p. 1384.

Chicago Tribune Books, November 1, 1992, pp. 1, 9; January 30, 1994, pp. 1, 9.

Christian Science Monitor, February 14, 1994.

Entertainment Weekly, November 6, 1998, p. 82; April 16, 1999, p. 12.

Horn Book, January-February, 200, p. 62.

Kenyon Review, spring, 1992.

Kirkus Reviews, September 1, 1994, p. 1162; July 15, 1999, p. 1140; August 1, 1999, p. 1214.

Library Journal, February 15, 2000, p. 26.

London Review of Books, March 11, 1993, p. 9.

Los Angeles Times, January 4, 1987.

Los Angeles Times Book Review, November 1, 1992, p. 3; July 19, 1999, p. 3.

Nation, February 12, 1996, pp. 25-28.

New Republic, May 27, 1996, p. 29; February 21, 2000, p. 32.

Newsweek, November 15, 1971; September 28, 1981; October 18, 1982.

New York, January 31, 1994, p. 62.

New York Review of Books, April 11, 1968; August 8, 1974; April 3, 1975; November 19, 1981; November 18, 1982; November 24, 1983; June 14, 1984; December 4, 1986; February 29, 1996, p. 4; November 19, 1998, p. 8; March 23, 2000, p. 13.

New York Times, January 11, 1959; October 7, 1982; August 27, 1986; November 5, 1990, p. A20; January 25, 1994, p. C19.

New York Times Book Review, March 18, 1962; April 7, 1963; April 7, 1968; June 21, 1970; November 14, 1971; September 27, 1981; October 17, 1982; September 18, 1983; August 31, 1986; April 26, 1987; November 1, 1992, p. 11; February 6, 1994, p. 1; January 28, 1996, p. 9; October 12, 1997, p. 9; May 31, 1998, p. 13; September 27, 1998, p. 32; October 25, 1998, p. 7; May, 1999, p. 8; September 26, 1999. P. 7.

Publishers Weekly, September 5, 1994, p. 88; January 8, 1996; p. 47; August 4, 1997, p. 62; July 20, 1998, p. 204; August 30, 1999, p. 82.

Spectator, April 9, 1994, p. 25.

Times (London), January 14, 1982; February 5, 1995.

Times Literary Supplement, January 15, 1982; January 20, 1984; September 28, 1984; October 24, 1986; February 25, 1994, p. 21; April 1, 1994, p. 21; February 6, 1998, p. 22; January 1, 1999, p. 20.

World Literature Today, winter, 1994, p. 128; spring, 1998, p. 374.*

—Sketch by J. Sydney Jones

Wendelin Van Draanen

■ Personal

Married; children: two.

■ Addresses

Home–California.

■ Career

Writer and former educator.

■ Awards, Honors

Edgar Award for Best Children's Mystery, and Best Book for Young Adults selection, American Library Association, both 1999, for *Sammy Keyes and the Hotel Thief.*

■ Writings

How I Survived Being a Girl, HarperCollins, 1997.

"SAMMY KEYES" SERIES

Sammy Keyes and the Hotel Thief, illustrated by Dan Yaccarino, Knopf, 1998.

Sammy Keyes and the Skeleton Man, illustrated by Dan Yaccarino, Knopf, 1998.

Sammy Keyes and the Sisters of Mercy, illustrated by Dan Yaccarino, Knopf, 1999.

Sammy Keyes and the Runaway Elf, illustrated by Dan Yaccarino, Knopf, 1999.

Sammy Keyes and the Curse of Moustache Mary, illustrated by Dan Yaccarino, Knopf, 2000.

■ Work in Progress

Sammy Keyes and the Hollywood Mummy, "in this story, Sammy and Marissa hop a bus to Hollywood to confront Sammy's mother, or, as Sammy puts it, 'to shake some bubbles out of the GasAway Lady's head,'" for Knopf, expected 2001; *Flipped*, "a 'substance over style' coming-of-age story told from two perspectives (a boy's and a girl's)," for Knopf, expected 2001.

■ Sidelights

Wendelin Van Draanen is the author of the popular "Sammy Keyes" mystery series for young readers, featuring an indomitable tomboy with a penchant for landing herself in trouble. The misunderstood heroine, whose formal name is Samantha, often starts out as the primary suspect in some sort of minor crime and finds the real culprit through efforts to clear her own name. The junior-high schooler also combats some tough family and social situations with the same sense of humor and adventure. Van Draanen's first book in the series—only her second ever published—won the Edgar Award for Best Children's Mystery in 1999. "The audience I have in mind is the kid who's coming to a place where they have to make decisions on their own," the writer told *Authors and Artists for Young Adults* (*AAYA*). "I try to shed a little light on the merits of being good, heroic, and honest. I hope that kids come away from reading my work with a little more strength and belief in themselves and the sense that they *can* shape their own destiny."

Until she was in the fourth grade when her sister was born, Van Draanen grew up the sole daughter in a family with three children, having an older and a younger brother. The situation provided the inspiration for her intrepid, tomboy protagonists of her books, though the future author described her own juvenile persona as tentative and shy. "My parents immigrated to the United States, so there was always something 'foreign' about our family," Van Draanen told *AAYA*. "I never really felt like I fit in unless I was with my family." Still, she admitted to a daring streak when backed up by her siblings. "I did a lot of 'boy stuff,'" she recalled. "We spied on the neighbors, played in the school yard across the street— roller-skating, kickball, dodgeball, hide 'n' seek— we also loved to go swimming at the Plunge (community pool) and ride bikes. Indoor activities included reading (loved mysteries) and endless hours of chess. We also had chores, chores, chores!"

Growing Up on YA Books

Like other shy children, Van Draanen found comfort in the world of books. She particularly enjoyed popular teen sleuth series, including *Nancy Drew,* the *Hardy Boys,* and *Encyclopedia Brown.* "My father would read to us at bedtime," she told *AAYA.* "He'd gather my brothers and me up in a bed and read from a collection of stories for children. We relished storytime and the way he read. My mother did this, too, but I remember the times

Thirteen-year-old Sammy witnesses a crime from her grandmother's apartment, but has trouble convincing people about what she saw in this 1998 Edgar Award-winning novel.

with my father the best." Van Draanen remembered learning to read at an early age, thanks to one of her siblings. "I began to read by watching my older brother learn to read. I'd hang over his shoulder while he got help from my mother, and that's how I picked it up. My mother worked with all of us, teaching us reading and mathematics at a very early age. One of my favorite pictures of me as a young girl was taken at the age of about eighteen months—I'm sitting on the toilet, feet dangling, engrossed in a book that's in my lap."

Entering adolescence was a time of added uncertainty for Van Draanen, however. Her coming-of-age adventures would form the basis for the comical problems she later forces Sammy Keyes to suffer. "I liked elementary school, but beginning in junior high I felt terribly awkward and on the outskirts of social circles," she remembered in the interview with *AAYA*. "I guess you'd call me a straight-A student. Academics were important in our family. I liked learning." She remained rather shy throughout her teens, and did not even have her first date until the night of her senior prom.

Van Draanen looked forward to an impressive career. "My parents were both chemists, so I was sure I'd become something scientific," she told *AAYA*. "I really wanted to be a singer, but was much too shy to put that forward, so I stuck to science and math. I certainly did not want to be a writer! It seemed so dull!" But when she was in college, a catastrophe in her family would inadvertently open up a new door for her: their family business was destroyed by arson, and she took time off from school to help out. For a time, they were financially ruined, and Van Draanen was troubled by feelings of anger and helplessness. She began to have problems sleeping, and to help alleviate some of the stress, she decided to write about the incident, with the hope of turning it into a screenplay.

Van Draanen discovered that writing was not only cathartic but enjoyable. What she found most rewarding, she would later note, was the ability to create a happy ending, to have her characters make positive gains through personal difficulties. Van Draanen would eventually find hervocation as a teacher of computer science to high schoolers, but she also had ten finished novels, each around four hundred pages long, by the mid-1990s. By then she had married and had begun a family of her own in California.

Van Draanen was inspired to try her hand at writing for children as a result of a chance gift. "My husband gave me *Dandelion Wine* (by Ray Bradbury) and told me it was one of his favorite books. I read it and it reminded me of all the wonderful mischief my brothers and I got into when we were young, and decided it would be fun to write a book like *Dandelion Wine* about my experiences growing up." The result was *How I Survived Being a Girl,* published in 1997. It is Van Draanen's sole work for young readers outside of her Sammy Keyes series, but the works share a heroine with pointed similarities. Carolyn, the narrator of *How I Survived Being a Girl,* is a tomboy who feels herself somewhat alienated from the

girls in her neighborhood and at school. She much prefers tagging along with her brothers and their friends, especially a neighbor boy named Charlie. During the summer of her twelfth year, Carolyn spies on neighbors, digs foxholes with Charlie, steals a book, and helps her brother with his paper route.

The setting of *How I Survived Being a Girl* is vague, but reviewers seemed to agree that Van Draanen placed her story at some point in the relatively recent past. Girls must still wear dresses to school, for instance, and are strongly discouraged from becoming newspaper carriers—official and unofficial biases that had vanished by the end of the 1970s. Carolyn manages to skirt the skirt issue by wearing shorts under hers; meanwhile,

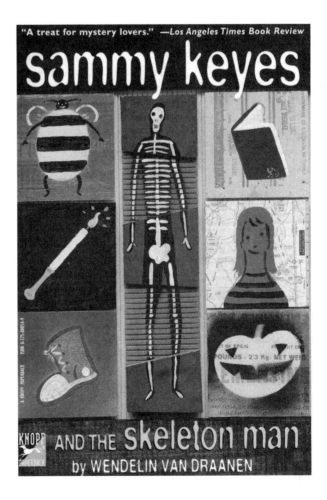

In this second book of the "Sammy Keyes" series, Sammy stumbles upon a decade-old family feud and witnesses a burglary by someone dressed in a skeleton costume.

she derides her peers who play with dolls and wear frilly, impractical clothes. Yet as she begins a new school year in September, Carolyn finds that some of her attitudes are beginning to change. She sees Charlie in a new way, and starts to speak out and become more politically active. She even starts a petition drive to force some changes at her school. When a baby sister arrives in her family, this softens her attitude, too. "I tell her . . . how being a girl is actually all right once you figure out that you should break some of the rules instead of just living with them," says Carolyn at the end.

A *Publishers Weekly* review called *How I Survived Being a Girl* an "energetic first novel" and "a sunny, funny look at a girl with a smart mouth and scabby knees." Writing in *School Library Journal*, Kathleen Odean found some fault with the premise that a new sibling can bring out an adolescent girl's feminine instincts. "Perhaps the unspecified time setting . . . makes it inevitable that she will be 'tamed a bit,' as she puts it," remarked Odean. Yet a *Kirkus Reviews* assessment praised Van Draanen's style and the narrative voice of her alter ego, Carolyn. "Her irreverent narration is engaging," stated the reviewer about the book's heroine, "and she's refreshingly astute about family and neighborhood dynamics."

The Debut of Sammy Keyes

Van Draanen found that "I loved writing in the voice of a twelve-year-old so much that I haven't gone back, and have no desire to go back, to writing for adults," she said in the *AAYA* interview. She began writing a teen-detective story that would evolve into a popular and much-praised series. The first of these arrived in 1998 with *Sammy Keyes and the Hotel Thief*. Here, readers are introduced to the feisty, intelligent title character who lives with her grandmother in a seniors-only apartment building. Because of this, Sammy is forced to sneak around just to get to school; naturally, her social life is severely curtailed as well. Sammy lives with her grandmother, readers learn, because her mother, to whom she refers as "Lady Lana," has moved to Hollywood.

Sammy has some formidable enemies. One is the nosy Mrs. Graybill, who lives down the hall; another is a girl, Heather, who torments her daily at school. To keep herself amused at home,

Sammy often observes the goings-on of the outside world with a pair of binoculars from her fifth-floor window. "Usually you just see people looking out their windows, pointing to stuff on the street or talking on the phone," Sammy states, "but sometimes you can see people yelling at each other, which is really strange because you can't *hear* anything."

Sammy is particularly fascinated by the shady Heavenly Hotel across the street, and one afternoon spots a fourth-floor resident moving about a room rather quickly. She then sees the man rifling through a purse while wearing gloves. As Sammy tells it: "And I'm trying to get a better look at his face through all his bushy brown hair and beard, when he stuffs a wad of money from the purse into his jacket pocket and then looks up. Right at me. For a second there I don't think he believed his eyes. He kind of leaned into the window and stared, and I stared right back through the binoculars. Then I did something really, really stupid. I waved."

The man flees the room, and she wonders whether she has just witnessed a crime and if she ought to tell someone about it. But her grandmother is making dinner, and she can't call 911 from the kitchen; getting to a police station is also problematic. Then, her grandmother calls her into the kitchen and reminds her to feed the cat. When the doorbell rings, Sammy is so agitated that she does not quietly make for the closet, as is her usual drill when an unexpected visitor arrives. "This time, though, I jumped. I jumped and yelped like a puppy. And all of a sudden my heart's pounding because I know who it is," Sammy panics. "It's the guy I saw at the Heavenly Hotel, come to shut me up for good."

Eventually, Sammy manages to tell the police, who fail to take her seriously at first. Meanwhile, Heather is plotting against her at school, but Sammy's cleverness uncovers the plot in time. She also learns that a burglar has indeed been stealing from purses in the neighborhood. Other characters in the book include a pair of comical detectives, her friend Marissa, a local DJ, and an eccentric astrologer who is also a robbery victim. They all help Sammy bring the thief to justice. "The solution will likely come as a surprise, and the sleuth delights from start to finish," asserted a *Publishers Weekly* review of *Sammy Keyes and the Hotel Thief*. A *Horn Book* review by Martha V.

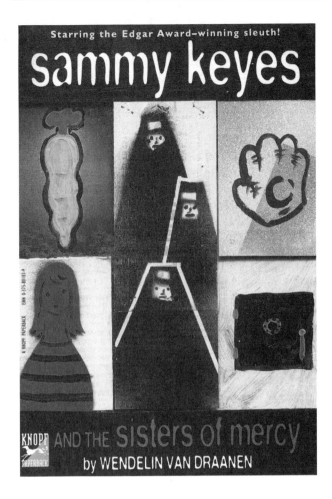

Starring the Edgar Award–winning sleuth!

sammy keyes

KNOPF AND THE **sisters of mercy**
by WENDELIN VAN DRAANEN

Sammy fills her days trying to solve the St. Mary's church burglaries and defeating a bitter rival in a softball tournament in this 1999 mystery.

Parravano described Van Draanen's protagonist as "one tough, smart, resourceful seventh grader," and compared the heroine and structure of the lighthearted detective novel to popular adult mystery writers such as Sue Grafton, who are adept at "making the investigator's character and private life at least as interesting and complex as the plot," noted Parravano.

Van Draanen followed the success of the first Sammy Keyes book with a second that same year, *Sammy Keyes and the Skeleton Man.* As it opens around Halloween time, Sammy still lives with her grandmother and is eagerly outfitting herself as the Marsh Monster for the holiday. While trick-or-treating, she and her friends bravely approach the "Bush House," a scary manse with wildly overgrown shrubbery. But then Sammy is nearly knocked down by a man wearing a skeleton costume and carrying a pillowcase. She and her friends advance and discover a fire in the house, and Sammy puts it out. They also find that a burglary has just taken place, and severalvaluable books are missing from the house.

Sammy, naturally, finds herself drawn into the drama and wants to solve the whodunit. She learns that the Bush House is neglected because its owners, the LeBard brothers, are feuding with one another. Once again, her cleverness helps her find a solution, and also helps her keep one step ahead of Heather, who continues to plot against her. Sammy, for instance, sneaks into Heather's Halloween party and plants a baby monitor in her room—which provides Sammy with evidence that Heather has been making prank phone calls in Sammy's name. Yet Sammy's natural talent for making friends also helps her forge an unusual bond with Chauncy LeBard, and she even gets the two warring brothers to agree to talk. In the end, she unmasks the skeleton man and recovers the missing rarities. Parravano, reviewing the story for *Horn Book,* praised it as a "highly readable mystery [that] hits the ground running." Critic Lynda Short also offered positive words in *School Library Journal:* "Readers will enjoy the mystery, hijinks, plotting, and adult comeuppance."

Series Is a Hit

Van Draanen's third entry in the series, *Sammy Keyes and the Sisters of Mercy,* was published in 1999. Still walking that fine line between intellectual brilliance and juvenile delinquency, Sammy finds herself sentenced to twenty hours of detention, which she must fulfill by helping out at the local Roman Catholic church. One day, cleaning the windows of St. Mary's, she sees a girl she does not know and approaches her, but the girl vanishes and Sammy is suddenly alerted to the distress of Father Mayhew, who has just discovered his valuable ivory cross missing. Sammy, of course, is the first suspect in the theft. Yet other possible culprits surface as well, and in order to clear her own name, she resolves to catch the thief herself. On another day, she again sees the mysterious girl at the church's soup kitchen and eventually learns that she is homeless.

Again, Van Draanen tries to make Sammy a typical adolescent. There is more enmity with Heather,

---

If you enjoy the works of Wendelin Van Draanen, you may also want to check out the following books:

Betsy Byars, *The Dark Stairs*, 1994.
Cynthia DeFelice, *The Light on Hogback Hill*, 1993.
Mary Downing Hahn, *Following the Mystery Man*, 1988.

---

and she is determined to beat her foe in the local softball league championships. In the end, it is Sammy's offer to help a group of musical nuns who do missionary work out of an old school bus that helps solve the mystery of Father Mayhew's missing cross. "As always, quirky characters are Van Draanen's strength," remarked Kay Weisman in a *Booklist* review. An assessment from Jennifer Ralston in *School Library Journal* praised the main plot of *Sammy Keyes and the Sisters of Mercy* as well as the other story lines, both recurring and new. Ralston noted the story lines provide "depth and interest to an already engrossing mystery while capturing the angst of junior high school." Beth E. Anderson, reviewing it for *Voice of Youth Advocates*, commended Van Draanen's heroine. "Sammy is genuine, funny, devoted to her friends and blessed with a strength of character that lets her reach for a peaceful solution," Anderson wrote.

Van Draanen wrote another in the series that also appeared in 1999, *Sammy Keyes and the Runaway Elf.* Set during the Christmas season, Sammy is still in seventh grade and becomes involved in her community's holiday parade. She is assigned to the "Canine Calendar Float" and is charged with babysitting a famous Pomeranian, the calendar cover dog, Marique. Parade chaos ensues, however, when a trio of culprits dressed as the Three Kings throw cats onto the hound-laden float. The prized Marique vanishes, and its owner, wealthy Mrs. Landvogt, blackmailsSammy into finding Marique in order to avoid paying the fifty thousand dollar ransom demanded. An elfin girl, Elyssa, turns out to be a runaway, and Van Draanen weaves her plight and the dognapping together and ties it up with another satisfying conclusion. Once again, however, several suspects must first be eliminated and comical plot twists

steered through. This time, Sammy manages to befriend the formidable Mrs. Graybill, too. Remarking upon Sammy's penchant for making friends both younger and much older than herself, *School Library Journal* reviewer Linda Bindner noted that "Van Draanen handles the relationships with style and sensitivity."

A fifth book in the series, *Sammy Keyes and the Curse of Moustache Mary,* was published in 2000. Like all of her books, Van Draanen finds that the complex plots seem to come to her slowly. "I get an idea and just let it stew and stew in my brain until it's boiling over," she told *AAYA*. "Then I start writing and can't stop until the story's out." She conducts all of her research herself and then sits down to writing in her inimitable character's voice. "I need to be able to get into the 'Sammy-zone,' where I feel like I'm channeling her. I work best when the computer can just suck me in and trap me. That's when things start cookin'!"

The success of her career as an author led Van Draanen to give up her teaching job. "This is my first year as a full-time writer," she said in the summer of 2000. "All those years before I'd get up when my husband got ready for work (5:00 AM) and just stumble over to the computer to get in an hour or two before I had to get the kids up (I have a six year old and a nine year old) and go off to teach school. I still get up early with my husband and find that early morning is still my most productive time."

Van Draanen says she plans to continue writing for adolescents. "They're growing, they're changing, and they're receptive to making the world a better place," she enthused. "They have big dreams that they want to reach for. I try to give them the strength to believe that—with determination, thought, and persistence—they can attain them. Growing up's not easy. Everyone feels awkward through adolescence, but when you're a kid it seems that you're the only one who's not fitting in. Everyone else seems to have it together, or be comfortable with themselves. It's not true, but that's how we feel when we're kids."

The author concluded, "It's my goal to get kids through those awkward years and onto adulthood safely. The choices they make in the areas of honesty, convictions, friendships, and compassion now will effect them their entire lives."

■ Works Cited

Anderson, Beth E., review of *Sammy Keyes and the Sisters of Mercy, Voice of Youth Advocates*, April, 2000, pp. 40-41.

Bindner, Linda, review of *Sammy Keyes and the Runaway Elf, School Library Journal*, September, 1999, p. 229.

Review of *How I Survived Being a Girl, Kirkus Reviews*, December 1, 1996.

Review of *How I Survived Being a Girl, Publishers Weekly*, January 6, 1997, p. 73.

Odean, Kathleen, review of *How I Survived Being a Girl, School Library Journal*, February, 1997, p. 106.

Parravano, Martha V., review of *Sammy Keyes and the Hotel Thief, Horn Book*, July-August, 1998, pp. 498-499.

Parravano, Marcha V., review of *Sammy Keyes and the Skeleton Man, Horn Book*, November-

December, 1998, p. 743.

Ralston, Jennifer, review of *Sammy Keyes and the Sisters of Mercy, School Library Journal*, July, 1999, p. 101.

Review of *Sammy Keyes and the Hotel Thief, Publishers Weekly*, April 27, 1998, p. 67.

Short, Lynda, review of *Sammy Keyes and the Skeleton Man, School Library Journal*, September, 1998, p. 211.

Van Draanen, Wendelin, in an interview for *Authors and Artists for Young Adults*, June 14, 2000.

Weisman, Kay, review of *Sammy Keyes and the Sisters of Mercy, Booklist*, April 1, 1999, p. 1415.

■ For More Information See

PERIODICALS

Booklist, September 1, 1998, p. 131; September 1, 1999, p. 146.

San Luis Obispo Tribune, September 27, 1999.

School Library Journal, July, 1998, p. 100; August, 2000, p. 190.

—Sketch by Carol Brennan

Phyllis A. Whitney

Personal

Born September 9, 1903, in Yokohama, Japan; daughter of U.S. citizens, Charles Joseph and Lillian (Mandeville) Whitney; married George A. Garner, July 2, 1925 (divorced, 1945); married Lovell F. Jahnke (in business), 1950 (died, 1973); children: (first marriage) Georgia. *Education:* Attended public schools in Chicago, IL. *Hobbies and other interests:* "My only hobby is collecting backgrounds for new books, and that takes most of my time, since I visit these places and do a great deal of research."

Addresses

Agent—McIntosh and Otis Inc., 310 Madison Ave., New York, NY 10017.

Career

Writer, 1941—. Children's book editor with the *Chicago Sun* (now *Chicago Sun Times*), 1942-46, and *Philadelphia Inquirer*, 1946-48. Teacher of juvenile

writing at Northwestern University, Evanston, IL, 1945-46, New York University, New York City, 1947-58, and at writers' conferences.

Member

Authors League of America, Mystery Writers of America (member of board of directors, 1959-62; president, 1975), Malice Domestic, American Crime Writers League, Society of Children's Book Writers, Children'sReading Round Table, Midland Authors.

Awards, Honors

Youth Today contest winner, and *Book World*'s Spring Book Festival Award, both 1947, both for *Willow Hill*; Edgar Allan Poe Award for best juvenile mystery, Mystery Writers of America, 1961, for*Mystery of the Haunted Pool,* and 1964, for *Mystery of the Hidden Hand*; Edgar Allan Poe nominations, 1962, for *The Secret of the Tiger Eyes,* 1971, for *Mystery of the Scowling Boy,* and 1974, for*The Secret of the Missing Footprint*; Sequoyah Children's Book Award, 1963, for *Mystery of the Haunted Pool;* "Today's Woman" citation, Council of Cerebral Palsy Auxiliaries of Nassau County, 1983; Grandmaster Award, Mystery Writers of America, 1988, for lifetime achievement; Malice Domestic Award, 1989, for lifetime achievement; Romance Writers

of America Award, 1990, for lifetime achievement;
Agatha Award, 1990, for lifetime achievement.

■ Writings

JUVENILE NOVELS

A Place for Ann, illustrated by Helen Blair,
Houghton (Boston), 1941.
A Star for Ginny, illustrated by Hilda Frommholz,
Houghton, 1942.
A Window for Julie, illustrated by Jean Anderson,
Houghton, 1943.
The Silver Inkwell, illustrated by Frommholz,
Houghton, 1945.
Willow Hill, McKay (New York City), 1947.
Ever After, Houghton, 1948.
Linda's Homecoming, McKay, 1950.
Love Me, Love Me Not, Houghton, 1952.
Step to the Music, Crowell (New York City), 1953.
A Long Time Coming, McKay, 1954.
The Fire and the Gold, Crowell, 1956.
The Highest Dream, McKay, 1956.
Creole Holiday, Westminster (Philadelphia), 1959.
Nobody Likes Trina, Westminster, 1972.

JUVENILE MYSTERIES

Mystery of the Gulls, illustrated by Janet Smalley,
Westminster, 1949.
The Island of Dark Woods, illustrated by Philip
Wishnefsky, Westminster, 1951, published as
Mystery of the Strange Traveller, 1967.
Mystery of the Black Diamonds, illustrated by John
Gretzer, Westminster, 1954 (published in England
as *Black Diamonds*, Brockhampton, 1957).
Mystery on the Isle of Skye, illustrated by Ezra Jack
Keats, Westminster, 1955.
Mystery of the Green Cat, illustrated by Richard
Horwitz, Westminster, 1957.
Secret of the Samurai Sword, Westminster, 1958.
Mystery of the Haunted Pool, illustrated by H. Tom
Hall, Westminster, 1960.
Secret of the Tiger's Eye, illustrated by Horwitz,
Westminster, 1961.
Mystery of the Golden Horn, illustrated by
Georgeann Helmes, Westminster, 1962.
Mystery of the Hidden Hand, illustrated by Hall,
Westminster, 1963.
Secret of the Emerald Star, illustrated by Alex Stein,
Westminster, 1964.
Mystery of the Angry Idol, illustrated by Al
Fiorentino, Westminster, 1965.

Secret of the Spotted Shell, illustrated by John
Mecray, Westminster, 1967.
Secret of Goblin Glen, illustrated by Fiorentino,
Westminster, 1968.
Mystery of the Crimson Ghost, Westminster, 1969.
Secret of the Missing Footprint, illustrated by Stein,
Westminster, 1970.
The Vanishing Scarecrow, Westminster, 1971.
Mystery of the Scowling Boy, illustrated by Gretzer,
Westminster, 1973.
Secret of Haunted Mesa, Westminster, 1975.
Secret of the Stone Face, Westminster, 1977.

ADULT NOVELS

Red Is for Murder, Ziff-Davis, 1943, published as
The Red Carnelian, Paperback Library, 1965.
The Quicksilver Pool, Appleton, 1955.
The Trembling Hills, Appleton, 1956.
Skye Cameron, Appleton, 1957.
The Moonflower, Appleton, 1958 (published in En-
gland as *The Mask and the Moonflower*, Hurst &
Blackett, 1960).
Thunder Heights, Appleton, 1960.
Blue Fire, Appleton, 1961.
Window on the Square, Appleton, 1962.
Seven Tears for Apollo, Appleton, 1963.
Black Amber, Appleton, 1964.
Sea Jade, Appleton, 1965.
Columbella, Doubleday (New York City), 1966.
Silverhill, Doubleday, 1967.
Hunter's Green, Doubleday, 1968.
The Winter People, Doubleday, 1969.
Lost Island, Doubleday, 1970.
Listen for the Whisperer, Doubleday, 1972.
Snowfire, Doubleday, 1973.
The Turquoise Mask, Doubleday, 1974.
Spindrift, Doubleday, 1975.
The Golden Unicorn, Doubleday, 1976.
The Stone Bull, Doubleday, 1977.
The Glass Flame, Doubleday, 1978.
Domino, Doubleday, 1979.
Poinciana, Doubleday, 1980.
Vermilion, Doubleday, 1981.
Emerald, Doubleday, 1982.
Rainsong, Doubleday, 1984.
Dream of Orchids, Doubleday, 1985.
Flaming Tree, Doubleday, 1986.
Silversword, Doubleday, 1987.
Feather on the Moon, Doubleday, 1988.
Rainbow in the Mist, Doubleday, 1989.
The Singing Stones, Doubleday, 1990.
Woman without a Past, Doubleday, 1991.
The Ebony Swan, Doubleday, 1992.

Star Flight, Crown (New York City), 1993.
Daughter of the Stars, Crown, 1994.
Amethyst Dreams, Crown, 1997.

OTHER

Writing Juvenile Fiction (also see below), Writer, Inc. (Boston), 1947, revised edition, 1960.
Writing Juvenile Stories and Novels: How to Write and Sell Fiction for Young People (contains portions of *Writing Juvenile Fiction*), Writer, Inc., 1976.
Guide to Writing Fiction, Writer, Inc., 1982, second edition, 1988.

Contributor of articles to periodicals, including *Writer*.

■ Sidelights

Called "America's queen of romantic suspense" and the "Grandmaster" by reviewers, Phyllis A. Whitney, with over forty novels for young adults to her credit, is a master crafter of mysteries, romances, and intrigues about young women whose attempts to unlock secrets and solve puzzles oftenput them at the threshold of danger. A popular writer and commercial success—at one time she had over forty million copies of her books in print—Whitney also has garnered critical recognition for her artistry in the genre. She has received the prestigious Edgar Allan Poe Award for two of her young-adult mysteries, and award-nominations for three others.

Whitney's incredible plot twists, foreign settings, complex family dynamics, sinister villains, and spooky overtones echo the eighteenth-century Gothic motif, to which Whitney adds twentieth-century themes, issues, and characters. Critics esteem her works for their realistic, likable, and spunky protagonists, who unlike many traditional heroines of romantic and Gothic fiction, are not idealized nor sentimentalized, but rather are burdened with shortcomings that they must attempt to work out for themselves. Althea K. Helbig and Agnes Regan Perkins wrote in the *Dictionary of American Children's Fiction*: "Typically, [Whitney's YA suspense novels] are from the point of view of a young adolescent girl who feels unloved or inferior because of a lack of talent and who, with a boy her age or slightly older, unravels a series of mysterious events, often involving crime but not

murder, and in so doing comes to self-understanding."

Another distinguishing feature of Whitney's work is the incorporation of a variety of exotic locales and cultures culled from her own international travels. In *Secret of the Samurai Sword*, for instance, Whitney infuses thetext with hints of the Japanese traditions and customs she experienced as an American child growing up in Japan. Her stories also have been set in the Virgin Islands, the Isle of Skye in Scotland, China, and South Africa.

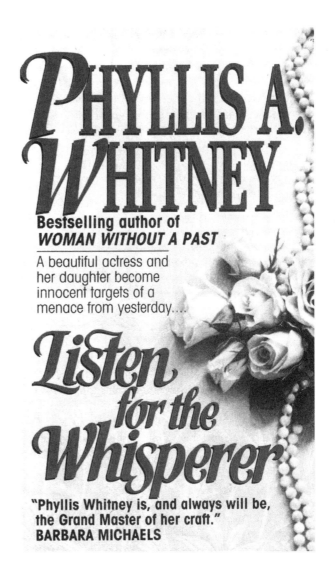

While Leigh Hollins searches for her Hollywood actress mother, she becomes entangled in a deadly mystery stemming from her mother's past in this 1972 thriller.

While her mysteries and romances have been occasionally criticized for formulaic and artificial plots, reviewers applaud their swift action and vivid settings and atmospheres. Thematically, Whitney has touched upon such issues as apartheid, race relations, and the plight of Native Americans; in addition, she is concerned with the social and emotional problems of adolescents. Above all, Whitney has a knack for telling suspenseful stories and for luring readers into the fantastic secrets and chilling situations of her fiction.

Grows Up in Asia

Like the plots in some of her books, Whitney's early life also featured exotic places and frequent travel. Whitney was born in Yokohama, Japan, in 1903 to American parents. She lived in Japan, China, and the Philippines until her father's death when she was fifteen. She then came to the United States with her mother, who passed away two years later. Settling in Chicago with an aunt, Whitney finished high school and married a year after graduation. By that time, she was already writing stories, and managed to sell a few to magazines.

In 1941, she published her first book, *A Place for Ann*, a young-adult novel that brought her a measure of success and self-sufficiency. Shortly afterdivorcing her husband in 1945, Whitney approached her editor about writing a book involving racial issues. "My editor objected to the story idea," Whitney related in *Library Journal*. "She didn't think I could do it. She doubted that it would sell, and she didn't want to publish it anyway." Despite her editor's reservations, Whitney wrote *Willow Hill*, a story about a white girl and her high school friends confronting the integration of a housing project into their community. Another publisher brought out the work in 1947. *Willow Hill* won the Youth Today contest and became one of Whitney's most popular children's books.

Critics have also admired the novel. "For all the problems involved," M. C. Scoggin comments in the *New York Times*, *Willow Hill* "is not a thesis hung on a clothes-horse of a plot. It is full of flesh-and-blood boys and girls." A *Saturday Review of Literature* critic agrees, noting that "this is a story that comes completely and excitingly to life. . . . A book with a message, it gains rather than

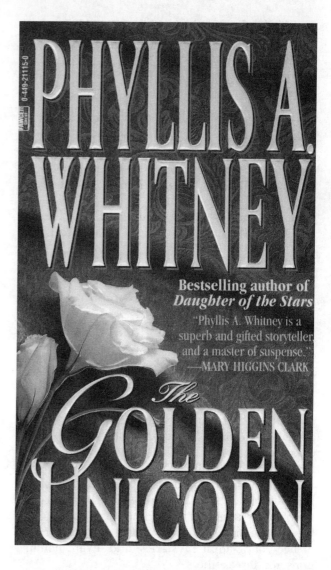

A tiny gold unicorn that Courtney Marsh wears around her neck is the secret link to the adopted girl's past—a past filled with mystery and murder.

loses by its preoccupation." As a result, Bobbie Ann Mason notes in *Twentieth-Century Children's Writers*, "the book seems daringly ahead of its time in its sympathy and in its honest portrayal of race relations."

Begins Penning YA Thrillers

Soon after *Willow Hill*, the author turned to writing stories of mystery and intrigue because, as she told Diana Gleasner in *Breakthrough: Women in Writing*, "I like mystery novels. It's a difficult form to masterbecause the plotting is so complicated;

you have to juggle so many balls at the same time." Whitney's young adult suspense novels "are lively, light mysteries," as Mason describes them, with young female protagonists "who tend to be normal kids with shortcomings and frustrations, rather than sophisticated, independent, idealized heroines. Thus Whitney has been praised for her honesty, realism, and intellectually stimulating themes." As G. P. Lancaster remarks in a *Christian Science Monitor* review of the Edgar-winning *Mystery of the Haunted Pool*, "The author has a fine flair for making her characters likable, lively, and natural."

Whitney combines history and culture with a gripping mystery in *Secret of the Samurai Sword*. Celia Bronson and her brother Stephen, fourteen and fifteen years old respectively, travel to Kyoto to visit their grandmother, who is writing a book about Japan. They soon find themselves absorbed in Japan's exotic scenery and classic customs, as well as embroiled in a mystery involving the uneasy ghost of a Samurai warrior. Critics praised the intriguing plot, the ornamental setting, and the information on ancient Japanese culture and ways of life. A *Kirkus Reviews* critic commented, "If the teen-age reader, ignorant of the structure of classical Japan, can absorb even half of the details of Japanese life offered here, this pleasant mystery will have been well worth the reading." Ruth Hill Viguers deemed *Samurai Sword* "an exceptionally good story," while Silence Buck Bellows, writing in the *Christian Science Monitor*, stated, "This book is quite a package, being a top notch mystery, a source of authentic information about Japan, and a wise and warm commentary on human relations."

While Celia and Stephen visit their grandmother, twelve-year-old Susan Price travels ahead of her family to stay with her aunt in New York in *Mystery of the Haunted Pool*. Shortly after she arrives, Susan becomes intrigued by a family secret attached to the large old house her parents are about to rent from a retired riverboat captain. Susan helps solve the mystery, and in the process makes friends with the captain's embittered grandson, who is having difficulty adjusting to a disability. Zena Sutherland deemed the book, "A good mystery story, with logical explanations but romantic atmosphere." She added, "The writing has pace and suspense; characterization and conversation are realistic." A reviewer for *The Booklist and Subscription Books Bulletin* noted of the book,

Jennifer Blake's mission to find her daughter who has been missing for seven years continues despite the dangers she encounters while following a mysterious lead.

"A plausible mystery with a well-developed plot and characterization that is above average for a mystery story."

For *Mystery of the Scowling Boy*, Whitney moved the action to the Pocono Mountains of eastern Pennsylvania, where Jan Sutton and her older brother Mike are spending the Christmas holidays with their grandparents while their parents are away. The mystery of this novel revolves around familial relationships rather than ghosts or sinister prowlers. When Jan discovers that her favorite movie star, Alanna Graham, is staying in a nearby estate, she is determined to meet her. As Jan gets to know the Graham family, shediscovers that all is not well and that Alanna is being blackmailed. A *Publishers Weekly* reviewer commented, "The author is at the top of her professional form in this improbable but appealing new mystery," while Raymond J. Morafino wrote that *Scowling Boy* "is another of [Whitney's] competently plotted but routine mysteries." Morafino concluded, "The complex plot and glamorous characters will keep young readers entertained until all the mysteries are predictably resolved in time for a happy Christmas." Althea K. Helbig and Agnes Regan

Perkins, writing in the *Dictionary of American Children's Fiction*, observed, "Though the story depends partly on the Gothic atmosphere of the old house and the grotesque sculptures, it is all plausible, and the ski-country setting is well evoked."

Secret of Haunted Mesa takes place in New Mexico. Jenny and her family visit Haunted Mesa Ranch, where her father is lecturing at a conference. At the ranch, Jenny meets up with Greg, one of the few young people she knows who is not smitten with her famous older sister Carol, a singer. A mystery unfolds as Jenny and Greg investigate strange-looking lights and the disappearance of Charlie, a Zuni Indian boy who steals food and kachina dolls. Although a reviewer for *The Children's Book Review Service* remarked that Whitney's "portrayal of Zuni Indians and their problems lacks accuracy, sensitivity, and depth," the reviewer concluded that the work was "a competently written mystery story." *Kirkus Reviews* was less kind. "A perfunctory mystery . . . is sandwiched in between clumsy lectures on Zuniculture and 'understanding' Anglos and a stock psychological problem—young Jenny's fear of being upstaged by her famous, folksinging sister." Sarah Law Kennerly, however, was more complimentary, concluding that the mystery will be "popular with Whitney's many fans."

Mysteries for Adults

More recently, Whitney has focused on adult novels of "psychological" or "romantic suspense," stories of young women who must unravel puzzles that often involve mysterious family relationships. But while Whitney's heroines often find romance along the way, they are also "liberated women," according to Barbara Mertz in the *Washington Post Book World*. "They may—and do—end up in the arms of the hero, but they have to solve their own problems before they get there." As Allen J. Hubin similarly notes in the *New York Times Book Review*, "Whitney seeks to create that mood of impending doom . . . without much recourse to the idiotic behavior common to heroines of the genre." The author explained in a *Parade* interview with Pam Proctor: "The girls in my books are out solving their own problems. They've always been women's libbers because I've always been a liberated woman. I've always done whatever I've wanted to do."

"Phyllis A. Whitney is a superb and gifted storyteller, and a master of suspense." —MARY HIGGINS CLARK

PHYLLIS A. WHITNEY

Author of *Amethyst Dreams*

DAUGHTER OF THE STARS

Lacey Elliot searches for her past—a past her mother refused to speak about for thirty years—in Whitney's suspenseful 1994 novel.

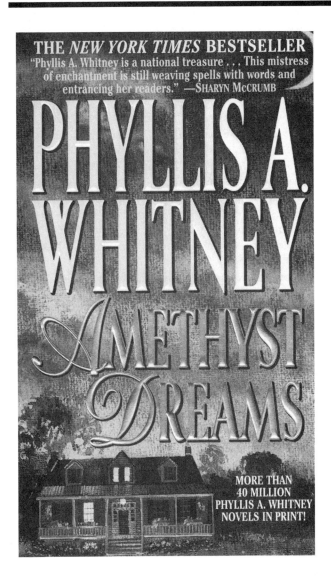

THE *NEW YORK TIMES* BESTSELLER
"Phyllis A. Whitney is a national treasure . . . This mistress of enchantment is still weaving spells with words and entrancing her readers." —SHARYN McCRUMB

PHYLLIS A. WHITNEY

AMETHYST DREAMS

MORE THAN 40 MILLION PHYLLIS A. WHITNEY NOVELS IN PRINT!

When her best friend Susan disappears, Hallie Knight discovers that a vast inheritance is the reason for Susan's disappearance in this 1997 thriller.

Another distinguishing feature of Whitney's mysteries is her striking use of unique settings. *The Stone Bull,* for instance, uses a Catskills setting that combines "mythology, drama, and botany," Irene M. Pompea remarks in *Best Sellers;* with this novel, "Phyllis Whitney has given her public an experience of genuine suspense." More recent offerings eschew exotic locations and time periods for modern situations such as child-custody disputes and kidnappings, a popular singer's widow coping with the press, and psychic phenomena. *Feather on the Moon,* besides including British Columbia's "lush scenery," is "a smoothly written tale," Sherman W. Smith states in *West Coast Review of Books.* "It is indeed an art to glue readers to the pages and Whitney has honed that art to its peak," another *West Coast Review of Books* writer similarly concludes of *Rainsong.*

In her most recent adult novels, Whitney has produced plot lines that feature rediscovered family secrets and murder. *Woman without A Past* follows a woman's search to uncover events surrounding her childhood after learning that she may have been kidnapped as an infant before arriving to her adoptive parents. Setting the novel in Charleston, South Carolina, Whitney evokes the atmosphere of the historic city and its old, traditional families to heighten the intrigue. In *The Ebony Swan,* Whitney crafts a suspenseful, psychological drama set in the scenic tidewater region of northern Virginia. The story centers on a woman's return to her childhood home, where twenty-five years earlier she witnessed her mother's murder. The woman encounters troubling mysteries surrounding the tragedy, including the implication of her maternal grandmother, a former ballerina.

Star Flight describes a woman's quest to uncover the truth behind two family deaths. Set in a resort town in western North Carolina, the complex plot links the protagonist's grandmother's suicide decades ago with her husband's recent accidental death while filming a documentary about a film star. As it turns out, an adulterous affair between the film star and her grandmother in the 1930s produced her own mother. Her husband's death arouses suspicion when she learns that he may have discovered new information suggesting that her distraught grandmother's death was not self-inflicted. The story is further complicated by the introduction of many characters and sub-plots, including UFOs and government conspiracies, drawing criticism from several reviewers on the grounds of excessive dialogue and an implausible plot. *Daughter of the Stars* similarly involves childhood revelations and domestic intrigue in historic Harpers Ferry, West Virginia. In this story, a children's book author revisits her birth place to investigate unresolved speculation surrounding the circumstances of her father's murder thirty years earlier. Whitney weaves an intricate plot involving Civil War ancestors, daunting matriarchs, and eccentric half-siblings which, according to a *Publishers Weekly* reviewer, "culminates in a gratifying surprise ending."

If you enjoy the works of Phyllis A. Whitney, you may also want to check out the following books:

Susan Howatch, *April's Grave*, 1969.
Barbara Michaels, *The Crying Child*, 1971.
Mary Stewart, *Nine Coaches Waiting*, 1958.

Whitney once commented: "I have always written because I couldn't help it. From the age of twelve on I loved to make up stories, and I've been doing it ever since. I believe in entertaining my readers, and I also hope to make them think and feel. I have great respect and admiration for fellow writers in the mystery-suspense field, and I read both to enjoy and to learn. I seem to have been born with a hunger for stories." Although shehas been publishing for over fifty years, Whitney shows no signs of slowing down. As she told Sarah Booth Conroy of the *Washington Post:* "These are my happiest years. I always want to live long enough to finish the book I'm working on and see it published. But then I start another book before the previous one is in the stores, so I always have a reason to go on."

■ Works Cited

Bellows, Silence Buck, review of *Secret of the Samurai Sword, Christian Science Monitor,* November 6, 1958, p. 17.

Conroy, Sarah Booth, "The Novelist's Spirited Path," *Washington Post,* September 2, 1991, pp. D1, D9.

Review of *Daughter of the Stars, Publishers Weekly,* August 8, 1994, p. 378.

Gleasner, Diana, *Breakthrough: Women in Writing,* Walker, 1980, pp. 126-45.

Helbig, Althea K., and Agnes Regan Perkins, *Dictionary of American Children's Fiction,* Greenwood Press, 1986.

Hubin, Allen J., review of *The Winter People, New York Times Book Review,* May 18, 1969, p. 31.

Lancaster, G. P., review of *Mystery of the Haunted Pool, Christian Science Monitor,* November 23, 1960, p. 11.

Mason, Bobbie Ann, "Phyllis A. Whitney," *Twentieth-Century Children's Writers,* 3rd edition, St. James Press, 1989, pp. 1037-39.

Mertz, Barbara, review of *Emerald, Washington Post Book World,* January 2, 1983, p. 4.

Morafino, Raymond J., review of *Mystery of the Scowling Boy, School LibraryJournal,* May, 1973, p. 92.

Review of *Mystery of the Haunted Pool, Booklist and Subscription Books Bulletin,* February 15, 1961, p. 368.

Review of *Mystery of the Scowling Boy, Publishers Weekly,* April 16, 1973, p. 55.

Pompea, Irene N., review of *The Stone Bull, Best Sellers,* September, 1977, pp. 173-74.

Proctor, Pam, "Phyllis Whitney: She Writes Best Sellers the Old-Fashioned Way," *Parade,* November 2, 1975.

Review of *Rainsong, West Coast Review of Books,* Number 1, 1985, p. 54.

Scoggin, M. C., review of *Willow Hill, New York Times,* April 6, 1947, p. 27.

Review of *Secret of Haunted Mesa, Children's Book Review Service,* February, 1976, p. 65.

Review of *Secret of Haunted Mesa, Kirkus Reviews,* August 15, 1975, p. 920.

Review of *Secret of the Samurai Sword, Kirkus Reviews,* August 1, 1958, p. 551.

Smith, Sherman W., review of *Feather on the Moon, West Coast Review of Books,* Number 6, 1988, p. 27.

Sutherland, Zena, review of *Mystery of the Haunted Pool, Bulletin of the Center for Children's Books,* October, 1961, p. 34.

Viguers, Ruth Hill, review of *Secret of the Samurai Sword, Horn Book,* February, 1959, p. 47.

Whitney, Phyllis A., "What Does a Writer Expect of an Editor?," *Library Journal,* October 15, 1963.

Review of *Willow Hill, Saturday Review of Literature,* September 6, 1947, p. 34.

■ For More Information See

BOOKS

Budd, Elaine, *Thirteen Mistresses of Murder,* Ungar, 1986, pp. 125-35.

Children's Literature Review, Volume 59, Gale, 1999, pp. 176-96.

Contemporary Literary Criticism, Volume 42, Gale, 1987, pp. 431-38.

Gleasner, Diana, *Breakthrough: Women in Writing,* Walker, 1980, pp. 126-45.

St. James Guide to Young Adult Writers, 2nd edition, St. James Press, 1999, pp. 888-91.

PERIODICALS

Best Sellers, September, 1977, pp. 173-74.

Booklist, June 1, 1992, p. 1748; September 1, 1993, p. 38; September 15, 1994, p. 115; October 15, 1995, p. 421.

Chicago Tribune, June 16, 1991, section 14, p. 8; July 26, 1992, section 14, p. 4.

Christian Science Monitor, May 26, 1960, p. 17; November 23, 1960, p. 11.

Cosmopolitan, May, 1989, p. 13.

Kirkus Reviews, April 15, 1992, p. 498; July 1, 1993, p. 817; July 1, 1994, p. 884.

Library Journal, October 15, 1963; November 1, 1989, p. 128; August, 1991, p. 161.

New York Times, April 6, 1947, p. 27.

New York Times Book Review, September 29, 1957, p. 41; May 18, 1969, p. 31; November 22, 1970, p. 61; February 20, 1972, p. 27; February 5, 1984, pp. 18-19; May 27, 1990.

Parade, November 2, 1975.

Publishers Weekly, May 4, 1992, p. 42; August 16, 1993, p. 88.

Rapport, Volume 18, number 4, p. 42.

Saturday Review, September 29, 1956.

Saturday Review of Literature, September 6, 1947, p. 34.

School Library Journal, August, 1990, p. 177; December, 1991, p. 150; March, 1995, p. 236.

Washington Post, September 2, 1991, pp. D1, D9.

Washington Post Book World, January 2, 1983, p. 4; January 6. 1985, p. 11.

West Coast Review of Books, Number 1, 1985, p. 54; Number 6, 1988, p. 27.

Writer, February, 1980, pp. 11-14, 46; June, 1985, pp. 9-12; July, 1987, p. 7; August, 1988, p. 9; December, 1989, p. 13; May, 1991, p. 11; August, 1992, p. 29.*

Diana Wieler

■ Personal

Surname is pronounced "wheeler"; born October 14, 1961, in Winnipeg, Manitoba, Canada; daughter of Heinz Egon (a chef) and Jean Florence (an accounts receivable manager; maiden name, Zebrasky) Petrich; married Larry John Wieler (a trucking parts national sales manager), May 2, 1981; children: Benjamin. *Education:* Attended Southern Alberta Institute of Technology (Calgary, Alberta, Canada), 1979-80. *Hobbies and other interests:* Painting, doll making, portraiture.

■ Addresses

Home—133 Spruce Thicket Walk, Winnipeg, Manitoba, Canada R2V 3Z1.

■ Career

Writer, 1980—. CKXL Radio, Calgary, Alberta, Canada, advertising copywriter, 1980-82; CJWW Radio, Saskatoon, Saskatchewan, Canada, advertising copywriter, 1982-89; *Star Phoenix*, Saskatoon, creative features writer, late 1980s-early 1990s; full-time writer, 1989—. Writers-in-Electronic-Residence (WIER) Program, York University Faculty of Education and the Writers' Development Trust, writer-in-electronic-residence, 1995-96.

■ Member

Manitoba Writers' Guild.

■ Awards, Honors

H. Gordon Love Award, Alberta Advertising Association, 1982, for excellence in advertising; CBC Radio Literary Competition, Children's Story category, first prize, 1985, for "To the Mountains by Morning"; Major Award, Saskatchewan Writers' Guild, 1985, for "The Lucky Charm"; Vicky Metcalf Short Story Award, Canadian Authors' Association, 1986, for "The Boy Who Walked Backwards"; Max and Greta Ebel Memorial Award for Children's Writing, Canadian Society of Authors, Illustrators and Performers, 1987, for *Last Chance Summer*; Governor General's Literary Award for Children's Literature (English text), Canada Council, 1989, for *Bad Boy*; International Honor List selection, International Board on Books for Young People, 1990, for *Bad Boy*; Ruth Schwartz Children's Book Award,

Ontario Arts Council, 1990, for *Bad Boy;* Young Adult Book of the Year Award, Young Adult Services Interest Group of the Canadian Library Association, 1990, for *Bad Boy;* Mr. Christie's Book Award (Best English Book for Twelve Years and Up), Christie Brown & Company, 1993, for *Ran Van the Defender;* Ruth Schwartz Children's Book Award finalist, Ontario Arts Council, 1994, for *Ran Van the Defender;* Governor General's Literary Award for Children's Literature (English text) finalist, Canada Council, 1995, for *Ran Van: A Worthy Opponent;* McNally Robinson Young Adult Book of the Year, 1997, for *Ran Van: Magic Nation,* and 1998, for *Drive;* finalist, Ruth Schwartz Children's Book Award, Ontario Arts Council, 1998, for *Drive.* Several of Wieler's books have been Canadian Children's Book Centre *Our Choice* selections, including *Last Chance Summer,* 1986-87, *Ran Van the Defender,* 1993-94, and *To the Mountains by Morning* and *Ran Van: A Worthy Opponent,* both 1995-96.

■ **Writings**

FOR CHILDREN

A Dog on His Own, illustrated by Diana Wieler, Prairie Publishing Company, 1983.
To the Mountains by Morning, Nelson Canada, 1987, reissued as a picture book, illustrated by Ange Zhang, Groundwood/Douglas & McIntyre, 1995.

FOR YOUNG ADULTS

Last Chance Summer, Western Producer Prairie Books, 1986, Delacorte, 1991.
Bad Boy, Groundwood/Douglas & McIntyre, 1989.
Ran Van the Defender, Groundwood/Douglas & McIntyre, 1993.
Ran Van: A Worthy Opponent, Groundwood/Douglas & McIntyre, 1995.
Ran Van: Magic Nation, Groundwood/Douglas & McIntyre, 1997.
Drive, Groundwood/Douglas & McIntyre, 1998.

OTHER

Short stories are represented in *Prairie Jungle: Songs, Poems and Stories for Children,* edited by Wenda McArthur and Geoffrey Ursell, Coteau Books, 1985; and *Canadian Children's Annual: Number Twelve,* edited by Brian Cross, Potlatch Publications, 1987.

Wieler's works have been translated into French, German and Danish.

■ **Work in Progress**

Another young adult novel.

■ **Sidelights**

Diana Wieler, author of short stories, picture books, and novels, is considered one of Canada's finest writers for young adults. Many of her works have won prestigious Canadian awards and honors, including the Governor General's Literary Award. Wieler's fiction is respected for both its style and its content, as the author writes openly, respectfully, creatively and with insight about themes and issues relevant to contemporary teens. Wieler also has the reputation of being a risk-taker; in the *Globe and Mail,* Elizabeth MacCallum called her "a good writer with more than a small dose of courage." Bridget Donald, in her *Quill & Quire* review of Wieler's novel *Ran Van: Magic Nation,* commented: "Wieler has not shied away from difficult subjects in any of her novels for young adults, but she brings them out . . . in full force and treats them with intelligence and grace."

Like the boy in Wieler's award-winning short story "The Boy Who Walked Backwards," who claims he's walking not the *wrong* way but the *other* way, Wieler's main characters are rebels and loners. A loner herself as a child, Wieler grew up without a father in the 1960s when single-parent households were the exception to the normal family unit. She remembers feeling very "different" from her friends. At first, she dealt with the difference by becoming introspective; then she became a rebel. During high school, where she ran with the "bad" crowd, one teacher told her she was like a pinball arcade, always busy but never going anywhere.

Born in Winnipeg, Manitoba, Wieler lived in Calgary, Alberta, during her teen years. After high school, she enrolled at the Southern Alberta Institute of Technology in Calgary, where she completed the first year of a two-year program in television, stage and radio arts. She left school to take a writing job. At nineteen, she was working as an advertising copy writer at CKXL, a Calgary radio station. Eighteen months later, she married and moved to Saskatoon, Saskatchewan, where she wrote advertising copy for another radio station by day and worked on her creative writing on evenings and weekends. In 1983, her first volume, the picture book *A Dog on His Own,* was published. The following year, Wieler left radio for a position as a creative features writer with the Saskatoon *Star Phoenix*.

Develops a Reporter's Eye

Newspaper writing occupied Wieler's working hours for the next five years. Meanwhile, she continued to pursue her own writing interests in her spare time. Prestigious short story awards from CBC Radio, the Canadian Authors' Association and the Saskatchewan Writers' Guild provided a steady

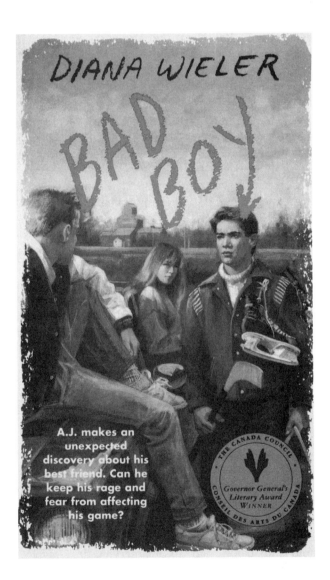

Wieler received Canada's prestigious Governor General's Literary Award for this 1989 work about a sixteen-year-old hockey player who learns his best friend is gay.

stream of encouragement. *To the Mountains by Morning,* one of Wieler's award-winning short stories, was published as a school reader in 1987. It was reissued as a picture book in 1995.

Wieler's day job, requiring the discipline to write to the newspaper's strict word limits and tight deadlines, helped fine tune a writing style that has characterized and distinguished her work as a novelist. Her first novel, *Last Chance Summer*, was published in 1986. In *Canadian Children's Literature*, book reviewer Douglas Thorpe described its prose as "refreshingly spare." The story, about a twelve-year-old, foster-home misfit, drew on Wieler's experience as a volunteer crisis worker with the Saskatoon Sexual Assault Centre. Tim Wynne-Jones, writing for the *Globe and Mail*, commented that Wieler "writes with imagination" and "exhibits insight and great compassion." The Canadian Society of Children's Authors, Illustrators, and Performers agreed and awarded *Last Chance Summer* the 1987 Max and Greta Ebel Memorial Award for Children's Writing.

Controversial Work

Wieler's impressive debut as a writer of fiction for young people created much anticipation for the author's second novel. As Wieler wrote *Bad Boy*, she realized it was controversial. Nevertheless, she was devastated when Western Producer Prairie Books declined to accept it for publication. Fortunately, there was an eager publisher waiting in the wings. Douglas & McIntyre's Groundwood Books snapped up the story of A. J., a sixteen-year-old severely shaken by the discovery that his best friend and hockey teammate is gay. Feeling betrayed, angry and confused, A. J. takes his emotional turmoil out onto the ice, becoming a hockey goon and earning a "bad boy" reputation.

While its sports orientation guaranteed that *Bad Boy* would be a hot potato in some circles, others were more interested in how Wieler handled the delicate subject of homosexuality in writing for teen readers. *Globe and Mail* book reviewer Elizabeth MacCallum maintained: "[Wieler] deftly integrates a difficult issue into the plot with tact and wisdom. Neither judgmental nor sanctimonious, Wieler still takes a stand. Homosexuality is treated as reality." *Bad Boy* won the 1989 Governor General's Literary Award for Children's Literature, the 1990 Canadian Library Association Young Adult Book

In this second work from the "RanVan" trilogy, Rhan Van's has difficulty adapting to small town life after he moves from the big city.

of the Year Award, and the 1990 Ruth Schwartz Children's Book Award. In *The New Republic of Childhood*, Sheila Egoff and Judith Saltman compared Wieler's *Bad Boy* to works by Kevin Major. "Like Major," they summarized, "Wieler writes prose that is brash and staccato, charged with youthful profanity, but sprinkles her narrative with tender moments."

By 1990, Wieler determined to make a full-time commitment to writing books; her target audience would be young people. "It's a tough audience who would just as soon flip on a TV as read a book," she told Kevin Prokosh of the *Winnipeg Free Press*.

"They're cynical, sophisticated and not very tolerant. That's what makes it exciting."

The "Ran Van" Books

Since then, Wieler has completed her Ran Van trilogy about a teenage loner whose video game alter ego transforms him into a super hero. In a *Quill & Quire* review of *Ran Van the Defender*, the series' first title, Patty Lawlor asserted: "Diana Wieler has her fingers firmly on the pulse of the mainstream teen reader. That she's confident enough in herself and in her readers to give conventional setting and staging a bit of a push is, in large part, what makes her the very distinguished author she is becoming." *Ran Van the Defender* won a Mr. Christie's Book Award. It's sequel, *Ran Van: A Worthy Opponent*, was a finalist for the 1995 Governor General's Literary Award for Children's Literature.

When it comes to writing, Wieler has always felt the pull to create. She recalls the journals she kept as a girl. "They were full of real literary stuff, all about the boys I had crushes on and the girls I was mad at," she commented. "It was a really good experience, though, putting my thoughts down. And then in junior high they started us writing journals in school and I found that to be a really positive experience as well." The experience was so positive that Wieler continues the practice today. "I write a minimum of three pages every morning, come hell or high water, to clear the gunk out of my system," she commented. "You put down all of the trivial stuff and the emotions and it clears the slate for writing."

When Wieler was thirteen, she read Ayn Rand's *We the Living*. "That book wasreally meat and drink to me," she commented. "The sheer drama and beautifully subtle prose carved itself on me, I know it did. Sometimes when I write, I can feel the cadence of those words, like an echo."

From the time her son Ben leaves for school in the morning until the time he comes home at night, Wieler thinks and rethinks her stories, often returning to her desk in the evening for a final three-hour stint before bed. In an interview in *Children's Book News*, she told the Canadian Children's Book Centre, "I think if I have anything, it's empathy. I don't think of myself as an exceptional writer or wonderful wordsmith. But ever since I was a little kid I was able to put myself in the other guy's

If you enjoy the works of Diana Wieler, you may also want to check out the following books:

Stephen Dobyns, *The Wrestler's Cruel Study,* 1993.
Neal Shusterman, *Speeding Bullet,* 1991.
Patricia Windsor, *The Hero,* 1988.

shoes and think what it would be like or imagine how that person would feel."

When she's not writing, Wieler prefers to spend time with family and friends, and is involved in artistic pursuits. She belongs to a local art group, paints, collects and makes dolls. Why the disparate interests? "I need that balance between hands and brain," she related. "It's a really absorbing way to relax."

Unexpected Insights

Wieler commented that her interest in dolls prompted an interesting remark from her son. "He said, 'Mom, I can't believe you can write such good boy stories when you're such a *girl.*'" His remark is a variation on a question many people ask Wieler about her writing. How can a woman who grewup in an all-female household know so much about the hearts and minds of teenage boys?

Wieler believes that it was precisely because she grew up in an all-female household that she has such an intense curiosity about men and has undertaken such a careful study of the male gender. "We are always told to 'write what you know,'" Wieler noted in comments to *St. James Guide to Young Adult Writers,* "but for me, I hunger to go places I've never been, look into experiences I probably will never have. As a woman, the most foreign and exciting landscape is the male perspective.

"'But how can you do this?' young writers ask. For me, research is about watching and listening and asking questions. I find that almost everyone is interesting: my doctor, my mechanic, the person who sits beside me in art class. The world is full of fascinating people who will share their stories if you are a good listener. I also draw on the expe-

riences of my husband and son. Just living with them is an adventure of discovery."

While lacking a male role model at home may have strengthened Wieler's observation skills, her parents' divorce weakened her self-esteem. "It was in the sixties when everyone was still married," she remarked. "I just felt so different and so poor. I felt so isolated. I wanted so desperately to be liked."

Today, a more confident Wieler reflects on her writing and her life. She believes good has come from the adversity she experienced as a child and ap-

Rhan experiences first love and meets his old nemesis, the Iceman, after he moves away from home in this final volume of the "Ran Van" trilogy.

Eighteen-year-old Jens Friesen quits school and becomes a car salesman, until a request for help from his younger brother changes everything in Wieler's 1998 work.

preciates the blessings that have come along the way. "I have to admit there have always been moments of magic in my life—corners I've turned that felt like the push of the universe," she commented. "I really believe that writing is an emotional and a spiritual process. It's not just what I do, it's who I am. My neighbors read my books and they say, 'Where are you? I can't see you in here.' I tell them it's all me."

Explaining why she has chosen to write for young adults readers, Wieler told *St. James Guide to Young Adult Writers:* "I write about the teen years because that was a vivid, terrible, exhilarating time of my life. So much happens in a short space, and lives change forever. As a writer, that's the promise I make to my reader: someone's life is going to change forever. I can't think of any work more exciting than that."

■ Works Cited

Canadian Children's Book Centre, "Meet the Author: Diana Wieler," *Children's Book News*, fall, 1990, p. 12.

Donald, Bridget, review of *Ran Van: Magic Nation*, *Quill & Quire*, October 1997, p. 36.

Egoff, Sheila, and Judith Saltman, *The New Republic of Childhood: A Critical Guide to Canadian Children's Literature in English*, Oxford University Press, 1990, pp. 75-76.

Lawlor, Patty, review of *Ran Van the Defender*, *Quill & Quire*, August, 1993, p. 38.

MacCallum, Elizabeth, review of *Bad Boy*, "Difficult Issues and Complex Sexuality," *Globe and Mail*, August 26, 1989, p. C19.

Prokosh, Kevin, "Bad Boy Vies for Top Prize," *Winnipeg Free Press*, February 25, 1990, p. 18.

Thorpe, Douglas, review of *Last Chance Summer*, "What Troubles Troubled Kids," *Canadian Children's Literature*, Number 46, 1987, pp. 86-87.

Wieler, Diana, comments in *St. James Guide to Young Adult Writers*, St. James Press, 1999, pp. 890-91.

Wynne-Jones, Tim, review of *Last Chance Summer*, *Globe and Mail*, February 21, 1987, p. E19.

■ For More Information See

BOOKS

Canadian Children's Book Centre, *Writing Stories, Making Pictures: Biographies of 150 Canadian Children's Authors and Illustrators*, Canadian Children's Book Centre, 1994, pp. 321-23.

PERIODICALS

Books in Canada, December 1986, pp. 15-17.

Canadian Book Review Annual, 1986, pp. 156-157; 1989, p. 328; 1993, p. 6195; 1995, pp. 490, 521.

Canadian Children's Literature, Number 76, 1994, pp. 22-30; spring, 1999,pp. 100-01.

Globe and Mail, October 30, 1993, p. C25; November 11, 1995, p. C21.

Quill & Quire, August 1986, p.35; August 1995, pp. 32-33.

School Library Journal, April, 1999, p. 142.
Voice of Youth Advocates, August, 1999, pp. 186-87.

Simon Wiesenthal

tation Center in Linz, Austria, 1947-54, building up a vast network of documents and informants to bring Nazi war criminals to justice; directed a number of Jewish welfare agencies in Linz, 1954-61, before establishing the Jewish Documentation Center in Vienna, Austria.

■ Personal

Born December 31, 1908; son of Asher (a businessman) and Rosa (Rapp) Wiesenthal; married Cyla Mueller, September 9, 1939; children: Pauline Rose. *Education:* Attended University of Prague, 1929-33; University of Lemberg, Engineer-Architect, 1939. *Religion:* Jewish.

■ Addresses

Home—Mestrozigasse 5, Vienna 19, Austria 1190. *Agent*—Robert Halpern, 225 Broadway, New York, NY 10007.

■ Career

Practicing architect in Lemberg, Poland, 1939-41; arrested in 1941, and spent World War II years in Nazi concentration camps of Janowska, Lvov, Gross-Rosen, Buchenwald, and Mauthausen; employed by War Crimes Commission, U.S. Office of Strategic Services, and Counter-Intelligence Corps, 1945-47; set up and directed the Jewish Documen-

■ Member

Association of Jews Persecuted by the Nazis (president), Union International des Resistant et Deportes (Brussels; past vice-president), Federal Association of Jewish Communities of Austria (past vice-president), B'nai B'rith.

■ Awards, Honors

Great Medal of Merit, German Federal Republic, 1985; Silver Medal of Honor, Vienna, Austria, 1985; nominee, Nobel Peace Prize, 1985; Knight of the Honorary Legion of France, 1986; Medal of Honor of the Yad Vashem Foundation, Jerusalem, Israel; Erasmus Prize, Amsterdam, 1992; Diploma of Honor of International Resistance; Needle of Honour, Austrian Resistance Movement; Diploma of Honour, League of the United Nations; Freedom Medals of Netherlands and Luxembourg; Dr. honoris causa, Hebrew Union College, Hebrew Theological College, Colby College, and John Jay College of Criminal Justice of the City University of New York; named Commandeur of Oranje-

Nassau, Commendatore de la Republica Italiana and Commandeur de ordre pour la merite, France; Commander's Cross of the Order Polonia Restituta, Warsaw, Poland, and Commander's Cross of the Order of Merit, Luxembourg; Congressional Medal of Honor; Jerusalem Medal. The Simon Wiesenthal Center, Los Angeles, California, was created in his honor in 1977. Wiesenthal has numerous honorary doctorates to his credit, as well as honorary citizenship of cities from Tennessee to Florida.

■ Writings

KZ Mauthausen (title means "Concentration Camp Mauthausen"), Landes Verlag, 1946.
Grossmufti-Grossagent der Achse (title means "Head-Mufti, Head-Agent of the Axis"), Ried Verlag, 1947.
Ich jagte Eichmann (title means "I Hunted Eichmann"), Siegberg Mohn Verlag, 1961.
(Editor) *Verjaehrung?* (title means, "Limitation?"), Europaische Verlagsansertalt, 1965.
The Murderers among Us: The Wiesenthal Memoirs, introduction and biographical note by Joseph Wechsberg, McGraw, 1967.
Die Sonnenblume, Hoffman & Campe Verlag, 1970, translation by H. A. Piehler published as *The Sunflower*, W. H. Allen, 1970.
Segel der Hoffnung: Die geheime Mission des Christoph Columbus, Walter Verlag, 1972, translation by Richard Winston and Clara Winston published as *Sails of Hope: The Secret Mission of Christopher Columbus*, Macmillan, 1973.
The Case of Krystyna Jaworska, Becht Verlag, 1975.
Max and Helen, Morrow, 1982.
Every Day Remembrance Day: A Chronicle of Jewish Martyrdom, Holt, 1987.
Justice Not Vengeance, Grove-Weidenfeld, 1989.

■ Adaptations

The Murderers among Us was filmed for an HBO movie starring Ben Kingsley, 1988; *Max and Helen* was filmed by Citadel Entertainment, 1990.

■ Sidelights

Simon Wiesenthal is a witness. He has spent more than half of his life ensuring that the horrors of the Nazi Holocaust will not be forgotten and that its perpetrators would be punished. A survivor of World War II and the concentration camps, Wiesenthal determined once he was freed to commit his life to the cause of justice. "Survival is a privilege which entails obligations," he wrote in his 1989 book, *Justice Not Vengeance*. "I am forever asking myself what I can do for those who have not survived. The answer I have found for myself (and which need not necessarily be the answer for every survivor) is: I want to be their mouthpiece, I want to keep their memory alive, to make sure the dead live on in that memory."

In both books and deeds, Wiesenthal has kept those memories alive. Working through the Jewish Documentation Center in Vienna, Austria, Wiesenthal has helped track down over one thousand Nazi war criminals, his most notable success being the assistance provided to Israeli agents in bringing Adolf Eichmann, one of the Nazi architects of the Final Solution, to trial. His documentation center has information on tens of thousands of war criminals who managed to escape punishment after the war. While the number of those Nazis is decreasing through old age and death, Wiesenthal has mounted his one-man campaign against intolerance and hate on a second front. In his ten books, most notably in *The Murderers among Us, The Sunflower,* and *Justice Not Vengeance,* Wiesenthal has spread a message of hope as well as redemption. Reviewing *The Murderers Among Us,* a *Booklist* critic noted, "Inspired not by hate but by a passion for justice Wiesenthal is motivated by the conviction that the inhumanity of the Nazi regime must be remembered, recorded, and publicized through legal action in order to prevent further atrocities." Summing up the achievement of this man in her biography *Simon Wiesenthal,* Hella Pick wrote that "Wiesenthal has been an exemplar, and yes, it has been a hero's life: not just a Jewish hero's, but a hero of our epoch."

Central European Beginnings

Wiesenthal was born just an hour before the New Year on December 31, 1908, in thetown of Buczacz, then a part of the Austro-Hungarian Empire. The area where Wiesenthal was born and came of age was known as Galicia at the time, long a contested region between Poland, Germany and Russia. Now it forms part of the Lvov Oblast section of the Ukraine. Growing up, however,

Wiesenthal, like most of the Jews of the region, looked to Vienna as their cultural center. His early life was relatively affluent, for his father, Asher, was a sugar merchant. The first of two children, Wiesenthal grew up speaking both Polish and Yiddish, and he learned German from his mother, Rosa.

"Survival is a privilege which entails obligations. I am forever asking myself what I can do for those who have not survived. The answer I have found for myself (and which need not necessarily be the answer for every survivor) is: I want to be their mouthpiece, I want to keep their memory alive, to make sure the dead live on in that memory."

—Simon Wiesenthal

When Wiesenthal's father was killed on the eastern front in Galicia in 1915 during World War I and the Russian forces overran their territory, Wiesenthal's mother took her small family to Vienna, where they stayed for two years until the danger passed in Buczacz. But after returning home, the next several years were anything but peaceful; while mother Rosa struggled to rebuild the family business, the region was overrun by consecutive bands of soldiers and marauding troops, one of whom, a Cossack, one day drove his saber into young Wiesenthal's leg.

At age fifteen, Wiesenthal entered the local secondary school where he met Cyla Mueller, the young woman who would later become his wife. When Wiesenthal's mother remarried in 1926 and moved with her husband to the foothills of the Carpathians, Wiesenthal pleaded to be left behind in Buczacz to finish his high school education. His mother lodged him in the Mueller household, and the relations between Cyla and Wiesenthal became even stronger. Graduating in 1928, Wiesenthal tried to enter the Polytechnic Institute in nearby Lvov, but was refused entry because of quota restrictions on Jewish students. Finally he found a place at the Technical University of Prague.

Wiesenthal had long loved sketching and drawing, but when he suggested to his mother and stepfather that he might want to study art, they strongly suggested he concentrate on something more practical. Architecture was the next best thing, and for four years in Prague, Wiesenthal experienced a new freedom he had never experienced in his hometown. Graduating in 1932, he went to Lvov, where he worked as an architect and also continued his studies at the Technical University. By 1936 he felt that he was on solid enough ground economically to marry his childhood sweetheart, and by 1939 he completed his degree, making him a full architectural engineer. However, by this time outside events came to play on Wiesenthal's life, and he would never again work as an architect.

War and Liberation

The German-Soviet non-aggression pact was signed in 1939, partitioning Poland between the two countries, and soon the Russian army occupied Lvov. A purge of Jewish merchants, factory owners, and intellectuals resulted in the death of Wiesenthal's stepfather and stepbrother; Wiesenthal himself was forced to cease his architectural work and take a job instead in a factory making bedsprings. He managed to save himself, his wife, and his mother from deportation to Siberia by bribing a Soviet secret police official. But when the Germans replaced the Russians in 1941, things became even worse. Narrowly escaping execution by the Nazis, he and his wife were assigned to a forced labor camp repairing the railroads near Lvov. When the Nazis set on their Final Solution—the annihilation of the Jews of Europe—in 1942, the first person to be lost to the Wiesenthal family was Wiesenthal's beloved mother, who was sent to the Belzec death camp.By September of 1942, eighty-nine members of both Wiesenthal's and his wife's families had died in the Holocaust.

Wiesenthal's wife managed a precarious existence during the war, passing herself as an "Aryan" because of her blond hair. This ruse was in part arranged by the Polish underground, for whom Wiesenthal provided valuable railway information in return. Wiesenthal later escaped from the labor camp just before its inmates were killed by the Nazis. Recaptured in June, 1944, he was placed in a concentration camp near Lvov, and finally ended up in Mauthausen, an infamous camp in

Austria, after retreating SS guards fled westward with a small contingent of inmates. There, on May 5, 1945, Wiesenthal, along with other walking skeletons, were liberated by the U.S. Army. He was thirty-six and weighed less than one hundred pounds. As far as he knew, his wife along with all the rest of his family had died in the war and camps.

From Inmate to Tireless Nazi Hunter

Recovering his health, Wiesenthal went to work for the U.S. military, documenting Nazi crimes and gathering evidence that was later used at the War Crimes Trials in Nuremberg. In late 1945 Wiesenthal and his wife, who had survived the war, were reunited. In 1946, their daughter, Pauline, was born. Wiesenthal continued working for the United States until 1947, when he and thirty others opened the Jewish Historical Documentation Center in Linz. This bureau operated for seven years, gathering information on Nazis who had eluded justice. Meanwhile, Wiesenthal also turned his hand to journalism to make financial ends meet. His first book, *KZ Mauthausen,* a book of caricatures and sketches of his time in the Mauthausen concentration camp, was published in 1946; a second, *Grossmufti-Grossagent der Achse,* appeared in 1947.

In 1954, Wiesenthal's Linz office was closed and its files turned over to the Yad Vashem Archive in Israel. However, Wiesenthal continued to place a special interest in one file left behind: that of Adolf Eichmann. He would not let the trail of this high-ranking Nazi grow cold, and he continued to monitor the man's movements through his worldwide network of informants, updating the Israelis periodically. While working as a salaried employee in Jewish relief and welfare agencies, Wiesenthal kept this private crusade alive, and was in large part responsible for making others take interest as well. When Mossad or Israeli agents captured Eichmann in Buenos Aires, where he was posing as Ricardo Klement, and spirited him off to Israel to stand trial in 1960, Wiesenthal's name suddenly became known worldwide and the true horrors of the Holocaust were played out in the evening news in countries around the world as the subsequent trial was broadcast.

Encouraged by this turn of events, Wiesenthal reopened the Jewish Documentation Center, but this

time in Vienna in modest offices and with a small budget and staff. Over the years, Wiesenthal has been involved in 1,100 cases and has brought to justice such men as Franz Stangl, the infamous commandant of Treblinka, Gustav Wagner, commandant of Sobibor concentration camp, Walter Ruff, the inventor of mobile gas vans that killed hundreds of thousands in Russia, and Karl Silberbauer, the man who arrested Anne Frank. Additionally, Wiesenthal was instrumental in exposing the Odessa network that helped Nazis escape to Latin America. The novelist Frederick Forsyth dramatized this in his *The Odessa File.* Wiesenthal has also campaigned to find out the truth of what happened to the Swedish diplomat

Fifty-three distinguished men and women from various walks of life respond to Wiesenthal's World War II experience of a dying Nazi officer asking for forgiveness.

RaoulWallenberg, who helped to save thousands of Hungarian Jews and who disappeared when the Soviets overran that country.

There have been failures as well, including the case of Dr. Mengele, the Auschwitz doctor who carried out horrendous medical experiments on inmates, and who managed to elude all Nazi hunters. Wiesenthal has also had his detractors, who criticize him for taking too much responsibility for the Eichmann capture, or for his stance vis-a-vis the Austrian president and one-time Secretary General of the United Nations, Kurt Waldheim, who was found to have been a Nazi. Wiesenthal argued for moderation in this case, noting that while the man had lied about his past, that did not necessarily make him a war criminal. Wiesenthal has also been the object of death threats and his Documentation Center the attempted target of bombings.

The Power of the Pen

Relying on the power of the pen to remind the world of the horrors of Holocaust, Wiesenthal published *The Murderers among Us* in 1967, chronicling his investigations up to that time. A later paperback edition of the book includes a further chapter on the Stangl investigation. "Simon Wiesenthal is a modern Sherlock Holmes," wrote a reviewer for the *Times Literary Supplement*. "Mr. Wiesenthal has written a stimulating book, full of new and disturbing information," this same reviewer noted. In 1988, the book was adapted for an HBO movie starring Ben Kingsley as Wiesenthal, who, eighty at the time, was on hand to oversee some of the production. As Wiesenthal told Jack Friedman in *People Weekly* during the filming, "I think I am one of the last witnesses. And a last witness, before he leaves the world, has an obligation to speak out. My work for half a lifetime is to inform people. My work is a warning to the murderers of tomorrow."

A companion volume to that book is the 1990 *Justice Not Vengeance*, which goes over much the same ground, detailing individual investigations from Stangl to Odessa and Eichmann. "What the book consists of mainly is a miscellany of cases and questions that have engaged . . . Wiesenthal . . . through the course of his unique career," noted Ronald Sanders in the *New York Times Book Review*. Sanders continued, "Mainly on account of

such stories, this book may best be described as a companion volume, or even as a supplement, to Mr. Wiesenthal's classic 1967 work, `The Murderers among Us.' But perhaps some progress in this gloomy area has after all been made; whereas the present book can dwell on the successful pursuits, `The Murderers among Us' stressed unfinished histories and was, implicitly at least, a plea for help." However, Otto Friedrich, writing in *Time* magazine, felt that while *The Murderers among Us* "had a clear thesis, coolly pursued, Wiesenthal's new memoir rambles through whole chapters on such marginal matters as whether Hitler had syphilis." Friedrich ultimately found the title of Wiesenthal's new memoir, *Justice Not Vengeance*, rather ironic: "One can argue that vengeance is a private reprisal, whereas justice comes from an impartial authority, but the two seem very tightly (and understandably) intertwined in the mind of Simon Wiesenthal." Wiesenthal has also traced Jewish persecution through the ages in his *Every Day Remembrance Day: A Chronicle of Jewish Martyrdom*, a "chilling calendar of horrors," according to a reviewer for *Library Journal*, and "a powerful yet bizarre work," as a *Kirkus Reviews* critic wrote. For each day of the year, Wiesenthal chronicles a list of atrocities directed against the Jews. "This book is a unique, fairly exhaustive, easy-to-use and concise source for YA research or reports," wrote Shelley WaitsmanRiskin in a *Voice of Youth Advocates* review.

While most of his writing has been related to the Holocaust, the inquisitive Wiesenthal has also turned his hand to a reassessment of Christopher Columbus in *Sails of Hope*. In this book, Wiesenthal attempts to prove that the Columbus sailing was actually an attempt by Spanish Jews to find India, the "place where Israel's original tribes were thought to have settled," according to Albert H. Johnston writing in *Publishers Weekly*. Wiesenthal also hypothesizes in the book that Columbus was a Jew. Johnston concluded that the book was a "news-making and plausible construction of one of history's legends."

One of Wiesenthal's most far-reaching and influential books has been, ironically, a small parable of his time in the concentration camps; a book about forgiveness rather than Nazi hunting. *The Sunflower* was originally published in German in 1969; the first English edition came out in 1970 and the U.S. edition in 1976. In 1997 a further English edition appeared. At heart, this book is

If you enjoy the works of Simon Wiesenthal, you may also want to check out the following books and films:

Anne Frank, *The Diary of Anne Frank: The Definitive Edition*, 1995.
Judgment at Nuremberg, a film about the famous Nazi war crimes trials, 1961.
Schindler's List, an Academy Award-winning film by Steven Spielberg, 1993.

simply the story of how Wiesenthal, an inmate at the Lvov camp in 1942, was forced to hear the deathbed confession of an SS man who wanted to unburden his soul to a Jew for the massacre of the Jews in a small Polish town. Wiesenthal listened throughout the gruesome details of the story, and then, instead of forgiving the dying man as the German had hoped, he turned around and walked silently out of the room. This scene troubled Wiesenthal over the years, and finally in *The Sunflower* he asks his readers what they would have done in the same situation. The 1976 edition includes responses to this troublesome question from Christian and Jewish theologians, while the 1997 editions broadens the scope to include responses from the Dalai Lama, the Chinese dissident Harry Wu, the Italian writer and survivor of the death camps, Primo Levi, the Nazi Albert Speer, who spent much of his life in prison, and the psychiatrist Robert Coles, along with more than two dozen other new responses to this timeless question of guilt and forgiveness. As a springboard for discussion and writing, *The Sunflower* has become a standard work in the schoolroom.

Reviewing the 1976 edition of *The Sunflower*, a writer for *Booklist* noted that an "imperative moral question is posed" in the book, while Robert McAfee Brown called Wiesenthal's tale "a gripping story" in the *New York Times Book Review*. Writing on the 1997 edition, Michael Rogers called the book "[h]eavy stuff" in *Library Journal*. A *Publishers Weekly* reviewer mentioned that *The Sunflower* "raises questions of ethics, responsibility, guilt, repentance and forgiveness" without "lapsing into the maudlin or self-pitying." The same reviewer concluded, "The mystery of evil and atonement remain, and the reader is left challenged on these most basic issues of meaning in human life." David Chanoff, in a lengthy review in the *Wash-

ington Post Book World*, concluded, "*The Sunflower* is a rich text, a quasi-Biblical parable. It bears reading, not only for its evocation of the Holocaust, but for its power to illuminate our own moral lives."

Wiesenthal continues his life's work today, going daily to the office of the Vienna Documentation Center. It has been said of him that it is as if he were married to the six million dead Jews of the Holocaust; he daily pours over dossiers of now old men still on the run from justice. But it is work vital to him and the world. "I don't think there is any other solution than constantly coming to terms with the past, and learning from it," Wiesenthal wrote in *Justice Not Vengeance*. "There is no point in minimizing guilt in order to make it easier for sons anddaughters to bear the failure of their fathers and grandfathers, their mothers and grandmothers." "The history of man is the history of crimes, and history can repeat," Wiesenthal told a journalist for the *Baltimore Jewish Times*. "So information is a defense. Through this we can build, we must build, a defense against repetition." Wiesenthal once also summed up his work of over fifty years to an interviewer in the *Jerusalem Post International Edition*: "The only value of . . . my work is a warning to the murders of tomorrow, that they will never rest."

■ Works Cited

Brown, Robert McAfee, review of *The Sunflower*, *New York Times Book Review*, September 12, 1976, pp. 36-37.

Chanoff, David, "When Should Healing Begin?," *Washington Post Book World*, May 4, 1997, pp. 1, 10.

Review of *Every Day Remembrance Day*, *Kirkus Reviews*, July 15, 1987, pp. 1058-59.

Review of *Every Day Remembrance Day*, *Library Journal*, November 1, 1987, p. 116.

Friedman, Jack, "On Location in Budapest, Nazi Hunter Simon Wiesenthal Relives the Horrors of His Past," *People Weekly*, August 1, 1988, p. 49.

Friedrich, Otto, review of *Justice Not Vengeance*, *Time*, April 23, 1990, p. 97.

Johnston, Albert H., review of *Sails of Hope*, *Publishers Weekly*, September 13, 1973, pp. 45-46.

Review of *The Murderers among Us*, *Booklist*, June 15, 1967, p. 1077.

Pick, Hella, *Simon Wiesenthal*, Weidenfeld & Nicolson, 1996, p. 323.

Riskin, Shelley Waitsman, review of *Every Day Remembrance Day, Voice of Youth Advocates,* April, 1988, p. 52.

Rogers, Michael, review of *The Sunflower, Library Journal,* August 1, 1997, p. 134.

Sanders, Ronald, "Nazi Hunting: Trails that Never Grow Cold," *New York Times Book Review,* May 13, 1990, p. 7.

"Searcher for Guilty Men," *Times Literary Supplement,* June 8, 1967, p. 499.

Review of *The Sunflower, Booklist,* April 1, 1976, p. 1076.

Review of *The Sunflower, Publishers Weekly,* April 28, 1997, p. 66.

Wiesenthal, Simon, *Justice Not Vengeance,* Weidenfeld & Nicolson, 1989.

Wiesenthal, Simon, interview in *Baltimore Jewish Times,* February, 1989.

Wiesenthal, Simon, interview in *Jerusalem Post International Edition,* February 5, 1994.

■ For More Information See

BOOKS

Ashman, Chuck, and Robert Wagman, *The Nazi Hunters: Behind the Worldwide Search for Nazi War Criminals,* Pharon Books, 1988.

The Cambridge Biographical Encyclopedia, second edition, Cambridge University Press, 1998.

Levy, Alan, *The Wiesenthal File,* Constable, 1993.

Noble, Iris, *Nazi Hunter: Simon Wiesenthal,* Messner, 1979.

PERIODICALS

Booklist, June 1, 1997, p. 1636.

Christian Science Monitor, June 2, 1997, p. 15; July 2, 1997, p. 15.

Commentary, October, 1990, p. 59.

Economist, November 24, 1989, p. 102.

Foreign Affairs, summer, 1990, p. 182.

Harper's, January, 1975.

Library Journal, February 1, 1990, p. 91; June 15, 1990, p. 146.

Maclean's, May 5, 1980, p. 36; December 9, 1985, p.6; May 25, 1987, p. 40.

New Statesman and Society, November 10, 1989, p.34.

New York Times, May 14, 1982; June 13, 1982, p. 5; June 26, 1988, p. H27; December 2, 1988, p. A15; December 1, 1993, p. 12; August 1, 1997, p. A5; June 18, 1998, p. A16.

New York Times Book Review, September 12, 1976.

Publishers Weekly, February 5, 1968, p. 69; January 5, 1990, p. 57.

Saturday Review, April 15, 1967.

Smithsonian, June, 1988, p. 158.

Time, March 31, 1967, November 19, 1973.

U.S. News and World Report, June 16, 1997, p. 71.

Vogue, June, 1983, pp. 208-9.*

—Sketch by J. Sydney Jones

Ellen Wittlinger

■ Personal

Born October 21, 1948, in Belleville, IL; daughter of Karl (a grocer) and Doris (a grocer and secretary; maiden name, Malzahn) Wittlinger; married David Pritchard (a reference editor), June 23, 1978; children: Kate, Morgan. *Education:* Millikin University, B.A., 1970; University of Iowa, M.F.A., 1973. *Politics:* Democrat. *Hobbies and other interests:* Photography, theater, folk music, gardening.

■ Addresses

Home—47 Beach Ave., Swampscott, MA 01907.

■ Career

Writer, 1970—; children's librarian, Swampscott Public Library, Swampscott, MA, 1989-92; writing instructor, Emerson College, Boston, MA.

■ Member

Society of Children's Book Writers and Illustrators, Swampscott Cultural Council (member, 1983-86, 1994-98), Friends of the Swampscott Library (second vice president, 1992—).

■ Awards, Honors

Finalist, Massachusetts Artists Fellowship, 1980 and 1983, for poetry, and 1989, for playwriting; Best Book for Young Adults selection and Recommended Book for the Reluctant Reader selection, both American Library Association, 1994, for *Lombardo's Law;* Michael R. Printz honor book, Lambda Literary Book Award, Best Books for Young Adults selection and Quick Picks for Reluctant Readers selection, both American Library Association, all for *Hard Love; What's in a Name* and *Gracie's Girl* are both Junior Library Guild selections.

■ Writings

YOUNG ADULT NOVELS

Lombardo's Law, Houghton, 1993.
Noticing Paradise, Houghton, 1995.
Hard Love, Simon & Schuster, 1999.

What's in a Name, Simon & Schuster, 2000.
Gracie's Girl, Simon & Schuster, 2000.

OTHER

Breakers (poetry), Sheep Meadow Press, 1979.
One Civilized Person (play), first produced by
Playwright's Platform, Boston, MA, 1982.
Coffee (play), produced by Egg Rock Players,
Swampscott, MA, 1985.

Contributor of short story "Stevie in the Mirror"
to *On the Edge,* edited by Lois Duncan, Simon and
Schuster, 2000; numerous short stories and poems
published in periodicals, including *Ploughshares,
Antioch Review,* and *Iowa Review.*

■ Sidelights

"I get a little aggravated when people label my
books 'romances,'" remarked young adult novelist Ellen Wittlinger in an essay for *Something about
the Author Autobiography Series* (*SAAS*). "I prefer
to think of my books as coming-of-age stories,
books that remember what it feels like to be thirteen or fifteen or seventeen and to feel for the
first time the tumult of adult emotions." In novels such as *Lombardo's Law, Noticing Paradise, Hard
Love,* and *What's in a Name,* Wittlinger explores
this adolescent landscape through the eyes of outsiders and loners. "I find I'm most interested in
those kids who are on the fringes," Wittlinger
noted in *SAAS,* "the slight oddballs and lovable
misfits who aren't quite comfortable in their own
skins, or if they are, their differentness makes
those around them uncomfortable. I want to cel-
ebrate their differences because they are likely to
be the most fascinating people the rest of us will
ever know." Often Wittlinger's protagonists are
artists in the making—writers, photographers, film-
makers. "I'm most interested in the kids with their
ears to the ground, the ones who can tell us secrets, and in my experience, that kind of person
is often an artist of one kind or another."

Wittlinger herself was the sort of kid she now
writes about. Born on October 21, 1948, in
Belleville, Illinois, she grew up an only child. Her
parents first managed and then later operated
their own mom-and-pop grocery in Belleville.
Much of the time as a young child she was under the eye of a watchful grandparent while both
her parents worked, and this increased the sense

of isolation that Wittlinger felt. "I felt always under surveillance—safe but too safe," the author
noted in *SAAS.* "Early on I longed for more freedom, for adventure, although the fear of it was
instilled in my heart too by the succession of well-
meaning old ladies who guarded my early life."
Her Uncle Walt, a roving jazz musician, gave her
a glimpse of a bigger world on his occasional
visits to town. But more importantly, books filled
her world.

"For children who find themselves alone a good
deal and thrown back onto their own resources,
reading often becomes their escape, their friend,
their adventure, their imaginary life," Wittlinger
reported in her autobiographical sketch. Wittlinger
became a regular at the local library, graduating
from the children's section to the young reader
section, and finally to adult works. The library
became for Wittlinger a "beloved refuge." She also
found refuge in a pet, a Welsh corgi named
Penny. "I think having the dog helped me move
from loneliness to an enjoyment of being alone,"
Wittlinger recalled in *SAAS.*

She gained much of her identity as the kid from
the local grocery, and when her parents operated
their own market, the family lived on the pre-
mises. No other parents in town could offer the
variety of after-school snacks Wittlinger's parents
could. She took to working in the store for her
allowance, and about this time also found a group
of kids who became her friends at school. Mostly
outsiders like herself, these kids provided another
refuge for the young Wittlinger. One group from
junior high school called itself the Horse and Pony
Club, though none of them were riders. They
traded horse figurines, read classic horse books
together, and sketched equine portraits. Wittlinger
was soon convinced that she would become a
painter when she grew up, and turned the small
living room of her home into an artist's studio in
pursuit of this dream.

By high school she had become certain that painting was her destiny; at the same time, however,
she had graduated from reading mushy romances
to experiencing plays. "I became particularly interested in the bizarre world of Eugene O'Neill's
characters, ravaged by drink or drugs and tiedto
each other by the bandages of love and need,"
Wittlinger noted in *SAAS.* From O'Neill she went
on to Tennessee Williams as well as poetry. Her
friends were still "an eclectic bunch who didn't

really fit in." Wittlinger was also particularly attracted to the Air Force 'brats' from nearby Scott Field. They, like her jazz-playing uncle, would bring a glimpse of the larger world to her small town environment. Together with these friends she shared the usual amusements of a teenager in the 1960s: going to the drive-in movie and then to a drive-in hamburger stand afterward. Or sneaking off to nearby St. Louis, across the Mississippi from her hometown, to sit under the newly constructed Arch, "an enormous silver croquet hoop over the Mississippi River, reflecting in the moonlight," as Wittlinger described it in *SAAS*.

From Painter to Writer

Wittlinger attended Millikin University in Decatur, Illinois, second choice to the Kansas City Art Institute, which did not offer her any scholarship money. She majored in art and sociology—the latter so as to satisfy her mother who felt a sociology degree would provide some employment possibilities. Actually, neither of Wittlinger's majors made her very employable. A young teacher and his wife became important in Wittlinger's college life when they encouraged her propensity for poetry, giving her books to read and reading her own writing efforts. Upon graduation, she moved west to Ashland, Oregon, influenced in her decision by a college friend who lived there. She loved the small town in southern Oregon and found work putting ads together for the local newspaper. By this time, however, Wittlinger was writing more poetry; she no longer thought of herself as an artist in the making. Accepted to the graduate program at the University of Iowa's Writers' Workshop, she reluctantly left Oregon to pursue this new goal.

Work at Iowa was intense and very competitive. Wittlinger stuck with it, learning fictional techniques of plot, setting, and characterization, as well as verse models. "This was . . . the first time in my life I had been *identified* as a writer," Wittlinger remarked in *SAAS*. "Just the fact of being in the program at Iowa empowered me to be able to say to people, 'I'm a writer.'" Another benefit of the program was the people she met there, including a young short story writer, David Pritchard, who would later become her husband.

From Iowa, Wittlinger moved to Cambridge, Massachusetts, and worked at a variety of part-time

jobs while pursuing a writing career. Fellowships at the Fine Arts Work Center in Provincetown, Massachusetts, from 1974 to 1976 gave her the time she needed to find her voice, both in poetry and in playwriting. Married in 1978, Wittlinger and her husband moved to Boston, where they could more easily find work. Her first publication, *Breakers,* a book of poetry, was published in 1979, not long before her first child, Kate, was born. "It was a surprise to me (who believed herself a feminist, and still do[es]) that of the two events, it was the birth of my child—not holding the hardcover book in my hands—which filled me with the most complete joy," Wittlinger noted in *SAAS*.

With husband David working as a reference editor for Houghton Mifflin, the couple moved to the oceanside suburban town of Swampscott, and Wittlinger became a full-time mom with the birth of her second child, son Morgan. "I wanted to be with my children when they were young, but also . . . I could sometimes sneak in a few hours of writing now and then." This writing consisted of poetry, as well as plays, which had increasingly captured her creative attention. Twoof these plays for adults, *One Civilized Person* and *Coffee*, were produced by local theatrical groups, and Wittlinger had hopes of larger productions. But the more she became involved with theater, the more she began to understand that such a career would mean traveling with the play and helping to develop it, something that would take her away from home and from her family too much.

When her son started school, Wittlinger took a job as children's librarian in the local Swampscott library. Soon she became self-educated in the world of children's literature, more specifically in YA novels. Influenced by the work of people such as Brock Cole, M. E. Kerr, Katherine Paterson, Gary Paulson, Avi, and Lois Lowry, Wittlinger began to see that here was a field she could happily take part in. "It seemed to me they took the YA genre and pulled it in new directions," Wittlinger recalled in *SAAS*. "And I wanted to try it too."

A YA Novelist

Engaged with her first young adult novel, Wittlinger soon realized that writing such novels was a lot like writing plays. Characterization is all-important, and the characters in YA books must

If you enjoy the works of Ellen Wittlinger, you may also want to check out the following books:

Joan Bauer, *Thwonk*, 1995.
Ellen Conford, *Crush*, 1998.
M. E. Kerr, *"Hello," I Lied*, 1997.

be established just as quickly as the central problem. Keep the plot simple, and the theme as well, and move the action forward at a rapid pace with dialogue-driven scenes. The ending needs resolution, but it need not always be a happy one. Such craft lore was a part of the bag of tools that Wittlinger had already developed in writing for the theater. "So you see, my transition from writing plays to writing young adult novels was not a difficult one," she wrote in *SAAS*. "I loved them immediately."

Wittlinger's first young adult novel, *Lombardo's Law,* is about Justine Trainor, a shy, intelligent, fifteen-year-old loner whose mother would like her to have more friends. As a result, her mother introduces her to Heather and her brother, Mike, who are new to the neighborhood. Justine is quickly snubbed by Heather, a beautiful, boy-crazy teen who easily adjusts to their high school. However, Mike, a thirteen-year-old junior high student, develops a close friendship with Justine due to their common interests and a shared desire to make a movie. As time goes by and they continue writing and then filming a screenplay together, Justine and Mike begin to secretly feel romantic interests toward one another. These two adolescents have a difficult time concealing their fondness from each other, as well as from people at school. At times, such an attachment proves awkward, as when her friends see the two together and wonder if Justine is not babysitting the younger boy.

Reviewing this debut novel in *Horn Book,* Nancy Vasilakis remarked that Justine's "qualms over this social transgression will seem much more compelling and real to young teens than other more serious problems that are currently topical. Wittlinger has hit the bull's-eye with her first try." Lucinda Snyder Whitehurst, a critic for *School Library Journal,* stated: "Beyond entertainment, the story's

value lies in its message of reassurance to young teens who feel out of step with their peers." *Lombardo's Law* also fared well with *Bulletin of the Center for Children's Books* contributor Kathryn Jennings, who wrote, "This first young adult novel by Wittlinger not only strikes at a real dating issue for teenagers, but also has a plot that is satisfying and not too crowded." Wittlinger's first novel earned not only positive reviews, but also spots on the 1994 ALA Best Young Adult Novels list, as well as on the ALA Best Reluctant Reader list for thesame year. Its success prompted Wittlinger to give up her day job as a children's librarian and work on YA fiction full time.

"Slight Oddballs and Lovable Misfits"

Wittlinger's next novel, *Noticing Paradise*, utilizes a trip the author and her family had taken to Ecuador and the Galapagos Islands as a setting. The story takes place on a boat in the Galapagos, involving the mysterious disappearance of endangered tortoises. Two lonely sixteen year olds, Cat and Noah, alternately narrate the action in first person, accounts that sometimes differ. The two are caught up in dramatic events in one of the most exotic if not romantic spots in the world and ultimately fall in love with each other. Noah, from Brookline, begins to question all that he was taught and all that he believes when his parent's divorce unhinges his reality. Cat, another passenger on this international summer excursion, is from Oregon, a reclusive and sheltered child who has never had a date. Noah, too involved in his own pain, does not even notice the paradise all around, until Cat "wakes him up and makes him see," according to *Booklist's* Hazel Rochman. Their romance is powered by the plot involving stolen endangered tortoises and a near drowning. "Wittlinger breaks new ground in YA romance," Rochman further noted, and her dialogue "is lively and immediate." Sharon Neff, reviewing the novel in *Voice of Youth Advocates,* felt that there was a "flatness" to the characters, but that Wittlinger's novel found its real strength in "its naturalist's view of a world of scientific and cultural significance."

Hard Love, published in 1999, features another sixteen-year-old boy torn apart by his parents' divorce. John is having trouble coping, until he begins publishing a zine called *Bananafish.* Here he puts down all his feelings about the divorce and his changed role vis-a-vis both his parents. Marisol, another zine writer, then makes her entrance, and these two troubled teens feel an attraction for each other, but on Marisol's part this can go only so far. She lets John know that she is a lesbian. But John cannot help himself; he finds himself falling in love with Marisol despite his conviction to feel no emotions. "John's simmering passions for Marisol, which come to a full boil at the prom, predictably lead to disaster," remarked a reviewer for *Publishers Weekly*. In a *School Library Journal* review of the book, Dina Sherman observed, "Teen angst is always a popular route for young adult literature, and Wittlinger has successfully created an intense example here." Sherman concluded, "This is a smart addition to YA collections."

A cast of ten teenagers fill the pages of *What's in a Name,* a book that explores personal identity. All residents of the small town of Scrub Harbor, Massachusetts, these teenagers start a search for their own identities when the residents of the town are contemplating whether or not to change the name of Scrub Harbor. Inspired by this naming quest, various teenagers share their own thoughts on personal meaning and identity, from the gorgeous country-club type, Gretchen, to bookish and gay O'Neill. These glimpses of each character intertwine into a larger story. While Mary Ann Capan, writing in *Voice of Youth Advocates,* felt that the characters in Wittlinger's book "lack the depth that could make them memorable," they still display emotions that "ring true." Wittlinger has also penned a novel dealing with homelessness. *Gracie's Girl* features middle-schooler Bess, who volunteers to work on the school musical. Another of Wittlinger's outsiders, Bess hopes that such involvement will lead to her fitting in. But when she and a friend get to know an elderly homeless woman, Bess begins to wonder what really is important in life.

For Wittlinger, the growing pains of adolescence are all too real and present. "I sometimes tell people I never got over being thirteen," she wrote in *SAAS.* "I got kind of stuck back there. But I don't only mean stuck with that feeling of being an oddball kid, with not quite the right looks or interests to fit in . . . but also I never quite got over what's so good about being thirteen. At that age . . . we're still optimistic, the world is right in front of us waiting to be embraced, and we have unlimited hope that it will open its arms to

us as well. . . . This is why I love writing young adult novels. Who lives a more exciting life than a teenager just moving from the safety of home and family into the wide world of emotional possibilities? It's the equivalent of boarding one of the first manned spacecrafts. And yet teenagers rush enthusiastically into this rare atmosphere, as they have always done and will always do. I hope only to show them there have been others there before them and they have survived."

■ Works Cited

Capan, Mary Ann, review of *What's in a Name, Voice of Youth Advocates,* April, 2000, pp. 41-42.

Review of *Hard Love, Publishers Weekly,* June 21, 1999, p. 69.

Jennings, Kathryn, review of *Lombardo's Law, Bulletin of the Center for Children's Books,* October, 1993, p. 63.

Neff, Sharon, review of *Noticing Paradise, Voice of Youth Advocates,* February, 1996, p. 380.

Rochman, Hazel, review of *Noticing Paradise, Booklist,* November 1, 1995, p. 464.

Sherman, Dina, review of *Hard Love, School Library Journal,* June, 1999, p. 102.

Vasilakis, Nancy, review of *Lombardo's Law, Horn Book,* November, 1993, p. 748.

Whitehurst, Lucinda Snyder, review of *Lombardo's Law, School Library Journal,* September, 1993, pp. 253-54.

Wittlinger, Ellen, essay in *Something about the Author Autobiography Series,* Volume 25, Gale, 1998, pp. 285-98.

■ For More Information See

PERIODICALS

ALAN Review, fall, 1999, p. 40.

Booklist, September 15, 1993, p. 144; September 15, 1998, p. 220; October 1, 1999, p. 355; March 15, 2000, p. 1370.

Choice, December, 1979, p. 1311.

Horn Book, July-August, 1999, p. 474.

Horn Book Guide, spring, 1994, p. 92.

Library Journal, December 15, 1979, p. 2626; March 15, 1980, p. 728.

Publishers Weekly, October 11, 1993, p. 89.

Voice of Youth Advocates, December, 1993, p. 304.

—Sketch by J. Sydney Jones

Cumulative Index

Author/Artist Index

The following index gives the number of the volume in which an author/artist's biographical sketch appears.